The Man Who Killed President Garfield

This edition is dedicated to
Eric M. Soehnlein,
skilled attorney and history enthusiast.

The Man Who Killed President Garfield

George H. Herbert's *Guiteau, the Assassin*

Edited and introduced by Paul Rich

WESTPHALIA PRESS
An imprint of Policy Studies Organization

The Man Who Killed President Garfield
George H. Herbert's
Guiteau, The Assassin

All Rights Reserved © 2013 by Policy Studies Organization

Westphalia Press
An imprint of Policy Studies Organization
dgutierrezs@ipsonet.org

All rights reserved. No part of this book may be reproduced or transmitted in any form or by any means graphic, electronic, or mechanical, including photocopying, recording, taping, or by any information storage or retrieval system, without the permission in writing from the publisher.

For information:
Westphalia Press
1527 New Hampshire Ave., N.W.
Washington, D.C. 20036

ISBN-13: 978-0-944285-83-1
ISBN-10: 094428583X

Updated material and comments on this edition can be found at the Policy Studies Organization website:
http://www.ipsonet.org/

Preface to the New Edition: Charles Julius Guiteau

CHARLES Julius Guiteau (1841-1882) spent five years as a young man in the Oneida Community in upper New York State, which at the time was a hotbed of theological experimentation, including group marriage. He turned against the cult and misadventures led him to Chicago, where he had an unsuccessful law practice. His early religious enthusiasms never left him and for a time he was an itinerant lecturer on religion. In 1880 he supported James Garfield's presidential campaign but only in a very small way, giving a couple speeches to limited audiences. However, he thought his support had won Garfield the presidency and he asked whomever he could buttonhole that he be made ambassador to Vienna or Paris as a reward.

Thwarted in his job search, in the spring of 1881 he began stalking Garfield in Washington. On July 2, 1881, he shot Garfield at the railroad station in the capital and the President died eleven weeks later. Guiteau was indicted for murder in October and brought to trial in November. The proceedings have a place in jurisprudence because they are among the first in which the so-called insanity defense was presented. The prosecuting attorney, George Corkhill, would have none of it and commented, "He was a deadbeat, pure and simple. Finally, he got tired of the monotony of deadbeating. He wanted excitement of some other kind and notoriety, and he got it."

The insanity defense was unsuccessful as was another ploy, that Garfield had been killed by medical malpractice and would have recovered but for his doctors. The jury quickly brought in a guilty verdict. Guiteau managed to shout at them, "You are all low, consummate jackasses!" but his court appeals went nowhere and he was hanged on June 30, 1882. The court record found in this unusual volume has a permanent place in legal history.

THE GREAT STATE TRIAL.

GUITEAU, THE ASSASSIN.

FULL DETAILS OF HIS TRIAL FOR THE MURDER OF

PRESIDENT JAMES A. GARFIELD.

THE CRIME, ITS CAUSES AND CONSEQUENCES.

GRAPHIC SCENES IN COURT; THE ORAL, DOCUMENTARY AND EXPERT
EVIDENCE; THE REMARKABLE STATEMENTS OF THE PRISON-
ER ON THE STAND; SPEECHES AND ADDRESSES OF
COUNSEL; SKETCHES OF THE PRINCIPAL
CHARACTERS ENGAGED IN THIS
WORLD-FAMOUS CRIMINAL
TRIAL.

By GEORGE B. HERBERT,
JOURNALIST AND AUTHOR OF THE LIFE OF GENERAL WINFIELD SCOTT HANCOCK, ETC.

PROFUSELY ILLUSTRATED.

PHILADELPHIA.
PUBLISHED BY WILLIAM FLINT,
623 Sansom Street.

LIST OF ILLUSTRATIONS.

Judge Walter S. Cox,
The Jury,
Hon. James G. Blaine Pursuing the Assassin,
The Jail at Washington,
Guiteau's Morning Toilet,
From the Jail to the Court House,
Guiteau on the Witness Stand,
Court Scene (Rush for Seats),
Hon. Geo. B. Corkhill, U. S. District Attorney,
Judge J. K. Porter, Prosecuting Attorney,
Walter W. Davidge,   "   "
The Prisoner on the Alert (Pretending to Read),
George M. Scoville, Attorney for the Defence,
The Scoville Family,
The Father of Guiteau,
John Guiteau—The Prisoner's Brother,

Viewing the Assassin,

Lunch at Recess,

A Strong-minded Woman—"Let me Pass, Sir,"

Receiving Dispatches,

Scene in Front of Court House—"It am Hot,"

From the Court House to the Prison Van,

Attempt on the Assassin's Life by Serg't John A. Mason

Dr. Bliss with Part of President Garfield's Vertebræ,

Shooting at the Assassin through the Prison Van,

Guiteau Examining his Wound,

Sergeant John A. Mason, U. S. A.,

W. J. Jones, the Supposed Assailant of Guiteau in the Prison Van,

Guiteau Preparing his Address,

CONTENTS.

THE CRIME.

CHAPTER I.

The Fatal Shot—Scenes at the Railway Depot in Washington—A Journey Interrupted and a Life's Work Terminated—Effect of the News upon the Country at Large—A Pistol Shot!.. 19

CHAPTER II.

The Details of the Assassination—The Documents Found on the Assassin—The Evidences of Preparation, and the Key-note of the Motives Prompting the Dastardly Deed. 25

THE CAUSES AND THE CONSEQUENCES.

CHAPTER I.

The Spoils System of Office—Its Growth and Contaminating Effects—Its Association with the Third Term Movement—The Stalwart Combination and the New York Collectorship... 32

CHAPTER II.

A "Seer's" Strange Statement—The Assassination of President Garfield Circumstantially Foretold at the Time of his Nomination—The Strong Impression Made by the Prediction upon General Garfield, Secretary Schurz, Marshal Henry and others................................ 36

(ix)

CONTENTS.

THE GREAT STATE TRIAL.

CHAPTER I.

The Grand Jury Presentment—Col. Corkhill's Remarkable and Exhaustive Bill of Indictment—The Full Text of the Six Counts of this Masterly Instrument............. 45

CHAPTER II.

Opening Scenes—Unpleasant Altercations between Counsel for the Defence—The Prisoner's Persistent Interruptions—The Panel Exhausted and only Four Jurors Obtained—Guiteau's Detestable Document................ 52

CHAPTER III.

The Excitement Increasing on the Second Day—Another Panel Exhausted without Completing the Jury—Curious Disqualifications and Comments........................ 77

CHAPTER IV.

The Jury Complete—Who and What the Jurymen are—Their Appearance, Occupation and General Characteristics—The Court Decks Cleared for Action............. 81

CHAPTER V.

District Attorney Corkhill's Opening Address—Guiteau's Grotesque Ghoulishness Begins to Show itself—Secretary Blaine on the Witness Stand—His Definition of the Word "Stalwart," etc.. 92

CHAPTER VI.

Guiteau Again Demonstrative—The Court Threatens to Remove Him—The Story of the Crime Continued by Eye Witnesses—The Letters Written to His Intended Victim. 135

CHAPTER VII.

Dramatic Scene in Court—A Fragment of the Martyred President's Vertebræ Produced on the Witness Stand—The Murderer and Murdered in Juxtaposition—Dr. Bliss as a Witness—End of the First Week of the Trial..... 156

CONTENTS.

CHAPTER VIII.

Mr. Robinson Retires From the Defence—The Prosecution Rests its Case—Guiteau Offers a Few Remarks in Place of a Set Speech—Mr. Scoville Commences His Opening for the Defence...................................... 176

CHAPTER IX.

Continuation of Mr. Scoville's Opening Address—Repeated Interruptions by the Prisoner—A Sensational Scene Between Mr. Scoville and Colonel Corkhill............... 188

CHAPTER X.

Guiteau Administers "Taffy" to the Colored Juror—He Denies Being a Fool, but Admits He did Not Draw as a Speaker—"I Presume I'd Draw Now"—Adjournment over Thanksgiving Day................................ 209

CHAPTER XI.

Guiteau Makes an Elaborate Statement of the Reasons for "Removing" the President—He Continues His System of Interruptions, and the Court Threatens to "Gag" Him. 221

CHAPTER XII.

Senator John A. Logan on the Stand—Guiteau's Bogus Political Career Described by Other Witnesses—Mrs. Scoville, the Prisoner's Sister and his Counsel's Wife a Witness.. 239

CHAPTER XIII.

The Prisoner's Sister, Mrs. Scoville, Again on the Witness Stand—Her Impressions as to Guiteau's Insanity—Other Witnesses think Him Crazy or a Fool—Guiteau's Brother John as a Witness—The Prisoner Sworn................ 253

CHAPTER XIV.

Guiteau on the Witness Stand—His Own Account of His Life—His Efforts to Obtain Possession of the INTER-OCEAN Newspaper—His Experiences of the Oneida Community.. 274

CONTENTS.

CHAPTER XV.

Guiteau Still on the Witness Stand—He Details his Applications for Office—His Book "Truth" and His Lectures on the "Second Coming"—His Aspirations for the Presidency of the United States............................ 300

CHAPTER XVI.

Judge Porter Cross-Examines the Prisoner Closely—A Terrible Ordeal for the Shifty Scoundrel—Guiteau Claims all His Acts to be Inspired and all Attacks on Him Mere Human Crimes.. 338

CHAPTER XVII.

Cross-examination of the Prisoner Concluded—He Deliberately Recounts the Circumstances of the Assassination—The Redirect Examination............................. 371

CHAPTER XVIII.

Emory A. Storrs Gives His Views About the Prisoner—Considers That He is "Off His Nut"—The Ponderous Form of David Davis on the Witness Stand—The Senator's Views About Matters in General.................. 390

CHAPTER XIX.

The Expert Testimony Commenced—Remarkable Hypothetical Questioning to Obtain Presumption of Insanity—Guiteau makes a Speech and Gives Advice to President Arthur.. 396

CHAPTER XX.

The Prisoner Insists on Having all His Distinguished Friends Put upon the Stand—The Evidence for the Defence Practically Closed............................... 409

CHAPTER XXI.

Another Cranky Speech—Rebuttal Testimony to Prove the Sanity of the Guiteau Family—If they were Insane, Nobody Knew it—The Prisoner Compliments President Arthur's Message.. 418

CHAPTER XXII.

The Rebuttal Testimony Continued—The Answers of President Arthur to the Interrogations—Some Further Chapters out of The Prisoner's Life........................ 429

CONTENTS.

CHAPTER XXIII.

Testimony that the Guiteau Family Have Denied Insanity in Insurance Policies—Guiteau's Threats Years ago to Imitate Wilkes Booth—His Pawning a Brass Watch for Gold... 443

CHAPTER XXIV.

An Expert Who is Convinced that the Prisoner is Insane—Dr. Spitzka's Remarkable Statements—He Objects to Veterinary Allusions—Guiteau in a Great Rage......... 456

CHAPTER XXV.

Dr. Spitzka Declines to State Whether he Believes in a God—He Gives His Views upon Experts in General and Lawyers in Particular—Dr. Fordyce Barker, Expert on the Prosecution Side.................................. 479

CHAPTER XXVI.

A Short Session in Consequence of Juror's Illness—Several Witnesses who did not Admire the Prisoner's Character and One who Thought he Ought to be Hung............ 490

CHAPTER XXVII.

Guiteau's Divorced Wife on the Witness Stand but Withdrawn—Another Egotistical Address to the American Public—Some Lively Scenes in Court................... 497

CHAPTER XXVIII.

The Prisoner's Ex-Wife Again on the Stand—She Never Considered Guiteau Insane—More Medical Expert Testimony to Establish the Prisoner's Sanity................ 510

CHAPTER XXIX.

Death of the Wife of Juror Hobbs—The Court Adjourns until Wednesday without Further Action—Guiteau Expresses Confidence in the Jury........................ 520

CHAPTER XXX.

Another Day with the Experts — Testimony Bearing Strongly against the Irresponsible Theory—Guiteau again in several of his Raging Moods..................... 523

(xiii)

CONTENTS.

CHAPTER XXXI.

Another Tiresome Day with Expert Testimony—Guiteau Doing a Good Deal of Talking and Roundly abusing the Witness Shaw.. 534

CHAPTER XXXII.

Mr. Reed Comes into the Case as Counsel for the Defence—The Wilkes Booth Imitation Threat Confirmed—More Expert Testimony and More of Guiteau's Insolence...... 543

CHAPTER XXXIII.

A Weary Court and Jury—Guiteau's Abominable Interruptions and Insolence Lead to a Threat of his Removal to the Dock—His Anticipations of a "Happy Christmas." 551

CHAPTER XXXIV.

After the Christmas Holidays—The Dreary Farce Resumed Guiteau Claims to Belong to the Abraham School of Insanity—He Sneers at Experts and Expects to Go to a Lunatic Asylum....................................... 555

CHAPTER XXXV.

The Prisoner Placed in the Dock After an Exciting Contest between Counsels—The Assassin from this Time Forward to be Recognized as an Alleged Criminal...... 559

CHAPTER XXXVI.

Guiteau Again in the Dock—Some Expert Testimony on "Heads"—The Prisoner Interpolates Some Anxious Remarks about his own Safety—He Dreads Cranks.... 578

CHAPTER XXXVII.

Guiteau Puts Himself in Nomination for the Presidency—A Suggestion that the Jury Separate for a Rest is Promptly Negatived by that Body—Another Lively Day. 585

CHAPTER XXXVIII.

The Last Day of the Old Year Consumed in a Wearisome though Careful and Critical Analysis of Guiteau and his Character by an Expert....................... 590

CONTENTS.

CHAPTER XXXIX.

The Prosecution Closed at Last—Sur-rebuttal Testimony Offered—Counsel on Both Sides Getting Ready for the Closing Arguments.................................... 595

CHAPTER XL.

All the Evidence in—Mr. Scoville Presents his Affidavit—The Prosecution Submit their "Prayer for Instructions." 598

CHAPTER XLI.

The Prayers for the Defence, Fourteen in Number, Formally Presented to the Court—The Defence Commences the Closing Argument 613

CHAPTER XLII.

The Arguments Continued—Mr. Scoville and Mr. Davidge on the Question of Malice—The Prisoner on Everything in General.................................... 626

CHAPTER XLIII.

Judge Porter Closes the Argument on the Prayers—Guiteau Interrupts and "Catches a Tartar"—Judge Cox gives his Decision on the Prayers............................. 633

CHAPTER XLIV.

Mr. Davidge Makes Argument on the Prayers for Instructions—The Question Raised as to Whether Guiteau shall Speak—Much Feeling Exhibited by Counsel on both Sides.. 642

CHAPTER XLV.

The Court Refuses to Allow Guiteau to Speak—Mr. Reed Makes his Argument—He also Makes the Startling Discovery that Charlotte Corday was Insane.............. 647

CHAPTER XLVI.

Mr. Scoville Commences his Argument and Speaks for five Days—A General Summary of a Long Argument Made Against Time.. 651

CONTENTS.

CHAPTER XLVII.

Guiteau Makes the Closing Argument for the Defense, and Showers his Thanks upon the New York Court of Appeal, his Previously Malignant Counsel and the American Press 663

CHAPTER XLVIII.

Judge Porter's Masterly Closing Argument for the Prosecution—The Calm, Consciencious, Comprehensive Charge of Judge Cox to the Jury—Retirement and Deliberation of the Jury for only Thirty Minutes—The Verdict—"Guilty! and so say all of us." 666

CHAPTER XLIX.

Argument for a New Trial—Some Lively Scenes Between Counsel—Judge Cox Takes the Papers................ 715

CHAPTER L.

The Application for a New Trial Refused—The Prisoner Sentenced to be Hanged June 30—End of the Trial..... 728

JUDGE WALTER S. COX.

THE CRIME.

CHAPTER I.

The Fatal Shot—Scenes at the Railway Depot in Washington—A Journey Interrupted and a Life's Work Terminated—Effect of the News upon the Country at Large—A Pistol Shot!

THE whizzing flight of a bullet.

Another sharp detonation and the dull thud of a bullet's impact.

Echoes spreading, commingling, returning and again spreading, till the pines of Maine and the rocks of Texas; the plashing ripples on the Pacific and the bellowing billows on the Atlantic coast, had heard and hurled back in sorrowful indignation, the portentous sound.

The collapsing form of a man in the flower of manhood, in the midst of a startled group; the fleeing form of a guilty, conscience-stricken wretch; a little wreath of pale blue smoke.

Such were the sounds and sights at the B Street depot of the Baltimore and Potomac R. R. in the City of Washington at 9.45 A. M. on Saturday, July 2, 1881, when President James A. Garfield, fell beneath the cowardly aim of the skulking assassin, Charles Jules Guiteau.

The pale blue wreath of smoke from that murderous weapon floated lazily, innocently upward and disappeared; but it had blurred forever one page of the national history; it had tarnished the brightness of that July morning, and had cast a sable shadow across the coming "Glorious Fourth," for which such happy anticipations had been entertained.

There was a hushed suspense amid that startled throng thus suddenly brought face to face with treachery and crime; a numb sense of inexplicable woe; a deadening perception of a dread calamity for a moment chained heart and hand with icy fetters; then there came a rush of hurrying feet, a brief scuffle, and as the wounded President sank into the arms of grief-stricken friends, his dastardly assailant was seized by the indignant hands of an outraged people.

Like the beast at bay, cowardly yet defiant, he bellowed forth a challenge in words, the import of which could not be misunderstood; and false as it is fervently to be hoped they were, in implication, their utterance sent a chill to the very marrows of their hearers.

"I AM A STALWART! AND ARTHUR IS PRESIDENT!"

Not a word of Conkling, the Achilles sulking in his tent; but there came up, involuntarily memories of the Chicago battle and discomfiture, when amid the huzzas which proclaimed the nomination of a true patriot, a beaten clique and a Star Route ring moulded the fatal bullet and planted the avenging hemp, not actually—but metaphorically—for the purposes of selfish safety and craven revenge. Yes! Guiteau was " a Stalwart of the Stalwarts," as he avowed, and if crazy, then crazed by the pernicious example of men older, wiser and better favored than he, who had essayed to do politically, that which he in his animal instinct had done physically—strike down the chosen chief of fifty millions of people under the shadow of the Capitol of the United States.

The journey thus rudely interrupted was to have been one of the crowning joys of an eventful existence. The man upon whom a Republican nation had bestowed its highest honors, was returning to that *alma mater* from which a quarter of a century before he had emerged a diffident youth, blushing beneath the humble honors of a graduation at Williams' College, earned by intense application and keen privation.

The closely written pages of twenty-five years' mutations, the varied details of a life at the teacher's desk, in the preacher's pulpit, on the field of battle and amid the keen strifes of the forum, were spread out before him, with the sharp angles of early struggles rounded off by the crowning glory of an earnest career, and mellowed by time and distance. The timid, diffident student, the bashful graduate, was to re-enter those college halls an honored guest, conferring honor by his very presence. Such were the hopes and the aspirations, but, "Finis" had been written by inexorable fate. Life's work for him had been accomplished, and the anguished form of one of America's truest sons was borne reverently, sorrowfully through the portals of the White House at the same moment that the wretched carcase of one of her meanest abortions, was hustled into the corridor of a jail.

God's servant and the Devil's agent were alike helpless, the one already in the grasp of death and the other crouching beneath the mailed hand of its deliberate minister—the Law.

With lightning rapidity the sad news had flashed along the wires till every city, town and hamlet stood aghast with bated breath, in the presence of a giant horror. Men looked askance at each other, and the wildest surmises as to the causes and the consequences of the detested deed were rife.

It happened that we, during a brief release from journalistic labors, had sought rural rest at Doylestown, in Bucks County, Pa., when the first vague rumor reached that community. Words are inadequate to paint its immediate effect. Indignant Republicans at once assumed that Democratic revenge for recent defeat had found fiendish expression, and "another shot at Fort Sumpter" was the sneering comment. Later on the details cast shame upon those who had been so prompt to accuse and now failed to find wherewith to excuse so foul a crime within their own ranks. Hurrying to the city we found excitement at fever heat. The streets crowded by surging masses craving information and muttering maledictions on the assassin till midnight dispersed the stricken citizens to fitful, troubled slumbers. The wildest theories were advanced and eagerly caught up till the incensed community became as one Destroying Angel seeking victims that it might rend them in its righteous rage.

Meanwhile, the heroic wife of the wounded President, herself barely released from a couch of suffering, had been hurried from the seashore, and now knelt by the bedside of what was dearest to her upon earth, and which it seemed was but too certainly to be snatched from her.

There are hours in which human beings live a lifetime, and in which a nation passes through an entire history. This was one of those periods, and it is indelibly imprinted on the memories of all who passed through the sad, eventful day and night of July 2, 1881.

CHAPTER II.

The Details of the Assassination—The Documents Found on the Assassin—The Evidences of Preparation, and the Key-note of the Motives Prompting the Dastardly Deed.

IN order to present the facts of the assassination in the order of their occurrence, it may be expedient to make a brief running summary of the reports collected on the spot by the attaches of the great daily newspapers of the different cities, and those distributed by the Associated Press. Slight variations of detail occur in the course of the evidence given at the trial, but they do not affect the main features, and merely tend to prove the time-worn assertion that no two people ever see the same incident through precisely the same colored spectacles.

President Garfield had arranged to make an extended trip through Massachusetts, New Hampshire, Vermont, and perhaps other of Eastern or New England States, a principal feature of the journey being a visit, in accordance with a cordial and impressive invitation, to his *alma mater*, Williams' College, Williamstown, Massachusetts. The start was to be made on the morning of July 2d, from Washington; and Mrs. Garfield, just

FROM THE JAIL TO THE COURT HOUSE.

convalescing from a severe illness at Long Branch, was to join the party in New York.

By appointment made the previous evening, Secretary Blaine called at the White House shortly before 9 o'clock, and, after a brief conversation, entered the carriage with the President to be driven to the Baltimore and Potomac depot, on B Street. Secretaries Lincoln, Windom and Hunt, and Postmaster-General James, accompanied by their wives, had reached the station, and had taken their seats in the special car which had been provided for the Presidential party on their trip, before the President arrived. At about 9.20 the President's carriage arrived at the Sixth Street entrance to the station, and after a moment's delay the occupants alighted, assisted by Officer Kearny, who met them at the door. The President and Secretary Blaine then started leisurely through the waiting room, arm in arm, and had passed but a short distance from the door when two shots were fired in quick succession. At the second shot the President turned quickly to the right and fell heavily to the floor, in a position diagonally across the passage-way between the seats, the blood flowing rapidly from a jagged wound in his side. The people in the vicinity were paralyzed with horror for a moment, being unable to realize the terrible deed. Secretary Blaine was the first to act, and turned toward the assassin, but discovering that he had been secured, he then gave his attention to his prostrate chief. Word was carried at once to the other members of the party, who were awaiting the arrival of the President, and they at once hurried to his side. Medical aid had been summoned at once, and about five minutes after the shooting Dr. Townshend, Health Officer of the District, arrived. The President by this time was vomiting freely and in a fainting condition. After administering some stimulants, a mattress was procured and he was carried to a room in the second story, where he remained for nearly an hour. Other physicians arrived in a short time after his removal, and on making an examination of the wound it was resolved to take him to the White House, where absolute quiet and rest could be obtained. An ambulance was accordingly brought, and accompanied by Colonel Rockwell, Doctors Townshend and Smith, and a guard of mounted police the President was tenderly removed.

ARREST OF THE ASSASSIN.

Meanwhile, the assassin, who proved to be Charles Jules (or Julius) Guiteau, had started at a deliberate pace for the centre door, but being headed off at that exit, rapidly retraced his steps and hurriedly attempted to escape by the ladies' entrance on B Street. Here, however, he was seized by an officer, who said, in reply to remonstrance and attempted resistance, "I heard two shots, and I am going to arrest you." Finding flight impossible, for by this time the crowd had recovered self-possession, and volunteer aid in the name of the law was ample, Guiteau surrendered with the remark, "All right! I did it, and will go to jail for it;" adding, after a brief pause, "I AM A STALWART, AND ARTHUR IS PRESIDENT." He also said: "I want General Sherman to know; I want him to have this"—referring to a letter which was subsequently taken from him on being searched at police headquarters.

THE ASSASSIN'S DOCUMENTS.

The trash found in the pockets of the prisoner, and in a package left by him at the news stand in the depot, addressed to Byron Andrews, correspondent of the Chicago *Inter-Ocean*, consisted of a lot of newspaper slips, being editorial expressions from various parts of the country anent the political situation; something which purported to be a diary or reflex of the prisoner's mental condition for some time previously (and this was probably a concoction of devilish ingenuity, intended for use in the event of his capture after the commission of the deliberate, diabolical crime he had planned). There was also a letter addressed to Vice-President Arthur, informing him of the assassination of President Garfield, an act by which he became President of the United States. It further contained advice as to the formation of a Cabinet, recommending Mr. Coulsburg for Secretary of State; Levi P. Morton for Secretary of the Treasury; Emory A. Storrs, of Chicago, for Attorney-General, and John A. Logan for Secretary of War. This precious document also suggested that as Postmaster-General James was doing so well, he might be retained; and as the Departments of the Navy and Interior were not of much account, it would be hardly worth while to make any fuss by changes in them at present. The actual text of this letter, for some reason not very clearly defined, was not made public, but the following are verbatim:

JULY 2, 1881.
TO THE WHITE HOUSE :

The President's tragic death was a sad necessity, but it will unite the Republican party and save the Republic. Life is a flimsy dream and it matters little when one goes. A human life is of small value. During the war thousands of brave boys went down without a tear. I presume the President was a Christian, and that he will be happier in Paradise than here. It will be no worse for Mrs. Garfield, dear soul, to part with her husband this way than by natural death. He is liable to go at any time any way. I had no ill-will toward the President. His death was a political necessity. I am a lawyer, a theologian and a politician. I am a Stalwart of the Stalwarts. I was with General Grant and the rest of our men in New York during the canvass. I have some papers for the press, which I shall leave with Byron Andrews and his co-journalists at No. 1420 New York Avenue, where the reporters can see them. I am going to the jail.

CHARLES GUITEAU.

Another, bearing the address, "Please deliver

HON. JAMES G. BLAINE PURSUING THE ASSASSIN.

at once to General Sherman or his first assistant in charge of the War Department," contains the following declarations:

To GENERAL SHERMAN:

I have just shot the President. I shot him several times, as I wished him to go as easily as possible. His death was a political necessity. I am a lawyer, theologian and politician. I am a Stalwart of the Stalwarts. I was with General Grant and the rest of our men in New York during the canvass. I am going to jail. Please order out your troops, and take possession of the jail at once.
Very respectfully,
CHARLES GUITEAU.

Having been searched, the prisoner was removed to the District jail, Lieutenants Austin and Eckloff and Detective McElfresh being added to the escort. The detective promptly entered into conversation with his charge, and gave the following as the result of his inquiries:

"I asked him, 'Where are you from?'"

"I am a native-born American. Born in Chicago, and am a lawyer and a theologian."

"Why did you do this?"

"I did it to save the Republican party."

"What are your politics?"

"I am a Stalwart among the Stalwarts. With Garfield out of the way, we can carry all the Northern States, and with him in the way we can't carry a single one."

Upon learning that McElfresh was a detective, Guiteau said: "You stick to me and have me put in the third story, front at the jail. General

Sherman is coming down to take charge. Arthur and all those men are my friends, and I'll have you made Chief of Police. When you go back to the depot, you will find that I left two bundles of papers at the news stand which will explain all."

"Is there anybody else with you in this matter?"

"Not a living soul. I have contemplated the thing for the last six weeks, and would have shot him when he went away with Mrs. Garfield, but I looked at her, and she looked so bad that I changed my mind."

On reaching the jail, the officers of the institution did not seem to know anything about the assassination, and when taken inside, Mr. Russ, the deputy warden, said: "This man has been here before."

The detective then asked Guiteau, "Have you ever been here before?"

"No, sir," he replied.

"Well, the deputy warden seems to identify you."

"Yes; I was down here last Saturday morning, and wanted them to let me look through, and they told me that I couldn't, but to come Monday."

"What was your object in looking through?"

"I wanted to see what sort of quarters I would have to occupy."

Continuing, the detective said: "I then searched him, and when I pulled off his shoes he said, 'Give me my shoes; I will catch cold on this stone pavement.' I told him he couldn't have them, and then he said, 'Give me a pair of pumps then.'"

The prisoner having been safely locked up, a conference was held between Secretary Lincoln and General Sherman, when it was resolved that in view of the rapidly increasing public excitement, and the very natural fears that an attempt would be made to lynch the assassin, the District militia should be put under arms, and three companies of United States Artillery were called out from the Arsenal, one company being mounted as cavalry, and the other two as infantry. These were again sub-divided, and placed partly about the White House grounds and partly around the jail.

The dastardly deed had been done: the cowardly criminal caged; and then public attention turned sadly to the prostrate patriot President, stricken down in the path of duty, and perishing on that political Pisgah whence he had viewed the Promised Land of his career; that purified administration which he had hoped for as the crowning glory of his life, and the proud boast of every American citizen.

THE CAUSES AND THE CONSEQUENCES.

CHAPTER I.

The Spoils System of Office—Its Growth and Contaminating Effects—Its Association with the Third Term Movement—The Stalwart Combination and the New York Collectorship.

THE sometimes subtle, but always interesting, relations of cause and effect are at any time worthy of attention and study. They are of especial interest to every American citizen in considering the crime of Guiteau. While it is perfectly true that nothing can extenuate the character of the dastardly act, nothing can take from it the stigma of personal malice and disappointment, it may not be denied that the inciting causes were above, below and beyond the mere petty promptings of his miserable, vicious vanity. Guiteau was the willing, and therefore contemptible, exponent and tool of the spoils system of office holding, and office seeking, which originating Democratically, was seized upon and adopted by the Republican party at the close of the war; transplanted and nurtured into bloom under the Grant administrations; conserved

JAIL AT WASHINGTON (GUITEAU'S PRISON.)

throughout the career of that amiably obstinate, apology for a President, Rutherford B. Hayes; forced to fruit by the hot-house atmosphere of the Chicago Convention, and ripened by the conscienceless contumacy of Conkling, till it scattered its seeds in the fatal shot of July 2, 1881. Beneath the shadow of this Upas tree of our political development, public probity had perished, and party purposes or personal profit became alone the considerations which entered into the conditions of the public service. The prolific parent of fraud, of treachery, and of brutality, the spoils system, had brought this coun'ry to that revolutionary state when, in the words of Talleyrand, "everything solid and valuable sinks to the bottom, and only straws and things worthless float upon the surface." The official turpitude which became so rampant in the days of Grant's second administration, aroused the fears of the people, and the Third Term scheme was reluctantly abandoned, but the poison in the political veins was not extirpated; partly because Democratic degeneracy had kept pace with Republican rascality, and the vitiated system of the entire nation was too sluggish to throw off the virus. The appalling fraud of 1876 could only have been possible in such a condition of moral disease. The subsequent quiescence was but the consequent stupor. Meanwhile the rank weeds were growing apace; the Star Route frauds were developing and extending their area, and "Stalwartism," the shibboleth of a bandit brotherhood, had been coined.

But meanwhile, also, a healthy reaction had taken place; a vigorous undergrowth, which pestiferous vegetation could not choke, had asserted itself, and the result was the remarkable outcome of the Chicago Convention, crushing out the revived Third Term heresy, re-asserting the sovereign will of the people in opposition to the domination of the "Bosses," and inscribing on the renovated banner of a re-awakened nation the potent legend,

"GARFIELD AND CIVIL SERVICE REFORM."

It is needless here to enter upon the details of that campaign; they are too well known and too widely apprehended, as matters of universal interest, to require recapitulation; but the subsequent movements of the New York Stalwart ring, in regard to the Collectorship struggle, though equally matters of pertinent national interest, were, from their sectional character, less generally known and appreciated. It is, however, amid the details of the warring, selfish ambitions, which were rampant in their hydra-headed repulsiveness at the time of the Conkling revolt and resignation: amid the scenes of shameless bribery in the Senate and House of Representatives at Albany, New York, which followed in the desperate struggle for reinstatement and vindication: amid such episodes as that of the Delevan House, when the moral record of ex-Senator Platt was smirched by the disgraceful trick of a depraved and dissolute clique who sought to throw off the track the candidate for the long term, and thus clear the path along which "Conkling and his Curl" might march triumphant towards the National Capitol, with the avowed intent of braving, bearding and defying under its sacred dome, the chosen ruler of fifty millions of free people. Amid all these must be sought, and can readily be found, the causes which afforded the egotistical assassin a colorable pretext for his pretended inspiration.

While reviewing this branch of our subject, it it will not be inappropriate to incorporate just here, a strange chapter of secret history in connection with the assassination, which has just come to light. It is for others to judge of its value and significance, and we therefore give the story just as we find it in the *Cincinnati Enquirer* of January 8th, 1881.

CHAPTER II.

A "Seer's" Strange Statement—The Assassination of President Garfield Circumstantially Foretold at the Time of his Nomination—The Strong Impression Made by the Prediction upon General Garfield, Secretary Schurz, Marshal Henry and others.

CLEVELAND, OHIO, January 6, 1882.

EDITOR CINCINNATI ENQUIRER:

"I have just unearthed a chapter in the Garfield tragedy which reads like a romance. It is no romance, however, but cold, unadulterated facts.

In a quiet street along the lake side, in this city, resides a remarkable man, one about whom there is an air of mystery which, so far has baffled official scrutiny. He impresses one with his learning, his intimate acquaintanceship with affairs of State in foreign countries, and his knowledge of politics, men and measures of this nation.

The bare assertion, unsupported by the incidents I am about to relate, that this interesting man foretold the assassination of President Garfield weeks, aye months before the act was done, would make no impression on the reader, for "cranks" with predictions are as thick as blackberries.

But this prediction is well known to at least two influential men in this city, one of them holding a position of honor and trust in the municipal government, the other an officer of the Federal Government.

The "man with a vision" has been a resident of Cleveland for several years, emigrating to this place from a Jesuit college in Georgetown, D. C.

Last July a year ago, he first came to the notice of certain officials here. These gentlemen, up to the present time—when the awful calamity is a thing of the past, and the minutest details of the assassination of President Garfield corroborate just what had been foretold—are astounded, and know not what to think. The sober second thought, the early training and the education of these gentleman were all against the theory that that this singular man knew that the

GUITEAU, THE ASSASSIN. 37

assassination would take place, but they are confronted with the cold facts—they saw the terrible tragedy unravel itself as predicted by him, and they stand aghast at what they cannot fully comprehend.

One afternoon, about four o'clock, at the time stated above, this man called at the private office of one of the gentlemen mentioned. The other official was sent for and the interview was had.

The "Seer," for by this name he will be distinguished in this article, in obedience to an implied promise that his identity should not be revealed, began his business by a remarkable statement to the the effect that the powers of Europe, with the exception of two governments, were in league against the perpetuity of the American Republic, and that there were machinations then on foot to destroy our republican institutions, and plant upon its ruins a monarchy. This sounded like the ravings of a distempered imagination, and these cool-headed, business men concluded that their visitor was daft. He convinced them, however, that there was at least method in his madness, by taking from his pocket a bundle of letters from foreign Ministers, among them being a number from Prince Bismarck. The letters were in German, and, as neither of the Seer's auditors could read the language, they were not read at that time. The man kept on, and finally, by his reasoning, the power of his eloquence and his earnestness, so impressed them that they became convinced that there should be some heed taken of his utterances. This remember, was during the Presidential campaign.

"What can we do?" was asked by the attentive listeners to this visionary. "What is necessary to be done? You are certain Garfield will be elected President, and you are just as certain he will be murdered," said they; "now, what do you advise us to do?"

"Give me," said he, "a letter or note to Mr. Garfield. You gentlemen are both acquainted with him. You are his intimate friends. Write me a letter which I may take with me, and I will do the rest." This was the substance of his reply.

The note to Garfield was written almost under protest, and ran something like this: "The bearer has a matter of a remarkable tenor to communicate to you. Give him a hearing."

The Seer departed from the office satisfied, and at once made preparations for his journey to Mentor, to hold an interview with Garfield.

After he had left the office, one of these gentlemen, a man, by the way, well known in Cleveland, the holder of an important Government position, and one whose name, if given here, would be recognized all over the State, was so impressed with the singular interview, was so convinced that the man would go to Mentor on his self-imputed mission, that he became alarmed. He thought to himself (and he has since given expression to the thought) that it would be wrong for him to send this man to Mentor, to the home of Garfield, with the uncertainty as to what were his intentions himself towards Garfield.

He didn't know but that his visitor was a murderous crank, who made the prediction, and then intended to kill his victim to make sure that such prediction would be verified.

The more he thought about it, the firmer he became convinced that it was his duty to go to Mentor himself and warn Garfield of the proposed visit.

The whole circumstance was related to Garfield. He was told of the strange prediction, the trustworthiness of the man who made it, his earnestness, his eloquence, and his determination to come to Mentor on this business.

Garfield listened attentively, but showed no signs of fear or trepidation. The narrative, however, made a marked impression upon his mind, and he told his Cleveland friend that he had had warnings a few days previous that his life was in danger.

One of these warnings came from a man who traveled all the way from New York City, for the express purpose of putting him on his guard. Another one came from Boston. A man from that city visited Mentor, and asked Garfield, during the course of the conversation which ensued, what room he slept in at night.

"Right there," said Garfield, "on the gound floor, next to the portico."

"For God's sake, General Garfield," replied the man, "do not sleep there any more. Your life is in danger. Occupy the most obscure room in this house, for I tell you an attempt will be made upon your life."

As a matter of fact, well attested by the members of the Garfield household at that time, General Garfield heeded that warning, and moved his bed to an upper floor—not the night immediately following, but the change was made soon after, and this room he occupied until after his election to the Presidency, and his removal to Washington the following March.

So when the Cleveland friend took him the tidings of this prediction he was the more impressed with it. The friend remained at Mentor until one o'clock in the morning, and then rode back to Cleveland, making the return trip in a little over two hours.

The incident of the above visit is incorporated in Colonel Rockwell's recent article in the "Century Magazine" upon the subject of Garfield's life and death.

GUITEAU, THE ASSASSIN. 39

Before the Cleveland man left Mentor, he heard Garfield request Colonel Rockwell and Major Swaim, who then formed part of his household, to keep watch of the expected visitor and see what he meant to do.

The Seer took the train the next day for Mentor, arriving there about one o'clock.

He carried with him an American flag, made of silk and of a small pattern. On the top of the flagpole on small streamers, about a foot long, were worked the names of "Washington" and "Lincoln."

Garfield gave him an audience immediately, and for two hours this man held the future President spell-bound with the eloquence of his words, the deep knowledge of State affairs and political measures which he evinced, and the terrible earnestness of his manner. He rehearsed to him in detail the subject touched upon in the Cleveland office at the interview above alluded to; told him that he would be elected President, and warned him that there was a conspiracy on foot to murder him, and that the weapon of death would be a pistol.

This reads like the mouthings of a "crank," but Garfield did not regard his visitor in that light. He told him that he was impressed with his words; that he would take every precaution against assassination, and that he would write a letter to any person his visitor would name in Washington, so that when he went there, as the Seer intended, he could make arrangements to thwart any conspiracy, if there was one, against Garfield's life.

The Seer suggested the name of Hon. Carl Schurz, then Secretary of the Interior. President Hayes at that time was on a visit to California.

The letter to Schurz was written. The substance of it was, that the bearer had made to him some astounding statements which bore evidence of truth, and that he and his statements should be given careful consideration.

Before he made arrangements, however, to visit Washington, Schurz came on to Cleveland, where he had a personal interview at the Kennard House with this strange man. He made the same impression upon Schurz, as he did upon all with whom he talked on this subject, and was treated with great distinction by the German statesman.

Captain Henry, Marshal of the District of Columbia, before he went to Washington to take the position given him by Garfield after the election, was put in possession of the outlines of the Seer's story and prediction, and during an interview held at the office of the gentlemen alluded to as a Government officer, Henry was present and became acquainted with him.

"Who would hurt Garfield?" asked Henry of the Seer upon one occasion soon after the election.

"Wait and see," were the prophetic words of the Seer. When next they met (Henry and the Seer) Garfield was suffering at Elberon from the wounds made by the assassin's bullet, and he had nothing to say to the words of the Seer, "What did I tell you?"

After the election and Garfield had been inaugurated, this singular man called upon ex-President Hayes. He told him his fears as to the awful fate of the President, spoke in burning language of the foul conspiracy, as he termed it, of killing the President to make way for a man who was in league with the Powers who had determined to sound the death-knell of the Republic, and place on its ruins a powerful monarchy. It is in evidence in the handwriting of ex-President Hayes, which he wrote to a relative in this city a day or two after the Seer's visit to him at Fremont, that he had never met a man who so interested him, or one who seemed to be better informed upon subjects of which the average citizen never thought. He had his misgivings of the man, however, and wrote to the Government officer mentioned above that he must be mad—not that his words or actions denoted insanity, but that the stupendous and wicked conspiracy he spoke of, of which the death of Garfield was the forerunner, and of which he talked about with so much earnestness and reason, was too monstrous for belief. Said the Federal officeholder to the Seer upon one occasion after Garfield's death:

"You must be crazy."

"I know you think I am," he replied, "and so do other men, but I am just as certain of what I tell you as I am that Garfield is dead —cut off by the hand of an assassin."

His remarkable prediction did not rest with the mere declaration that Garfield would be killed. He described the looks of the assassin and the make of the pistol whose sound shocked the world, and in every detail his prophecy was fulfilled to the letter. This is the literal truth, and will be sworn to, if necessary, by at least two of the most reputable men in Cleveland.

When the nation was cheered up with the messages from the President's bedside, and Hope spread her wings with joy over the intelligence flashed by wire that Garfield would live, this man doggedly said: "No; he will die. If the bullet wound does not kill him, his end will be encompassed some other way. He has been doomed to die."

Under cover of a letter addressed to Dr. Boynton, one of Garfield's physicians, and a relative of Mrs. Garfield, this man wrote a note to Mrs. Garfield, the President's wife, telling her not to be buoyed up with false hopes; that her husband would never arise from his bed; that if the wound made by Guiteau's bullet did not prove sufficient, the conspirators would end his life by poison, or some other sure and certain means. Dr. Boynton can tell whether or not he ever received such a missive, and will no doubt corroborate this part of the story.

The Seer made a trip to Washington just previous to the assassination, but met with no encouragement from Captain Henry, upon whom he called, but was told by that official that he had better go back to Cleveland. He did go back, and when the news came to Cleveland that Garfield was shot at the Potomac Depot, while about to take the train for Long Branch, this man was engaged at his work at a private house on Kennard Street.

The lady of the house ran to him with a paper in her hand and said, in an excited manner, "My God! President Garfield has been shot."

"I am not at all surprised to hear that," said he. "I have been looking for it for some time."

He did not stop to make any explanations, and the horrified lady pronounced him a fool. He started towards his home, and, meeting an acquaintance, he asked if he had heard that the President had been shot. The reply was in the affirmative and the Seer went on, while the citizen stood and uttered curses upon the miscreant that fired the shot.

He kept on until he reached the City Hall. He ascended the steps and entered the Mayor's office. Mayor Herrick had read the startling announcement from Washington, and when the Seer stood before him he was speechless with amazement and horror. Herrick knew of the prediction.

The two citizens and officeholders, whom I have referred to in this article, have kept their knowledge of this remarkable story a profound secret. They cannot explain it away, and are powerless to suggest a solution. They cannot believe that there is any superhuman agency about it. They only know that this man told them what would occur long before it was done, and they saw his prediction verified in all its essential features. Upon the subject of political conspiracies they pronounce him a monomaniac, but they accord to him a wonderful knowledge of European and American secret history; they acknowledge that he is a keen, self-contained man, with none of the wild-eyed, suspicious cranky actions or manners of a lunatic; they agree that he is a quiet, good citizen, an affectionate husband and a kind father; there never has been the breath of suspicion against his good name, but still they are unsettled as to his status. Say they, he has perhaps made hundreds of predictions that never were fulfilled. Perhaps he has blundered on to this. But yet they cannot forget that his prediction in this instance was so circumstantial, and was so fully borne out by subsequent events, that again they are troubled as to what category he belongs.

The man is modest in the extreme. He does not wish to get into print, and made me promise solemnly that his name should not be given to the public. He fears the vengeance of these conspirators, whoever they may be, and does not care to run the risk of being made away with. This again sounds like the ravings of a demented brain, but to hear him talk you would almost be convinced that his fears are not groundless. He does not trade upon his alleged powers as a seer. He makes no money at it. He has made no predictions like the one in question. He is a poor man, but keeps his family comfortable on the proceeds of his labor in an entirely legitimate field of industry.

I asked him to-day if Guiteau would be hanged.

"No, sir; he will not; but he will be killed, and there will be others killed at the same time."

The truth or falsity of this prediction may be tested in a few weeks, and if he is right, the Seer will go down to history as the greatest guesser of the age—a man who blundered on to the truth, but whose words must be taken with all the allowance due an unfortunate whose mind is unbalanced. Let us wait and see.

(Signed), BEVERLY.

THE GREAT STATE TRIAL.

CHAPTER I.

The Grand Jury Presentment—Col. Corkhill's Remarkable and Exhaustive Bill of Indictment—The Full Text of the Six Counts of this Masterly Instrument.

THE first formal and specific step in the preliminary proceedings of this most remarkable criminal trial was, of necessity, the finding of a true bill by the Grand Jury of the District of Columbia. We have, in a previous section, detailed the conferences held with the authorities of the State of New Jersey upon the question of jurisdiction arising from the fact that, while the wounding took place in Washington, D. C., the resultant death occurred at Elberon, N. J., so that the mere allusion will suffice at this point.

THE GRAND JURY PRESENTMENT.

On the 4th of October, 1881, the following presentment was made:

In the Supreme Court of the District of Columbia, holding a Criminal Term. District of Columbia, County of Washington, to wit: June Term, 1881.

We, the Grand Jurors of the United States for the District aforesaid, upon our oath, do present Charles J. Guiteau for murder, in causing the death of James A. Garfield, President of the United States, by wounding him with a bullet fired from a pistol, with malice aforethought, by the said Charles J. Guiteau, in the building known as the Baltimore and Potomac Railroad Depot, situated at southwest corner of Sixth and B Streets, northwest, Washington, D. C., on or about the 2d day of July, A. D. 1881, on the evidence of Joseph K. Barnes, Surgeon-General U. S. A. ; Dr. D. F. Lamb, Medical Museum ; George W. Adams, EVENING STAR ; Sarah V. E. White, Baltimore and Potomac Depot ; Patrick Kearney, Metropolitan Police ; Robert A. Parke, Bal'imore and Potomac Depot ; Jacob P. Smith, Baltimore and Potomac Depot; Edwin A. Bailey, attorney ; Edmund L. Du Barry, Baltimore and Potomac Depot.

C. CHURCHMAN, Foreman.

THE FORMAL INDICTMENT.

Based upon this presentment, Colonel George B. Corkhill, District Attorney for the District of Columbia, drew up the following indictment, which, as a masterly sample of involved diction, covering, in its length, breadth, depth and subtle earnestness, every possible avenue of escape, deserves to go on record as a model instrument. Whether, like the frog in the fable, Col. Corkhill made one mighty effort, and burst, is matter for others to decide; but we may mention, regretfully, in passing, that the anticipations of a cold, keen, consistent and powerful prosecution, which this document aroused, were doomed to bitter disappointment. It may never be known, perhaps, what influences, if any, were brought to bear, or whether this mighty flow of legal acumen was merely a spasmodic outburst like that of a torpedoed petroleum well, or the unique development of an artfully "salted" mining claim; but certain it is, that the prosecuting attorney who commenced the proceedings with all the sternness of a Spartan, gradually sank to to the role of a Greek chorus in the course of the tantalizing travesty of a trial, which converted into a comedy that which was in reality, a te.rible tragedy. But these comments are anticipatory, and we, therefore, without further preface, present in its entirety, one of the most potent and peculiar legal productions of the period:

In the Supreme Court of the District of Columbia, holding a Criminal Term. District of Columbia, County of Washington, to wit: June Term, 1881.

The Grand Jurors of the United States of America, in and for the county and District aforesaid, upon their oath present that Charles J. Guiteau, late of the county and District aforesaid, on the second day of July, in the year of our Lord one thousand eight hundred and eighty-one, with force and arms, at and in the county and District aforesaid, in and upon the body of one James A. Garfield, he, the said James A. Garfield in the peace of God and the United States of America then and there being, feloniously, wilfully and of his malice aforethought did make an assault, and that the said Charles J. Guiteau, a certain pistol of the value of five dollars, then and there charged with gunpowder and one leaden bullet, in which said pistol he, the said Charles J. Guiteau, in his right hand then and there had and held, then and there feloniously, wilfully, and of his malice aforethought, did discharge and shoot off to, against and upon the said James A. Garfield ; and that the said Charles J. Guiteau, with the leaden bullet aforesaid, out of the pistol aforesaid, then and there, by force of the gunpowder aforesaid, by the said Charles J. Guiteau discharged and shot off as aforesaid, then and there feloniously, wilfully and of his malice aforethought, did strike, penetrate and wound him, the said James A. Garfield, in and upon the right side of the back of him, the said James A. Garfield, giving to him, the said-

James A. Garfield, then and there, with the leaden bullet aforesaid, so as aforesaid discharged and shot out of the pistol aforesaid by the said Charles J. Guiteau, in and upon the right side of the back of him, the said James A. Garfield, one mortal wound of the depth of six inches and the breadth of one inch, of which said mortal wound the said James A. Garfield, from the second day of July, in the year last aforesaid, until the nineteenth day of September, in the year of our Lord one thousand eight hundred and eighty-one, at and in the county and District aforesaid, did languish, and languishing did live, on which said nineteenth day of September, in the year of our Lord one thousand eight hundred and eighty-one, at and in the county and District aforesaid, the said James A. Garfield of the mortal wound aforesaid died; and so the Grand Jurors aforesaid, upon their oath aforesaid, do say that the said Charles J. Guiteau, him the said James A. Garfield, in the manner and by the means aforesaid, feloniously, wilfully and of his malice aforethought, did kill and murder, against the form of the statute in such case made and provided, and against the peace and Government of the United States of America.

THE SECOND COUNT.

And the Grand Jurors aforesaid, upon their oath aforesaid, do further present that the said Charles J. Guiteau, late of the county and District aforesaid, on the second day of July, in the year of our Lord one thousand eight hundred and eighty-one, with force and arms, at and in the county and District aforesaid, in and upon the body of one James A. Garfield, he, the said James A. Garfield, in the peace of God and the United States of America then and there being, feloniously, wilfully and of his malice aforethought, did make an assault, and that the said Charles J. Guiteau, a certain pistol of the value of five dollars, then and there charged with gunpowder, and one leaden bullet, which said pistol he, the said Charles J. Guiteau, in his right hand then and there had and held, then and there feloniously, wilfully and of his malice aforethought, did discharge and shoot off, to, against, and upon the said James A. Garfield, and that the said Charles J. Guiteau, with the leaden bullet aforesaid, out of the pistol aforesaid, then and there, by force of the gunpowder aforesaid, by the said Charles J. Guiteau discharged and shot off as aforesaid, then and there feloniously, wilfully and of his malice aforethought, did strike, penetrate and wound him, the said James A. Garfield, in and upon

GUITEAU, THE ASSASSIN. 47

the right side of the back of him, the said James A. Garfield, giving to him, the said James A. Garfield, then and there, with the leaden bullet aforesaid, so as aforesaid discharged and shot out of the pistol aforesaid, by the said Charles J. Guiteau, in and upon the right side of the back of him, the said James A. Garfield, one mortal wound of the depth of six inches and of the breadth of one inch, of which said mortal wound he, the said James A. Garfield, then and there instantly died, and so the Grand Jurors aforesaid, upon their oath aforesaid, do say that the said Charles J. Guiteau, him, the said James A. Garfield, in the manner and by the means aforesaid, feloniously, wilfully and of his malice aforethought, did kill and murder against the form of the statute in such case made and provided and against the peace and Government of the United States of America.

THE THIRD COUNT.

And the Grand Jurors aforesaid, upon their oath aforesaid, do further present that the said Charles J. Guiteau, late of the county and District aforesaid, on the second day of July, in the year of our Lord one thousand eight hundred and eighty-one, with force and arms, at and in the county and District aforesaid, in and upon the body of one James A. Garfield, he, the said James A. Garfield, in the peace of God and of the United States of America then and there being, feloniously, wilfully and of his malice aforethought, did make an assault, and that the said Charles J. Guiteau, a certain pistol of the value of five dollars, then and there charged with gunpowder and one leaden bullet, which said pistol he, the said Charles J. Guiteau, in his right hand then and there had and held, then and there feloniously, wilfully and of his malice aforethought, did discharge and shoot off, to, against and upon the said James A. Garfield, and that the said Charles J. Guiteau, with the leaden bullet aforesaid, out of the pistol aforesaid, then and there, by force of the gunpowder aforesaid, by the said Charles J. Guiteau discharged and shot off as aforesaid, then and there feloniously, wilfully and of his malice aforethought did strike, penetrate and wound him, the said James A. Garfield, in and upon the right side of the back of him, the said James A. Garfield, giving to him, the said James A. Garfield, then and there, with the leaden bullet aforesaid, so as aforesaid discharged and shot out of the pistol aforesaid, by the said Charles J. Guiteau, in and upon the right side of the back of him, the said

James A. Garfield, one mortal wound of the depth of six inches and of the breadth of one inch, of which said mortal wound he, the said James A. Garfield, from the said second day of July, in the year last aforesaid, until the nineteenth day of September, in the year of our Lord one thousand eight hundred and eighty-one, as well at and in the county and District aforesaid, as at and in the County of Monmouth and State of New Jersey, did languish, and languishing did live, on which said nineteenth of September, in the year of our Lord one thousand eight hundred and eighty-one, at and in the County of Monmouth and State of New Jersey aforesaid, the said James A. Garfield, of the mortal wound aforesaid, died, and so the Grand Jurors aforesaid, upon their oath aforesaid, do say that the said Charles J. Guiteau, him, the said James A. Garfield, in the manner and by the means aforesaid, feloniously, wilfully and of his malice aforethought, did kill and murder, against the form of the statute in such case made and provided, and against the peace and Government of the United States of America.

THE FOURTH COUNT.

And the Grand Jurors aforesaid, upon their oath aforesaid, do further present that the said Charles J. Guiteau, late of the county and District aforesaid, on the second day of July, in the year of our Lord one thousand eight hundred and eighty-one, with force and arms, at and in the county and District aforesaid, in and upon the body of one James A. Garfield, he, the said James A. Garfield, in the peace of God and of the United States of America then and there being, feloniously, wilfully and of his malice aforethought, did make an assault; and that the said Charles J. Guiteau, a certain pistol of the value of five dollars, then and there charged with gunpowder and one leaden bullet, which said pistol he, the said Charles J. Guiteau, in his right hand then and there had and held, then and there feloniously, wilfully and of his malice aforethought did discharge and shoot off to, against and upon the said James A. Garfield; and that the said Charles J. Guiteau, with the leaden bullet aforesaid, out of the pistol aforesaid, then and there by force of the gunpowder aforesaid, by the said Charles J. Guiteau discharged and shot off as aforesaid, then and there feloniously, wilfully and of his malice aforethought, did strike, penetrate and wound him, the said James A. Garfield, in and upon the right side of the back of him,

HON. GEO. B. CORKHILL,
U. S. District Attorney.

the said James A. Garfield, giving to him, the said James A. Garfield, then and there with the leaden bullet aforesaid, so as aforesaid discharged and shot out of the pistol aforesaid by the said Charles J. Guiteau, in and upon the right side of the back of him, the said James A. Garfield, one mortal wound of the depth of six inches and of the breadth of one inch, of which said, mortal wound he, the said James A. Garfield, from the said second day of July, in the year last aforesaid, until the nineteenth day of September, in the year of our Lord one thousand eight hundred and eighty-one, as well at and in the county and District aforesaid, as at and in the County of Monmouth and State of New Jersey, did languish, and languishing did live, on which said nineteenth day of September, in the year of our Lord one thousand eight hundred and eighty-one, at and in the County of Monmouth, and State of New Jersey, aforesaid, to wit, and in the County of Washington, and District of Columbia, the said James A. Garfield of the mortal wound aforesaid died; and so the Grand Jurors aforesaid, upon their oath aforesaid, do say that the said Charles J. Guiteau, him, the said James A. Garfield, in the manner and by the means aforesaid, feloniously, wilfully and of his malice aforethought, did kill and murder, against the form of the statute in such case made and provided, and against the peace and the good Government of the United States of America.

THE FIFTH COUNT.

And the Grand Jurors aforesaid, upon their oath aforesaid, do further present that the said Charles J. Guiteau, late of the county and District aforesaid, on the second day of July, in the year of our Lord one thousand eight hundred and eighty-one, with force and arms, at and in the county and District aforesaid, the said District constituting a judicial district of the United States, in and upon the body of one James A. Garfield, he, the said James A. Garfield, in the peace of God and of the United States of America then and there being, feloniously, wilfully and of his malice aforethought, did make an assault; and that the said Charles J. Guiteau, a certain pistol of the value of five dollars, then and there charged with gunpowder and one leaden bullet, which said pistol he, the said Charles J. Guiteau, in his right hand then and there had and held, then and there, feloniously, willfully and of his malice aforethought, did discharge and shoot off to, against and upon the said James A. Garfield, and that the said Charles J. Guiteau with the leaden bullet aforesaid, out of the pistol aforesaid, then and there by force of the gunpowder aforesaid, by the said Charles J. Guiteau discharged and shot off as aforesaid, then and there, feloniously, wilfully and of his malice aforethought, did strike, penetrate and wound him, the said James A. Garfield, in and upon the right side of the body of him, the said James A. Garfield, giving to him, the said James A. Garfield, then and there, with the leaden bullet aforesaid, so as aforesaid discharged and shot out of the pistol aforesaid by the said Charles J. Guiteau, in and upon the right side of the body of him, the said James A. Garfield, one mortal wound of the depth of six inches and of the breadth of one inch, of which said mortal wound he, the said James A. Garfield, from the said second day of July, in the year last aforesaid, until the nineteenth day of September, in the year of our Lord one thousand eight hundred and eighty-one, as well at and in the county and District aforesaid, as at and in the County of Monmouth and State of New Jersey, the said State of New Jersey constituting another Judicial district of the United States different from the Judicial district of the United States consisting of the District of Columbia, did languish, and languishing did live; on which said nineteenth day of September, in the year of our Lord one thousand eight hundred and eighty-one, at and in the County of Monmouth and State of New Jersey aforesaid, the said James A. Garfield of the mortal wound aforesaid died; and so the Grand Jurors aforesaid, upon their oath aforesaid, do say that the said Charles J. Guiteau, him, the said J. A. Garfield, in the manner and by the means aforesaid, feloniously, wilfully and of his malice aforethought, did kill and murder, against the form of the statute in such case made and provided, and against the peace and Government of the United States of America.

THE SIXTH COUNT.

And the Grand Jurors aforesaid, upon their oath aforesaid, do further present that the said Charles J. Guiteau, late of the county and District aforesaid, on the second day of July, in the year of our Lord one thousand eight hundred and eighty-one, with force and arms, at and in the county and District aforesaid, in and upon the body of one James A. Garfield, he, the said James A. Garfield, in the peace of God and of the United States of America then and there being, feloniously, wilfully and of his malice aforethought, did make an assault, and that the said Charles J. Guiteau, a certain pistol of the value of five dollars, then and there charged with gunpowder and one leaden bullet, which said pistol he, the said Charles J. Guiteau, in his right hand then and there had and held, then and there feloniously, wilfully and of his malice aforethought, did discharge and shoot off to, against and upon the said James A. Garfield; and that the said Charles J. Guiteau, with the leaden bullet aforesaid, out of the pistol aforesaid, then and there, by force of the gunpowder aforesaid, by the said Charles J. Guiteau discharged and shot off then and there, feloniously, wilfully and of his malice aforethought, did strike, penetrate and wound him, the said James A. Garfield, in and upon the right side of the back of him, the said James A. Garfield, then and there, with the leaden bullet aforesaid, so as aforesaid discharged and shot out of the pistol aforesaid, by the said Charles J. Guiteau, in and upon the right side of the back of him, the said James A. Garfield, one mortal wound of the depth of six inches and of the breadth of one inch, of which said mortal wound he, the said James A. Garfield, from the said second day of July, in the year last aforesaid, until the nineteenth day of September, in the year of our Lord one thousand eight hundred and eighty-one, as well at and in the county and District aforesaid, as at and in the County of Monmouth and State of New Jersey, did languish, and languishing did live; on which said nineteenth day of September, in the year of our Lord one thousand eight hundred and eighty-one, at and in the County of Monmouth and State of New Jersey aforesaid, the said James A. Garfield of the mortal wound aforesaid died; and that thereafter, to wit: On the twenty-first day of September, in the year of our Lord one thousand eight hundred and eighty-one, the dead body of him, the said James A. Garfield, was removed from the said County of Monmouth, and State of New Jersey, and brought into the County of Washington, and District of Columbia, within which last-mentioned county the dead body of him, the said James A. Garfield, lay and remained from the said twenty-first day of September, in the year of our Lord one thousand eight hundred and eighty-one, until the twenty-third day of September, in the year of our Lord one thousand eight hundred and eighty-one; and so the Grand Jurors aforesaid, upon their oath aforesaid, do say that the said Charles J. Guiteau, him, the said James A. Garfield, in the manner and by the means aforesaid, feloniously, wilfully and of his malice aforethought, did kill and murder, against the form of the statute in such case made and provided, and against the peace and Government of the United States of America.

CHAPTER II.

Opening Scenes—Unpleasant Altercations between Counsel for the Defence—The Prisoner's Persistent Interruptions—The Panel Exhausted and only four Jurors Obtained—Guiteau's Detestable Document.

ON the morning of Monday, November 14, 1881, the formal proceedings in the trial of Charles J. Guiteau for the murder of President James Abram Garfield began in the District Supreme Court at Washington, D. C.

THE COURT ROOM.

A low ceilinged, large sized, square apartment, in the eastern wing of the City Hall, was arranged specially for this important trial. At the eastern end was located a platform, containing the Judge's seat, the clerks' desk being immediately below it. The large table which usually occupies the greater part of the space allotted to the Bar had been removed, and several small tables placed for the accommodation of counsel and reporters. At the northeastern end were the seats assigned to the jurors, and the western half of the room was occupied by a raised platform with a few hundred chairs for spectators. There was but little interest

THE JURY.
THE GREAT STATE TRIAL OF GUITEAU THE ASSASSIN.

GUITEAU, THE ASSASSIN. 53

manifested at the outset, and beyond the usual scramble in a criminal court for front seats, the opening proceedings were uneventful. A few ladies were present, including Mrs. Scoville, sister of the prisoner, and wife of his counsel. But few men of note, other than those engaged in the case, were observed, and the majority of the spectators belonged to the rougher element; still there were in all some four hundred persons present, when the crier, in the old Norman form, opened the Court with his

OYES! OYES! ETC.

Judge Walter S. Cox had taken his seat punctually at 10 o'clock, and the counsel were arranged at their tables in the following order: District Attorney Corkhill, of the District of Columbia, Judge Porter, of New York, Mr. Davidge, of Washington, and Mr. E. B. Smith, of New York, ex-Assistant Attorney-General, who had been retained as assistant counsel, represented the prosecution, and had seats to the left of the table facing the judge. Mr. E. B. Scoville, of Chicago, and Mr. Leigh Robinson, of Washington, who was assigned by the Court to aid in the defence, sat next, and when the proceedings had commenced the prisoner sat on the right of Mr. Robinson, his sister Mrs. Scoville being next him, and his brother John W. Guiteau, of Boston, beyond her. Between the attorney's table and the railing to the forum were the press tables, while on either side, and in the immediate rear, were the seats for the local Bar.

THE PRISONER APPEARS.

The drawling tones of the crier had barely died away when Guiteau, who had been brought from the jail at half-past nine o'clock, was escorted by the marshal and his deputies to the seat arranged for him next to his sister. There was a general murmur among the crowd, which for a moment had been silent with intense expectation, and many rose to their feet in order to get a good view of the prisoner. His step was elastic and his manner nervous. His face evidenced fear in all its features. His eyes gleamed and danced as if their owner was inspired with the utmost dread of some pending danger. He gave a quick but timid glance at the crowd, and then stood with his head downward. Immediately the handcuffs were removed and Guiteau threw his black slouch hat on the table, at the same time taking his seat. Back of him were four officers. The change in the prisoner's features was now visible. After using his handkerchief he turned to the right and shook hands with Mrs. Scoville and his brother. With the former he engaged in earnest conversation for a minute apparently unmindful of the gaze of those around him. After his fright had subsided, his face assumed a dull expression, characterized by a vacant stare, occasionally varied by a scowl. He gradually became more composed and was for the first time seen to smile when Mr. Robinson began to speak.

District Attorney Corkhill then stated that the Government was ready to proceed with the trial of Charles J. Guiteau.

Mr. Robinson rose and said that when he had been assigned to this case, neither of the eminent counsel now assisting in the prosecution had been been retained by the government. At the time referred to, also, a gentleman in Chicago had been expected to assist in the defence. Shortly afterward it had been stated that he would not be able to be present. The presence of the able counsel whose services the government had been able to command, whatever other advantages it might possess, did not make him (Robinson) feel more satisfied with the condition of the defence. It would be truly remarkable if he were not very sensible of the great disparity of force which had been created by the addition to the prosecution. A few days ago, his Honor had been kind enough to express his regret that he had not been at liberty to accede to his request for an extension of time, and had suggested that he could assign the defence additional counsel. As soon as it had been in his (Robinson's) power he had sought the aid of such additional counsel. He had applied to a well-known member of the District Bar, and laid before him the situation of the case, stating to him that it was absolutely imperative that he should have assistance. The gentleman in question had said that he did not see how he could at this time come into the case. He had then asked the gentleman whether he could do so in two weeks, and whether he would if he was ordered to do so by the Court. He, therefore, was going to ask his Honor to give him the time necessary for the Court to made the order. It would be remarkable, if in this case in which he was practically alone, he would not have assistance. On the day of the prisoner's arraignment Mr. Scoville had stated that he was not familiar with the practice of criminal law. The relationship of that gentleman to the accused also disqualified him, in the estimate of many, from rendering that assistance which he (Mr. Robinson) required as an associate. For the fair trial of this man assistance was absolutely necessary. He had no other motive than to acquit himself faithfully to the profession. He had other grounds upon which to base his request for the delay. There were at least three material witnesses for the defence who were absent from this district, and could certainly not be here before the 1st of December. He would give the names of those witnesses to the Court, and he would make an affidavit of the fact if the prosecution required it. He then filed the affidavit to which he had referred, preferring doing that to reading it himself.

No sooner had Mr. Robinson taken his seat than the prisoner rose, and in an excited manner, addressed the Court: "I was not aware that my counsel, Mr. Robinson, intended this morning to make an application for postponement, and I desire to be heard in my own behalf in this matter, at the very threshhold of this case. I am charged here with a murderous attempt, and I desire to be heard in my own behalf."

The Court: "This is not the proper time to enter upon the defence. The only question before the Court is whether further time shall be allowed counsel to prepare for the defence."

The prisoner (emphatically): "So far as I am concerned I do not want further time. We are ready to try this case now."

The Court: "The question is whether further time ought to be allowed the counsel."

The prisoner (persistently): "I do not want that, if the Court please."

District Attorney Corkhill then said: "The Government must insist, as far as it can, on this trial proceeding now. The Court will recollect that the Goverment, as represented by your Honor, has extended to the defence all the courtesy, all the liberality, that could possibly be demanded by any prisoner. This crime was committed on the 2d of July last. The prisoner was arraigned on the 8th of October. He was at that time represented by counsel—by counsel, of reputation, of ability—a gentleman fully able to take entire charge of the case, notwithstanding his relations to the prisoner. The time fixed for the trial on that occasion was fixed with the understanding that the trial was to proceed on that day. When the statement was made that the risoner was unable to procure the attendance of witnesses, your Honor not only ordered the processes of the Court to which the prisoner was entitled, but allowed him the same right as the Government had to have the expenses of his witnesses paid by the United States. The Government could never get to trial in a case of this importance, if such reasons as are now alleged, were regarded as sufficient for the continuance of a case. It may well be that with all Mr. Robinson's ability he may shrink from taking the responsibility of going on with the case. Almost any lawyer would shrink and prefer to have more time in such a case. But there are other interests which must be considered. A great crime has been committed. There is a public demand that if this prisoner be guilty he should be punished; and if not guilty that the jury should say so. Mr. Robinson says that he has consulted with an eminent gentleman whom he wishes to have associated with him, and who will give him an answer at some future time. That is a matter which could have been presented to your Honor at the time the trial day was fixed. The witnesses are here from great distances and at great expense to the Government and to the great injury of their private business. No less than twenty witnesses have called upon me this morning begging to be relieved from attendance on the trial. They are here by process of the Court, in obedience to its order. They are here from all parts of the country as witnesses, both for prosecution and defence. A continuance of the case would do no good. It would accomplish nothing, except the allowing of Mr. Robinson (as he says) to prepare his case properly. He says that there are three important witnesses whose names he declines to divulge, lestt heir publication might interfere with their coming. If, during the progress of the trial, it should be found that these witnesses are not here, the process of the Court can enforce their attendance without any trouble. We are ready this morning to proceed with the trial, and if an emergency should arise during the progress of the case requiring the compulsion of a witness' attendance, he can be brought here through the process of the Court."

Mr. Robinson then addressed the Court as follows: "I will now swear to the affidavit and will give to the Court the names of three witnesses, from which the Court will see that is impracticable to have them here now, but that they can be here in the course of the next three weeks. If I had it in my power to carry this case over to the next term, I would not want to do it. I wish it begun in this term, that a jury shall be obtained, and that we shall have a week before the trial begins. In asking for this assignment of counsel, it will be obvious as soon as I give the name of the gentleman that I am asking for an auxiliary, which will be accepted by this community as a guarantee (I trust I may say without presumption, an additional guarantee) of the character and integrity of this defence."

He proceeded to the clerk's desk and swore to the affidavit, which he then handed to the Judge.

All this time Guiteau had been making frantic efforts to interfere, and was with the greatest difficulty restrained by Mr. Scoville and the deputy marshals.

SCENE BETWEEN COUNSEL.

At this point Mr. Scoville complained that the proceeding was unprecedented; he had no notice of it, and had not even seen the affidavit. Mr. Robinson remarked that he could do so, and Mr. Scoville replied: "Very well. Wait a moment. I say this is an unprecedented proceeding. Your Honor is aware that I have been here six weeks, leaving my business at home at great disadvantage to myself, and solely from a sense of personal duty which I could not shirk. I have undertaken in good faith to prepare for this defence. I have my witnesses subpœnaed and have done my best to be ready. I understand full well that I am not competent for a criminal trial of this kind. I supposed that, with the assistance of Mr. Robinson, who is competent, as I have understood, we could safely go to trial. I care nothing about prestige in this matter. 1 simply want to have what is done openly and in order. Personally I am willing to confine my work to the subpœnaing of witnesses. I seek no notoriety. I only ask that justice may be done, and that the character of this man may be vindicated. I shall withdraw from the case if the defence is to proceed longer in this manner. I will give whatever information I have to counsel for the defence, and I will step out. I do not want to have this case continued, and the prisoner does not want to have it continued. I do not know the gentlemen who Mr. Robinson says has been consulted. That fact, at least, should have been communicated to me. I have had no communication with Mr. Robinson for the last four days, although I have sought him. I certainly should have had conference with him at least with reference to the testimony and to the management of the case. I hoped for Mr. Robinson's assistance in this case, or, at least, I hoped to be permitted to assist him. If that cannot be done I cannot help it. All that I have to say is, that I am, in my feeble manner, ready for trial. I do not want the case continued. I do not want any further connection with the case unless, when a motion is to be made, I am advised of it long enough beforehand to know something about it. Unless the defence can go on harmoniously with me in it I will withdraw."

Guiteau again managed to get on his feet as Mr. Scoville sat down, and exclaimed, with a motion of his clenched fist: "I indorse every word of that, and I tell Mr. Robinson that if he does not do this thing just as I want it done, he can get out of the case. That is short."

Mr. Robinson rose to address the Court.

Guiteau (persistently): "I do not want to hear any more speeches of Mr. Robinson's. I want him to get out of the case." (To the deputy marshals who were pulling him back into his seat.) "Let me alone. You have nothing to do with me here."

Mr. Robinson, in reply, said: "I must express my unaffected regret that it should be supposed by Mr. Scoville that I intended any disrespect to him. I told him some time ago that I wanted assistance, and he knew, of course, that I wanted an extension of time. The Court will see the great delicacy which I had in regard to the name of the counsel whom I wished to have assigned. I had to see the gentleman and to press and urge him, and when I came into Court this morning I was fresh from an interview with this gentleman which justified me in making this application. I am very sorry not to have seen Mr. Scoville for the past two or three days; but it was only because I have been employed in preparing for the defence. I should have been happy to meet him. I did not intend him the least disrespect. I have thought very seriously over the matter, and I know that what I have asked is indispensable. I will give the name of the counsel as soon as I know that he can be assigned. I am sure that his assignment will strengthen the defence, especially where it most needs strengthening."

The Court: "The trouble is that I have no assurance that at the expiration of the time mentioned this gentleman will go into the case."

Mr. Robinson: "I give you my assurance that, if ordered by the Court, he will feel the obligation to accept the assignment."

The Court: "There is this much to be said about this application: the time that was first fixed for the trial was a week sooner than the time asked by Mr. Scoville, and when Mr. Robinson was assigned to the case he was not granted, by a week, the extension of time which he asked. So that the present application is not for any longer time than was originally asked by Mr. Robinson. I feel very much the embarrassment of the question. It is important that this trial should proceed without delay, and I intend that it shall proceed without unnecessary delay. I intend, also, that the prisoner shall have a fair trial, and that the reproof shall not rest upon the Court that the prisoner was sent to the gallows without a fair trial in order to appease public indignation. My inclination is to allow a week's time to Mr. Robinson, which is the time originally asked by him. I shall assign the counsel of whom he has spoken to assist him, leaving that counsel to make his arrangements to come into the case (if he cannot do so sooner) in two weeks' time. I do not think that I should give any more indulgence than this, and I find embarrassment in giving that much."

Guiteau (escaping the control of the deputy marshals and getting to his feet): "I do not want Mr. Robinson to act as my counsel. I want to say, emphatically, that Mr. Robinson came into the case without my consent. I know nothing about him, and I do not like the way he talks. I ask him peremptorily (pronouncing this word 'pre-emptorily') to retire. I expect in some time to have money to employ any counsel that I please. I am not a beggar nor a pauper."

Guiteau was made to resume his seat, and Mr. Scoville said: "I do hope that the Court will consider to some extent at least my position in this case. The only near relatives of the prisoner here present are his brother and his sister, and they will indorse all that I say. In our opinion the prisoner is not a person fit to take charge of or to arrange or to dictate his defence. Those who are responsible for that defence are the persons whom I have named. It does seem to me that in the assignment of counsel at least the name of the person proposed should be communicated to some of us."

The Court: "Of course it shall be."

Mr. Scoville: "Yes, your Honor; but I do not want it arranged until we know it in advance. I do not want Mr. Robinson, or any other man, to come in here and suggest the name of a counsel, and arrange with him, without the near relatives of the prisoner knowing the names or circumstances until it is too late. Your Honor is aware that I came here unacquainted with a single member of the bar, with one exception—Mr. Merrick. I went to Mr. Merrick and asked him whether he would accept an assignment by the Court. He said that his arrangements were such for several weeks that he could not do it. At the same time I understood from Mr. Merrick that if the trial could be fixed far enough ahead so that he could attend to it consistently with his other engagements, he would take part in the defence. Now, if the case is to be continued from time to time for the accommodation or satisfaction of any one, can it not be for the accommodation and satisfaction of the nearest relatives of the prisoner? Again, when Mr. Merrick declined I applied to General Butler, whose reply was substantially the same as Mr. Merrick's. All this was done by authority of the nearest relatives—the responsible persons charged with the defence of the criminal. I am also informed authoritatively that General Butler will come into the case if he gets sufficient time to prepare for it. Which of the two would be better counsel for the prisoner—General Butler or the person proposed by Mr. Robinson unknown to me—I do not know. But I do know this—that General Butler is the choice of the prisoner's relatives and of the prisoner himself. If the matter is to be continued, let it be continued long enough so that we can get such counsel as we want, and we will be prepared with counsel who will be fit to cope with the eminent counsel on the other side. We do not want the Court to assign counsel. We will employ counsel ourselves if the case be continued."

The Court: "I hardly know what to do in the matter. I think, however, that if it is the desire of the prisoner and his relatives for the case to proceed, I shall allow it to go on now. After a jury is obtained, and the testimony for the prosecution is put in, then if Mr. Robinson needs time to prepare his case I will give him time."

Guiteau had meanwhile persistently kept up his running interruptions and statements that he did not want Mr. Robinson in the case, till, losing patience, the Court said: "Let the case be commenced to-day." A further movement of the prisoner led to a peremptory order for his silence, to which the irrepressible prisoner replied: "I will do what the Court says, but not what that gentleman (pointing to the District Attorney) says."

After a further explanation between the Court

and counsel, during which Mr. Scoville was informed that no counsel should come into the case without his consent, this unpleasant scene terminated, and the Court acceded to the wish of the District Attorney to proceed with the case.

GETTING A JURY.

About 11 o'clock the work of swearing the jury panel was commenced, and the first juror, D. Lewis Blackford, took the witness stand. Before questioning him as to whether he had formed an opinion about the case, Judge Cox stated that he desired to address a few observations to the jury.

"Under the Constitution," he said, "the prisoner is entitled to be tried by an impartial jury. But an idea prevails that any impression or opinion, however lightly formed or feebly held, disqualifies from serving in the character of an impartial juror. This is an error. As the Supreme Court says, ' In these days of newspaper enterprise and universal education, every case of public interest is almost as a matter of necessity brought to the attention of all the intelligent people in the vicinity, and scarcely one can be found, among those best fitted for jurors, who has not read or heard of it, and who has not some impression or some opinion in respect to its merits.' If the prevalent idea I have mentioned were correct, it would follow that the most illiterate and uninformed people in the community would be the best qualified to discharge duties which require some intelligence and information. It is now generally, if not universally, agreed that such opinions or impressions as are merely gathered from newspapers or public report, and are mere hypothetical or conditional opinions, dependent upon the truth of the reports, and not so fixed as to prevent one from giving a fair and impartial hearing to the accused, and rendering a verdict according to the evidence, do not disqualify. On the other hand, fixed and decided opinions against the accused, which would have to be overcome before one could feel impartial, and which would resist the force of evidence for the accused, would be inconsistent with the impartiality that the law requires. There is a natural reluctance to serve on a case like this, and a disposition to seek to be excused on the ground of having formed an opinion, when in fact no real disqualification exists. But it is your duty as good citizens to assist the Court in the administration of justice in just such cases unless you are positively disqualified, and I shall expect you on your consciences to answer fairly as to the question of impartiality according to the explanation of it, which I have given to you."

The selection of a jury proved a difficult task, the three who first presented themselves being disqualified, two on the ground that they had formed fixed opinions on the case, and the other on the ground that he had conscientious scruples on the subject of capital punishment. In examining the jurors Mr. Scoville went over a large range of questions, inquiring as to their religious and political belief.

By 12.50 P. M. only the following five jurors had been obtained and sworn in: John P. Harlin, restaurant keeper; Fred. W. Brandenberg, cigar maker; Charles G. Stewart, flour and feed dealer; Henry J. Bright, retired from business, and Thomas H. Langley, grocer. The panel having been exhausted by them an order was issued, on the suggestion of the District Attorney, for the drawing of seventy-five additional names from the box, and it having been agreed that the sittings of the Court should be from 10 A. M. to 3 P. M. daily, allowing half an hour for recess, the Court at five minutes past one adjourned.

ANOTHER SCENE.

Just before the Court rose, however, Guiteau addressed Judge Cox, stating that he should desire to make a speech next morning, meanwhile fumbling with a manuscript which he had from time to time from the opening of the Court alternately withdrawn from his pocket and replaced, in deference to significant gestures from Mr. Scoville. The Court ordered him to take his seat.

He then passed the manuscript of his speech to a newspaper reporter, but before the latter could leave Mr. Scoville called him back and compelled him to return it. This raised the anger of the prisoner, who excitedly declared that he was not under the control of his counsel; that he was a lawyer and knew the law himself; that when he wanted help he would ask for it, and that he desired his speech to be published for the purpose of influencing public opinion.

The remarkable document, however, found its way into the hands of the press, and is here given in full. As a specimen of combined cunning, audacity, special pleading and blasphemy, it has probably never been equalled, and for the credit of humanity, it is to be hoped that it never will be.

GUITEAU'S STATEMENT.

If the Court please, I desire to address your Honor at the threshhold of this case. I am in the presence of this honorable Court charged with "maliciously and wickedly murdering one James A. Garfield." Nothing can be more absurd, because General Garfield died from malpractice. The syllogism to prove it is this:—Three weeks after he was shot his physicians held a careful examination and officially decided he would recover. Two months after this official announcement he died. Therefore, according to his own physicians, he was not fatally shot. The doctors who mistreated him ought to bear the odium of his death, and not his assailant. They ought to be indicted for murdering James A. Garfield, and not me. But I have been indicted and must stand my trial for the alleged homicide. General Garfield was President of the United States and I am one of the men who made him President. His nomination was an accident; his election the result of the greatest activity on the part of the Stalwarts, and his removal a special providence. General Garfield was a good man, but a weak politician. Being President, he was in a position to do vast harm to the Republic, and he was doing it by the unwise use of patronage, and the Lord and I took the responsibility of removing him. I certainly never would have sought to remove him on my own account. Why should I shoot him? He never harmed me. From him I expected an important office. I considered him my political and personal friend. But my duty to the Lord and to the American people overcame my personal feeling and I sought to remove him. Not being a marksman, he was not fatally shot; but incompetent physicians finished the work, and they and not me are responsible for his death. Nothing but the political situation last spring justified General Garfield's removal. The break in the Republican party last spring was widening week by week, and I foresaw a civil war. My inspiration was to remove the late President at once, and thereby close the breach before it got so wide that nothing but another heartrending and desolating war could close it. The last war cost the nation a million of men and a billion of money. The Lord wanted to prevent a repetition of this desolation and inspired me to execute his will. Why did he inspire me in preference to some one else? Because I had the brains and nerve probably to do the work. The Lord does not employ incompetent persons to serve him. He uses the best material he can find. No doubt there were thousands of Republicans that felt as I did about General Garfield wrecking the Republican party last spring, and had they the conception, the nerve, the brains, and the opportunity they would have removed him. I, of all the world, was the only man who had the conception. On the trial of my case, I propose to summon some of the leading politicians of the Republican and Democratic parties; also, the leading New York and Washington editors, to show the political situation and the perils which surrounded the Republic last spring. I propose to go into this branch of my defence exhaustively.

Another reason the Lord inspired me to remove the President in preference to some one else is because he wished to circulate my theological work, "The Truth." This book was written to save souls, and not for money, and the Lord in circulating the book is after souls. By it He preaches the Gospel, and prepares the world for their judgment, which some people think, and with reason, is not far distant. I have been delayed in getting out a new edition of this book, which will include a graphic narrative of my life, but I expect it will be issued shortly. More than one hundred witnesses have been summoned by the prosecution. Two-thirds of them I know nothing about, and the Court, I presume, will decide they are irrelevant. The issue here is: The Deity seems well disposed to father it thus far, and I expect He will continue to father it to the end. It is not likely He will allow me to come to grief for obeying Him. How do you know it was the Deity? I was so certain of it that I put up my life on it, and I undertake to say the Deity is actively engaged in my defence. I am confident He will checkmate the wise heads on this prosecution. I beg they go slow. They cannot afford to get the Deity down on them. "He uttered His voice," says the Psalms, "and the earth melted." This is the God whom I served when I sought to remove the President, and He is bound to take care of me. Recently a Washington newspaper lithographed a cramped piece of paper I had carried in my vest pocket a week under the title of "Guiteau's Plea." It was written, when I had the malaria, at odd times, and I could hardly read it myself, and so told the gentleman I gave it to, but he thought he could read it, and took it, as he was in haste. I next heard of it as a lithograph. Owing to circumstances beyond my control, I have been forced to ask your Honor to assign me counsel and furnish me witnesses. I formerly practised law in New York and Chicago. In 1877, I left a good practice in Chicago and went out lecturing, but I had small success. I had ideas, but no reputation. My theological work, "The Truth," contains "My Theology." It was written during a period of five years, and cost me a great deal of trouble, and I have no doubt but it is official. It left me in reduced circumstances, and I have had no chance to recuperate my finances since. I easily could have made $5,000 at the law in Chicago in 1877, and worked myself into a splendid position, but I had other work to do. As I know something about the law I propose to take an active part in my defence. My brother-in-law, George Scoville, Esq., of Chicago, is a true and active friend, but I disapprove of some of his movements in this case. Notably his mixing me with "Oneida Noyes," who for 25 years was the curse of my father's life, and for six years I lived under the despotism he wielded in the Oneida Community. I expressed my detestation of Noyesism then. To-day John H. Noyes, the founder of the Oneida Community, is an American fugitive on British soil. Noyes is a cold-blooded scoundrel. He has debauched more young women; broken up more reputable families, and caused more misery by his stinking fanaticism and licentiousness than any man of this age. Had Noyes had his due he would have been hanged thirty years ago for crimes committed with his own flesh and blood, and it would have been a Godsend to a great many decent people if he had

GUITEAU'S FATHER.

GUITEAU'S BROTHER (JOHN.)

THE SCOVILLE FAMILY.

been. During my residence in the Oneida Community I, like most of the men in that community, was practically a Shaker. * * * Mr. Scoville is developing a theory of hereditary insanity which may have an important bearing on this case. Insanity runs in my family. My father had two sisters and a nephew and a niece in an insane asylum. He himself was a monomaniac for twenty-five years on the Oneida Community. He could see no evil in that concern and no good out of it. He thought Noyes a greater man than the Lord Jesus Christ. He was rational enough outside of the community ideas. On that he was a lunatic. He would get greatly excited in discussing that, and look and act like a wild man. All this time he was a good business man. He was cashier of a bank, and attended to his duties promptly and faithfully. It was owing to his fanaticism and insanity that I got into the Oneida Community when a boy. Once under Noyes' influence it was impossible to get away, and I lingered there in the greatest distress for six long and weary years. I was in the community from 1860 to 1866. Since then I have known and cared nothing for them. One Smith, whom I knew there, has taken upon himself to write on this case, and among other silly and impertinent statements, he says I was in the habit of connecting my name with the words "Premier to England," &c. These statements are false. My father was a frequent visitor at the community, but never resided there. He wanted to go; but my step-mother opposed it. I wish this Oneida Community business to pass into oblivion.

My ex-wife has been summoned by the prosecution. Our marriage was premature. I only knew her ten weeks, and we married on ten hours' notice. She was a poor girl. She had been unfortunate, and I had no business to have married her. We were married in 1869, separated in 1873, and divorced in 1874, without issue I was practising law then, and we lived at hotels and boarding-houses. I have known little about her since 1873. I understand that she married well, four years ago, and is living in Colorado. I have been strictly virtuous for six or seven years. I claim to be a gentleman and a Christian.

I have been in jail since July 2. I have borne my confinement patiently and quietly, knowing my vindication would come. Twice have I been shot at, and came near being shot dead, but the Lord kept me harmless. Like the Hebrew children in the fiery furnace, not a hair on my head has been singed, because the Lord, whom I served when I sought to remove the President, has taken care of me. I have been kindly treated by the jail officials, and have no complaint, save that my letters have been intercepted going out and coming in, and I have been cut off until recently from reporters and newspapers, which I consider illegal and impertinent. Certain parties, whom I need not name, have been greatly benefited financially by my inspiration, and I am going to ask them to contribute to my defence. I have no right or wish to ask my lawyers to work for nothing. There are hundreds of persons who are and will be benefited financially by the new administration. They are all indebted to me for their positions, from the President down.

I confidently appeal to them and to the public at large to send me money for my defence. The money can be sent quietly by express (withholding the name, if you wish to) to George Scoville, Washington, D. C. It will be sacredly used for my defence. Certain politicians seem perfectly willing to fatten at the public crib on my inspiration; but they pretend to be horrified out of their senses by the late President's removal, and want nothing to do with me. They say I am "a dastardly assassin." The word "assassin" grates on the mind, and yet some people delight in using it. Why am I an assassin any more than a man who shot another during the war? Thousands of brave boys on both sides were shot dead during the war, but no one thinks of talking about an assassination. There was a homicide—i. e., a man was killed. But in my case the doctors killed the late President and not me, so that there is not even a homicide in this case. The President was simply shot and wounded by an insane man. The man was insane in law, because it was God's act and not his. There is not the first element of murder in this case.

To constitute the crime of murder two elements must co-exist:—1. An actual homicide. 2. Malice—malice in law or malice in fact. The law presumes malice from the fact of the homicide. There is no homicide in this case and therefore no malice in law. Malice, in fact, depends on the circumstances attending the homicide. Admitting that the late President died from the shot, which I deny as a matter of fact, still the circumstances attending the shooting liquidate the presumption of malice either in law or in fact. Heretofore political grievances have been adjusted by war or the ballot. Had Jefferson Davis and a dozen or two of his co-traitors been shot dead in January, 1861, no doubt our late Rebellion never would have been.

I am a patriot. To-day I suffer in bonds as a patriot. Washington was a patriot. Grant was a patriot. Washington led the armies of the Revolution through eight years of bloody war to victory and

GUITEAU, THE ASSASSIN. 75

glory. Grant led the armies of the Union to victory and glory, and to-day the nation is happy and prosperous. They raised the old war cry, "Rally round the flag, boys, rally round the flag," and thousands of the choicest sons of the Republic went forth to battle— to victory or death. Washington and Grant by their valor and success in war won the admiration of mankind. To-day I suffer in bonds as a patriot, because I had the inspiration and nerve to unite a great political party to the end that the nation might be saved another desolating war. I do not pretend war was immediate, but I do say emphatically that the bitterness in the Republican party last spring was deepening hour by hour, and that within two or three years or less, the nation would have been in a civil war. In the presence of death all hearts were hushed; contention ceased. For weeks and weeks the heart and brain of the nation centred on the sick man at the White House. At last he went the way of all flesh, and the nation was a house of mourning. To say that I have been misunderstood and villified by nearly the entire American press— nay, more, by nearly the entire American people—is a true statement. But Providence and time rightens all things, and to-day, by the gradual change of public opinion, I am justified in passing with laudable contempt the continual venom of certain newspapers. Let the newspapers change from "Guiteau, the assassin," to "Guiteau, the patriot."

I appeal to the stalwart and liberal press of the nation for justice. I appeal to the Republican party, especially the Stalwarts, of whom I am proud to be one, for justice. I appeal to the President of the United States for justice. I am the man that made him President. Without my inspiration he was a political cipher, without power or importance. I was constantly with him in New York last fall during the canvass, and he and the rest of our men knew that we had all that we could do to elect our ticket. Had General Hancock kept his mouth closed on the tariff or had the Morey letter been delayed a week Hancock would certainly have been elected. Then no man could tell what would have happened to the Republic. I am more than glad that President Arthur is proving himself a wise man in his new position, and I expect he will give the nation the finest administration it has ever had. I appeal to this Honorable Court for justice. I am glad Your Honor is a gentleman of broad views, Christian sentiment and clear head. I count myself fortunate, indeed, that my case is to be tried before so able and careful a jurist. I appeal to the District Attorney and his learned associates for justice. I beg they go slow in prosecuting this case, that they do no injustice to the Deity, whose servant I was when I sought to remove the late President. At the last great day they and all men will stand in the presence of the Deity crying for mercy and justice. As they act here so will be their final abode hereafter. Life is an enigma. This is a strange world. Often men are governed by passion, and not by reason. The mob crucified the Saviour of mankind, and Paul, his great Apostle, went to an ignominious death. This happened many centuries ago. For eighteen centuries no man has exerted such a tremendous influence on the civilization as the despised Gallilean and his great Apostle. They did their work and left the result with the Almighty Father.

This speech was written in a cramped position in my cell.

COURT SCENE—RUSH FOR SEATS.

CHAPTER III.

The Excitement Increasing on the Second Day—Another Panel Exhausted without Completing the Jury—Curious Disqualifications and Comments.

THE proceedings of the second day were marked by a vast increase in the excitement about the court-room and a greater pressure for admission, which the ushers checked by exercising the right of selection, and affording seats to a number of well-dressed persons before opening the doors to the general public. Very shortly after 10 o'clock Judge Cox took his seat, and the prisoner was brought in, taking his place, after the removal of his handcuffs, between his brother and sister and his counsel. As a precaution, he was warned by a Deputy Marshal that he must remain quiet, and he promised to comply. He seemed more cheerful and had a less scared look. The five jurors already selected having taken their seats, work was commenced on the new panel of seventy-five. The defence peremptorily challenged three and accepted four, one of the latter, Ralph Wormley, being a colored plasterer and formerly a well known Republican politician in the District of Columbia. Of the above number the prosecution challenged one, three or four were excused, but the rest were disqualified by reason of their opinions, which, they said, would render it impossible for them to give the prisoner a fair and impartial trial. The cross-examination of talesmen by Mr. Scoville was conducted ingeniously and excellently. Nearly every person examined made some remark that caused general laughter, and even Guiteau smiled several times at the witty answers.

He, however, frequently requested Mr. Scoville to ask certain questions, and made suggestions which he deemed absolutely necessary. He especially objected to any one as a juror who believed him insane, and insisted that Mr. Scoville should challenge any person who held such an opinion. He said that he did not wish this to be made an issue, but preferred the trial to be on the merits of the case. Mr. Scoville humored the whims of Guiteau, and whenever he accepted a juror consulted the prisoner before doing so.

VIEWS OF THE TALESMEN.

John P. Buckley said he could not do the prisoner justice, and was, therefore, declared disqualified. John Lynch, a white man, when asked by the Judge as to the character of the opinion he had formed on the matter said:

"I think the prisoner ought to be hung or burnt. There is nothing in the United States to convince me otherwise."

Joshua Green said he was of opinion that the

prisoner should be hanged. This opinion was also expressed by a colored man, Alexander Peterson. John Judd, being called up, said he thought the prisoner should be hanged, as he had swindled him out of fifty dollars. William F. Poulton said his opinion was such that no amount of evidence could change it. He believed the prisoner ought to have a rope put around his neck. A good deal of laughter was elicited by L. C. Bailey, a colored man, who in defining his opinion said he believed Guiteau was crazy. Much amusement was caused by the answers of Mr. Dade, a typical colored gentleman of the old school. Dade wore a puffed bosom shirt and across his right shoulder hung carelessly a grey toga. With thorough composure of manner, and a wooden toothpick in one corner of his mouth, he answered shrewdly and wittily every question propounded. He was the second colored man challenged by the defence, the other being Mr. Howard, who was too ignorant to tell whether he had any opinion.

The four additional jurors accepted were Mike Theeran, an Irish grocer, who says he had never worked for nor earned a cent from the Government; Samuel Hobbs, a native of Maryland, aged sixty-three and a plasterer by trade ; George W. Gates, aged twenty-seven, a native of Washington and a mechanic in the Government navy yard (Mr. Gates testified to-day that one of his uncles was insane), and Ralph Wormley, the colored plasterer already mentioned.

The list having been again exhausted, a further panel of seventy-five was ordered to be drawn, and the Court at 12.20 adjourned.

On being handcuffed and led out of the building to the van, the prisoner exhibited considerable trepidation, which was not to be wondered at, as there was a considerable number of persons in the hallway and quite a crowd outside. As he passed through the crowd several jeers were heard, and Guiteau became nervous and excited. When the van door was opened, it was with difficulty that he could mount the steps, although there was no overt demonstration. Still it needed only a good opportunity for some crank to try to kill Guiteau. Among those in the hallway was Bethard, who wanted to shoot Guiteau at the time he was arraigned. Going outside of the hall Bethard said as Guiteau passed by:

"Oh, how I wish I had a pistol!"

The crowd clustered around the van until the horses were started, and then there were threats of vengeance loud enough to reach the ears of the trembling prisoner, who crouched in the dark vehicle. The horses were put out at full speed, and in a short time the prisoner was safely landed at the jail.

CHAPTER IV.

The Jury Complete—Who and What the Jurymen Are—Their Appearance, Occupation and General Characteristics—The Court Decks Cleared for Action.

THE attendance on the third day did not differ much in number or character from that on the previous days, though it was evident that many of those present had never before seen the prisoner. On the opening of Court, Guiteau, manacled as usual, was brought in and as soon as released from his handcuffs, commenced his customary conference with his counsel, bringing down his right hand with sledge-hammer force to emphasize his remarks. After he had taken his seat a couple of officers stationed themselves near him to be ready to repress the violence which he had already given evidence of. Mr. Scoville promptly addressed the Court, and it became evident at once what had been the nature of the excited colloquy between him and his client, or as Guiteau himself would have it, his associate counsel in the case.

Mr. Scoville said: "Before this trial commenced, on Sunday evening, several reporters called on me and I gave them, as usual, such items as I thought of public interest, and I told them I should not entertain any more visits from reporters during the progress of the trial, but that they must get information as the case progressed. I also at that time intended to prevent anything getting into the papers except what came out properly during the progress of the trial. There was a paper obtained from the prisoner by some member of the press that was published, I think it was called an 'Address to the Public.' I did not see it before it was published and I did not know its contents. To-day I understand that another paper has gone out without my consent. I had not intended that anything of this kind should go out to the public in the manner indicated. That paper was presented to me this morning by the prisoner, who asked me to indorse it. I refused to do it and said I did not think it proper that anything of that kind should go out. I understand, however, that it has gone out. What I want to say is this:—I would like to have the public understand that that paper has gone out without my consent. Not that I care for its influence on the public or anything of the kind, but because it is of that character that it might have (if it were understood to have gone out with my consent) an influence in some quarters which I should very much regret. For instance, I have received this morning, two letters from gentlemen that I think are fully competent to take part in the management of this case, whose services may be obtained. They are not residents of the District and may see this thing in the newspapers, and supposing it has gone out with my sanction, it may have some influence upon them. Of course I could not meet all these things with private letters to persons in sympathy with me and giving me valuable assistance, and I simply want to have it understood that from this time anything that gets into the papers is entirely without my consent and approval.

GUITEAU CLAIMS TO BE COUNSEL.

Mr. Scoville's statement excited the prisoner to the boiling point, and he sprang to his feet despite the efforts of the officers. Addressing the Court, he said. "I desire to be heard. I appear here in a dual capacity—first, as prisoner, and second as counsel—and I want to have the final say in this matter. When I request counsel the Court can assign them. That paper was addressed to the legal profession, and I expect many responses to it. I want it understood that I appear here in part as my own counsel, and until I request counsel I propose to defend myself.

The extraordinary document which produced this storm in a tea pot ran as follows:

"To the Legal Profession of America"

"I am on trial for my life. I formerly practised law in New York and Chicago, and propose to take an active part in my defence, as I know more about my inspiration and views than any one. My brother-in-law, Geoge Scoville, Esq., is my only counsel, and I hereby appeal to the legal profession of America for aid. I expect to have money shortly so I can pay them. I shall get it partly from the settlement of an old matter in New York and partly from the sale of my book and partly from public contribution to my defence. My defence was published in the *New York Herald* on October 6, and in my speech published November 15th (yesterday). Any well-known lawyer of criminal capacity desiring to assist in my defence will please telegraph without delay to George Scoville, Washington, D. C. If for any reason an application be refused, the name will be withheld from the public."

Charles J. Guiteau.

In Court, Washington, D. C., Nov. 16, 1881.

This matter having been disposed of, the task of securing three jurors to complete the requisite twelve was proceeded with. Some sixty talesmen were examined and of these four were excused, four were challenged by the Government, seven the defence objected to, forty-two were disqualified on account of their opinions and the other three were accepted and sworn. The examination of the talesmen reflected great credit on the tact, and the honorable disposition of Mr. Scoville, who displayed a praiseworthy anxiety to secure men of thought and honest purpose, rather than those likely to be swayed by mere eloquence on either side. In order to secure the twelve jurymen, 159 persons had been drawn as talesmen, a clear indication that the jury was far from a hap-hazard aggregation—the often sneered at "twelve men in a box." Just here it may be pertinent to note some of the objections to the talesmen, their peculiar replies and the remarks which indicated how wide-spread was the popular indignation against the prisoner.

In selecting from the last tales, the first challenge was by the defence in the case of Edward Thomas, who said he could not read and had "never formed any opinion whatsoever." Mr. Scoville remarked that while this was such a person as the law qualified, the defence did not want him. The second challenge by the defence was S. H. Williams, a barber, who thought the act dastardly, but had "since modified his opinion on the subject." The next challenge by the defence was Thomas H. Barron, a carpenter, who twenty years ago had employed Mr. Davidge, now of Government counsel. John Hughes, a colored man, who could not read, was also challenged by the defence.

Charles Hopkins a bartender, who objected to serving on the case because he thought "the duty would be too confining," was challenged by the defence. Frederick C. Revels (colored) was challenged by the defence because he is employed under his father, a deputy marshal in the police court. Perhaps, however, the most striking peculiarities of the day, were the outspoken opinions which the examinations of Mr. Scoville and Judge Cox elicited. One talesman replied.

"My opinion is such that no evidence whatever will change it."

Another said:—"There is nothing under the sun that can change my opinion."

Again came the emphatic answer:—" My opinion is unchangeable, and I know that no evidence will modify it."

One person said:—" I am satisfied of the prisoner's guilt and it will have to be proved that he is not guilty before I would change my opinion."

Three talesmen were positive as to what disposition should be made of Guiteau. One said his opinion was such that nothing save the rope should be used.

Enoch Edmundson, upon being examined, said:—"No amount of torture is too great for the prisoner."

Allison Naylor, a livery stable keeper, said:— " No amount of proof can remove my opinion but that the prisoner should be hung."

As a matter of course these expressions made use of in open Court, and under oath, had an inflammatory effect upon the audience.

THE LAST THREE JURORS.

Of the jurors picked from the last sixty talesmen, William H. Browner, the first selected was a grocer and commission merchant, having been in the business thirty-one years. According to his answers he believes in different phases of insanity, and has given the subject some consideration. Though not a church member he believes in God and a future state of rewards and punishments; though not a spirituallist, he had been spiritually inclined.

The second, Thomas Heinlein, said he had never belonged to any organization to lynch the prisoner. "I am an American," said he; "these institutions are not American. I am a mechanic, and not a politician." The third, who completed the panel, was Joseph Prather, a commission merchant. He admitted having some prejudice, but believed he could render a fair verdict. He acknowledged that he, like one juror previously sworn, had a relative who was insane.

There was a general hum and bustle in the court-room when it became known that the jury was complete, and a recess of half an hour was taken by the Court. From the number of lunch baskets which suddenly made their appearance, it was evident that many of the audience, the ladies especially, had come prepared to see the matter out.

On re-assembling the Court, District Attorney Corkhill administered the oath to the jury, as a whole, composed of the following persons: John P. Hamlin, restaurant keeper; Fred. W. Brandenburg, cigar dealer; Henry J. Bright, retired merchant; Charles J. Stewart, merchant; Thomas H. Langley, grocer; Michael Sheehan, grocer; Samuel F. Hobbs, plasterer; George W. Gates, machinist; Ralph Wormley (colored), laborer; W. H. Browner, commission merchant; Thomas Henlein, iron worker; Joseph Prather, commission merchant.

It was the openly expressed opinion of Mr. Davidge, of counsel for the prosecution, and of Mr. Scoville, as counsel for the defence, that a better jury was never assembled than that which subscribed to the following oath: "You and each of you do solemnly swear, that you will well and truly try and a true deliverance make between the United States and Charles J. Guiteau, the prisoner at the bar, whom you shall have in charge, indicted for the murder of James A. Garfield, and a true verdict give according to the evidence, so help you God."

The preliminaries being now complete, District Attorney Corkhill stated that it was usual in a case of such magnitude, and which was likely to be of such long duration, to afford the jury time to arrange their private affairs, and he, therefore, moved the immediate adjournment of the Court, which was assented to by Judge Cox at 1.45 P. M.

The effect of the talesmen's remarks was visible in the conduct of the crowd outside as the prisoner was led to the van; hoots, yells and groans voiced the popular indignation, but beyond this there was no attempt at molestation.

PEN PORTRAITS OF THE JURY.

The following graphic sketches give an idea of the men into whose hands this important case was consigned: John P. Hamlin, the foreman, is about fifty years old. He has a kindly face, white hair aud moustache, is of medium height and build, and dresses in grey. He is a restaurant keeper, and has been engaged in that business in Washington for thirty years. Frederick W. Brandenburg, juror No. 2, is a Prussian by birth. He has lived in Washington ever since he came to this country thirty-one years ago. He is not now fifty. In stature he is small, and he has a rather pinched and shrewd but withal a frank face. He wears a moustache which is dark, and he has black hair. By trade he is a cigar manufacturer, working for himself. Henry J. Bright, No. 3, is a retired merchant, and has the rotundity of form and benignity of expression indicative of satisfaction with the world. His head is large and his face genial. He has a double chin, of course, and allows only brown tufts in front of the ears to grow as beard. Dressed in cockade and epaulets, he could sit for an excellent portrait of a Revolutionary patriot. He is fifty-two years old, and a man of family. Charles J. Stewart, No. 4, is middle-aged. He has deep-set eyes, whose expression tells how serious a thing life has been with him. A light-colored beard, considerably frosted, covers his face. His manners, dress and looks suggest an overworked farmer, not the least trying of whose duty has been to rear a family, who should never forget that Sunday meant three times to Church, and Sunday-School between services. Mr. Stewart is in the flour and feed business. Thomas H. Langley, No. 5, is a grocer and provision dealer. He was born in Maryland, of parents evidently very Irish. He lacks only a brogue to fit him for a real old Irish squire, for he is portly, has a ruddy appearance, dresses comfortably, including a chokee and white necktie. He is over fifty, slightly grey, shaves clean, has lived in Washington for forty-five years, and now does business in groceries and provisions. Michael Sheehan, No. 6, is a neat-appearing Irishman, under forty. He has brown side whiskers, and the most guileless face on the jury. Samuel F. Hobbs, No. 7, is an earlier edition of Mr. Stewart, No. 5. Their resemblance is remarkably close, and the examinations showed them to be of a like cast of mind. Mr. Hobbs is quite gray; plastering is his trade. George W. Gates, No. 8, is the youngest member of the jury, being about thirty-five. He has an agreeable, frank face, full of grit and strength. He is a machinist, and is employed in the navy yard. Ralph Wormley, No. 9, merits the distinction of being the only colored man of the twelve. The ace of spades is not darker. He is quite good-looking, with a round, laughing face and perfect teeth. He is about forty, and sprinklings of white have grown into his beard. He is a man-of-all-work in the pension office. William H. Browner, No. 10, is a commission merchant. He is middle-aged and has gray hair and moustache. He has the appearance of a man worn with business, and in need of the rest that this temporary change of occupation will probably give him. He has given the subject of insanity some consideration. Thomas Heinlein, No. 11, is a machinist. He is not forty. He has practised his trade here since leaving the army at the close of the war. He is tall, as straight as a soldier, and has dark eyes, hair and moustache. Joseph Prather, No. 12, is the only juror, excepting Wormley, with a full beard. He is a commission merchant, and on the wrong side of fifty. He declined to answer a question put by Mr. Scoville to ascertain if he had ever had experience with insanity in his family or among his relatives.

CHAPTER V.

District Attorney Corkhill's Opening Address—Guiteau's Grotesque Ghoulishness Begins to Show itself—Secretary Blaine on the Witness Stand—His Definition of the Word "Stalwart," etc.

THE fourth day of the proceedings was, certainly, in many of its incidents, as dramatic as anything ever seen in a Criminal Court. The knowledge that the jury had been empanelled, and that the formal presentation of the case by the District Attorney would be followed by the evidence of actual eye witnesses of the assassination, had attracted an audience so large that not an inch of standing room was unoccupied, and when, ultimately, the Secretary of State stood on the witness stand, and in the presence of the unblushing, hardened, defiant assassin, related how the beloved President of a great nation had been stricken down on that fateful 2d of July, the scene was one to which neither the pen of the ready writer nor the brush of the skilled limner could do adequate justice.

At ten minutes after 10 o'clock, the Court was formally opened, and the prisoner, looking paler and more flurried than on previous occasions, was brought in by the deputy marshals and policemen.

VIEWING THE ASSASSIN.

ON THE ALERT PRETENDING TO READ.

When his handcuffs had been removed, he threw one eager, furtive glance at the densely packed audience—a glance in which the cold, steely glitter of a serpent's eye, the ferocious fire of a tiger's dilated orb, and the cowardly, cunning, hungry gleam of the carrion-hunting hyena, were curiously blended. It was a truly typical glance. Then, sullenly, with a bare notice of his relatives, he ostensibly busied himself with his papers. He had looked at his prey; he was hungry for applause; he was waiting for a chance to spring to his feet, and by some exhibition of ghoulish grotesqueness, provoke a ripple of that inane laughter and applause as congenial to his depraved, notoriety seeking intellect, as is the music of the spheres to the senses of the rapt Seraph.

The jurors having been called, and having responded, Mr. Scoville rose and said: "I merely want to say a word with the consent of the District Attorney, in explanation it may be, at any rate with relation to a little occurrence here on the first day of the trial between my associate and myself. On consulting in relation to the matter and reference to the defence generally, we became satisfied that the press of the business on each of us, working as we were, at a disadvantage, resulted in something that may appear and actually did go to the country as a disagreement between us. I merely wish to say that there has been nothing, in fact or reality, of that kind, and since we have been able to confer together fully and freely, we are in perfect accord in regard to the defence and the different steps which are to be taken. Mr. Robinson will cordially give his assistance in this case, just as I supposed he would all the time. I do not know that it needs an explanation, but at all events I have thought it best to make one."

Guiteau saw his chance and was swift to take advantage of the opening. Springing up suddenly, with flashing eyes and violently demonstrative gestures, he exclaimed in a high pitched voice:

"May it please the Court, I object to Mr. Robinson appearing in this case."

The Court (severely).—"Take your seat, prisoner. I wish you to understand distinctly that your labors as counsel in this case, as you claim to be, shall be confined to consultation with the associate counsel in this case. If you disobey," he continued, as the prisoner again jumped to his feet and commenced another wild speech, "the Court will be under the necessity of ordering your removal from the court room and proceeding with the trial in your absence."

"Your Honor said that I could be heard, and I have a speech."

"You cannot be heard until the close of the case."

The prisoner.—"I desire to be heard throughout

the case. Your Honor has no right to cut me off, and I am going to make a noise to the country about it. When I want counsel I will notify your Honor."

The Court: "Counsel have been assigned, and you must keep silence."

Struggling against the deputy marshals, who were pressing him into his seat, the prisoner cried out: "The law is that when a man wants counsel they are assigned to him. If your Honor does not coincide with me I will make a noise to the country about it. The country is broader than this court is." After a pause (and speaking in a fierce tone): "There is not a word of truth in that *Post* special from Chicago. It is an absolute lie from beginning to end."

The Court (sternly): "Keep quiet now; let me have no more discussion;" but the prisoner was irrepressible. He continued to argue with Mr. Scoville, who attempted to quiet him; he broke out again with the remark that he would not trust his case with the best lawyer ever made. "I know my case and my position in this matter," he cried; "one or two blunderbuss lawyers will compromise my entire defence, and I will not have it." Another pause ensued, and then lifting his eyes from the newspaper before him, he declared that if Robinson had proper respect he would get out of the case.

"That is my opinion on him." I would not

trust him with a $10 note case; that is my opinion on him."

The prisoner, then, apparently, became more passive; but, while the District Attorney was preparing to open the case, he once more, violently brandishing his arms, addressed the Court. "I come here," he cried, "in the honorable capacity of being the agent of the Deity on this occasion, and I propose to appear as such. I do not come on my hands and knees, and that is all there is about it. That is the view I supposed your Honor to have taken." This exclamation had the effect of causing a ripple of laughter, which spread among the spectators, who had listened to his previous utterances in an excited silence; and, apparently satisfied with his success in obtaining some manifestations from the public, the prisoner became quiet.

Nearly half-an-hour had been wasted in this manner when Secretary of State James G. Blaine, accompanied by his son, Walker Blaine, and Chief Clerk Brown, of the State Department, entered the court room. They were assigned seats by Messrs. Davidge and Porter, and then District Attorney George B. Corkhill proceeded to open the case for the Government.

COL. CORKHILL'S ADDRESS.

MAY IT PLEASE THE COURT AND GENTLEMEN OF THE JURY: The prisoner at the bar stands before you charged with the murder of James A. Garfield. Under any circumstance there rests a grave

GUITEAU, THE ASSASSIN.

and responsible obligation upon every man who is called upon in the discharge of his duty under the law, to render a decision upon which depends the life of a fellow creature. And while it is true that the offence charged in the present case is no greater in legal gravity and consequences to the prisoner, than if by his act he had taken the life of the humblest and most obscure citizen of the Republic, still it is idle to overlook the fact that the eminent character of the man whose life was taken, his high official position, and the startling effects of the commission of the crime, render the case one of unusual and unparalleled importance. It is the second time in our history that the citizen chosen by the people of the United States to discharge the high and responsible duties of President, has fallen a victim to a lawless assassin during the period of his incumbency of the office.

But in the former case we were just emerging from the shadows of a long and bloody war. The country had been racked by commotions and stirred by civil feuds. Throughout the length and breadth of the land, nearly every household mourned the loss of relatives or friends, slain on the hotly contested battlefields of the Republic. It was a danger that thoughtful men had anticipated. It was a calamity that patriots had feared. And when it came, with all its dread consequences, it was accepted as one of the results of the then disordered and discordant conditions of public affairs.

But we had passed from the arena of the war; the sword had been beaten into a ploughshare and the spear into a pruning hook; the country was united—peace reigned at home and abroad. There were no local dissensions; there were no intestine strifes; seed-time and harvest had come and gone; the battlefields, redeemed from the scars and havoc of their bloody contests, were blossoming with the fruits of peaceful labor. Suddenly the startling fact was proclaimed throughout the land and around the entire world, that the President of the United States had fallen a victim to the assassin's bullet in the Capital of the nation.

Murder, under all circumstances and upon all occasions, is shocking. The life of which we know so little, and which we hold by so fragile a tenure, is dear to us all; and when it is brought to a close, not in the usual order and course of nature, but prematurely by violence, no matter what may be the condition of the person, the human mind is appalled with terror. When a man, holding a position of eminence and power, falls a causeless victim to the murderer's stroke, we realize still more fully the awfulness of the deed which produces the result.

This trial is a remarkable illustration of the genius and spirit of our Government. Although our chief ruler was murdered; although the effect of that death was felt in every station of life, in every avenue of business, in every department of society, yet the prisoner, his murderer, stands before you to-day entitled to the rights, to the same privileges, panoplied by the same guarantees of the Constitution, as if he had killed the lowliest member of this community. I doubt whether, in the world's history, there can be found another instance like the present. In no age, under no government, has there been seen such a situation as we have here before us. Defended by eminent counsel, demanding of right the full benefit of every provision of law, and the protection of every guarantee of the Constitution, with the power, exercised carefully, to see that the jury selected is unbiased and free from prejudice; every right is extended to the prisoner that would be granted to a criminal charged with the most insignificant offence.

It has been a subject of the deepest anxiety and gravest consideration on the part of the admirers of our form of government, whether the fundamental principles which underlie it did not contain elements fatal to its permanency and success. With the individual citizens are its absolute destinies for weal or woe. The choice of your proper rulers, the enactment of laws and their prompt execution, depend upon his character. No matter how important the trust, or how grave the responsibility, upon the individual citizen rests its final decision.

The simplicity of the forms under which our Government is administered, constitute for us one of its greatest attractions, but the easy accessibility to all of those charged with its administration exposes them to many dangers from the visciously disposed. The President of the United States, without pomp and parade, but after the manner of the humblest citizen, and with no other safeguard than those common to all citizens, leaves the scene of his official labors for a brief recreation. In a public depot the prisoner at the bar, without warning, fires at him with a pistol, inflicting wounds which result in his death. And to-day this, the greatest case ever presented to a court of justice, is trusted entirely to you, who have been selected from the body of the community, to weigh the evidence and the law, and then to say upon your oaths whether the man charged with the crime is guilty. While this trial will attract unusual attention, while every stage of its progress will be watched with intense interest throughout the entire world, yet its final decision rests with you. You are to determine, after you shall have heard the evidence and been instructed in the law, whether or not the prisoner at the bar is guilty of the murder of James A. Garfield.

The time and the scene of that occasion were generally disseminated by the press, and are still fresh in the minds of every citizen of the Republic, and they will remain with all their sad and gloomy results until the present generation shall pass from among men. After we are dead they will live in tradition, in history, song and story till the latest hour of time. There is an enormity about the immediate occurrences as they will be detailed to you by the witnesses for the Government, that makes them horrible to contemplate. No words can faithfully depict the scenes of that fatal July morning. It was bright and beautiful, and the morning sunlight gilded the dome of the Capitol, the rays fell upon a city adorned with all the loveliness of summer leaf and flowers.

The President, wearied with official cares, was specially joyous at his approaching vacation.

He started from the Executive Mansion, in company with the Secretary of State, for the depot, buoyant and glad. Early on the morning of July 2d, last; the prisoner at the bar made preparation for the murder. Breakfasting at the Riggs House, he took the fearful weapon that he had previously obtained, and going to the foot of Seventeenth Street, away from residences and beyond observation, he planted a stick in the soft mud on the river bank where the tide had gone out and deliberately practised his aim and tested his weapon. He intended there should be no failure in the accomplishment of the crime for which he had been preparing. Returning he took with him a small bundle of papers and went to the Baltimore and Potomac Railroad Depot at half past eight o'clock A. M., an hour before the arrival of the President.

After reaching the depot he went to the news stand and left certain papers with a letter addressed to Byron Andrews a correspondent of the CHICAGO INTER-OCEAN, and a paper addressed to Mr. Preston of the NEW YORK HERALD, and then went into the closet, carefully examined his weapon, placed it in his pocket, returned and went outside to the pavement, had his boots blackened, and then, in order to avoid the swift vengeance of an outraged community, which he properly feared, engaged a carriage to take him, as he said, to the Congressional Burying Ground, this point being near the jail, and then entered the waiting room to watch for his victim.

All unconscious of the preparation for his murder, President Garfield in company with Secretary Blaine, arrived at the depot and for a few moments remained in the carriage in conversation. While thus occupied the assassin stood gazing at them, waiting and watching for a favorable opportunity for the perpetration of the deed. The President and the Secretary of State alighted from the carriage. With his usual courtesy President Garfield hesitated a moment on the step to acknowledge the salution of the policeman at the door, and then entered the depot. He had gone but a few steps when the assassin lurking in the rear, stepped up behind him, and pointing his pistol with deliberate aim fired at his back, the first shot, no doubt, doing its fatal work. The President shuddered, staggered and attempted to turn, when another shot was fired and he fell bleeding to the floor—unconscious.

The horror that seized upon everybody may be imagined but no words can describe it. The ball from the assassin's pistol had entered the middle of the back of the President about three inches to the right of the back bone, inflicting a fearful wound which resulted in his death after nearly three months of pain and suffering—and here the story of the crime might legally end, for the unlawful killing of any reasonable creature by a person of sound memory and discretion, with malice aforethought, either expressed or implied, is murder.

The motives and intentions of an individul who commits a crime, are of necessity known to him alone—no human power can penetrate the recesses of the heart—no eye but the eye of God can discern the motives for human action. Hence the law wisely says, that a man's motives shall be judged from his acts, so that if one kill another suddenly without any provocation, the law implies malice. If a man uses a deadly weapon it is presumed he intended to commit murder, and in general the law presumes a man to intend the natural consequences of the act.

Were there nothing more against the accused than the occurrences on the morning of July 2d, the evidence of his crime would be complete, and you would be authorized to conclude that he feloniously, wilfully and with malice aforethought did kill and murder, James A. Garfield. But crime is never natural. The man who attempts to violate the laws of God and society, goes counter to the ordinary course of human action. He is a world to himself. He is against society, against organization, and of necessity his actions can never be measured by the rules governing men in the every day transactions of life. No criminal ever violated the laws, who did not leave the traces of his crime distinct and clear when once discovered. So in this case we can only add to the enormity of this offence by showing you its origin, its conception and the plans adopted for its execution.

One year ago, the 11th of the present month, the prisoner addressed to Hon. Wm. M. Evarts, the Secretary of State, the following letter:

"NEW YORK, November 11, 1880.

"HON. WM. EVARTS.

"DEAR SIR:—I wish to ask you a question. If President Garfield appoints Mr. A. to a foreign mission, does that supersede President Hayes' commission for the same appointment? Do not all foreign ministers appointed by President Hayes retire on March 4th next?

"Please answer me at the Fifth Avenue Hotel at your earliest convenience. I am solid for General Garfield, and may get an important appointment from him next spring.

"Yours, very truly, CHARLES GUITEAU."

At this time, over a year ago, it will be seen he had in his mind an application for and expectation of receiving an office under the approaching administration. In pursuance of that hope the prisoner came to this city on the afternoon of the 5th of last March, no doubt believing that he would receive at the hands of an administration he supposed he had assisted in placing in power, such recognition as according to his own opinion of his merits, he deserved. He was outspoken and earnest in his demands, and in his various conversations seemed to feel confident of success. From his own letters it is evident that during October and January he had written to President Garfield, calling attention to his services in the campaign, and soliciting an appointment. On the 8th of March he addressed a letter to the President, calling his attention to the fact of his desire to be appointed to the Paris Consulate. On the 11th of May, he wrote Secretary Blaine the following letter:

"March 11, 1881.

"SENATOR BLAINE:

"In October and January last, I wrote General Garfield touching the Austrian Mission, and I think he has filed my application and is favorably inclined. Since then I have concluded to apply for the Consul Generalship at Paris, instead of the Austrian Mission, as I prefer Paris to Vienna. I spoke to the General about it, and he said your endorsement would help it, as it was in your department. I think I have a just claim to your help on the strength of this speech (a speech was enclosed), which was sent to our leading editors and orators in August. It was about the first shot on the rebel war-claim idea, and it was the idea that elected General Garfield. Mr. Walker, the present Consul at Paris, was appointed through Mr. Evarts, and I presume he has no expectation of being retained. I will talk with you about this as soon as I can get a chance. There is nothing against me, I claim to be a gentleman and a Christian. Yours, very respectfully,

"CHARLES GUITEAU."

He followed this communication by persistent personal appeals and by writing notes and letters urging in various ways his claim for this position. Not only did he besiege the Secretary of State and the officers of the State Department, but the President and the officers of the Executive Mansion. Generally treated with courtesy and kindly dismissed, as his wants and necessities became more urgent, he became more persistent and determined. On the 8th of March, he commenced writing to the President, stating his reasons why the position should be given him, and urging in various ways his claims for the place. Finally, his importuning became such a nuisance, that Secretary Blaine ordered him to keep away from the State Department, and he was forbidden admittance to the White House.

Soured and indignant at this treatment, disappointed and enraged, on the 23d of May he wrote President Garfield a letter in which—in the light of the fearful tragedy that followed—it needs no discerning eye to detect the threat of murder. This is the first premonition of the conception of this crime. That letter was the first indication that disappointment had turned his heart to malice, and that he had determined in revenge to commit the crime with which he stands charged. He was still smarting under the indignity cast upon him by the Secretary of State: he was still suffering from the rebuffs he had received at the hands of the employees of the Executive Mansion. Of inordinate vanity and of unparalleled self-esteem he had keenly felt the personal outrages he supposed had been committed upon him, and he determined to avenge them. That letter is a remarkable one; remarkable as indicating the motive that prompted this terrible crime; remarkable as giving an insight into the reasons that impelled this man to nerve himself up to a condition to commit this deed. It was as follows:

"(Private.)

"GENERAL GARFIELD:

"I have been trying to be your friend. I do not know whether you appreciate it or not; but I am moved to call your attention to

the remarkable letter from Mr. Blaine which I have just received. According to Mr. Farwell, of Chicago, Blaine is a vindictive politician and an evil genius, and you will have no peace till you get rid of him. This letter shows Mr. Blaine is a wicked man, and you ought to demand his immediate resignation, otherwise you and the Republican party will come to grief. I will see you in the morning if I can, and talk with you. Very respectfully,
"May 23. CHARLES GUITEAU."

You see in these sentences his bitterness of spirit, inspired by the treatment he claims to have received at the hands of the Secretary of State, and the demand for his removal and the threat, if it was not done, what would result. Yet we will find on the 21st of March he wrote to Secretary Blaine:

"I am very glad personally that the President selected you for his premier. * * * * You are the man above all others for the place."

That is one chapter in the history of this crime. The letter standing above, and independent of every other circumstance, would not of itself, attract attention to its peculiar and significant expressions. But it will be shown, that among the papers left by this man for publication, is found one dated the 16th day of June, 1881, in which he uses this significant language: "I conceived the idea of removing the President four weeks ago." So that at the time he wrote that letter, he in effect said, I want my office, Mr. Blaine stands in my way, I demand his removal, if it is not done, ruin for you and the party will be the result. It will be for you to consider whether this was not as near a threat of his determination to do this crime, as he dared then to make with his knowledge of the law, and the danger of exposure. When he conceived the idea he had been rebuffed and, as he thought, insulted by the Secretary of State. He had been driven from the White House. He was disappointed in his grand expectations. He was without money, and also an almost destitute wanderer upon the streets, and he determined to do the cruel deed. But here is the first conception; the original inspiration. Here the ground-work of his settled determination. Once the idea conceived that he was a wronged and outraged man, it took but little time for him to decide to represent his actions as being the result of his desire to vindicate some great principle. He knew, and well knew, that he must hang some screen in front of the real motive for his crime. His heart was wicked enough to conceive from its own malignity the crime itself, but his shrewdness and vanity demanded that the public should not gaze upon the real motives. This will account for all of the extraordinary circumstances connected with the crime. This will explain many of his lofty and egotistical utterances. It is true there was a period during this time when there existed dissensions in the party in power. It is a well-known fact, that as between the Executive and certain prominent and eminent men there was a difference of opinion, as to the course to be pursued and the policy to be inaugurated by the administration then just at its commencement. It is true that there were grave differences of opinion, and earnest expressions of sentiment on questions of great gravity and importance to the peace and welfare of the country, and as attendant upon these, there were frequent utterances of bitterness by partisans on either side. To this man's wicked and revengeful mind it immediately occurred: "Here is the opportunity to commit the crime; to avenge myself and shelter my actions under the claim that it was the outgrowth of the present strife;" and he systematically and cunningly prepared an apology and defence of his crime in accordance with this. You will learn by the testimony that will be presented to you, that from the time of his arrival in this city, and until he had lost the expectation of favors to be received, and made up his mind to kill the President, a period of nearly three months, he was an earnest, so-called Garfield man. He announced to the President, as will be shown by his own letter, his devotion and fealty to him; he desired constantly to impress upon the President that he was for him as against every one else. You will find him on May 7th announcing to the President, that in the contest going on, he stood by him; but when he had lost all hope of the appointment he desired under the administration of President Garfield, and all expectation of official recognition from this source, he resolved to seize upon the pretext afforded by the situation, to gratify his revenge and kill the President, and shield his real motives from the public. After this had been fully settled in his mind, with his experience of human affairs; with his observations of society (for he is a man of no ordinary ability in these directions), he carefully determined to make the situation of advantage to him, and when he had fully conceived the idea; when it had fastened itself on his mind, he went to work to accomplish his purpose with a spirit of vindictiveness; with a cruel determination that has scarcely a parallel in the annals of crime. How many efforts to do the deed, or when and where he decided upon the exact method of its commission, no human mind can tell.

On the 8th day of June, he borrowed from an acquaintance in this city fifteen dollars, representing that he was out of money, and desired the amount to pay his board bill. After procuring this loan, he at once visited the store of Mr. O'Meara, on the corner of Fifteenth and F Streets, for the purpose of purchasing a weapon. In this, as in all other acts connected with the commission of this crime, he displayed the malignity of his determination, and the wickedness of his motives. He asked for a pistol of the largest calibre, and one that would do the most effective work, and was shown and purchased the pistol which he finally used; a weapon terrible to behold, carrying a ball of the largest size; a weapon that was self-cocking, in order that there might be no delay in its use, when an emergency occurred.

How for twenty-four days he carried that deadly weapon, and how often he dogged the footsteps of the unsuspecting President; how he watched his carriage; how he made his arrangements at the church; how he followed him from the residence of Mr. Blaine, watching and waiting for the fatal hour, he alone can tell; but on the morning of the 18th of June, he ascertained from a publication in the newspapers, that the President would go to Long Branch, and he determined to kill him at the depot. How he went there fully prepared for that purpose, and was deterred from its accomplishment his own words best tell. Returning to his room he wrote:

"WASHINGTON, Saturday Evening, June 18.

"I intended to remove the President this morning at the depot, as he took the cars for Long Branch. Mrs. Garfield looked so thin, and clung so tenderly to the President's arm, my heart failed me to part them, and I decided to take him alone; it will be no worse for Mrs. Garfield to part with her husband this way, than by natural death; he is liable to go at any time anyway. C. G."

After this commenced the period of watching and waiting. It might be a story of thrilling interest to know how often the fatal danger threatened the lamented dead, and how often while buoyant with life the shadow of death haunted him. But again, we are in the field of conjecture, until we come to the morning of the murder, the occurrence of which I have already described. And this completes the story of the crime. This ends the recital of the circumstances attendant upon this National bereavement; for it cannot be forgotten that the effects of that fatal shot were felt throughout the land; that not only one family mourned, but around every hearthstone and about every fireside there hung a shadow, and it is not surprising that many for a time forgot law, and doubted Providence, for it seemed so terrible that this man, in the full tide of his career of eminence and usefulness, should fall murdered without warning or notice.

No verdict of yours can recall him. He "sleeps the sleep that knows no waking," on the peaceful banks of the beautiful Lake Erie, whose limpid waters wash the boundaries of his native State, overlooking the city he loved so well, and beneath the sod of that State, whose people had crowned his life with the highest honors. It is too late to call that husband back to the bereaved wife and fatherless children. For that waiting little mother, whose face will never fade from the Nation's memory, there can be no relief in this world. The fatal deed is done, and its horrors and griefs must remain.

You have each been asked whether you were governed by religious convictions, and upon your oaths you have answered affirmatively. Eighteen hundred years ago, it was written by the pen of inspiration as the law of that merciful God whom you revere: "Woe unto the world because of offences, for it must needs be that offences come; but woe to that man by whom the offence cometh. It were better for him that a mill-stone were hanged about his neck, and that he were drowned in the depth of the sea." And the honest, patriotic, law-abiding people of this country are waiting for your verdict, to see whether the man by whom this great offence came, shall not suffer the just and merited punishment of the law.

The conclusion of this masterly address, which Court, jury and audience had listened to with the closest and most respectful attention, and the prisoner, save once, with sullen indifference, was marked by an outburst of applause, which for a few seconds the Court vainly attempted to check.

The prisoner's interruption was in regard to Col. Corkhill's allusion to Guiteau's threat that ruin would come to Garfield and on the Republican party if he was neglected. At this point the prisoner broke in with the exclamation: "Political ruin, if you please; not personal ruin."

Then, in solemn tones, Mr. Porter, one of the counsel for the prosecution, said: "The administration of justice, and especially of criminal justice, should never be distracted by the clamor, the disorder, or the contumacy of the prisoner. I must insist on the execution of the order of the Court."

Judge Cox.—"I think it within the power of the Court to order the removal of the prisoner and to have the trial conducted in his absence."

Guiteau (in a more subdued manner).—"I will not do it again, your Honor. I will control my feelings, but I do feel very deeply in this case."

Judge Cox.—"You must control yourself, or you will be removed from the Court room."

Mr. Robinson announced that the defence would reserve their opening, and the District Attorney called to the stand

HON. JAMES G. BLAINE.

The Secretary threw aside his overcoat, walked rapidly through the crowd to the box and affirmed. Attired in a plain, black suit, with a black tie, the well-known political chieftain stood facing the District Attorney, looking calm and healthful, but, naturally, somewhat sad. In his crossed hands he carelessly twirled a lead pencil, and he answered the questions put to him in that clear, emphatic voice which has been so oft and so potently heard in the Senate Chamber and on the platform. A large diagram of the Baltimore and Potomac Depot was spread out before him for reference in the course of his thrilling narrative.

As the significance of many of the replies in this examination, the key note of the case for the prosecution, depends in a great measure on the form and intent of the relative question, it will be expedient to deviate from the general plan of this history, and give Secretary Blaine's evidence mainly in the form of question and answer.

SECRETARY BLAINE'S EVIDENCE.

The District Attorney asked: What is your name and busiess? A. My name is James G. Blaine; at present Secretary of State for the United States.

Q. Were you acquainted with James A. Garfield? and how long? A. I was acquainted with him from the year 1863 to the hour of his death.

Q. Are you acquainted with the prisoner at the bar? have you ever seen him? A. I saw him occasionally during the months of March, April and May; not so frequently in May.

Q. Were you in company with the President at the time of the shooting? A. I was by his side.

Q. Will you relate to the jury an account of the proceedings, in your own manner, so that they will obtain a full narrative of the circumstances as they are familiar to you?

Sec'y Blaine. I wish to take directions as to the point at which to begin the narrative.

Q. Did you meet the President by appointment on the morning of the assassination? A. Yes, sir. On the night of July 1, I was engaged with the President until near midnight on public business. On parting he suggested that I had better call and see him in the morning before he left, because there might be some matters to which he desired to call my attention. I went to the White House in the morning, reaching there about nine o'clock; not later than three minutes past. I was detained some little time in conference with the President in the Cabinet room and library: a very few minutes. I then started with him for the depot, he riding in the carriage in which I went to the White House, the State Department carriage, in daily use by myself; following out of the White House grounds came his own carriage, in which his children were carried, under the conduct of Colonel Rockwell. We rode down the avenue without any noticeable incident and at a moderate speed.

On reaching the depot, on the B Street side (the ladies' entrance, commonly called), we sat a moment, finishing the subject on which we were then conversing, and the President turned round to say good-bye. "No," said I; "I will escort you." I thought it not proper that the President should go entirely unattended. "I will escort you," I said; "and, besides, I wish to see the gentlemen of the Cabinet who are going to leave with you." With that he alighted. He got in, of course, first at the White House, and that brought him on the side next to the pavement at the depot, and as the carriage was a small coupe he got out first. He took my arm as he went up the steps, and turned to the left (he was on my left) to speak to some one, I think a police officer, the same officer who told us that we had ten or twelve minutes time remaining. When he turned to speak to him our arms became disengaged, according to my impression, and as we walked through the ladies' waiting room we were not arm in arm. We had got two-thirds across the room when suddenly, without any premonition whatever, there was a very loud report of a pistol discharged, and, in a very brief interval, followed by a second shot. At the instant that I first heard the report it occurred to me that it was some trouble between persons to whom we were in no way related; some such deed of violence, and I touched the President as though to hurry him on, as I thought there might be some danger to his person or my own. Just as I did that the President kind of threw his hands up, and said; "My God! what is this?" It seemed to have been almost between the shots that he said that. Of course, in so exciting and horrible a scene I can only give an impression, not an absolute statement. Then there rushed past me a man. According to my recollection he passed on my right, though I am aware that this statement must be taken merely as my impression. I immediately followed after the man, instinctively, and when, I suppose at the distance of eight feet; I remember I stopped just outside the door which led from the ladies' waiting room to the main room. Then the shout came up, " We have got him." I found that the President had quite sunk; he was sinking as I left. When I got nearly back to him (I was the first or second person who got back to him) he was vomiting, and I think, at that moment, was unconscious. Of course, immediately, a very large crowd surrounded him, and mattresses were brought, I think, from a sleeping car and he was removed to an upper room in the depot. Medical aid was soon at hand, and an examination was made. He was returned to the White House, reaching there I should say in about fifty minutes, or possibly an hour. I knew that I returned to my own room and wrote a despatch to the public, especially to the European public, directing it to the Minister at London. In the despatch I said, that at the hour 10.20 A. M., the President being shot about 9.30. That enabled me to identify time at which the President got to the White House. He got there about the time I got to my house, possibly a little before. These are the circumstances connected with my observations.

When in the upper room of the depot, there was a gathering around of the Cabinet Ministers, who immediately repaired there from the cars. There had as yet been no report made of whom it was, but I gave information that the man I saw run and whom I went after, and whom I saw fall into the hands of the police was Guiteau. I recognized the man. I made that statement to the Cabinet, the attending surgeons and General Sherman before the police had discovered the name. Of course, the shot being behind my back, I did not see him with the pistol in his hand. He did not in running have the pistol exposed.

QUESTIONS BY THE DISTRICT ATTORNEY.

The District Attorney then produced a diagram of the depot in which the tragedy occured, and at his request the witness indicated the positions occupied by the President and himself at the time the fatal shot was fired. He also stated that though the second shot was fired immediately after the first, it did not follow it as rapidly as shots could be fired from a self-cocking revolver.

Q. How often have you seen the prisoner to the best of your recollection? A. Very often; numerical statements are apt to be exaggerated when we are recalling a statement of this kind. According to my recollection he visited the State Department twenty or twenty-five times. It might possibly not be over ten; but eight or ten visits of that kind are apt to make the impression of twenty or twenty-five.

Q. Did you have any conversation with him on that subject? A. Several times. I never gave him the slightest encouragement that he would receive the appointment.

Q. Do you recollect to have made use of any particular expression to him with regard to that appointment? A. I remember, after persistent and repeated visits, that I told him that there was, in my judgment, no prospect whatever of his receiving the appointment, and that I did not want him to continue his visits. I wanted to bring them to an end, and I told him there was no prospect whatever of him receiving it.

Q. Do you recollect the time of that remark? A. There was no fact of special importance that I could note, but I am very positive that it was in the month of May.

Q. You saw him personally? A. Yes; very frequently.

Q. Was he an applicant for office? A. He was a very persistent applicant for the Consul-Generalship at Paris.

Q. Had he written quite a number of letters? A. Several.

Q. You have seen the letters? A. I have.

Q. You are familiar with the handwriting? A. I am.

Q. Will you look at these letters (producing a

bundle of letters and handing them to the witness)? A. (After examination). These are letters taken from the files of the State Department on the request of the Government, to which I complied, and I have endorsed them. The letters which bear my signature, with the date of the delivery to the Government, are genuine letters which were received from Guiteau, and believed to be in his handwriting. I observe that the letters contain the signature made on them for identification, and this (indicating a paper) is the speech that was inclosed in one of the letters which he alleged to have made during the political campaign, and on which he based his claim for office. Here (indicating) is a letter that came over from the White House with the ordinary Executive Mansion blank. It is a mere endorsement," Guiteau, Charles, applicant, Austrian Mission." That letter came from the White House in this envelope?

By Mr. Porter.—Was that the letter Mr. Evarts found on the floor of the State Department? A. That was on the regular files of that department before I became Secretary of State. I observed the handwriting that came to me, and I merely marked it for identification.

By the District Attorney.—On the morning of the commission of the crime, you say you did not see the assassin fire the shot? A. No.

Q. Did you see the body of President Garfield

when it was brought to the District after he was dead? A. I came with the funeral train, and did not see the body of the President after the return here. It was not a pleasant sight, and I did not go to the rotunda of the Capitol to see it. I saw the body after death at Elberon, in the Francklyn Cottage, where he died on the 19th of September.

Q. In what place did he die? A. He died on the coast of New Jersey, in what was called the Francklyn Cottage, belonging to C. F. Francklyn, a well-known citizen of New York, who had very kindly tendered to us the use of the cottage for the President.

This ended the direct examination. The District-Attorney then proceeded to read the letters which had been identified by Secretary Blaine, and which consisted of the written applications of the prisoner to the President, and to the Secretary of State for an appointment in the diplomatic service of the United States, covering a period from March 11, 1881, to April 2, 1881. The District Attorney also read the letter addressed by the prisoner to Mr. Secretary Evarts, on November 11, 1880, asking him whether the terms of foreign ministers who had been approved by President Hayes did not expire on the 4th of March. He also read the speech which the prisoner claims to have delivered during the late Presidential campaign, entitled; " Garfield against Hancock."

THE CROSS-EXAMINATION.

The counsel for the defence then held a short consultation, and the witness was cross-examined by Mr. Robinson as to the position occupied by the President and himself at the time of the shooting. Mr Scoville then rose and proceeded to cross-examine the witness, as follows:

Q. When did you first become acquainted with the prisoner? A. I cannot say exactly that I ever was acquainted with him in the sense of acquaintance. He visited the State Department frequently, especially after my accession to this office. I can hardly claim that persons visiting there are acquaintances, but I know him and I identified the man from time to time as I see him before me now. As to the identical day that I first saw him I cannot say. It was early in March.

Q. Did you ever see him and observe him before that time? A. I did not.

Q. Did you meet him during the campaign last year? A. It is possible that I did. He corresponded with the Maine Committee, attempting to get into the campaign as a speaker.

Q. One moment. You are stating now the instance of his correspondence. How do you know it? A. There were letters addressed to me.

A. Have you got them? A. No.

Q. Are they in your possession? A. No; I

think not. My private Secretary, Mr. Sherman would know more about that than I.

Q. What makes you think that he wrote any letters? A. I know that there were several puerile letters from Charles Guiteau, of whom I then heard for the first time, desiring to speak in Maine.

Q. Can they be produced? A. I do not think they can. The debris of a campaign is generally swept away into the waste basket or fire. It is wholly unimportant. Very often persons try to get into the campaign as speakers. This is not an exceptional case. It is a transaction every speaker in the country is familiar with, the general rule being never to take a speaker who himself applies to speak.

Q. What is the reason of that rule? A. Because a man of reputation enough to be of influence is of consequence enough to be sought and not to seek.

Q. Had your attention been directed to this man or his name sufficiently that that name should be familiar to you when you came into the State Department? A. No, sir; it made no impression on me at all. The thing had passed out of my mind until my private Secretary said that this man had persistently applied to speak on the Maine campaign. I never should have recalled the fact in the world.

Q. You then remembered the name? A. I

did. It was a peculiar name. Probably if it were an ordinary one I would have been unable to identify it at all.

Q. How was he introduced to you? A. By himself.

Q. Alone? A. Yes, sir.

Q. Where was that? A. In the State Department.

Q. What was the purpose of it? A. He desired an office.

Q. What office? A. According to the correspondence, it seems he first wanted the Austrian Mission. What had impressed itself on my mind was the Paris Consulate. I do not recall much personal talk about the Austrian Mission. I do recollect several conversations about the Paris Consulate, but the whole matter was one that I did not give very strong personal attention.

Q. Did you give any personal notice to the individual who was making this application? A. So as to be able to identify him?

Q. So as to notice him—his appearance? A. Yes, sir.

Q. Did he come at any time with any backing for office, either written or personal? A. I do not recall that he did. He continually referred to the fact of General Logan being his friend, and I am not sure that I did not have some letters. That is a fact I cannot now state.

Q. Had it been a usual thing in applications for

office that the applicants came without any backing? A. Very common. He would often be one of forty in a single morning.

Q. All alike, substantially? A. All alike in desire, and pretty nearly all alike in disappointment. The case was not a peculiar one.

Q. At any time during this continued application for office did anything strike you as peculiar in his case; in regard to the man? A. No, sir.

Q. How did you treat him? A. Possibly if I had never seen but one office seeker I might have thought that he was persistent. Having seen so many of the same kind I did not notice him.

In response to further inquiries on this head, the witness substantially said that he had always treated Guiteau with civility as he did any gentleman who came to the State Department. After persistent applications, he had finally informed Guiteau that he need not have the faintest expectation of receiving the Consulship, and did not wish to be spoken to again about it. This was said firmly, but without any harshness. Witness had certainly never said that he should not object to the appointment, for he had great objections. The Paris Consulate was an office of great consequence, and he did not consider Guiteau as belonging to the rank and class of men that would naturally be assigned to it. When pressed for a further reason in explanation the Secretary said: "For the very simple reason that I think a man of sufficient consequence would have been a well-known public man. Such an important office is always assigned to gentlemen of a conspicuous rank for intelligence and public service." The question was then asked: "Do you mean party service?" Witness replied: "It may be party services. The incumbent at that time, Mr. George Walker, can illustrate my meaning. He was a gentleman, who had performed public services in the Finance Department of Massachusetts; had been Financial agent in Massachusetts and Europe, and was a gentleman of high character, widely and favorably known. I do not think there are any grounds for misunderstanding me." When further pressed as to whether offices were usually distributed as the reward of party services, witness replied that while such services were sometimes considered in that connection, yet in point of fact, men who hold conspicuous positions in diplomatic stations are not those who have applications on file for them in the Department. At this point Mr. Scoville began to narrow his questions down to the main point of attack, and asked: "To come nearer home, how about the Collectorships in the leading cities?" Witness replied: "I am not in the Treasury Department. I know nothing about it except from hearsay, and that I suppose would not be accepted. I never appointed a Collector in my life."

GUITEAU INTERVIEWED IN PRISON.

After having elicited the statement that witness never told Colonel Harper, of the Republican Committee that Guiteau was to have a Consulship, and that he had no recollection of making a remark about Guiteau's mental condition at the time of the shooting, Mr. Scoville suddenly wheeled round into a revival of

THE GARFIELD-CONKLING CONTROVERSY.

The first question indicated the range this cross-examination was now to take. It was as follows:

Q. What was the condition of the Republican party, as to unanimity and harmony, for six weeks before the shooting of the President? A. (After a pause.) There were some dissensions in it.

Q. They were considerable, were they not? A. Yes, sir.

Q. They created a good deal of excitement in the country? A. I should not say in the country.

Q. I mean among the people? A. The dissension was largely local. There were differences between the President and some members of the party about some matters in New York.

Q. They were agitated in the press all over the country? A. They were commented upon.

Q. I wish you would state briefly to the jury the substance of the dissensions, here in Washington and in New York, as a matter of evidence. I refer to the differences that culminated in the resignation of the Senators from New York. A.

I do not exactly know the scope of the question.

Q. Were there any such troubles? A. Oh, yes; there were very sharp differences of opinion.

Q. Were there not acts as well as opinions? A. Yes.

Q. What did they consist of? A. The act that created the difference.

Q. There was more than one act in that connection? A. If you will specify any particular one I will give my opinion upon it.

Q. Perhaps if I call your attention to the conduct of certain individuals you can answer. How was it with Senator Conkling, of New York. Did he do anything, or say anything, that led to the trouble that fanned the difference and promoted it? A. What difference?

Q. In the Republican party? A. About what?

Q. Oh, of course, if you do not know, you need not answer. A. If Senator Conkling spoke, he must have spoken about some particular thing.

Q. I do not want any long disquisition. I simply ask you to state to the jury the substance of the trouble in the Republican party.

The witness.—I do not exactly see the point about which the counsel desires me to testify. I have no reluctance to testify, and I hope he will not construe my answer in that way. The President had appointed Mr. Robertson as Collector of Customs at New York, and on that and the propriety of it there grew up a feeling between him and his administration, and the Senator from New York.

Mr. Scoville.—Now, if you will go a little further, and state what happened after that disagreement grew up. What resulted from it?

The witness.—I am sure that I can make a political speech of two hours and a half on the subject. If you ask specific questions I will answer them.

Q. What was done, if anything, by the Senators from New York after the disagreement arose with the Administration? Did they resign? A. They resigned. Yes, sir.

Q. When was that? A. I think that the resignation was on the 28th of May. Of that I will not be positive. [To the District Attorney.] Am I correct?

The District Attorney.—It was earlier than that—about the 15th.

Guiteau (quietly).—The 16th of May.

Mr. Scoville.—We will say the 16th of May. What was the cause of their resigning? A. Discontent with the President's action in appointing Robertson.

Q. What followed immediately after in relation to the election of their successors?

The witness.—I am very certain that I do not see what the counsel desires me to testify about.

Mr. Davidge.—In your cross-examination, Mr.

Scoville, you are at liberty to ask leading questions. You ought to question more specifically.

Mr. Scoville.—Did not considerable feeling exist for several days here, in the Senate and in Washington, over that matter of disagreement? A. Yes.

Q. That resulted in the resignation of those Senators, did it not? The witness nodded assent.

Q. The next step was to elect successors in New York? Another nod.

Q. And the matter came before the Legislature and resulted in a struggle there? Another nod.

Q. How long did that continue? A. That struggle continued until long after the President was shot.

Q. And commenced immediately after the resignations? A. Yes.

Q. Did that struggle generate or keep up the feeling that existed and that caused the resignations?

Mr. Davidge.—I must object to that. The examination is taking too wide a range.

Mr. Scoville.—If the Court please, it may be, and we consider it important to show that there was a quarrel in the Republican party; that it was outspoken and persistent, and that instead of being healed it was growing wider, if possible, so that even the death of the President did not interrupt the daily bickerings and strife that existed in the Legislature at Albany, in which leading men of the country were taking part. We wish to show the extent of the feeling that prevailed in the community in order to show, in proper relation, the influence that was brought to bear on the mind of the prisoner.

Mr. Davidge.—In order to save time, we withdraw any objection.

Mr. Scoville.—When did that contest terminate at Albany?

The witness.—I think that the termination of it was in the election of the second Senator—Lapham. My recollection would be that it was about the 20th or 21st of July; it may have been later. I did not charge my mind with it. The reason I did not was that I was very deeply absorbed and engrossed in the condition of the President. I can say to counsel that, after the President was shot, the political canvass gave me as little concern and elicited from me as little observation as any individual in the country.

Mr. Scoville.—No doubt of that.

The witness.—I took no part whatever in the contest in the New York Senate.

Mr. Scoville.—I never understood that you did. I did not question you with that idea. I wish to know if those factions in the Republican party were classified under certain heads, and, if so, what were they denominated? A. I believe that they were commonly designated as "Stalwarts" and "Half-breeds."

Q. Did not this term "Stalwart" date back to the political campaign last year, including Grant, Logan and Conkling? Were they not designated "Stalwarts," and was not that term used in 1880? A. Yes; the term is older than that.

Q. Did it not become prominent before the people in connection with the Chicago Convention? A. It was used there

Q. As applicable to the delegates that stood by Grant—was it not. There were 306, I think? A. Oh, yes.

Q. I believe Guiteau refers to the term "Stalwart" in some of his letters? A. I believe he does.

Q. What would any one understand properly from the use of that word? A. Well, if counsel is wishing a chapter in political history to form part of the testimony it ought to be a correct one. The term "Stalwart" originated before that. I invented the term myself, in a despatch to the *Boston Herald*, in 1875.

Q. Then you are just the man we want to have explain it. When Guiteau, in his letters or speeches, in the latter part of 1880 and first of 1881, refers to himself as a "Stalwart," what did he mean? A. I suppose he meant to class himself with the personal supporters of General Grant.

Q. Did not those supporters, after Garfield was nominated, become his supporters? A. Naturally.

Q. Was it not a fact? A. Of course. They were Republicans, and all Republicans supported Garfield.

Q. The "Stalwarts" worked for the election of Garfield? A. Very heartily and very cordially.

Q. Yes, sir, I was one of them. What was understood by the "Half Breeds" in New York? A. They included all the Republicans in New York that were not included among the "Stalwarts."

Q. Then there were only two divisions there? A. Yes.

Q. To what branch did the person appointed as Collector belong? He was classed in the nomenclature of New York with the "Half-Breeds."

Q. To what branch did Senator Conkling belong? A. He was understood to be a "Stalwart."

Mr. Scoville.—That is all.

Secretary Blaine then left the witness stand, and at 12.30 P. M. the Court took a recess for half an hour.

The prisoner, as he was being taken from the room, addressed his counsel in a violent and angry manner, making use of such expressions as "There is going to be a big row," and "I am going to have a fight:" but the Deputy Marshals prevented any further demonstrations.

AFTER THE RECESS.

The recess lasted until 1 o'clock. Before the session was resumed, Guiteau (who had just been brought in by the officers) said: "Will your Honor allow me to address the Court a moment? In spite of counsel I have rights here which should be recognized. I want to state my position."

Judge Cox.—"You cannot be heard now. The Court is satisfied with your counsel."

The prisoner.—"But I am not. I think it an outrage to have incompetent counsel forced upon me. Mr. Scoville is doing splendidly. I most distinctly appreciate his services. I want a chance to defend myself, and there will be a row all the way through if I don't have it." (All this time Guiteau was resisting the efforts of the officers to make him take his seat, and was talking in his usual jerky, disconnected way.) "I am not satisfied with this business (striking the table with his fist), and I will not have it."

Judge Cox (severely).—"If you do not keep silence I will have you removed."

The prisoner.—"I do not care if you do. The American people have something to say about this matter. It is an outrage that I should not be heard in my own defence."

Mr. Simon Camacho, the Venezuela Minister, was the next witness called. Before he was sworn, the District Attorney stated that, under the law governing diplomatic relations, Mr. Camacho could not be subpœnaed or required to testify, but that his government had given him instructions to appear and testify just as any citizen of the country.

Mr. Camacho was then sworn and examined. He spoke with a strongly marked foreign accent, so that it was rather difficult at times to understand him.

In the course of his testimony this witness was asked if, when he saw Guiteau in the hands of an officer at the depot, the prisoner seemed to be afraid, and the answer was "Very much, indeed."

In his cross-examination the witness explained how the prisoner wore his hat, and Mr. Scoville placed Guiteau's hat upon his (Guiteau's) head, partly on the side. Witness stopped counsel, saying: "That is the way he wore his hat."

Guiteau said: "That is false; I wear my hat this way." (Placing it on his head perfectly straight.) He added: "I wear my hat this way, and do not go sneaking around." Further cross-examination elicited nothing of importance from this witness.

Mrs. Sarah B. White, matron of the Baltimore and Potomac Depot Ladies' Waiting Room, was then called. She explained the circumstances of the shooting in detail, substantially as published in her statement obtained soon after the shooting.

She recognized Guiteau as the person who fired the shot.

She had seen the prisoner walking up and down the Gentlemen's Room previous to the arrival of the Presidential party on the morning of July 2. She did not observe the pistol in the assassin's hand when she went to the President's assistance. "Guiteau," she said, "was only about three feet back of the President when he fired at him."

Cross examined. Witness saw nothing remarkable in the prisoner's appearance, excepting that he walked to and fro in the Gentlemen's Room, keeping his eyes constantly on the Ladies' Room, as if awaiting the arrival of some one.

She explained the manner in which Guiteau wore his hat, stating that it was on his head straight. Guiteau's hat was here placed on his head again in the manner indicated by witness, and she said that was the way he wore it. The prisoner bowed his approval at the reply of the witness.

Robert A. Parke, Secret Agent, employed in the Baltimore and Potomac Depot, was the next witness. He testified that he was looking through the window of his office into the Ladies' Room, when the shooting took place. He was not in a position to see the prisoner when he fired the first shot, but he saw him move two steps into the Ladies' Room and fire the second shot. He then rushed around and was the first to seize the prisoner and to give him in charge of two police officers.

On cross-examination the witness stated, that on his pursuing the prisoner, the prisoner seemed to be starting towards the Ladies' Retiring Room; there he turned around and was facing the witness when he was arrested.

Q. Was there anything to prevent the prisoner from getting out by the B Street door? A. So far as I saw there was nothing to prevent him from getting out by that way.

Q. Did you notice how the prisoner wore his hat? A. He wore a slouched hat pulled pretty well over his head.

Guiteau (putting on his hat and wearing it a little back of his head).—"This is the way I wore it."

Q. Was there anything particular about his appearance at that time? A. Nothing particular.

Q. Did he say anything when you seized him? A. He spoke about a letter and said that the letter was for General somebody.

Guiteau (interrupting).—"For General Sherman."

The witness—"His language was unintelligible. The letter was in his left hand."

Q. What was the first thing he said when you arrested him? A. He said that this letter was for General somebody.

After getting out in the main waiting room,

he said that he wanted to go to jail. I caught him by the back of the neck with my right hand, and by the left wrist with my left hand. He didn't make much resistance. I arrested him just on the threshold of the Ladies' Room. There was some little force necessary to get him into the main room. All that he said was about this letter to General somebody, which would explain everything. I did not look at the letter. I cannot say that I noticed his appearance or his countenance. I had not seen him there before.

Judson W. Wheeler, a young man from Elizabeth, City County, Virginia, was in the Ladies' Waiting Room at the time of the occurrence. He said that when the first shot was fired, the pistol was not more than a few inches from his face, and that the smoke from the discharge made him cough. His account of the occurrence did not vary from that of the other witnesses.

George W. Adams, publisher of the *Washington Evening Star*, was the next witness. He testified that he was in the railroad depot on the morning of the 2d of July, having reached there about twenty minutes past nine o'clock. The President and Secretary Blaine had just alighted from their carriage and stepped into the Ladies, Waiting Room. The President stopped to speak to a policeman at the door, and Mr. Blaine stepped in ahead of him. Witness did not see the first shot fired but in a few seconds afterwards another shot was fired. At this shot, the President turned half around, raised his arms and sank gradually to the floor. The man who fired the shot started toward the main waiting room and then turned and was seized by the officers. The whole thing had not occupied ten seconds. The witness, with the aid of a diagram, described the various positions. He saw the prisoner's face just for a moment. The prisoner did not seem to him to be very much excited. Had understood him to say it was all right, and at first thought the prisoner was a countryman who was trying to quiet the people.

Jacob P. Smith, janitor of the Baltimore and Potomac Railroad Depot, described the scenes in the depot as far as they had come under his observation, but the only point of special notice in his testimony was that he insisted that it was the second shot fired by Guiteau which took effect on the President, and that when that shot was fired, Mr. Blaine was at the door leading to the main saloon. Witness was the first who laid his hand upon the President after he fell. His impression was that the President just settled down after he was shot. His legs gave way under him. When the witness reached him he was very pale and did not say a word. His eyes were open. Witness did not know whether the President was then unconscious or not. He tried to get the President into a sitting position, but finding that he could not do so, he lowered his head, ran to the door and gave the alarm. Nobody was yet with the President when the witness left him. Witness had not seen the prisoner there before the President's arrival. He was pretty confident that the second shot had been fired when the President began to fall. The President did not turn round until the second shot had struck him. At the close of this testimony the Court at 3 P. M. adjourned.

CHAPTER VI.

Guiteau Again Demonstrative—The Court Threatens to Remove Him—The Story of the Crime Continued by Eye Witnesses—The Letters Written to His Intended Victim.

ON the opening of the Court on the fifth day of the trial, Mr. Scoville requested the Court to take some measures to prevent the prisoner from giving unauthorized communications to the public press, and also to prevent the annoying interruptions of the prisoner in the Court room. This aroused Guiteau's anger, and an unseemly wrangle ensued, during which the prisoner shouted: "Mr. Scoville talks one thing to me in private and another thing in public. Last night he spent an hour in jail with me, and showed a different spirit from now. That is his way. I do not propose to put my case in his hands. He is no lawyer and no politician. I want first-class talent on this business, and I am going to have it, or there is going to be trouble. Mind your business," he continued, fiercely struggling with the deputy marshals, who were trying to suppress him. After a further wordy war with the prisoner Mr. Scoville said to the Court : "I do not propose to be interrupted here by the prisoner every day, nor to spend an hour or two at the jail every day to prevent his giving out communications. Struggling with the deputy marshals Guiteau exclaimed wildly, addressing his remarks, which were uttered very rapidly, to Mr. Scoville: "You are no criminal lawyer, and I have no confidence in your capacity. I propose to get two or three of the first-class lawyers in America to manage my case; and I want to say a word upon the law," cried the prisoner, addressing the Court. "If you expel me from the Court room, the Court in banc will reverse you. If the Court puts me out—confounded fools you," he cried, turning and struggling with the deputy marshals who were pressing him into his seat, from which he had half risen, "the Court will understand that he will be reversed by the Court in banc. Mind your business; you aint got no sense," he said, turning upon the deputies, with whom he continued to argue violently for several moments.

The Court.—On several occasions in the Courts of the United States the prisoner has been, on occasions of disorderly conduct, removed from the Court and the case continued in his absence. It was done in this very Court in the case of Lawrence.

The prisoner.—(interrupting and striking the table with his fist) "It's totally illegal, and not a Court in America—"

The Court.—"I will not resort to that unless it

FROM THE COURT-HOUSE TO THE PRISON VAN.

is necessary; but I admonish the prisoner in advance that if the case requires it, it will be done. I have told you that at the proper time, you can be heard in your defense, and you shall be heard at the close of the evidence if you desire it. Until that time you must preserve silence."

"I came here as counsel, and I want to be heard," cried the prisoner.

The Court.—(sternly) "You cannot be heard."

Guiteau.—"I accept your Honor's ruling, and will let it go up to the Court in banc. If I am convicted the Court in banc will reverse you and give me a new trial."

The Court.—(to Mr. Scoville) "I shall pass any order you desire in regard to the communications."

The prisoner.—(impulsively) "I want two or three of the best lawyers in America, and I expect to get them."

The Court.—(severely) "We will not talk about that.

"I don't care if you don't. I have had my say," exclaimed the prisoner, as a parting shot, and he then relapsed into comparative quiet.

The District Attorney then put in evidence formally the letters identified by Secretary Blaine.

Joseph K Sharp, Assistant Train Master of the Baltimore and Potomac Railroad Company was called. He testified that he had been standing on the western platform, waiting to start the limited express. He heard two shots fired, hurried into the main waiting room, and there found Guiteau in the hands of Mr. Parke with two police officers closing in on him. Parke was shouting: "This is the man," as if he wanted assistance. Then witness went into the Ladies' Waiting Room. Mr. Garfield was lying on his back, supported by Mrs. White; and he gave the witness (as the witness then thought) a serious, dying look, with his eyes fixed. Witness then went out of the B Street door and sent two colored boys to the police station to get police officers to keep out the crowd. When he returned the President had been taken up stairs.

On cross-examination witness said that he had heard nothing said by the prisoner while he was held by Parke. He repeated his account of the incident and illustrated his story by reference to the diagram.

Miss Ella M. Ridgley was the next witness, and testified that on the morning of July 2d, she had been standing at the B Street door at the depot, waiting for a street-car, when she saw the prisoner. A hackman came up to him and asked him where he wanted him to drive to. The prisoner said to the Cemetery, and told him to wait there till he came out. This was about four minutes before the President and Secretary Blaine entered the depot. Then she saw the prisoner in the Ladies' Waiting Room with his right hand in his pocket. He drew out a weapon and the witness noticed the sunlight shining on the barrel, although she did not realize at the moment that it was a pistol. After firing the first shot the prisoner took two or three steps nearer to the President, and fired a second shot when about four feet from him. On the first shot the President threw up his hands and half fell back. He kept sinking all the time as the second shot was fired. She was not sure whether the second shot touched him at all. After the prisoner fired the second shot he stepped to the B Street door, and the witness lost sight of him, as her attention was directed to the President. When she next saw the prisoner, the officers were passing through the room with him.

On cross-examination witness said that when the prisoner was talking to the hackman he looked distressed and troubled, so that she had the idea that he was going to the Cemetery to visit dead friends. After he was in the hands of the officers he held some paper in his hand, and witness heard him say that he wanted it given to General Sherman. He seemed to be more calm then, than he was before he fired the pistol. His countenance did not look so distressed or troubled as it did when he was talking to the hackman. He looked rather pale. He did not run after the second shot, but just turned round and walked to the B Street door; not very rapidly. In reply to further questions as to how the assassin held the pistol, witness said he just extended his hand out, and when he fired the second shot he held his hand higher. The President was falling when the second shot was fired. The whole thing was so quick that witness did not think much aim was taken. The prisoner just took the pistol out of his pocket and extended his arm.

Joshua A. Davis, a gentleman at the depot, and *William S. Crawford*, driver of a wagon, were next called, but their testimony was unimportant, having reference only to the way the prisoner wore his hat, and upon this they were often contradicted by the prisoner.

John A. Scott, special officer at the railroad depot, was the next witness. He was the first officer to reach the prisoner after Parke seized him. The prisoner said that he wanted to go to jail, and that he had a letter which he wanted sent to General Sherman. Witness, however, did not see any letter in his hand; they took him out of the Sixth Street door to the Station House, and when passing Sixth and B Streets he looked up and said: "I am a Stalwart and Arthur is now President of the United States." He then kept repeating about the letter he would send to General Sherman, and he said: "I am a gentleman and a lawyer." At the Station House the prisoner was searched, and a packet of papers, some change, and a revolver were taken out of his pocket. (Here the revolver was identified and exhibited to the jury—four of the chambers being still loaded.)

On cross-examination, witness said that the prisoner did not repeat more than once the expression that he was a "Stalwart" and that "Arthur was President;" but he referred repeatedly to the letter to General Sherman, which he said would explain the whole matter. Witness made no reply, except to say that General Sherman would have the letter. The prisoner had a kind of fierce, fresh, bright look out of his eyes.

Edmund L. Du Borry, a civil engineer, was the next witness, but there was nothing of importance in his direct testimony. In the cross-examination he was closely questioned by Mr. Scoville as to the appearance of the prisoner on the day of the shooting. He had thought that it was a bad countenance, but was unable, though searchingly examined by Mr. Scoville, to state what peculiar features of the prisoner had given that impression. It was merely his knowledge of human nature that had led him to the conclusion that the prisoner was a bad character. Witness admitted that he had several times expressed an opinion that the man should be hanged.

Patrick Kearney, police officer, was then called, and slowly gave the following graphic narrative: "The first time I saw the prisoner was at 8.55 on the morning of July 2. I saw him standing with two hackmen—one white and one colored. They were both "bucking a job" from him—that is, soliciting him for a job. Then I saw the President's carriage coming around from Pennsylvania Avenue to the B Street entrance. I went around and stood by the lamp-post. The President's carriage stopped outside the curbstone, and the President had his hand on Mr. Blaine's shoulder. The President said to me, "How much time have I, General?" I took out my watch and showed him that he had ten minutes. He made no reply, and I went back to the lamp-post. After awhile Mr. Blaine got out of the carriage and went into the depot, out of my sight. The President then got out and walked ahead. As he moved past I took up my hat and saluted him. He went up as far as the third step, and then he turned round smiling, lifted his hat to me, and went into the depot out of my sight. Then I was moving down to Sixth Street, when I heard the report of a pistol. I turned back quickly and ran down to the B Street door, and then I heard another report and a scream. I went to the door, and the first thing I saw was the prisoner coming against me. I grabbed him. He said: "I want to send this letter to General Sherman immediately." "Hold up," said I, "there were two shots fired, and you are coming from the direction in which they were fired. I will hold you to know the result. If you are in the wrong I will keep you, and if not, you can get off. But now I put you under arrest." Then I turned his back to the door. The first man that I saw was Du Borry (the last witness); he was right by my side. Then I could see the smoke rising out of the carpet, and saw that I could not advance in that way with him. The prisoner jerked and pulled me down towards the heater in the Ladies' Room, and I pulled out my club to hit him, but I thought of the Grand Jury, and not knowing what the man had done, I did not hit him, but I gave him a good shaking and brought him along. After that he went along with me. When I stopped he stopped, and when I moved he moved. We went out of the Ladies' Room into the main room, and stood by the indicator. One or two men passed and tapped the prisoner on the shoulder with: " I arrest you, I arrest you!" I said nothing, but I thought they were fools, because I had arrested him at the door and brought him back. Parke was standing at the jam of the door, near the ticket office, with a linen duster on him, and with his hands behind his back, as mildly as now. The prisoner passed Parke at that corner, and he and I went and stood by the indicator. Then Parke advanced toward the ticket office. I was standing along with the prisoner, and there was a crowd in a circle around us. I saw Lowry snatch the paper that the prisoner held in his hand; then Parke, the ticket agent, made a run and grabbed at Guiteau and threw his hat off. I lifted the hat up and put it right on the prisoner's head again. Then Scott came from the platform over to where I was with Guiteau, and got hold of his wrist and twisted it. Guiteau complained, and asked him not to break his wrist. As he did not repeat the complaint I said nothing. After Parke made the grab at Guiteau, he said: "That is the man who shot the President." That was the first I knew of what had happened. I did not know until then that the President or any other man had been shot. I took the prisoner out of the Sixth Street door, and when we came to the sewer trap on the street he said: "I did it; I will go to jail for it. Arthur is President, and I am a Stalwart." Scott and I took him along to Pennsylvania Avenue, and then we took an oblique direction eastward, till we came to the Mount Vernon House, and then we walked along till we got to the Police Headquarters on Four-and-a-Half Street. When I went in I sang out: "This man killed (or shot) the President." Lieutenant Eckloff said: "You are giving us taffy." I said: "No." Then I took the pistol out of the prisoner's pocket and laid it on the table, and then two pieces of silver; and then I went for these letters. He resisted, and I was going to throw him, but one of the officers catched him by the arm and held him till I got them letters from him. He said he wanted them letters to go to Byron

RECESS.
(LUNCH IN THE COURT ROOM.)

"IT AM HOT." SCENE IN FRONT OF COURT HOUSE.

Andrews, on Fourth Street. Lieutenant Eckhoff asked him if he had anything to say. "I have nothing to say" said he. "The papers speak for themselves." I asked him what his name was. He said: "Charles Guiteau, of Illinois, a theologian and a lawyer." After I got through his pockets I went to search him about the breast. He said, "don't get excited, take your time, you have plenty of time to search me." He was put into a cell for about ten minutes and then he was sent to jail. I never saw him again until I saw him here.

Mr. Scoville then cross-examined the witness as follows: "Did Parke ever touch him until you brought him into the main room?"

Witness (solemnly)—"Never; so help me God —never." It was up by the heater that Parke rushed at him, grabbed at him, knocked off his hat, and said: 'I seize the assassin.' At that I knew that somebody was hurt. On the way to Headquarters the prisoner spoke to me once or twice about his fear of being hurt, and I says to him: 'Now the quicker that you and me get to Headquarters, the better for both of us.' I never had no trouble with him after that. In repeating his description of the arrest of the prisoner, he said the prisoner had a paper in his hand, but I saw no writing on it, and took it as a 'bluff.'"

When Mr. Scoville ceased the cross-examination, Guiteau said in his usual flurried manner:

"Allow me to examine the witness. He came nearer the truth than any one else who has been on the stand." Mr. Scoville succeeded in suppressing the prisoner; and then he further examined the witness as to whether he was much excited when he arrested the prisoner. "No," said the witness, "when I catched that man I did not know what he had done. I knew that there were two shots fired, and that he was running from the direction where the shots were fired."

The prisoner.—"As a matter of fact I was standing still; and the witness came up and seized me by the wrist. I had just got my pistol put up, and you (addressing the witness) seized me simultaneously. I did not attempt to run at all. I told the officer that I wanted to go to jail at once. I made no disposition to escape at all."

The witness.--"No. I will say that for you. After the difficulty in the corner of the room, you gave up and went along with me, and stood by me all the way to Headquarters. Is not that so?"

The prisoner.—"Yes, sir."

Thompson H. Alexander, the next witness, related his recollection as to the incidents in the Baltimore and Potomac Depot on the morning of the shooting. His impression was, that the President was falling when the second shot was fired. The second shot was fired at an interval of about three seconds after the first. The cross-examination elicited nothing new; the witness merely stating

GUITEAU, THE ASSASSIN. 147

his impression that the prisoner had looked desperately in earnest. The Court then, at 12.20, took a recess for half an hour, during which time the prisoner was removed to the Marshal's room, and the Jury was taken for a walk around the Court House grounds.

AFTER THE RECESS.

On the reassembling of the Court, Guiteau calmly addressed the Court. "I understand, your Honor," he said, "that Judge Magruder, of Maryland, is willing to assist in the defence. I hereby publicly invite him to meet me here on Monday at the trial. I do not know whether Mr. Scoville wants him or not. The only way to make that known to him is to make it public. He has written a very fine letter. I have two or three other names I shall mention. Mr. Scoville is doing splendidly, but I want him to have help."

John Taylor and *Aquilla Barton*, both colored hackmen were then severally called. Their testimony was unimportant, being that the prisoner had bargained about a week before the shooting, over the charge to convey him to Benning's Station, just beyond the Congressional Cemetery, and in the other that in the absence of Taylor he made a fresh arrangement with Barton for the same purpose, stipulating that he was to be driven very rapidly. The latter witness having qualified his identification of the prisoner with the remark, "He was fleshier then than he is now," Guiteau seized the chance to raise a laugh, that solace to his sinful soul, by remarking: "I may state here that I had the first square meal to-day, I have had since the 2d or 3d of July."

Byron Andrews, correspondent of the *Chicago Inter-Ocean* and *New York Graphic*, testified that he had not received any papers from the prisoner, had no acquaintance with him, in fact did not know him.

THE INSANITY DEFENCE MOOTED.

While waiting for another witness, Mr. Scoville arose and said: "I give notice now that the defence in this case is insanity, and we will claim that the burden of proof is on the prosecution. If they intend to introduce evidence on that point they must introduce it before they close."

Mr. Davidge.—"We think otherwise and we will act according to our own convictions of what is proper. The defence has made no opening."

Mr. Scoville.—"I give you notice now before you close your proofs. I simply want to make it a matter of record."

Judge Cox.—"I understand."

Mr. Sevillon A. Brown, Chief Clerk of the State Department was the next witness. He testified as to the frequent visits of the prisoner to the Department, and of the witness giving orders not to send any more of his cards to the

Secretary, nor to let him see the Secretary. On cross-examination he said that he was quite sure that the place for which Guiteau applied was beyond his reach. The prisoner did not look to be the kind of a man who would be appointed to such a position. He had excluded his card from the Secretary "because it was hardly worth while to take up the Secretary's time. The Secretary had not ordered the exclusion of Guiteau's cards nor did Guiteau know they were excluded." Witness had also refused to permit the prisoner to make use of the library of the Department. He did not want to give him any excuse for being there. He wanted to "rid the Department of him." He did not notice anything peculiar about him except that he was a " nervous individual," and that he seemed to have a reluctance to "look one in the eye."

Guiteau.—"I looked in your eye, Mr. Brown."

Adolphus Eckhoff, Police Lieutenant, confirmed the identification of the revolver. In cross-examination he said the man seemed frightened on the way to the jail, but there was nothing particularly wild about his looks. Witness heard the man tell McElfresh that he was a Stalwart of the Stalwarts and that he had shot the President to save the Republican party and the Country.

Mr. J. Stanley Brown, Private Secretary to the late President, was the next witness. He testified as to Guiteau's very frequent calls at the

White House, and of his (witness) finally about the 15th of May, telling the usher that Guiteau must no longer trouble the office. He had told Guiteau himself and had reiterated it twice that his application, being in the consular service, must go to the State Department. Witness identified a large number of letters from Guiteau to the President, which the District Attorney proceeded to read.

THE ASSASSIN'S PRECIOUS PRODUCTIONS,

were worded as follows:

(Private.)

MARCH 8, 1881.

GENERAL GARFIELD:

I called to see you this A. M., but you were engaged. In October and January last, I sent you a note from New York touching the Austrian Mission. Mr. Kasson, of Iowa, I understand, wishes to remain at Vienna till fall. He is a good fellow. I should not wish to disturb him in any event. What do you think of me for Consul-General at Paris? I think I prefer Paris to Vienna, and, if agreeable to you, should be satisfied with the Consulship at Paris. The enclos d speech was sent to our leading editors and orators in August. Soon thereafter they opened on the rebel war-claim idea, and it was this idea that resulted in your election. Mr. Walker, of New York, the present Consul at Paris, was appointed through Mr. Evarts, and I presume he has no expectation of being retained. Senators Blaine, Logan and Conkling are friendly to me, and I presume my appointment will be promptly confirmed. There is nothing against me. I claim to be a gentleman and a Christian. C. G."

(Private.)

GENERAL GARFIELD:

I understand from Colonel Hooker, of the National Committee, that I am to have a Consulship. I hope it is the Consulship at Paris, as that is the only one I care to take. Now that Mr. Phelps has the

Austrian Mission, I think I have a right to press my claim for the Consulship at Paris. I think General Logan and Secretary Blaine are favorable to this, and wish you would send in my name for the Consulship at Paris. Mr. Walker, the present Consul, I do not think has any claim on you for the office, as the men that did the business last fall, are the ones to be remembered. Senator Logan has my paper, and he said he would see you about this.

Very respectfully,
March 26.   CHARLES GUITEAU.

(Private.)

GENERAL GARFIELD:

From your looks yesterday, I judge you did not quite understand what I meant by saying: "I have not called for two or three weeks," intended to express my sympathy for you on account of the pressure that has been on you since you came into office. I think Mr. Blaine intends giving me the Paris Consulship, with your and General Logan's approbation, and I am waiting for the break in the Senate. I have practiced law in New York and Chicago, and presume I am well qualified for it. I have been here since March 5th, and expect to remain some little time, or until I get my commission.

Very respectfully,
April 8.   CHARLES GUITEAU.

GENERAL GARFIELD:

I wish to say this about Mr. Robertson's nomination. Would it not be well to withdraw it, on the ground that Mr. Conkling had worked himself to a white heat in opposition. It might be done quietly and gracefully, on the ground that since the nomination many merchants and others in New York had petitioned for the retention of General Merritt. It strikes me that it would be true policy to do this, as Mr. Conkling is so determined to defeat Mr. Robertson, and the chances are that he may do it. It is doing great harm all around. I am very sorry you have got Conkling down on you. Had it not been for General Grant and Senator Conkling we should have lost New York. The loss of New York would have elected Hancock. Mr. Conkling feels you ought to have consulted him about the appointments in his own State, and that is one reason he is so set against Mr. Robertson, and many persons think he is right. It seems to me that the only way out of this difficulty is to withdraw Mr. R., on the ground that since his nomination the leading merchants of New York have expressed themselves as satisfied with General Merritt, who certainly is NOT a "Conkling man." I am on friendly terms with Senator Conkling and the rest of our Senators, but I write this on my own account and in the spirit of a peacemaker. I have taken the liberty of making this suggestion to Mr. Blaine, and wish you and he would give it due attention.

Very respectfully,

April 29. CHARLES GUITEAU.

(Private.)

GENERAL GARFIELD.

I am sorry you and Senator Conkling are apart, but I stand by you on the ground that his friends, Morton, James, Pearson, and the rest of them have been well provided for, and Mr. Conkling ought to have been satisfied. Very respectfully,

May 7. CHARLES GUITEAU.

(Private.)

TO GENERAL GARFIELD:

I have got a new idea about '84. If you work your position for all it's worth, you can be nominated and elected in '84. Your opponents will probably be General Grant and Mr. Blaine. General Grant will never be as strong again as he was just after his trip around the world. Too many people are dead set against a third time, and I don't think he can be nominated, much less elected again. Two National Conventions have slaughtered Mr. Blaine on account of his railroad record and connections. The Republican party are afraid to run him. This leaves the way open for you. Run the Presidency on your own account; strike out right and left. The American people like pluck, and in 1884 we may put you in again. C. G.

WHITE HOUSE, May 10.

P. S.—I will see you about the Paris Consulship to-morrow, unless you happen to send in my name to-day.

(Private.)

GENERAL GARFIELD:

Until Saturday, I supposed Mr. Blaine was my friend in the mat- of the Paris Consulship; but from his tone on Saturday, I judge he is trying to run the State Department in the interest of the Blaine element in '84. You are under small obligations to Mr. Blaine. He almost defeated your election by the loss of Maine. Had it not been for Hancock's blunder on the Tariff, and the decided efforts of the Stalwarts, you certainly would have been defeated after the loss of Maine. You recalled Mr. Noyes for Mr. Morton, and I wish you would recall Mr. Walker for me. I am with Mr. Morton and General Arthur, and I will get them to go on my bond. General Logan and Senator Harrison and the rest of my friends will see that it is promptly confirmed. "Never speak to me again," said Mr. Blaine Saturday, "on the Paris Consulship as long as you live."

Heretofore he has been my friend, but now his eye is on a "Blaine man" for the position, that will help him in '84. Two National Conventions have slaughtered Mr. Blaine, and he ought to see that there is no chance for him in 1884. I want to get in my work for you in 1884. I am sorry Mrs. Garfield is sick, and hope she will recover soon. CHARLES GUITEAU.
May 16.

(Private.)
GENERAL GARFIELD:

I hope Mrs. Garfield is better. Monday I sent you a note about the Paris Consulship; Tuesday, one about '84. The idea about '84 flashed through me like an inspiration, and I believe it will come true. Your nomination was a providence, and your election a still greater providence. Had Hancock kept his mouth shut on the Tariff, he would have been elected probably, notwithstanding Grant and Conkling and the treachery of Kelly. Business men were afraid to trust a man in the White House, who did not know anything about the Tariff, and this killed Hancock. You are fairly elected, and now make the best of it. With two terms in the White House, and a trip around the globe, you can go into history by the side of General Grant. May I tell Mr. Blaine to prepare the order for my appointment to the Paris Consulship, vice George Walker recalled. CHARLES GUITEAU.
WHITE HOUSE, May 13.

Another letter was read in which Guiteau refers to Secretary Blaine as a wicked man, and which was read by the District Attorney in his opening address. In reply to the District Attorney, witness stated that these were all the letters from this person that he found on the files of the Executive Office; and the prisoner immediately remarked: "They are all that I ever wrote."

The District Attorney then proposed to identify

by this witness, the letters and papers left by the prisoner at the depot news stand, and in spite of Guiteau's prompt admission: "Those letters are all correct; every one of them;" the witness formally identified the handwriting.

On cross-examination, Mr. Scoville inquired as to two letters written by Guiteau to General Garfield at Mentor. Witness remembered the letters referred to. One written in October, 1880, and the other in January, 1881, and said that they were probably now among the papers belonging to the estate, of which there were twenty-nine boxes full in a fire-proof vault, in the building occupied by the Bureau of Engraving and Printing. The prisoner remarked that those two letters, as he understood, had been published last July, and Mr. Scoville suggested that the printed copies be put in evidence; but the District Attorney objected, as he had never seen them.

Mr. Scoville then said.—"The October letter was dated from New York, and was substantially like this: "General Garfield: I am an applicant for the Austrian Mission. I expect to marry a lady of this city of great wealth in a few days."

The prisoner.—"Not correct. Better let me reproduce it from memory. I can do it if you want me to."

The witness.—"I have seen that letter."

The prisoner.—"The January letter was a repetition of that. There is no use in putting this gentleman, the witness, to the trouble of hunting up those letters."

James L. Denny, in charge of the news stand at the depot, then identified the package left with him by the prisoner, on the morning of the shooting, for Byron Andrews and his co-journalists.

After the District Attorney had read these letters and scraps of various kinds found in the package, he formally placed them in evidence, together with Guiteau's book and annotations to it, and the Court at 3 P. M. adjourned.

CHAPTER VII.

Dramatic Scene in Court—A Fragment of the Martyred President's Vertebræ Produced on the Witness Stand—The Murderer and Murdered in Juxtaposition—Dr. Bliss as a Witness—End of the First Week of the Trial.

During Friday it became evident that public sentiment had been much embittered against the prisoner by his brazen bearing in Court, and his offensive exhibitions of temper and insolence. Quite a number of demonstrations were observed by the officers, and promptly checked inside and outside the Court, and it was an open secret, that among some belligerent looking groups near the entrance, knives and pistols had frequently been displayed. Even the gentler portion of the audience seemed to be worked up. One strong-minded female, who had been taking notes, was heard explaining on the east portico, that it was her belief the Court would clear Guiteau; the Government was spending all the money, and making a show of him when he could be killed and got rid of. With an ineffable sniff of disdain she concluded: "What is wanted here is less freedom and more despotism."

Perhaps by reason of its being Saturday, and

DR. BLISS,
With part of President Garfield's Vertebræ.

perhaps on account of the rapidly increasing excitement, the rush for admittance this morning, November 19th, was greater than ever. Long before Court opened, an eager and very much mixed crowd began to assemble, and in a short time the steps, halls and corridors of the building were thronged with people. The crowd extended from the entrance along the corridors to the steps in front of the building. It was an annoying crush, the majority of visitors being women, who were veritably squeezed, and to such an extent as to have their hats and ruchings somewhat disfigured. By half-past nine it was useless for anyone to try to get within the building. In a short time the crowd had so increased that it was impossible for Deputy Marshal Williams to make way for the admittance of counsel and reporters, many of the latter being jammed in the main hall and unable either to go forward or retreat. Once within it was necessary to wait until the crowd by slow degrees pressed onward, and one by one gradually forced their way through the Marshal's office into the Court room, which in a short time was filled to its utmost capacity. At least one-half of the number were ladies, well dressed and intelligent in appearance. A great many ladies were unable to secure seats, but were so deeply interested in the proceedings as to stand among the crowd for three hours or more.

For a marvel, however, the Court opened without special incident, though the prisoner, when brought in, looked anything but calm, despite the satisfaction with which he regarded his bright new hand-cuffs, which had been procured for him in consequence of his complaint that the other "old bracelets" did not fit him. This remark evidencing his objection to the æsthetic craze may be scored as the only real symptom of insanity that had come to the surface. Hurrying to his seat, with his round bundle of newspapers, he at once became the centre of attraction, and this somewhat pacified him.

George C. Maynard, electrician, was placed on the stand, and testified to loaning Guiteau ten dollars at one time, and fifteen dollars at another. Guiteau protested against this line ot evidence; did not think it anybody's business whether he owed twenty-five dollars, or some one owed him. "Maynard is a good fellow, and I owe him twenty-five dollars; that's all there is in it." District Attorney Corkhill desired to prove by the witness that Guiteau borrowed the fifteen dollars with which he bought his revolver. In cross-examination witness said he thought Guiteau looked seedy and hungry. This at once irritated the prisoner, who angrily declared that he lived in first-class style, and wore a seventy dollar suit of clothes; he knew plenty or public men, and had all the money he wanted; his mental condition and not physical was at fault; he had a big load on his mind about that time. Witness did not notice anything particular about the prisoner's manner except a sort of skulking gait.

Joseph N. Burkart, clerk to Mr. Maynard, also testified to the loan of the fifteen dollars, and thought Guiteau's walk and the way he held his head, a little peculiar.

John O'Meara testified to selling the pistol to Guiteau. He could not identify it as there were thousands just like it. The charges were then drawn from the revolver at the suggestion of counsel, and much to the relief of the audience.

Pending the examination of the pistol, Guiteau desired to announce to the Court that he invited John B. Townsend, of New York, and Leonard Swett and A. S. Trude, of Chicago, to assist him. There was plenty of brains on the other side and he desired as much on his, in the interest of justice.

Colonel A. S. Rockwell, the next witness, began to detail the occurrences at the depot, when Mr. Scoville interposed, acknowledging the killing. Guiteau quickly shouted: "*No, your Honor; we acknowledge the shooting, but not the killing.*" Colonel Rockwell briefly stated the facts within his knowledge, and was dismissed without cross-examination.

General Swaim came next. He described briefly his attendance with the President during his illness. An impressive scene occurred during his testimony. "What were the President's last words?" asked District Attorney Corkhill. "His last words," replied the witness, with emotion, were, "Oh, Swaim!"

DR. BLISS TESTIFIES.

Dr. D. W. Bliss was then called, and his appearance, as well as the ghastly paraphernalia which had been prepared for his surgical explanation, created a decided sensation. A human skeleton of polished whiteness, which had been brought from the Army Medical Museum rested on the stand before him, and the horrid spectacle, as the doctor began handling the rattling bones, chilled the marrow of all present, the ladies in particular looking ashy pale.

In response to the District Attorney's questions the witness gave a succinct narrative covering the entire history of President Garfield's sufferings, from the time witness was called to his side, fifteen or twenty minutes after the shooting, down to the hour of his death. With these details the public is unfortunately too familiar, and they will be found briefly sketched in a previous section of this book. Dr. Bliss detailed at great length the progress and symptoms of the case, indicating, by means of the wired skeleton, the course the ball had taken, and the manner in which death had been produced. The witness in

GUITEAU, THE ASSASSIN. 161

concluding his examination in chief, said the immediate cause of death was hemorrhage. The wound made by the ball was the direct cause of death.

The cross-examination was opened by Mr. Robinson, with the following very comprehensive question:

"State concisely but accurately what was observed on each date from the time of the shooting until the time of the death. Describe all the symptoms observed each day, and also what was done. Begin with the first day."

The witness proceeded to make the statement called for. The statement was interrupted by inquiries and responses as to the medical consultations held prior to the arrival on the 4th of July of Drs. Agnew and Hamilton. Then the witness was asked to describe again minutely the course of the ball.

A TRAGIC EXHIBIT.

About this time there was a movement in Court. A sensation of some kind seemed imminent, though nobody understood just what to expect. A small pasteboard box had been handed to the District Attorney, and suddenly opening it he produced a small section of

A HUMAN VERTEBRÆ.

Holding it up, he solemnly asked: "Dr. Bliss, do you recognize this?" There was a gasping sensation among the almost breathless audience, as with straining eyes and craned necks they waited for the answer. Slowly and solemnly it came. "*I do; it is a portion of the vertebræ of the late President, James A. Garfield.*

An indescribable expression passed over the features of the spectators, and not a few of them turned their eyes from the sickening sight, and gazed upon Guiteau, in a manner that could not be misunderstood. Could lightning glances blast a man, a shriveled, crumbling heap of cinders would have been all that remained of the hardened wretch, who merely glanced up from the perusal of his papers, with an air of one who is bored by the recital of matters having no earthly interest for him.

Dr. Bliss then made use of the exhibit, pointing out the hole made by the bullet. Then Mr. Robinson inquired as to the location of the abscess, the incision into the pus sac, the muscles or organs through which the ball passed, the inclination at which the ball struck the spinal column, its force, the fragments of bone that were found during life and at the autopsy, and the condition of the wound as discovered in the autopsy.

Meanwhile the District Attorney showed the vertebræ to the jury, each member making an examination, so as to see how and where the bullet ranged. The piece, which was about four inches in length, and was removed at the time of the autopsy, was broken, one piece having been knocked off by the force of the bullet striking against it. The portion shown was decayed, the purulent pus having partially destroyed the cartilage between the sections of the backbone, which had been broken by the bullet. The main part of the broken bone was also eaten into by the pus. After the jury had finished their inspection, the fragment was laid on the edge of the Judge's desk, where it remained an object of morbid curiosity for some time. Then it was handed to the Judge for his personal inspection, and afterwards passed over to Mr. Scoville, who put on his spectacles for a critical examination, in which he was joined by Guiteau, in the most cold-blooded manner. The prisoner, however, did not attempt to touch it, a fortunate omission for him, as this would probably have been the last straw which human patience could have borne.

Mr. Robinson then reverted to the consultations that were held, up to the arrival of Drs. Agnew and Hamilton. He wanted to know exactly what was said by the physicians. Witness said that he could not give that information, but he could state the conclusions, and Mr. Robinson called for those conclusions, which the witness proceeded to state. Then Mr. Scoville took up the cross-examination and inquired minutely as to the formation, growth, and final rupture of the sac formed on the artery, which had been cut by the ball. He also inquired as to who had authorized the witness to take charge of the case. Mr. Davidge suggested that that had nothing to do with the matter, but the witness answered by saying that the request had been made to him on the morning of the 3d of July, by the President, no one else being present but Mrs. Garfield and the witness. Mr. Scoville also inquired minutely about the probing of the wound; about the supposed internal hemorrhage the first day; about the pus cavity and the openings made to it, and about the quantity of morphine administered.

The cross-examination had not been finished when the Court, at half-past twelve, took a recess.

On reassembling after the recess, the cross-examination of Dr. Bliss was resumed by Mr. Scoville. It ran upon the probing and washing of the wound, and the possibility of its having been thoroughly probed, if the real track of the ball had been known from the first. To the question on that point the witness gave a negative reply. He was also asked by what authority most of the doctors who had been originally in attendance were discharged, and he said it was by authority of the President, given in the presence of Mrs. Garfield and the witness. He was asked as to where the ball had been found, and replied that all the viscera had been taken out and placed in a bowl, and that in that bowl the ball was found in its cyst. Then Mr. Robinson again took up the cross-examination, and asked the witness to reply in detail to the question as to the symptoms observed during the first four days. In order to do that, it was necessary for him to refer to the data kept by Dr. Reyburn, and as there was some difficulty in reading the manuscript, Dr. Reyburn was sworn, and stood beside him to aid him in the task. The process was slow and the results uninteresting. When the reading had continued some twenty-five minutes, the District Attorney interposed with an objection to the waste of time, which was the result of the reading. He desired to know the purpose of the defence in having the record read. Mr. Robinson stated that he wished that the testimony as to the character of the wound should be perfectly accurate.

At this point Mr. Davidge said that he objected, with great reluctance, to the introduction of any evidence, that in the judgment of the counsel representing the defence benefited in any degree the case of the prisoner, but it appeared to him that the reading of this record was not only not pertinent to the issue, but had no pertinence whatever to the examination in chief, which had been studiously confined to the character of the wound. He could only infer from the cross-examination that it was the intention of the defence to endeavor to show that the death of President Garfield, had resulted from maltreatment on the part of the surgeons, who had had charge of the case; when the defence undertook to offer that evidence, the prosecution might have something to say in respect of its admissibility; it would be a novelty, indeed, if one human being could put a ball into the body of another, and, when arraigned for murder, defend himself on the ground, that possibly or probably, some other treatment than that adopted by the surgeons called in might have been used to advantage. He did not concede the truth of the averment, that the President had died of maltreatment, but conceding for the purpose of argument, that there was a shadow of truth in the pretension set up on the other side, he did not know what relevancy it could have to the present case. Until it was asserted here that the surgeons killed the President, and that the ball planted in his body was not the agent, or at least a contributing agent, any evidence of malpractice was wholly inadmissible. In order to save time, he suggested that the doctors record could be handed to the counsel for the defence, and by them examined.

This proposition was acceded to by Mr. Robinson, who thereupon proceeded with the cross-examination of the witness, insisting on details and the record of the symptoms throughout, based upon the physician's notes.

Mr. Robinson then continued his questions, which, written upon two or three sheets of foolscap, bore the indications of having been drawn

GUITEAU, THE ASSASSIN. 167

up by a medical expert, and related to the conditions in which the organs of the President were found at the time of the autopsy. The answers were given in a clear straightforward manner, and when Mr. Robinson had concluded, Mr. Davidge subjected the witness to a short redirect examination.

Q. What elements of danger are there attendant on a wound such as you have described the President's to have been? A. The injury to the body of the backbone and the vertebræ in gunshot wounds is liable to produce blood poison, and more especially so, because the vessels that are running through it are surrounded by firm walls; the vessels when torn still remain open and will take up the products of the pus that has formed, which is poisonous and produces septicæmia; the laceration of the splenic artery I should consider a fatal injury—that sooner or later the aneurism would give way and death would ensue; the carrying of the debris or the broken fabrics of bone through the spine—each one a point of suppurative inflammation—would be liable to produce blood poisoning; these are three elements of danger, in my judgment, in an injury of that character.

A MORTAL WOUND.

Q. What was the character of the wound? is it a mortal wound? A. Yes, it is a mortal wound. This concluded Dr. Bliss' examination.

The District Attorney.—"May it please the Court, we had expected confidently to close the case for the Government this afternoon. I did not suppose that there was any doubt about it, but Mr. Robinson informs me that the medical gentlemen who follow Dr. Bliss will be subjected to the same interrogatories which he has propounded to Dr. Bliss, which are, of necessity, interminable, and I do not see the use of going further this afternoon on this subject. The question may be submitted to the Court Monday morning as to the admissibility of the evidence at all.

Here the District Attorney paused, and the prisoner half rose to his feet, with an exclamation addressed to the Court.

"I wish to say further——" said the District Attorney.

"With the permission of the prisoner," satirically interjected the Court.

"With the permission of the prisoner," repeated the District Attorney. He merely wished to ask the consent of the defence to have the jury allowed to take a carriage ride to-morrow, which consent was given, the prisoner himself assenting in a pleasant way.

The Court then at fifteen minutes past two adjourned until Monday.

GUITEAU ON THE WITNESS STAND.

GUITEAU, THE ASSASSIN. 169

THE ASSASSIN ASSAILED.

A Daring Attempt to Shoot Guiteau on His Way From the Court to The Jail—Arrest of the Alleged Assailant—Details of the Sensational Scene.

During the course of the proceedings this day, and in fact for the past two days at least, Guiteau had been uneasy lest some other agent of the Deity, as he expressed it, should be commissioned to retaliate on him. His brother, J. Wilson Guiteau and Mr. Scoville had also evinced some apprehension of danger, probably from a sense of the aroused indignation as shown in the hissing and hootings when the prisoner was removed in the van. Taking advantage of a temporary pause in the Court during the morning session, Guiteau first asked to have additional counsel assigned, and then exclaimed: " I desire to say something else in this connection. I understand that there are one or two disreputable characters hanging around this Court. The Chief of Police has kindly given me a guard. I have a body guard. I want to notify all disreputable persons that if they attempt to injure me they will probably be shot dead by my body guard. I have no fears for my personal safety. There has been a good deal of loose talk about this subject for the past week and I want this matter understood."

To his sister he said: " You need have no anxiety about my being shot or killed as the Lord will take care of me and protect me. I am delighted at the week's work and the case is progressing splendidly. We have got a good jury and of course we will be given a fair trial."

That this feeling was not without some warrant will be seen by the sequel, as well as by the following incident in the Court room. A man approached the bailiff and remarked that he wanted to get a seat near District Attorney Corkhill. The bailiff asked why he wanted that particular position and received for answer: "I want to see him. I came a thousand miles to see him. I must have a seat by his side." As the man appeared to be under the influence of liquor and his actions were very suspicious, he was removed from the Court room, and thus a sensational scene in that locality was probably prevented.

THE ATTACK ON THE VAN.

When Guiteau was put in the van, there was a man, about twenty-seven years of age, on a sorrel horse, within a few feet of the vehicle. He followed at some distance, and when it had reached the intersection of East Capitol and First Streets, about three-quarters of a mile from the Court House, he stopped his horse and fired into the left side of the van. Guiteau was standing in the front of the van, looking through the small hole of the vehicle, a policeman being on the left and the driver on the right of the seat. The colored guard,

GUITEAU, THE ASSASSIN. 171

Perry Carson, was on the steps at the back. Guiteau had shifted his position after the starting of the vehicle, and thus it came that the horseman having miscalculated Guiteau's exact location, the ball penetrated the side of the van a foot in front, grazing the top of his left arm two inches below the elbow, making a flesh bruise, but no wound. Guiteau's coat and shirt sleeves were torn by the bullet, which, striking the opposite wall of the van, rolled down on the floor, where it was found.

There were several conflicting accounts of the affair, but the most correct appears to be that of James Leonard, the driver of the van, who made the following statement: "When we left the Court House, I noticed a red-faced man on a sorrel horse, who followed along in the rear, but at first there was nothing unusual about his doings. We kept watching him as he gradually neared the van. As we reached the intersection of First Street, he rode abreast of the van and halted his horse, as I thought, to turn into the other street. As soon as we had passed, to my astonishment, he presented a pistol and fired, the bullet crashing into the left side of the van. We were, of course, excited by the unexpected event, and the horses of the van began to plunge, requiring my best efforts to manage them. The unknown horseman then rode a little to the front, and I was sure he was going to shoot either me or Policeman Edelin. The policeman said: "You scoundrel," and drew his own pistol. As soon as Edelin got to his feet, he leveled his pistol and fired at the horseman. The assailant, dropping to the side of his horse, galloped up First Street towards the boundary. He got three blocks the start of us, but I turned my horses and put them out in full speed. We gradually gained on him, but did not get near enough to do any good. At the time he shot into the van, a crowd of boys was yelling and hooting around the vehicle. The chase, which continued for six or eight squares, was very exciting. The noise caused several teams that were on the street to run away. We yelled as loud as we could, and the people sprung out to see what was up. The fleeing horseman motioned them back with his hand, and they obeyed as if afraid he would do them some injury. Of course they did not know what was the cause of this novel chase, where a prison van, like a small locomotive, was pursuing an armed horseman. The horseman was dressed in brown clothes and looked like a country person.

When Guiteau found that he was shot at, which he realized at once, he crouched down in the bottom of the vehicle, not knowing but what this was the first demonstration by a mob. He cried to the driver and guard to make for the Court House as fast as possible, the jail being a mile distant.

GUITEAU, THE ASSASSIN. 173

ARREST OF THE ALLEGED ASSAILANT.

As the police suspected that the man who fired at Guiteau was a farmer named William Jones, who lived about two miles north of the city, detachments of mounted men were at once sent in search of the fugitive. Jones, instead of going home, rode out near Bladensburg, and is said to have told several persons of what he had done. By dint of careful inquiry, and describing the man, an officer soon got on the trail, but did not recognize Jones when he met him. Jones was very communicative, and at last the officer told him he would arrest him. Thereupon Jones put spur to his horse, and, falling to one side, whirled his steed into the woods and made good his escape. The officer fired at Jones, but the bullet went wide of the mark. This increased the vigilance of the pursuing party, which scoured the country in every direction, so as to make sure of surrounding him. Between eight and nine o'clock at night, Officer Cole met a man in Mr. Lyon's house, out on the Bladensburg road, but did not know who he was. After talking awhile, he discovered that it was Jones, and at once arrested him. He conveyed the prisoner to the Second Precinct Station.

VISIT TO THE PRISONER.

J. W. Guiteau, the prisoner's brother, was down

town at the time of the occurrence. Mr. Scoville, hearing of the attempt to kill Guiteau, went with his wife immediately to the jail, where they visited the prisoner. They found Guiteau in his bed, tranquil in mind and unusually calm. He expressed himself to the effect that the Lord was still shielding him. He said: "The Lord is taking care of me, and looking out for my case, and for the third time has saved my life;" referring to the attacks made by McGill and Mason. To the jail officials he remarked: "The Lord has saved my life so often, I think it time the Government was taking steps to give me an escort that will prevent any more attempts upon my life."

William Jones, who is charged with being the would-be avenger of President Garfield, is twenty-nine years of age, and of rather muscular build. He is well connected, and is a respected, well-to-do farmer in the neighborhood where he resides, a locality seven miles west of Washington, on the Metropolitan Branch of the Baltimore and Ohio Railroad. He was married, about six years ago, to a lady somewhat his senior. His wife is said to be wealthy. He is reputed to be a man of much courage, and is considered by his neighbors as a terror to all evil doers. Jones has held a commission from the Commissioners of the District of Columbia as a local detective, and has operated very successfully in the rural districts in bringing many criminals to trial. He is not considered a rowdy, but is said to be an advocate of law and order, and only resorts to extreme measures when the law lags, but at times he is a little eccentric.

Jones was subsequently arraigned before Judge Snell, in the Washington Court, and committed in default of $5,000. A few days later, bonds were entered for his release on bail. A true bill was afterwards found by the Grand Jury on the charge of assault with intent to kill, etc., and there the matter has since rested.

CHAPTER VIII.

Mr. Robinson Retires From the Defence—The Prosecution Rests its Case—Guiteau Offers a Few Remarks in Place of a Set Speech—Mr. Scoville Commences His Opening for the Defence.

THE opening day of the second week of the trial, Monday, Nov. 21st, indicated that the excitement and interest had in no way abated; in fact, partly, perhaps, on account of the sensational rumors in connection with the attack on the prison van on Saturday evening, and the very natural impression that Guiteau would seize upon the circumstance as an excuse for a melodramatic exhibition at the opening of Court, the crowd around the Court House, from an early hour, was even more dense than on previous occasions, and included a large proportion of women and children, many of whom had never seen the prisoner. By half past nine o'clock the assemblage had taken possession of the portico, main hall and corridors of the building, the crowd being so great that when the Jury, in charge of three court officers had made its way through the long basement hall to the stairway leading to the rooms above, further progress was barred, and for fifteen minutes they were thus halted until a body of police, under direction of Deputy Marshal Williams raised the blockade. This was no easy task, for

GEO. M. SCOVILLE,
Attorney for the Defence.

removing persons from the centre of the jam was merely like picking up a handful of sand from a heap, the space was immediately filled by natural expansion. Then the police went vigorously to work and the cries of those who were being almost crushed against the walls were heartrending. When, eventually, a passage way was cleared, the debris of demoralized humanity with its scattered ornamentation and impediment, produced a scene eclipsing the wildest dream of the screaming farce writer. Men, women and children in every attitude, and with every variety of facial expression; the taller specimens swaying about over the heads of their fellows like reeds shaken by the wind; obese individuals fairly smothering the slim, shadowless samples; hats of every shape, and want of shape; ostrich feathers, lunch baskets, lorgnettes, beads, bits of lace and ribbon, fragments of flounces and handfuls of artificial hair were inextricably blended. As a consequence of this confusion, the opening of Court was considerably delayed. When the prisoner was brought in manacled as usual, the effect produced was similar to that which marks the appearance of a great actor, and the similie is not inappropriate, for with an air of supreme nonchalance, Guiteau took his seat and assumed a careless attitude, with well simulated indifference to the crowd and the general surroundings.

As soon as the Court was formally opened, Mr.

Robinson, associate counsel for the defence, rose and said that his own self-respect required him to notice a statement in yesterday's *Washington Post* in which Mr. Scoville is represented in finding fault with his line of cross-examination of Dr. Bliss on Saturday, looking to the plea of malpractice, and as saying that he would ask the Court to-day to relieve him of Mr. Robinson's association. Mr. Robinson reviewed his early connection with the case, intimating that only a high sense of duty prevented him long since from asking the Court to relieve him. If he had acted upon impulse he would have asked the Court some time ago to relieve him from the case; but he did not feel at liberty to follow his inclinations, far less his impulses. Reflection had satisfied him that it would never do to desert in the midst of trial a defendant under such a ban as man had never rested under upon this continent, except on the ground which all men must say, left him no other choice. After adverting to the fact that Mr. Scoville had made no objection during the progress of the cross-examination on Saturday, Mr. Robinson said, in conclusion. "And, now, please Your Honor, I have to say that I am not accustomed to learn from an associate counsel his objections to my examination of a witness for the first time from the paper of the following day. The same counsel who thinks it such a breach of etiquette for me to make without consultation with him, a motion which originally had his concurrence and approval, esteems it no breach of etiquette to announce his concurrence with me in the expediency of my retiring from the case, through the columns of the press. It is unnecessary to say that I can have no further association of any kind with such a counsel; it would be impossible for me to remain in this case unless he were to go out of it; and as I conceive that, from his relation to the accused and from his knowledge of the facts of the defence, he is indispensable to the defence, it only remains for me to ask that I be instantly relieved. I will add that no odium attaching to this prisoner, no animadversions of the public, no difficulty of the case, no sacrifice required from it, would ever have induced me to abandon this defence."

GUITEAU IS GRACIOUS.

The prisoner.—(interrupting impetuously) "I want Mr. Robinson to stay now."

Mr. Robinson.—"I only ask to be relieved because there is no other alternative, and inasmuch as I can no longer continue in the honorable discharge of the trust committed to me, I must ask your Honor to give me an honorable discharge from it."

The prisoner.—"That is an able speech, and I agree with most of it. If it had been made last Monday, there would have been no disturbance between us. I sympathize with Robinson; not with you (Scoville) in this matter of malpractice. He has got the true idea of it."

Mr. Scoville replied to Mr. Robinson's speech, regretting that any difficulty had arisen between them, and attributing it to their different dispositions. He complimented Mr. Robinson on the ability which he had shown in arranging the defence, but made no opposition to his retiring.

Judge Cox then said the thanks of the Court are due to Mr. Robinson, for the promptness with which he responded to the request of the Court, and participated in this defence, at a great professional sacrifice, as I know, and nobody questions his professional ability, and the sentiments which governed him throughout. I perceived from the start that he was placed in a position of unpleasantness, and I have felt recently that I ought, if he desired it, to relieve him from connection with the case, especially as I perceived that Mr. Scoville was thoroughly master of the case. I feel constrained to grant Mr. Robinson's application, and to grant him a most honorable discharge.

Mr. Scoville was explaining that he did not anticipate being entirely without assistance, as he was still negotiating with a gentleman from Chicago, when the prisoner, in his usual abrupt way, broke in, and addressing the Court, said: "I understand that Judge Magruder is anxious to assist in the defence. I have sent him public notice that I want him, also John D. Townsend, of New York—not John B. And again, I desire to hear from those gentleman, either publicly or privately. I wrote them publicly to meet me here, also Mr. Trude and Mr. Swett, of Chicago. On the question of malpractice," broke in the prisoner, after a pause, " we do not propose to insist on that here, but I desire the record to show that I appear here in my own capacity as counsel. The idea of malpractice is this—that according to the physicians' statements, the President was not fatally shot on the 25th of July, at the time they made the official examination, and said he would recover. If he was not fatally shot on the 25th of July, we say that his death was caused by malpractice. We do not desire to press that, but I desire it to go on the record for the Court in banc, if necessary. (After a pause) My defence here is that it is the Deity's act, and not mine, and I expect that He can take care of it. He has taken care of it very well so far."

Just here it may be as well to note that every interruption by the prisoner was a signal for a burst of laughter from the audience, but rarely reprehended by the Court, and evidently a source of great gratification to Guiteau.

Mr. Robinson retired from the Court room, and then the examination of witnesses was resumed.

Dr. Joseph K. Barnes, Surgeon General of the

United States Army, was called, and testified that he had assisted in dressing President Garfield's wound, from the 3d of July to the 7th of September; that he was present at the autopsy, and that the wound was mortal, and was the cause of Mr. Garfield's death.

Dr. Joseph D. Woodward, Acting Surgeon United States Army, gave testimony of substantially similar effect.

Dr. D. S. Lamb, Acting Surgeon United States Army, testified that he had made the autopsy; that the gun-shot wound was the cause of the death; that he had examined the records, and had found no case of an injury to the same extent in which the man had recovered; it was a mortal wound. At the request of the District Attorney, he produced the bullet which Guiteau fired into the President. He opened a large envelope, sealed with red wax, which contained the following paper, the bullet secured to it by a wire:

I hereby certify, that the within pistol ball was, in the presence of Surgeon General J. K. Barnes, Surgeons J. J. Woodward, Robert Reyburn, Frank H. Hamilton, J. Hayes Agnew, S. C. Boynton, D. S. Lamb, (who made the autopsy), General D. G. Swaim, Colonel A. F. Rockwell and Mr. C. O. Rockwell, taken from the body of James Abram Garfield, late President of the United States, at the post-mortem examination, held in Francklyn Cottage, at Elberon, N. J., during the afternoon of September 20, 1881.

D. W. BLISS.

The bullet which was indented and partially flattened on one side and end, was shown to and

GUITEAU, THE ASSASSIN. 183

examined by the jury. According to the testimony of Dr. Bliss this bullet was found in a basin at the time of the autopsy. Mr. Scoville did not ask any of these witnesses a question. Guiteau was engaged in reading a paper, and did not appear to take any notice of the bullet.

THE PROSECUTION RESTS.

The District Attorney announced that the prosecution here closed its case, except that he wished it to go on the record, that Elberon was in Monmouth County, in the State of New Jersey, and that the railroad depot where President Garfield was shot, was on a public reservation, belonging to the United States. These facts were admitted by Mr. Scoville.

Mr. Scoville then suggested that at this stage of the proceedings the prisoner should be heard in his own defence, and intimated a desire to have such permission accorded. To this the Court assented, and expectation was on tiptoe, amid the vast audience.

GUITEAU RELUCTANTLY SPEAKS.

Without leaving his seat, and in a half hesitating manner, the prisoner said: "I was not aware that I was expected to speak this morning."

Mr. Scoville leaned over and whispered to him, evidently urging him to stand up, out of respect to the Court, but Guiteau snappishly replied in a loud tone of voice : " I will not stand up, I am not afraid to, however, but I have only got a moment to speak. I do not care to say anything more than was published in my address last Monday afternoon in the *Evening Star*. That paper was addressed to your Honor and the public, and I presume that most of the jurymen have heard it. I have no set speech to make. So long as I appear, in part, as my own counsel, the best way is for me to make corrections as the case proceeds just as I have done during the last three or four days. I mean no discourtesy to anybody in the case. I only want to get at the facts. If somebody says that I owe him twenty dollars and it is not true, I will deny it on the spot simultaneously with the false charge—and that as the case proceeds. Of course I will go on the stand at the proper time and be examined and cross-examined. My idea is, however, to correct a misstatement while it is hot, and at the moment the statement is made, and that disposes of it, instead of waiting a number of weeks till the matter is digested and misunderstood. A great deal of the bad feeling in this matter has come from enforced silence, or from the suppression of my papers. I think that the true way is to interject statements as the case proceeds. I have no set speech to make. I am much obliged to your Honor and my counsel for the courtesy of the invitation."

GUITEAU PREPARING HIS ADDRESS.

This little interlude over, Mr. Scoville commenced his address to the jury, making the

OPENING FOR THE DEFENCE.

Mr. Scoville began in a plain, matter of fact manner, to define the position of the defence before the jury. He made no attempt at oratorical display and therein exhibited his sound common sense in contradistinction from the sensational interjections of his client, a proceeding which at once demanded and obtained the respect of all his hearers.

He criticised the course of the District Attorney in presenting the testimony so much in detail. The simple questions in the case were whether the prisoner had committed the act (which was not denied), and whether he was, at the time, in such condition of mind as that he should be held responsible for the act. On this point there would be a great deal of expert and therefore contradictory testimony. The jury should note carefully the expert witnesses, hear their testimony, see how they stand examination and cross-examination, and then come to the best conclusion they could arrive at. The difficulty would come when the jury came to weigh the evidence on both sides. The jury should then consider that the experts on the part of the Government are being paid one hundred dollars or two hundred dollars a day, and that even these scientific men have not reached that height beyond passion and feeling and love of money, as that those things could have no influence whatever on their feelings or their judgment. On the other hand, not a single expert witness for the defence would be paid, and their testimony, if in favor of the prisoner, would expose them to condemnation and ostracism in the community where they reside. These were things to be taken into consideration in weighing the expert testimony. The popular feeling against the prisoner had been manifested in three separate attacks on his life—the last one was being commended by the newspapers all over the country. The popular feeling would also show itself in the testimony of the expert witnesses. He contrasted his own inexperience in criminal cases with the experience and ability of the counsel for the prosecution, and in view of this display he asked the jury to be considerate and candid toward the defence. Still he did not ask for any odds when it came to questions of fact. He expected that the defence would erect an impregnable wall and fortress which all the power on the other side could not overthrow. If he came short in law, he knew that he could rely confidently on the Court's learning, integrity and sense of justice. With the array of facts which he would present, an honest jury and an upright Judge, he felt that he was not entirely at a disadvantage.

After speaking for about half an hour, Mr. Scoville asked the Court to adjourn until next day, when he would be prepared to proceed with his address. Judge Cox promptly acceded to this request, and the Court, at 12 o'clock, adjourned.

THE PRISONER AND THE PUBLIC.

When the Court adjourned Guiteau was taken to his room and waited there until one o'clock, when the van arrived and took him back to jail. A large crowd collected around the Court House to see the prisoner removed. While waiting for the van a hot lunch was served to the prisoner. He was also provided with pen and ink and wrote his autograph for several persons who applied for it. Neither his appetite nor his vanity seemed to be diminished by his varied experience. He ate very heartily and wrote his autograph with a bold flourish, as though he was proud of the name he bore. The crowd about the east wing meanwhile kept augmenting, and when the van arrived extended to the middle of the roadway. There was also a line of spectators on the opposite side of the street. The prisoner was brought out through the basement and was almost completely hidden from the crowd by his guards. The van was driven rapidly away under guard of a troop of mounted police. The journey to the jail was accomplished without incident.

CHAPTER IX.

Continuation ot Mr. Scoville's Opening Address—Repeated Interruptions by the Prisoner—A Sensational Scene Between Mr. Scoville and Colonel Corkhill.

WHEN the Court opened on the morning of Nov. 22d, there was a marked decrease in the number of spectators, probably occasioned by the serious inconveniences from crowding on the previous day. Still the attendance was large, and among the prominent persons present, were Chief Justice J. B. Prince and bride, of New Mexico; Mrs. Blaine, Mrs. Corkhill, wife of the District Attorney; Dr. A. E. McDonald, Superintendent of Ward's Island Insane Asylum; Dr. Walter Dempser, Superintendent of the Wisconsin State Asylum; Dr. James H. McBride, Superintendent of the County Asylum, Milwaukee, and Dr. Rice, of Illinois, these latter gentlemen being experts, who had been subpoenæd. The Court was called to order promptly at 10 o'clock, and the prisoner was brought in. He looked more subdued than on former occasions, and a close observer might have noticed expressions flit across his face, at intervals, which were much like spasms of despair. Still he was outwardly cool, and when his handcuffs were removed, he deliberately unlocked his table-drawer for the officer to put his "bracelets" in, that they might be handy for the lunch recess. Mr. Scoville then faced the jury, and in a calm conversational tone, continued his address, which had been suspended at the adjournment on the previous day.

PRECIS OF SCOVILLE'S OPENING.

Mr. Scoville commenced by calling the attentention of the jury to the defence set up—insanity. He said he knew there was considerable antipathy against that defence, in criminal cases, but he asserted that it was quite as often put forward as a perfectly just defence as it has availed as an unjust defence. He expected the jury to treat it fairly and candidly, and to weigh it upon the evidence. The prisoner, since he had been in Court, had done many things which might have influenced the minds of the jurors. They might already have come to a conclusion as to what sort of man the accused was. It was impossible for it to have been otherwise, but it was not exactly the proper thing to do. The jurors should keep their minds open, so that when the sworn evidence was produced before them, they could weigh it, and accept what was shown to be the fact. He proceeded to state the progress of the Courts on the question of insanity, explaining the various kinds of insanity, and citing decisions on the subject, and claimed that it was the duty of the jury to ascertain the fact, whether the defendant was trying to deceive or not, because if not, he was entitled to the protection of the law. In the first place it was a very difficult thing to feign insanity so as to deceive experts. It would appear from the evidence that the defendant did not know anything about insanity; had never visited an insane asylum, and had never given the subject any thought or attention. Yet it was said that he was simulating, and the newspapers and a good many people in the community had been as hasty in passing judgment on this subject as on others. If the newspapers were correct, the District Attorney himself had repeatedly said that the prisoner was only feigning insanity. It was absolutely impossible for a man who never knew anything about it to feign insanity so as to deceive an expert.

Mr. Scoville continuing, said, that having been acquainted with the defendant since he was a boy, the first thing he had said when he heard of the act was: "He is crazy," just as many others had said, just as President Garfield had said, "What is the man doing; he is crazy;" just as Secretary Blaine had said; "Why was this done; the man must be crazy."

District Attorney Corkhill interrupted with an emphatic denial, that President Garfield had made such a remark, and reminded Mr. Scoville that Secretary Blaine had never considered Guiteau insane, but had stated, under oath, that he believed him to be sane. Mr. Scoville explained that he had seen statements in the newspapers to the contrary effect, and the point occurred to him at the moment as an illustration.

Mr. Scoville then resumed, and dwelt upon the difficulty of a person simulating insanity. A person feigning insanity forgets things, and pretends to be muddled and confused. Certainly nothing of that kind could be found about Guiteau. He did not profess to forget anything; on the contrary, he professed to remember everything. A person feigning insanity always felt it incumbent upon him to be insane all the time, while one really insane was in different moods at different times. The former always hesitated in speaking, the latter never. The prisoner did not act like one simulating insanity.

A SKETCH OF THE GUITEAU'S.

Mr. Scoville then proceeded to give an interesting sketch of the Guiteau family, and its peculiarities, as bearing on the question of insanity. The family was of Huguenot descent, imbued with the same intense religious spirit which had led half a million of the best people of France to leave their homes and possessions, and go out destitute into foreign lands. The prisoner's grandfather was a physician, who settled in Utica, N.Y., over ninety years ago—Dr. F. Guiteau. He (Scoville) did not know whether he could produce any evidence as to the grandfather and grandmother. They had ten children, and some of their very names would show this religious tendency. They were Abraham, Luther (the prisoner's father), Martin, (dividing Luther's name between two of the sons) and Calvin. As to a portion of the family he had not been able to obtain authentic information, but he had information as to certain members of it. Two of the girls were Julia and Mary. Julia married a Mr. Raymond, who had settled in Michigan, and Mary married a Mr. Parker. Julia was deranged during the last weeks of her life; her delusion being that her family was going to the poorhouse, although her husband was a very successful and prosperous merchant in Ann Harbor. Among her children was a daughter, Abby, who was a bright, interesting girl until fifteen or sixteen years of age, when she began to lose her reason on the subject of religion. Her first remark to an acquaintance would be: "Do you love Jesus?" She was now in an insane asylum, hopelessly insane. Another daughter of Mrs. Raymond was partially deformed, one side of her head not being fully developed. He did not know how far that might be of importance, but he understood that these things had weight on the question of hereditary insanity. Mrs. Parker (Mary) afterward married a music teacher, returned to Oswego insane, and died in that condition. He did not know what her special delusion

RECEIVING DESPATCHES.

A STRONG-MINDED WOMAN.
"Let me pass, sir."

was. Mrs. Parker had a son, Augustus, who inherited the musical talent and face of his father, and the insane taint of blood of his mother. He lived in Chicago, and a disappointment in getting the piano agency of the Deckers' of New York, threw his reason from the base. He became violently insane, was sent to the insane asylum of Cook County, and died there. This accounted for two of the sisters of this family of ten and for their children. As to the other three sisters, he knew very little about them. He expected some witnesses in regard to them, but they had not yet arrived. One of the brothers, Abraham, lived till he was about sixty years of age, and died in Freeport, Illinois. During the latter years of his life, he was what might be called foolish—not insane, but weak-minded, having no control over himself—and he died in that condition. The second son (Francis W.), while a young man living in the neighborhood of Utica, N. Y., became disappointed in love, and challenged his rival to fight a duel. The duel came off, but the pistols were loaded with blank cartridges. When he came to know that, his mortification and disappointment were so intense that he became insane. He had lucid intervals, but he died in the Bloomingsdale Asylum, New York, in the year 1820, when he was twenty-nine years of age. Another of the five brothers, Luther, was the prisoner's father, and the last survivor of the ten children. While Luther was not insane, he was eccentric and peculiar, especially in his religious views. He was a man of undoubted integrity, of excellent disposition and one whom everybody loved. On the subject of religion however, he was unreasonable and strange, going to such extremes as might properly be termed insanity. One of his beliefs was, for many years, that he had come to such a vital union with Christ that he was part and parcel of the Saviour himself, spiritually, and that their union was so complete that he would live on forever, just the same as the Saviour. He imagined that his daughter, in whom his heart seemed entirely bound up, was going to commit suicide, and he grieved over it and cried over it like a child. At another time, he imagined that a great Masonic celebration that was in preparation in Chicago and which he read of in the newspapers, was for the purpose of his funeral, and in travelling from Wisconsin to Freeport, Illinois, he refused to go through Chicago, because he did not want any such demonstration made over him. He died in 1880. During the last six weeks of his illness he was deranged most of the time. These were the facts as to the family history.

THE PRISONER'S OWN HISTORY.

Mr. Scoville paused for a second, and then said: "Now we come to the prisoner himself. His mother was an amiable woman, gentle and affectionate, and his father had the same traits. He was gentle as a woman, loving as a little girl. They lived at Freeport, Illinois. The mother was sickly. She had six or seven children, and died at thirty-five. She was twenty-eight when the prisoner was born. Before his birth she was sick with fever, so that the physicians deemed it necessary to shave her head. Her hair was shaved off close, and would be shown here as it was taken from her head forty years ago. The prisoner was born during that sickness. Afterwards two more children were born, one of them deformed, and both died in infancy. The mother died when the defendant was seven years old. There was nothing peculiarly noticeable in him when he was young. His father was an intense religionist, and did not give proper attention to the boy, but the latter, nevertheless, grew up bright, intelligent, gentlemanly, gentle and loving. He had no wayward ways or habits. For about a year he lived with his mother in Chicago, and went to school there, when he was about fourteen. Then his father married again, and the son went home to live with his stepmother, and helped his father, who was then Recorder of Freeport. There he worked for two years, and up to that time there was nothing specially noticeable about him, except one or two little circumstances. He could not pronounce the word " quail," but always called it " pail;" so in the little song, " Come along, old

Dan Tucker," he would always say: "Ped along." As he was old enough to know better, his father one day gave him such a whipping as an intensely religious man can give, and immediately afterward he looked up at his father and said unconsciously: "Ped along." He (Scoville) did not know that these things had any influence, but he merely mentioned them. At the age of eighteen, he began to feel the want of an education, and ambition began to stir him. He also began to have his attention directed to religious matters. His father's attention had been directed to the doctrines of the Oneida Community. He believed in their doctrine of community of goods and of living together in the Community. He believed that the religious character of the inmates would be better developed in that way, and that they could better perform their duties, and live more comfortable in that way. The father, in fact, had gone from one denomination to another, finding none of them sufficiently advanced to come up to his ideas. He had finally struck the Oneida idea, and it seemed to commend itself to his mind. He had taken their publications, and had been plying his son with their arguments. But the son wanted to be a lawyer, and wished to go to school. He had $1,000 left him by his maternal grandfather, and finally his father told him that he might take this money and go to school. Thereupon he went to Ann Harbor to enter the

University; but he was found unqualified, and he went to the high school, where he remained for some months, studying at the same time his lessons, his Bible, and the doctrines of the Oneida Community. Finally he left school and went to Oneida, where he joined the Community, and put his money ($900) into it. He fully believed that that was the only road to heaven. This was in June, 1860, and he stayed there until April, 1865. All the time that he was there he was convinced that their religious system was the correct one; that it was designed to supplant all the kingdoms of the world, and that he himself was to be the ruler and head of that system. He believed that thoroughly and clearly. That might be said to be egotism. He (Scoville) believed that insane people were often possessed of extreme egotism. Lawrence, who attempted to assassinate President Jackson, believed that he was entitled to the crown of America, and of England; and when he was arraigned in Court, he asked why he was brought before such a tribunal. He showed just as much egotism as Guiteau did. Of course the leaders of the Community did not recognize his pretensions, but considered him a very common sort of person. Finally, they "sat down on him." He endured the restraints imposed upon him as well as he could till April, 1865, when he told them that he wanted to go to New York. They fitted him out with new clothes, gave him some books and one hundred dollars, and let him go. His idea was to start a religious newspaper, which would advocate the principles of the Onieda Community, and revolutionize the world. He went over to Hoboken, where he lived on crackers and dried beef occasionally. His paper was to be a daily newspaper, and was to supplant or take the lead of all other papers. It was to be called *The Daily Theocrat*. He worked on that idea for weeks and months. Of course he had no success, and then went back to the Community, and remained there until November, 1866. The custom which prevailed among the members of the Oneida Community at that time—of meeting frequently, in a large hall, and publically criticizing one another's actions and behavior—was a custom which Guiteau, with his peculiarities and his egotism found particularly oppressive. He stood it as long as he could, and then wrote him (Scoville). All this time he had been fretting because he was hampered and kept from doing what he supposed he was fit to do, and what he considered it his duty to do, in promoting the kingdom of God on earth. He had never had any other controlling motive, from the time he was eighteen up to the present day, than this feeling of religious duty. He went away at night, feeling as though he were going away from the road to heaven, and almost involuntarily, he turned back two or three times. Yet he persevered and went to New

York. For some time afterward he was still wedded to the Community's religious belief, but when he came to reflect upon its practices, he finally became convinced that the Community's road was not necessarily the only way to heaven. He spent his time in New York, largely studying theological books, in reading his Bible, and in visiting the Young Men's Christian Association rooms. He then commenced studying law, and in a year or two drifted to Chicago, and was admitted to the Bar. The gentleman who passed on his qualifications was C. H. Reed, of Chicago. Reed asked him three questions, of which he answered two, and missed one. That was the way he got to be a lawyer. He attempted to practice law, but his practice soon ran off into a collection business. He was a man of great perseverance and intense devotion to a thing, and when he got after a debtor he gave him no peace until the man paid up or got away, so that in that department of business he succeeded well, and got a comfortable living for himself and wife, for he was at that time married. But if a man depended entirely on collecting bad debts, and did not have the capacity to bring a suit for a ten dollar note, to use an illustration made by the prisoner himself recently, he could not maintain his relations with his clients very long. It would appear in the evidence that he could not transact legal business.

Mr. Davidge at this point made an inquiry as to whether Mr. Reed made the motion for the admission to the Bar, and before Mr. Scoville could reply, Guiteau broke in with "Mr. Reed gave me the certificate; General Reynolds, the gentleman right behind you, made the motion. Go on! Scoville! that is an interesting story and correct in detail."

Mr. Scoville then proceeded with his narrative of the prisoner's life. He stayed in Chicago some time, and as long as he confined himself to the collection of bad debts he got along very comfortably. After the great fire he went to New York, and being a person of most excellent and gentlemanly address, pleasant and agreeable, he had no difficulty in going among entire strangers and getting collection business.

At that time and all times the prisoner was a gentleman, if being gentle in manner, gentle in speech, kind and considerate, constituted a gentleman. When in New York he never visited saloons, never used tobacco in any shape, never drank spirituous liquors, never visited gambling places and would not talk with any person who used improper or profane language. He (Mr. Scoville) related an incident of Guiteau's legal life in Chicago, where in a larceny case, to which he had been assigned, he made such a rambling speech that he convinced Mr. Reed, the District Attorney, that he was insane.

JUDGE J. K. PORTER.

WALTER W. DAVIDGE.

The Court then at half past twelve took a recess for half an hour.

After the recess Mr. Scoville continued the story of the prisoner's life. In 1874 he went to Chicago. His capacity for business (such as it was) began to diminish, and he was not able to support himself. He was not able pay his board, but that was not a capital crime; nor was it one that he might be shown in the evidence to have told a lie—that he said he wanted money to pay his board bill when he wanted it for something else. He had neither the mental nor the physical capacity for hard work.

Guiteau earnestly exclaimed, "I have brains enough but I have had theology on the brain. That's the reason I didn't run the law. There's no money in theology, but I am out of that business now. I was always well-dressed. I left a $5,000 law business to do that kind of work but you see how I came out. I was doing the same kind of business that St. Paul did. He got his reward after awhile and I expect to get mine from my book."

Mr. Scoville then related the story of Guiteau's threatening his sister with an axe, and concluded his narrative by stating how the family physician, Dr. Rice, had been called in and declared Guiteau to be insane but harmlessly so. Guiteau shortly afterwards went to Chicago. About that time Moody and Sankey were holding their meetings.

Guiteau became interested in them and became an usher. Hearing a minister saying one day that he was uncertain about the second coming of Christ, Guiteau applied great study to the subject and in January, 1879, started to lecture upon it. He met with failure everywhere.

This again aroused the prisoner's indignation, and he sullenly exclaimed—"I have heard that axe story before, but it is absolutely false." After a pause he added—"And I wasn't quite a failure either. I dead-headed from Toledo to Washington on the strength of the Lord, and I was only put off twice. I was travelling on my appearance. Not only did I visit Washington but all the other large cities. I am glad I did it. I was working for the Lord."

Mr. Scoville waited patiently while this safety valve was in operation, and then continued: "His idea was, that if he could not pay his hall rent, neither could the Saviour pay His. He was trying to serve the Lord, and he had to have some place to serve Him in. If he could not pay his hall rent it was not his fault; it was the fault of the people. That man never made a joke knowingly. He made one the other day, when he said that he had an interest in this case, but he did not know it until afterwards. He never make a joke in his life knowingly. Everything he ever did was done in earnest, and, therefore, since he has been confined in jail, he has in sober earnest given items of his life to Mr. Corkhill and to his stenographer, and concluded by saying that he was in search of a wife. He expected that the time would soon come, when the great danger which hangs over his head in this trial would be removed; when he would be vindicated, as he calls it, by your verdict; when he could go out a free man, and could reciprocate such attentions, and could make himself the honored husband of an honored wife. I say that he has done that in good faith, believing everything to be just as I stated. It was no joke with him, and yet the prosecution say that he is a sane man. Now beyond that it is true, as he says, that that notice, published to the world, brought one response, which shows that there is one woman in the United States that probably has lost her reason also.

This remark created an outburst of laughter among the audience, but it had a very different effect upon the prisoner, who in a loud, angry voice said: "It is not true that I think any lady would marry me. I did put a notice in my biography, which the *Herald* published, stating, that any young lady who wished to correspond with me would be properly received. There's no joke about the matrimonial proposition; that's business. I got a response from a lady worth $100,000. That's no joke, I am sure."

Then he smiled with characteristic self-complacency. When the audience, in obedience to the cry of "Silence!" uttered by the bailiff, had restrained its laughter, Guiteau resumed, saying: "I wrote her two letters, and she wrote me one. You suppressed the rest. I suppose you lied to me. I'll tell you so publicly. I intend to follow that girl after I am liberated."

Another outburst of merriment was quickly checked, and there ensued a more serious episode for which neither Court, counsel nor audience were prepared. District Attorney Corkhill interposed an objection with an evident offensiveness of tone, that at once challenged attention. Addressing the Court, he said: "May it please your Honor, Mr. Scoville knows as well as your Honor, that this testimony, if any is in existence, can never be produced in this trial; that if there were any such letters they never can reach the jury, and this attempt to get into a public colloquy with this man is reprehensible. Let him confine himself to the testimony which it is proper to introduce to the jury, and let this man play his part when the time comes."

"I am not playing a part," cried the prisoner excitedly and gesticulating wildly. "I knew Scoville was lying."

Mr. Scoville.—"I understand that this evidence is coming. I understand that it is perfectly competent."

"As a general thing testimony obtained from lying is not competent," retorted the prisoner.

Without paying any attention to Guiteau, Mr. Scoville, with calm dignity, turned towards the District Attorney, and mastering his emotion, said, partly to the Court, and partly to Col. Corkhill, whom he looked straight in the face:

"Notwithstanding my relationship to the prisoner, I never would have come into the case, except to lay the facts and real truth before the jury. If this is not competent evidence of the prisoner's mental condition, why have you, sir, in the name of the Government, had experts here and in the jail day after day? As to the insinuation, Mr. Corkhill will get his answer at the proper time."

The applause that greeted this declaration was so impetuous, so spontaneous and so unexpected, that the District Attorney and counsel for the Government looked amazed, for they seemed to interpret it as the first triumph won by the defence. The District Attorney could hardly believe his own ears, as he stood there, in anything but a pleasing mood. His associate counsel could conceal neither their vexation nor surprise. Mr. Davidge frowned; Mr. Smith looked a little startled, but his genial nature could not suppress a faint smile. Judge Porter, of New York, grew more thoughtful in look. Every eye was directed to the Government counsel. Judge Cox, unmoved, awaited further remarks, while the bailiff ordered silence, and Guiteau shouted to Mr. Scoville: "You have lied. You will not have any success from the Lord by lying. You lie. I have found you out. When a man lies to me once I never believe him again. You have lied to me once, and that is played out." Mr. Scoville, though evidently feeling the painfulness of his position acutely, attempted to continue his remarks by assuring the jury that he only required the truth to prevail; but the persistent prisoner was not yet satisfied, and in his sullen, dogmatic manner, remarked: "That is what I want, and I am going to have it, too."

Mr. Scoville then concluded his opening, in the following words: "All I want is that the truth shall prevail. If there is any evidence brought before you, you have an opportunity to criticize it any way you please, and if you believe I produce an item of evidence for theatrical effect, without an earnest conviction that it is just and proper to be done, I want you not only to reject it, but to charge it against me, with tenfold effect in your final verdict."

Mr. Scoville then proposed to read a bundle of letters, written by the prisoner, dating back to 1858, as showing the bent of his mind. A long discussion ensued between counsel, the District Attorney objecting to the introduction, as evidence, of a mass of matter, of which the prosecution knew nothing. The Court solved the difficulty, by suggesting that the letters would be read as part of the opening address, and Mr. Scoville reminded the District Attorney that he had produced similar documents in his opening, and the defence claimed the right to show insanity of twenty years ago, if it had existed. The District Attorney then waived the point, stating that it was his desire to afford the defence the greatest latitude in the case.

Mr. Scoville then proceeded to read the letters, most of them addressed to Mrs. Scoville, and some to himself. Those of the earliest date, 1858, showed nothing peculiar, but gradually they drifted into a religious turn, quoting texts of Scripture, and appealing to his sister to turn to God. This feature of them was more marked after he had gone to the Oneida Community, the first letter from which is dated in February, 1861. In this, he laid down and supported the doctrines of the Community. When this letter was read the prisoner said:—

"I forgot that letter. It is a very good representation of the influence under which I lived for six years. I was not aware that it was in existence."

The last letter from Oneida was dated October 12, 1866, and stated that his views had changed; that he desired to leave the Community and go to New York, to qualify for a position in some bank, and asking Mr. Scoville to send him fifty dollars.

The prisoner.—"I was recovering from my insanity then, got up under their influence. I was getting my eyes open then, away from those miserable people. I had been six years subject to their fanaticism."

Mr. Scoville explained that others of the prisoner's letters had been burned up in his office in the Chicago fire. These letters happened to have been kept at home. The next letters read were from New York and Brooklyn, 1867 and 1868. There were no striking peculiarities in any of these letters, except where they dealt with religious subjects.

At this point the opening was suspended, and the Court adjourned. There was no especial manifestations beyond curiosity, when the prisoner was brought out to the van, which was then escorted by six mounted police, as an additional guard to the two on the vehicle, driven rapidly back to the jail.

GUITEAU'S MORNING TOILET.

CHAPTER X.

Guiteau Administers "Taffy" to the Colored Juror—He Denies Being a Fool, but Admits He did not Draw as a Speaker—"I Presume I'd Draw Now"—Adjournment over Thanksgiving Day.

THE opening of Court on Wednesday, Nov. 23d, was marked by a display of feeling between the District Attorney and Mr. Scoville, in reference to the scraps of paper and newspaper articles found on the prisoner at the time of his arrest, and which Mr. Scoville declared to be material for the defence, while Col. Corkhill as resolutely maintained that they were properly in custody of the prosecution, as much so as the fatal pistol had been, and still remained. Pending discussion, Guiteau insisted on being heard, and said: "I can throw light upon this. At the time of my arrest I had forty or fifty editorial slips, showing the political situation in May and June last. These slips show the action and one of the forces that impelled me on to the President. They are very important, as showing the gist of the whole matter. There were forty or fifty slips denouncing President Garfield. It was living on such ideas as these that I was finally impelled to fire on the President with my inspiration."

The District Attorney offered to furnish copies, but these were refused, and finally if their production would enable Mr. Scoville to get through with his opening that day, he would send for them. This matter adjusted, Guiteau again broke in. He had evidently reflected over remarks of his the previous day in which he had stated that the dropping of the name "Julius" had been too suggestive of the negro race, and having remembered that there was a colored man on the jury, the astute criminal determined not to lose a chance by creating an antipathy. In a manner somewhat more cringing than his usual arrogant style, he asked permission to make an explanation of the remark in question, and said that he meant no disrespect to any person or any race, particularly to the colored race. His prejudices had been begotten twenty years ago, but he did not hold them now. Then with a covert glance at the jury he added: "It is getting now that colored men are a good deal better than white men."

Mr. Scoville then resumed his opening by reading some of Guiteau's letters. The first was dated April 10th, 1865, and contained a statement of the prisoner's reason for leaving the Oneida Community, and his purpose of starting a great theocratic daily paper in New York. He said that his paper was to be an illuminator, and to point out the devices of Satan's emissaries. "I claim," he said, "inspiration. I claim that I am a member of the firm of Jesus Christ & Co., the very ablest and strongest firm in the universe, and that what I can do, is limited only by their power and purpose." The prisoner interrupted by stating that he did not know the letter was in existence but admitted having written it. The next letter was dated from the Chicago jail in 1877, where as Guiteau expressed it: "he had been incarcerated by one of his clients, a miserable little whelp, about a difference of twenty dollars." He also said that he spent several days in the jail, and having been "on theology for some time, was out of money" the letter being to his father asking him to help him out.

As the reading of the letter was concluded Guiteau again interrupted, saying: "I never got much from my father. He got down on me because I left the Community—we could never after agree on that miserable, stinking Communty business. I'm mad every time I think of it. It kept me out of fellowship with my father up to the time of his death."

Mr. Scoville, resuming, alluded to Guiteau's career as a politician, and drew the conclusion that his intellect was deficient, when this view aroused the prisoner at once, and he began a series of interruptions, protesting against Mr. Scoville's conclusions as false. When reference was made to his running around from one committee-room to another, seeking to be employed as a campaign speaker, and his failure to obtain recognition was mentioned, Guiteau shouted angrily: "Twasn't because I had no ability, but I was not known. I had the ideas, but not the reputation. They wanted big guns like General Grant and Senator Conkling—men who would draw." Then he added, with a cunning grin: "I presume I'd draw now."

Mr. Scoville continued on in the same line, and criticized Guiteau's speech, entitled, "Garfield *vs.* Hancock." It was, he said, a mere jumble of ideas collated from the newspapers and from speeches of others. No one but a crazy man would have imagined, as Guiteau did, that this speech possessed any merit.

Guiteau became more and more restless, and in the most excited manner yet shown by him shouted to Mr. Scoville: "I object to your theory on that score, and when you try to make out that I'm a fool I'm down on you. I want you to tell the truth, but you needn't try to make me out a fool. I say the Deity inspired my act and he will take care of it. I want the truth, and that's all there is about it."

Col. Corkhill arose to protest against the interruptions of the prisoner, when Guiteau waved his hand to him, patronizingly, and said: "'Tis not necessary to make any remarks, Colonel; just let the matter drop."

Mr. Scoville expressed himself willing to join

the District Attorney in any measure to attain that end. The prisoner agreed to keep still if Mr. Scoville would only speak the truth. He then complimented the prosecuting attorneys for the liberal manner in which they were conducting the case, and finally, being so ordered by the Court, became quiet, and Mr. Scoville proceeded. He commented on his client's absurd ground for expecting to obtain an office, and then told how Guiteau finally came to the conclusion that the only way to restore peace in the party was to remove the President. He blamed the newspaper slips for bringing him to this frame of mind. The evidence would show that the matter was always preying on his mind, and it became his fixed and firm idea that his duty to his country and God, required him to remove the President. This course owed its origin to that office-seeking element of political contest, and the blame of it must be located on modern politics. If the jury found by their verdict that this man was insane, the same verdict would say that the blame rested on the politicians of the present day. It could not be otherwise.

In concluding his address, Mr. Scoville said: "It has to be determined here, whether your fellowman, with all his misfortunes and all his shortcomings, is to end his life on the gallows. This question will be submitted to you by the evidence, with the confidence that you will do what is right, according to your conscience and what will meet with the approval of your countrymen and of your God."

WITNESSES FOR THE DEFENCE.

The District Attorney then moved for the exclusion from the Court room of all the witnesses for the defence, except when called to the stand, and the order was made, with an exception in favor of Mrs. Scoville, whom the prosecution allowed to retain her seat. Mr. Scoville then began to call his witnesses for the defence.

H. N. Barton, a Congregationalist clergyman of Illinois, formerly a resident of Kalamazoo, Michigan, testified that he had there attended the lecture delivered by Guiteau on "The Second Coming of Christ." A question by Mr. Scoville as to the general opinion expressed on the lecture was ruled out, and in reply to the inquiry as to the opinion formed by witness, he said: "I cannot say that my opinion then was that he was so far insane as not to be responsible. I thought him not so much deranged as very badly arranged." The prosecution evidently satisfied with this, declined to cross-examine.

Hiram H. Davis, of Erie, Pennsylvania, formerly a resident of Kalamazoo, testified that when living there he knew the family of Wm. S. Maynard, the husband of Julia Guiteau, the prisoner's aunt. He knew of her complaining that she would have to go to the Poor House, her husband being a prosperous merchant. He also knew her daughter Abby. The boys used to call her "foolish Abby," she was a fool; she was always talking about religion, and always wore a large bonnet. The cross-examination drew out nothing important.

Thompson Wilcoxson, was then called. He was an old gentleman of eighty-one years, from Stephenson County, Illinois, who knew Luther W. Guiteau, father of the prisoner, intimately from 1840. One peculiarity of his was that he never expected to die. He was always sincere and honest. He was rather equivocating about religion, for he first belonged to the Presbyterians, then to the Methodists, and relapsed into the Oneida belief. Witness was not cross-examined.

John A. Rice, practicing physician of Myrtle, Wisconsin, for twenty-six years, testified that he first saw the prisoner in the summer of 1876 at Mr. Scoville's house. Mrs. Scoville called his attention to him for the purpose of inquiring into his mental condition. He observed the prisoner for that purpose. He had frequently been called upon for a like purpose with other persons, perhaps a dozen times a year. He came to the conclusion that he was insane, basing his opinion on certain facts which came under his observation. Among these facts were those of hereditary influence and the exaltation of his whole emotional nature. His exaltation was attended with explosions of emotional feeling, for which the witness could not discover any reason. He thought he could detect more or less incoherance of thought, also an excessive egotism. He was the subject of intense egotism, also of an intense pseudo-religious feeling. He was always talking about Christ and Christianity, without apparently having become impressed with the moral principles of Christianity. Witness made up his mind from the examination of the case, that Guiteau ought to be secluded, and so told his friends; but before steps could be taken to secure his confinement, the prisoner borrowed some clothes from the gentleman at whose house he was staying, and disappeared from that section. He had not seen him again until recently. Witness also knew the prisoner's father, Luther W. Guiteau. He had been called to attend him during his last illness, at Mr. Scoville's house. He did not observe any delusions in him, but did observe great obliquity of thought on religious subjects. He frequently exclaimed during his illness that his sickness was entirely unnecessary, that if he had lived with proper faith and had brought himself in proper relations with Christ, there was no necessity for him to be sick, and that he thought he might live forever. He noticed in him a feeling of petulance and fault-finding to the greatest extent he had ever known.

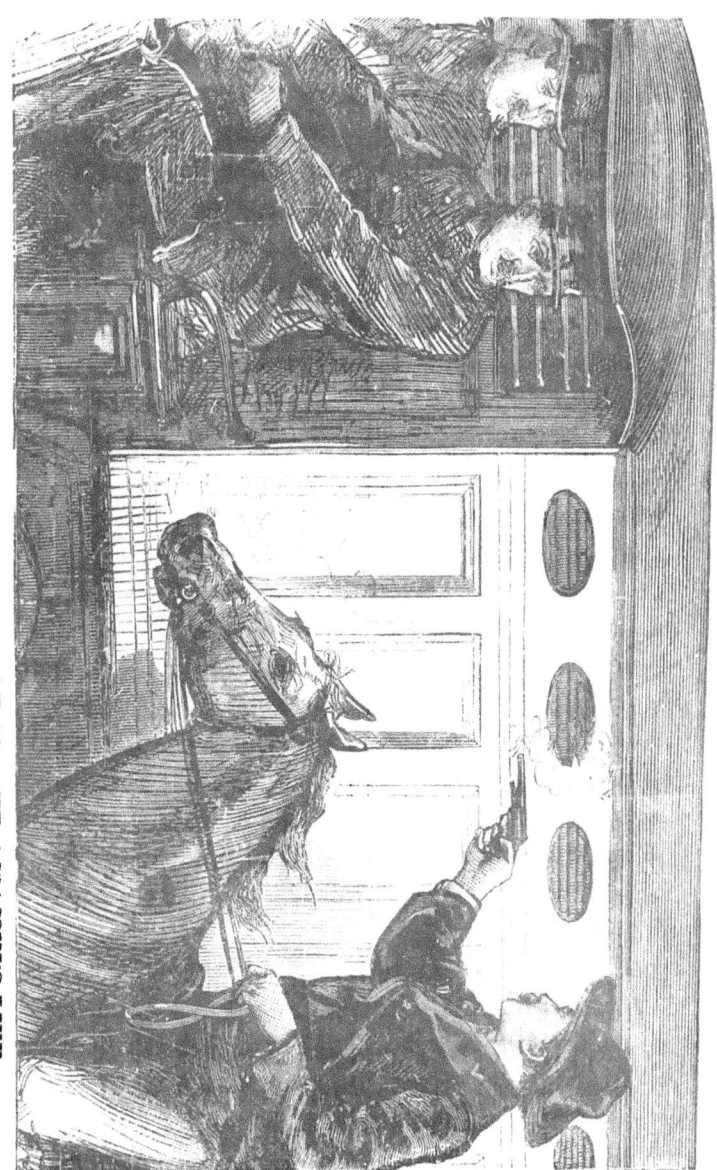

SHOOTING THROUGH THE VAN—ATTEMPT ON THE ASSASSIN'S LIFE.

Here the Court took its usual recess.

After recess the witness was briefly cross-examined by Mr. Davidge.

Frank L. Union, of Boston, testified that in September 1879, the prisoner had come to him to hire a hall in which to deliver a lecture. Witness had hired him "Investigator Hall" and then Guiteau had turned to him and told him that he had no money to pay for it, but that he would take up a collection and give him the first fifteen dollars raised. His programme was somewhat as follows: "Do not fail to hear the Hon. Charles J. Guiteau, the little giant from the West. He will show that two-thirds of the race are going down to perdition."

Witness did not notice any peculiarity about the man on the first day, but on the following day he talked queer, and said that he had challenged Ingersoll to debate, but he did not think that Ingersoll had courage enough to meet him, and witness then began to think him a little queer. There were about fifty persons present at the lecture. The lecturer brought in a manuscript. He commenced by reading some half-dozen lines and then skipping some half-dozen pages. He went on without any connection whatever. At the end of half an hour, the lecturer evidently became disgusted with himself and left the platform in a great hurry, evidently angered at something. Witness described the manner in which the lecturer had left the hall, and stated that after he had gone, the audience had held a conference and after speeches by Mr. Seever and Mr. Damon, agreed that the man was crazy.

The witness was cross-examined by Mr. Davidge. He stated that Investigator Hall was the resort of the liberals of Boston, the building having been erected in honor of Thomas Paine. He admitted having volunteered as a witness after reading Mr. Scoville's appeals in the newspapers. Guiteau interrupted the witness to explain that his idea of the doomed was a liberal one, and that he left in disgust at the audience.

Mary S. Lockwood, residing in Washington, was the next witness. She stated that the prisoner had boarded at her house for a month, beginning about the 12th of March, 1881. The only reason she knew of his leaving was that he did not pay his board. Guiteau interjected: "I was there a month. I paid five dollars and owe her twenty. I got money and paid five dollars, the rest I had to use. I stayed a week or two longer on the strength of that and that is all about it. This kind of evidence is irrelevant and I object to it. I presume there were people in the house who thought I was a little cranky. There is no doubt about that at all. If you want to prove it, prove it by them. I did not have any conversation with the ladies. It was all done by notes. They were too kind-hearted and polite to annoy me about board bills, and that is all about it. I want the facts. They are very nice ladies, Christian ladies, good people in every way. It is a good place to board. General Logan and a lot of high-toned people boarded there. I recommend it as a boarding-house."

The witness in the cross-examination admitted that there was nothing peculiar in Guiteau's manner except his abruptness.

Mr. Norwood Damon, of Boston, confirmed Mr. Union's testimony. Witness attended the lecture and supposed the man must be insane. No cross-examination.

George W. Olds, of Traverse, Michigan Co., Wis. next testified that he had been employed in the summer of 1876, on Mr. Scoville's summer place, at Beaver Lake, Wisconsin. He testified that on one occasion Mrs. Scoville called him to the house, and said in the presence of the prisoner, that he was crazy, and had attempted to kill her, and told witness to put him off the place. Witness took Guiteau into a back kitchen and talked with him. He seemed very much excited about Mrs. Scoville's saying that he was crazy, and he said that she was the crazy one, not he, and that if she were taken away and put in an insane asylum, everything would go along nicely on the place. Witness also related how Guiteau, when he was set to work to weed turnips and strawberries, pulled up more turnips and strawberries than he did weeds, and how, when he was sent out with a pan of soft-soap, to soap some young apple trees, he set to work soaping a grove of hickory trees, and persisted in saying that they were fruit trees. In reply to Mr. Scoville's question, as to what opinion witness had formed of Guiteau's sanity or insanity, he replied: "From the time that I made any remark about him, I said he appeared like a crazy man. That was my opinion. That was when he first came there. I never changed that opinion."

On cross-examination by Mr. Davidge, witness said he could not tell whether the prisoner did not know the difference between strawberries and weeds, or between turnips and weeds. He merely knew that he could not make the prisoner pull the weeds separate from the strawberries or the turnips. He seemed to be always willing to do what he was told. The cross examination was very searching, and the story of the axe having again been alluded to, the prisoner declared it to be a lie. "That was the short way to put it. He had never had any anger towards his sister at all, though, no doubt she thought so. As a matter of fact it was all nonsense."

At the conclusion of the examination of this witness, the Court adjourned over Thanksgiving day until Friday.

CHAPTER XI.

Guiteau Makes an Elaborate Statement of the Reasons for "Removing" the President—He Continues His System of Interruptions, and the Court Threatens to "Gag" Him.

AFTER the respite of Thanksgiving day, the trial was resumed on Friday, November 25th, with another audience, mainly composed of ladies, representing the most fashionable Washington circles, and filling the Court room to its utmost capacity. As soon as the Court had been called to order, Mr. Scoville stated that the prisoner desired to address the Court. Judge Cox having given permission to do so, Guiteau began to read from a manuscript, without rising from his seat. Mr. Scoville requested him to stand up, but this he firmly declined to do, stating, however, that he was not afraid to do so. (His position kept his head below the shoulder level of the officers standing behind him.) It was quite evident, in spite of his denial, that he feared to make a target of himself.

GUITEAU'S STATEMENT.

"I propose to have all the facts bearing on this case to go to the Court and the jury, and to do this, I have been forced to interrupt counsel and witnesses who were mistaken as to supposed facts. I meant no discourtesy to them or any one. Any fact in my career bearing on the question who fired the shot, the Deity or myself, is of vital importance in this case, and I propose that it go to the jury. Hence my personal, political and theological record may be developed. I am glad that Your Honor, and the opposing counsel, are disposed to give a historical review of my life, and I ask the press and the public to do likewise. All I want is absolute justice, and I shall not permit any crooked work. I have no idea my counsel want crooked work. They are often mistaken on supposed facts, and I shall have to correct them. Last spring certain newspapers in New York and Washington were bitterly denouncing the President for breaking up the Republican party, by improper appointments. I would like those newspapers to reprint those editorials now, and see how they would look and sound. In attempting to remove the President, I only did what the papers said ought to be done. Since July 2d they have been deifying the President, and denouncing me for doing the very thing they said ought to be done. I want the newspapers and doctors, who actually killed the President, to share with me the odium of his death. I never would have shot him of my own volition, notwithstanding those newspapers, if I had not been commissioned by the Deity to do the deed. But this fact does not relieve the newspapers from the supposed disgrace of the President's removal.

If he had been properly treated, he would have been alive to-day. It has been published that I am in fear of death. It is false. I have always been a religious man, and an active worker for God. Some people think that I am a murderer, but the Lord does not, for he inspired the act, as in the case of Abraham, and a score of other cases in the Bible. The assault made upon me on Saturday last by a crank, has been condemned by the press. The eyes of the civilized world are watching this case, and it behooves this Court and the Metropolitan police to protect me at all hazards. I hereby warn all cranks of high or low degree, to keep away from me, under penalty of instant death. He would have been shot dead on Saturday, but for the rearing of the horses in the van as the officer was shooting. The horses shook the van so that he lost his aim, and though the van pursued him, he temporarily escaped. I waste my arguments on cranks. All they can see in this case is a policeman's revolver. Again I say, if they value their lives, they must keep away from me. I desire the Court and the jury to dispose of this case on the facts and the law, and leave all the responsibility about it to the verdict."

Mr. Scoville again called attention to the fact that he had not yet been able to obtain the newspaper slips taken from the prisoner at the time of his arrest. Mr. Davidge asked him whether he had called at the District Attorney's office for them. Mr. Scoville replied that he had not and would not. He was entitled to them and should have them. The District Attorney insinuated that Mr. Scoville need not exhibit so much crankiness in the matter. A printed copy of these slips had been handed to him in Court the other day, and at the same time an envelope containing the originals had been passed over to him, but had not been looked at. He had now sent to his office for them, and would submit them for his inspection.

Joseph E. Smith, of Freeport, Illinois, took the stand. He testified that he was seventy-one years of age, that he had known Luther W. Guiteau, the prisoner's father from 1846 to the time of his death. He was a perfectly sincere man, standing well with the community, held several public offices and carried on a good business.

E. O. Toss, of Dover, New Hampshire, next testified that he was at the depot when President Garfield was shot; saw Guiteau taken in charge; from his appearance and the remark that he made about a letter to General Sherman which would explain all, the witness at the time was under the impression that the wrong man had been arrested.

Charles H. Reed, of Chicago, State Attorney

SERGEANT JOHN A. MASON.

W. J. JONES, ALLEGED ASSAILANT OF GUITEAU.

from 1864 to 1876, was called. He related an incident when the prisoner having been assigned to the defense of a small larceny case, he proceeded to deliver a rambling, wandering speech full of vagaries and quite illogical. He introduced all sorts of subjects that were foreign to the case. He talked about theology and divinity and the rights of man. Witness saw the prisoner at the Riggs House in Washington upon the Tuesday preceding the shooting of the President. He desired to borrow from witness fifteen dollars, promising to pay it back when he obtained the Paris Consulship. He stated that Mr. Blaine was on his side, and that in a few days the papers would announce his appointment. Witness had seen him several times previous to that, and on each occasion he introduced the subject of the Paris Consulship, and had become quite excited when witness suggested that he obtain some inferior office. Witness thought he was off his balance. He visited Guiteau a few days since in jail and asked why he killed President Garfield. The prisoner was lying down on his couch. He arose excitedly and began a rambling sort of speech, saying: "I didn't do it, the Lord did it. I was only the Lord's instrument in removing the President." At times the prisoner would show great excitement, striking his fists against the wall with considerable violence, then he would relapse into a perfect quiet state, speaking almost in a whisper. The witness received the impression that Guiteau was of unsound mind. Being pressed for a more direct answer, he replied: "I had not a doubt of it."

On cross-examinatiom the witness denied that he had told Colonel Corkhill that he had no doubt of the prisoner's responsibility.

Mr. Davidge.—"Do you mean to say that you did not state to Colonel Corkhill that while the man was unbalanced and cranky, you had no doubt of his responsibility?"

The witness.—"No, sir, I never said anything of the kind."

The witness at this point, and in response to questions propounded by Mr. Davidge, again detailed the conversation at the Riggs House, but was interrupted by the prisoner with a positive denial. "I do not want," he said, "to contradict Mr. Reed, because he is a good fellow, but there is not a word of truth in it. I spoke to Mr. Reed two or three months prior to July. I never spoke to Mr. Reed or anyone else about the Paris Consulship for two or three months prior to July. I want the exact truth and nothing but the truth and I don't care who hears it."

Mr. Davidge.—"We can dispense with these interruptions."

The prisoner.—"We want the facts, Judge."

Mr. Davidge.—"You have been indulged altogether too much."

The prisoner.—" And it is right that I should be. I appear as my own counsel."

The Court (severely).—" Be silent."

Mr. Davidge (firmly).—"You must keep quiet, at least while I am cross-examining a witness."

But neither Court nor counsel could repress the prisoner, who continued talking and struggling angrily with the deputy marshals. "This conversation," he said, "occurred about two months prior to July. You are right as to the conversation, but wrong as to the date. I say that it was in May. With that correction your statement is true."

Mr. Davidge (to the witness).—"You have heard the interruptions of the prisoner; what is your opinion about the time?"

The witness.—" I am very certain that it was on that Tuesday."

The prisoner.—" That was the time I spoke to you about getting fifteen dollars. You said you did not have the money. That part of the conversation is correct. I don't forget anything. Anything that goes into my head sticks."

Mr. Davidge (to witness).—" You said that he said that you would see his name in the papers in connection with the Paris Consulship?"

The prisoner.—" I never said that."

Mr. Davidge.—"Well he says, Mr. Prisoner, that you did say it, and he has a right to his opinion."

The prisoner in a persevering manner, declared that he had not said so. He also indignantly denied the witness' statement that he (witness) had not admitted him to the bar in Chicago. He did not want any trickery about this case.

The Court, impatient at the prisoner's constant interruptions of counsel and witnesses, in a stern and determined tone said: "If there is no other way of preventing these interruptions you will have to be gagged." "Well—" began the prisoner. "Keep your mouth shut," thundered the Judge, "and don't interrupt again during this trial. I don't desire it, but if the trial cannot go on without resort to gagging, it will have to be done." Even this threat, though it had a momentary effect upon the prisoner, could not entirely repress him, and he again denied the conversation detailed by the witness who "was a very good fellow but wrong there. "I'm going to have the facts in this case," he continued, "and nothing but the facts. I want the Judge and the jury to decide upon the facts and upon nothing else. The witness is entirely erroneous in his memory."

Mr. Davidge.—"Did Guiteau say that you would see his name in the newspapers in a few days as Consul to Paris or that he would make a fuss?"

The witness.—"He said: "If I do not forget it—" (reflecting to find his exact language).

The prisoner (interrupting).—" It is absolutely false. I never said any such thing. That has nothing at all to do with my intending to remove the President. I rest my defence entirely on the inspiration which came from the Deity for that act, and I will take my chances on the result. I do not want any lying or nonsense on this business and I will not have it."

Mr. Davidge (to the witness).—" Go on."

The witness.—" He said in connection with the administration, that if he did not get the Paris Consulate he would either make a fuss about it or would do something about it in the newspapers.

The prisoner.—" I never said anything of the kind and I never thought anything of the kind. That is the result of your own imagination, Mr. Reed. It is not true. You are a good fellow and I think a good deal of you, but you are mistaken in your facts. [After a pause.] I was not in the habit of telling my business in that kind of way to anybody."

Mr. Davidge (to the witness).—" Then your recollection is, that when Guiteau left you and threw up his arms as you have described, in an excited way, he said that in a few days you would see his name in the papers as Consul to Paris?"

The witness.—" Yes, that was the last part of the conversation."

At the close of the witness' examination the court took its usual recess.

After the recess Mr. Scoville asked for an attachment against Emory A. Storrs. He understood that Mr. Storrs had been served with a subpœna, but had positively refused to come. As there might be some doubt, however, as to whether the subpœna had been actually served, he would postpone his application for the present. The prisoner, in this connection, expressed his hope that Mr. Storrs would not be attached, unless it was absolutely necessary, because he was "a very nice fellow."

H. B. Amerling, at present a lawyer in Williamsport, Pa., who formerly resided in Freeport, Illinois, was the next witness. He had known Luther W. Guiteau intimately. He (Guiteau) believed that in order to be healed all that was necessary was to believe in Jesus Christ. Witness related an incident as to the sickness of his wife, when Luther W. Guiteau advised her to turn out the doctors and put her faith in Jesus Christ. He also had given witness the same advice upon another occasion. He believed that the pocket-books of all persons should be open to everyone, but that nothing more should be taken out than was right. Witness gave an account of a Presbyterian meeting which had assembled to call him to account for not attending Church. He gave as an excuse the fact that his wife was sick and he "turned the members up one by one," and gave them a severe lecture for not coming to attend his sick wife. Afterwards L. W. Guiteau had stated that witness had done right. He spoke to witness about a certain family which ought to have been sacrificed. The family was that of Martin P. Sweet. The son had remonstrated against the family becoming members of the Society of Communicants and for that reason L. W. Guiteau believed that the boy ought to be sacrificed.

The cross-examination, which was conducted by Mr. Davidge, was very amusing, the witness being rather prosy and desirous of giving explanations of almost every answer which he made. Mr. Davidge questioned the witness searchingly in regard to the letter which his son, at his request, had written to Freeport, Illinois, to a Mr. Oller, making inquiries as to the strange actions of Luther W. Guiteau. Witness replied that he had told his son to write the letter, not out of any love for Charles J. Guiteau, but out of respect for the family. "I loved L. W. Guiteau," said the witness, dramatically, "as I did my own brother."

Mr. Davidge.—"Did you think him an insane man?"

The witness.—"I consider that he was what we could say 'off' on religion and politics."

Mr. Davidge.—"What were his political views?"

The witness.—"He was a Republican."

Mr. Davidge.—"And you were a Democrat?"

The witness.—"Indeed I was."

Mr. Davidge.—"You have been a sort of consulting counsel in this case?"

The witness.—"I have been. I gave Mr. Scoville all the assistance I could. I prepared a brief on the question of insanity. I don't want to disguise nothing. I have assisted Mr. Scoville in every way, manner, and form in this case. I have no love for the prisoner—none whatever—because I say to you that I thought it was a terrible wrong in shooting the President and I think so to-day." Witness stated that he had no acquaintance with the prisoner, but subsequently said that the prisoner had made a threat against him. "Why," broke in the prisoner, "I never saw you before in my life until you came to the jail last Saturday." Mr. Scoville then proceeded in the re-direct examination to question the witness as to the occasion upon which he had been threatened by the prisoner.

"Well," began the witness, "we had a lyceum in Freeport. Mr. Horatio Burcham, Mr. Bailey and—" but here Mr. Davidge interrupted and cautioned the witness to be more brief.

The witness.—"We had a debate on the question of the taxation of national bonds."

Mr. Davidge.—"When was that?"

The witness.—"I can't fix no time."

The prisoner.—"I have not been in Freeport

for twenty years. It must have been when I was a boy."

The witness (contemptuously to the prisoner).—"I was not talking to you, sir."

The prisoner.—"But I was talking to you."

The witness.—"You are not fit to talk to. [To Mr. Davidge.] It must have been along about —Well (impatiently), I can't fix no time. It was about 1867. I do not pretend to fix the time. At the debate there was Mr. Coffin and Mr. Guiteau on one side, and myself and Mr. Dexter Nolton on the other side. I said a good deal. The old gentleman became angry with what I said and pitched into me. I had my opportunity at the close and I improved it. I said that the old gentlemen was well fitted to any position, but the one which he was best qualified to fill was with an apron from his chin to his toes, knife in his hands, and he in the kitchen of the Oneida Community, peeling potatoes.

The merriment in Court, which had been gradually increasing, as the witness related these funny incidents, became so pronounced at this point, that it was with difficulty that order was restored. The witness continued: "The old man became very angry, and afterwards I met this man, and he said that my life ought to be taken from me, but that God had ordered otherwise.

The prisoner.—"Are you referring to me or to my father?"

The witness maintained a contemptuous silence.

The District Attorney.—"I think that is a proper question to be answered."

The prisoner.—"If you refer to me, it is absolutely false; if to my father, it may be true, and probably is."

The witness.—"He (referring to the prisoner) is the one who mentioned that to me. Afterward I mentioned it to his father, and the father said that I must not mind what he said."

The prisoner.—"I have not lived in Freeport for twenty-one years."

Mr. Scoville.—"Where did you meet this man when this conversation took place?"

The witness.—"In Chicago."

The prisoner.—"You pretend that this conversation took place in Chicago?"

The witness (impatiently).—"Please let me alone."

The prisoner (excitedly).—"There is not a word of truth in it. That is the way to dispose of that statement."

Mr. Davidge.—"I want to know when this took place."

The prisoner.—"Find out the facts, Judge."

Mr. Davidge.—"I will bring them out."

The prisoner (alluding to the witness' statement).—"I have not heard that. It is the worst one we have had yet."

Mr. Davidge then attempted but in vain to

compel the witness to fix a date for the conversation with Charles Guiteau.

The prisoner expressed his approval of the witness: "Amerling appears to be a good fellow, but I never had the pleasure of his acquaintance before."

Thomas North, of Chicago, a lawyer, the next witness, testified that he had formerly lived in Freeport, Illinois, where he was intimately acquainted with Luther W. Guiteau. Witness was deputy clerk under him when he was circuit clerk and ex-officio recorder.

Mr. Scoville.—"What peculiarities were there in his religious views as to union with Christ, perfectionism, etc?"

The witness.—"He is what was called a perfectionist. He believed in perfect holiness. He believed in vital union with Christ by faith. He believed in inspiration by the Holy Ghost. He believed that inspiration would be carried so far as to save him from theological error, and to give him power over all diseases and maladies. He discarded doctors and would have nothing to do with them. He believed in immortality on earth by vital union with Christ. I have heard him say, perhaps a dozen times, that he never expected to die."

Mr. Scoville asked the witness how the prisoner and his father compared in regard to personal and mental characteristics.

Objected to by the District Attorney.

Mr. Scoville said he expected to prove that father and son were fac-similes.

The prisoner.—"That is true, they say. North has given a true statement of how father used to act with his family."

The objection being overruled, witness stated that the prisoner was an exaggerated fac-simile of his father.

The prisoner.—"I'm a little larger than he was."

The witness.—"I should say that mentally there was a very marked resemblance."

Mr. Scoville.—"What do you mean by the phrase: "an exaggerated fac-simile of his father?"

The prisoner.—"A chip of the old block."

The witness.—"I used the word "exaggerated" in reference to his mental characteristics."

The witness went on to narrate another incident that occurred one evening at the supper table. They were all seated round the table, he said, except the prisoner, who seemed to be a little dilatory. Certain graceful things to be done or said [to the District Attorney] I mean saying grace—

The prisoner.—"Tell them how they used to do that, how they used to confess Christ there. I want to get that out."

The witness.—"They were all seated around the table and they were all quiet for a few moments, and then if anybody felt like saying anything he did so. If not, nothing was said. What was usually said, was: 'I confess Christ in me with thankful heart for this food.'"

The prisoner.—"Thank Christ for this dinner and all similar expressions. That was the substitute for ordinary grace in the Christian families." The witness assented and went on to relate how Charles Guiteau, or Julius, as they called him then, came to the table late and was spoken to by his father in a peremptory and offensive tone; how Charles passing behind his father's chair, struck his father in the back or on his neck or shoulders, and how his father at once jumped from his chair; and how the two clenched and struggled, until finally Charles surrendered, and then how they withdrew from the table by themselves, talked the matter over, came back to the table and went on with their supper. There had been no previous quarrel between them, and this was a sudden outburst on both sides.

The prisoner.—"My mother died when I was seven years old, and my father remained a widower until I was twelve. During these five years we were exceedingly intimate. After he married there was more or less alienation between us."

Witness was questioned in regard to his knowledge of the prisoner, his appearance and manners, and said in reply that he always felt when in Guiteau's presence "that the quills might fly out at any time."

The prisoner.—" That's because we were not on good terms. I didn't like you at that time, but I think more of you now. I never thought so much of you before in my life as I do now." The witness was further cross-examined, but before his evidence was completed the Court adjourned.

CHAPTER XII.

Senator John A. Logan on the Stand—Guiteau's Bogus Political Career Described by Other Witnesses—Mrs. Scoville, the Prisoner's Sister and his Counsel's Wife a Witness.

SATURDAY morning, November 26th, at the opening of the Court for the last day of the second week of the trial, the attendance was fully as large and composed mainly of the same class of people, principally ladies, as on the previous day. The prisoner looked duller and less wild when brought in, and when his handcuffs had been removed, shook hands with his brother and sister. Then with a look of leaden stolidity he turned his attention to his usual bundle of newspapers. The Court having been called to order, Mr. Scoville stated that he had received a telegram from Emory A. Storrs, explaining his inability to attend at present. The application for an attachment would therefore be waived. Mr. Davidge remarked that Mr. Storrs would be permitted to testify at any time during the trial and this matter having been adjusted, the cross-examination of Thomas North was continued from yesterday. In reply to Mr. Davidge, witness again detailed the incident related yesterday of a quarrel which had occurred in Freeport, between Luther W. Guiteau and his son Charles at the supper table. The father had said something insulting to his son, who thereupon struck him, saying, "Take that, I have had enough of you." The father had then struck the son on the nose and made the blood flow.

The prisoner.—"I don't think there is a word of truth in this talk. I don't remember anything about it, and I remember most everything."

Witness repeated his statement that he never knew a man more intensely honest and sincere than Luther W. Guiteau.

Q. And of most accurate power in discriminating between right and wrong? A. I do not know anything in connection with his character contray to that view; I never knew him to violate the law of the land.

Witness was cross-examined as to the incident related yesterday in relation to the visit to Niagara in company with Luther W. Guiteau, but nothing of importance was elicited.

Mr. Davidge then questioned witness about the occasion of the sickness of Luther W. Guiteau's daughter Flora. Witness stated that Luther W. Guiteau had knelt by the bedside of his sick daughter and prayed, "Oh Lord Jesus Christ, let this, Thy daughter, be healed by Thy healing power. In the name of Jesus Christ, I rebuke this disease."

Witness said that Luther W. Guiteau was a

GUITEAU EXAMINING HIS WOUND.

man *sui generis;* he was a nervous, excitable man; he sympathized in politics with extreme abolition views. Witness then detailed the action of Luther W. Guiteau on the occasion of his visiting a sick lady, Mrs. Plummer, at witness' house. On this occasion he did not pray, he commanded the disease to disappear.

Q. Did that lady recover spite of the absence of the doctors? A. No, sir, she died; Flora recovered.

Witness stated that Luther W. Guiteau believed that there were persons living on the earth then, and he among them, who would never die; but he placed it on absolute conditions. He believed that the Oneida Community was the germ that was to work out the communistic idea of things. Witness stated that his belief differed from Luther W. Guiteau's only in degree. He believed that God might develop a new race of beings upon the earth somewhere in the indefinite future.

Mr. Davidge inquired whether witness knew of any other peculiarities of Luther W. Guiteau except those he had mentioned, and received an affirmative answer.

"There are scores of such cases," broke in the prisoner; "those are only two or three incidents. He was on that business all his life after he became acquainted with Noyes."

Some amusement was created during the cross-examination of this witness, but the officers checked the laughter until Mr. Davidge, in questioning the witness about his trip with the elder Guiteau to Niagara Falls, made allusion to the omission of drinks at the dinner there by the visitors. There was another titter when the witness stated that in addition to taking a bath, a dinner and a rest, he and the prisoner's father played a game of tenpins back of the church at Niagara Falls. Towards the close of the examination, Mr. Davidge tried to establish the disloyalty of the witness, who went to Texas in 1861, where he engaged in business. Mr. North said the Union had never lost him, nor had he gone to Texas to better his condition in anticipation of the rebellion.

When this witness left the stand, Guiteau, who had been reading a newspaper, suddenly looked up, and said: "I notice my friend, Henry Ward Beecher, is doing some cranky work on this case. I used to attend his Church and prayer meetings, and if Your Honor knew him as well as I do, you would not pay any attention to him. There are a good many people that think he is badly cranked, socially, and have no doubt that Mrs. Tilton told the truth, and that he lied about it, and I tell him so publicly."

"Oh, well, well, prisoner, that will do for you," said Mr. Davidge. Guiteau was apparently satisfied and nodded with a smile, saying, "That's all right, Judge; I have had my say on Beecher, I am satisfied."

Senator John A. Logan, of Illinois was the next witness. As he was sworn the prisoner greeted him with "How are you, Mr. Senator? I am glad to see you," but his greeting met no response.

In reply to questions by Mr. Scoville, the witness detailed two interviews which he had had with the prisoner. The first was about the 12th or 15th of March last, in the morning; the prisoner came to his room uninvited; witness was in the back room, and when he entered the reception room he found the prisoner there, sitting on a chair near the door; he did not know who he was. The first thing that the prisoner did, was to pull a pamphlet out of his pocket, and hand it to the witness, saying that it was a speech which he had delivered in the recent canvass, and asked witness to read it. Witness declined to read it at the time, but said that he would take pleasure in reading it afterwards. It was a speech entitled "Garfield against Hancock." The prisoner then said, "That speech elected Mr. Garfield President of the United States. He (the prisoner) then commenced talking about a position that he desired, saying that he had the promise of an appointment as Consul General to France; he said he had seen the Secretary of State, Mr. Blaine, who had promised him this appointment, provided he could get Senator Logan's recommendation. Witness said: "I do not know you, and cannot recommend you;" prisoner then went on to say that he resided in Chicago, and was a constituent of the witness, and that witness was under obligation to recommend him; he also told witness that he had been to New York during the canvass, to see the Republican National Committee there in regard to entering into the campaign; he said that the President was a friend of his, and that he had seen General Garfield somewhere, not in Washington; that he was satisfied that the President was favorably disposed to his appointment, and that he would get it, especially if he (witness) would recommend him; witness again declined; the prisoner then took out of his pocket a sheet of foolscap, with about three lines written very close to the top; it was a recommendation for his appointment; he wanted witness to sign it, but witness declined, and got rid of him as soon as he could.

Q. Why? A. He did not strike me as a person whom I would recommend for an office of that character, or any other office. I treated him as kindly and politely as I could, but I was very desirous of getting rid of him; I did not want to be annoyed by him.

Q. Was there anything particularly noticeable in his appearance? A. He was rather peculiarly clad for the season, there being snow on the street at the time. He had on his feet a pair of sandals or rubbers, or something of that kind; he had no stockings; he wore a light pair of pantaloons and a common, ordinary coat; a day or two afterward he came again to my room, uninvited; he still insisted on my signing his recommendation, reiterating the same statement as before, of his having a promise of the place if I would recommend him; I again declined; I had, in the meantime, out of curiosity, read the speech. He was a little more excited at the second interview than at the first; the second was a very short interview, for I tried to dispose of the matter as quickly as possible; I said to him: "The first time I see the Secretary of State I will mention your case to him." I did not say that I would recommend him, but simply that I would mention his case, and I intended to do so, but probably in a different way from what he supposed I would.

Q. From what you saw of the prisoner on those occasions, and from what was said and done by him, did you form any opinion, as to his mental soundness or unsoundness? A. I am not an expert, and do not know whether I should answer the question.

The Court.—"You may give an opinion in accordance with your observations."

The witness.—"I thought there was some derangement of his mental organization, but to what extent I could not say. When I went down to breakfast that morning I saw him at the table as a boarder; I called the landlady and asked her if she knew that gentleman: she mentioned his name and said he had told her he was a constituent of mine."

Q. What was your expression of opinion to the landlady at that time? A. I said this: "I do not think that he is a proper person to have in your boarding-house." She asked why; I said "I think he is a little off in his head," or some language of that kind. She asked me what I meant, and I said I thought he was kind of crazy, and that she had better not have him in her boarding-house; that is about the conversation we had at that time.

The cross-examination consisted mainly of the question: "When did this conversation take place?" And the reply: "I think it was about the twelfth or fifteenth of March."

George D. Hubbard, a farmer of Oneida County, N. Y., was then called. He testified that he lived less than half a mile from the Community, but (indignantly) was never connected with it as a member. In 1863 he worked for three months for the Community, to which the prisoner at that time belonged. He (Guiteau) worked in the same shop with witness; he was a nervous, quick-tempered man; if anything was said to disturb him he would get riled and would gesticulate wildly, and talk in a mysterious manner; he would sit for hours in a corner, saying nothing to anybody; at other times he would be cheerful. On one occasion he told witness that he aspired to be the leader of the Community.

On cross-examination witness stated that all persons were free to leave the Community when they pleased; that the doors were always open. Mr. Davidge here scored one laugh on his own account by quietly remarking: "I have no idea of going there." On re-direct examination, however, witness stated that an aunt of his was confined in the Community, and when she was finally found by his father she had been horsewhipped with a rawhide; she was afterwards sent to an insane asylum, but subsequently recovered.

The prisoner.—"I remember that case myself. There is no physical restraint there, but is it all spiritual and social. That is a good deal worse than physical restraint. If a man left there he was led to believe that he was forever damned. That is the way the Community was kept together."

Edmund M. Smith, of Chicago, next testified that he had been a clerk to the Republican Central Committee in New York during the last campaign; the committe sent out a large number of documents, "and we paid honest postage on all of it." Witness had seen the prisoner several times; he wanted to be placed on the rolls as a speaker; he did not appear as if he could put half a dozen sentences together, and witness did not think that he had received any assignment to speak.

The prisoner.—"The gentleman was not in a condition to know whether I did or not. He was only a clerk."

Mr. Davidge.—"That was what I thought."

The prisoner.—"Jewell was the fellow who did the business—Jewell and Hooker and Dorsey and the rest of us fellows."

Mr. Scoville then read the deposition of J. A. Turner, of Dakota Territory, who deposed to having known Mrs. Maynard and Mrs. Parker, sisters of Luther W. Guiteau, and to having regarded them as insane.

John A. Moss, a colored lawyer, who resides near the Government Asylum for the Insane, was the next witness. He had seen the prisoner at the Executive mansion fifteen or twenty times during the months of May and June; he thought he was a crazy man when he first saw him; witness had seen many crazy people and this man appeared to him to be crazy; he had never heard the prisoner say anything.

Mr. Davidge asked how the crazy man looked.

"Just as he does now," replied the witness, "except that he had a bundle of papers with him."

Mrs. Frances Scoville, sister of the prisoner and wife of his counsel was the next witness, and occupied the stand for an hour and a half.

Mrs. Scoville is a lady of prepossessing appearance for one of her age. She is of fair complexion, and has a smooth round face full of kindly expression, blue eyes and gray hair. She was dressed in a black suit and wore a dark bonnet. She did not stand, but occupied a chair and was quite composed in manner and voice while giving her testimony, although a little embarrassed as indicated by the mechanical manner in which she moved her fan. Her words were clear in tone and distinct in pronunciation. She was accorded special attention by nearly every one, the ladies being unusually quiet and deeply interested in hearing her recital of the family history and Guiteau's conduct. It was certainly an unusual scene wherein the wife was the witness and the husband conducted the examination. But in this, as in every other examination by Mr. Scoville, there was the same matter of fact style of putting the questions. Had not Mrs. Scoville been known, no one would have thought her the wife of the attorney asking the questions.

Mrs. Scoville stated her age at forty-five. Her father was Luther W. Guiteau, of Freeport, Illinois, and her mother, Jane Howe Guiteau. The prisoner is forty years old. He was about seven years old when her mother died. She remembered her mother from the time the witness was three years old. She was sick a very long time at the time that Charles was born; had been told that her sickness at that time lasted a year and a half; remembered seeing her head shaved perfectly bald; this was before Charles was born; her aunt had subsequently given her (among other keepsakes) the hair then shaved from her mother's head; after that time her mother always wore a cap; never saw her mother walk in the street after that; there were two children born subsequently; Luther Theodore, who died when he was two years old and who was born with a crooked foot and limb, and Julia Catherine, who died when twenty months old, six week's after her mother's death. Her mother's sickness was attended with a very severe pain in her head and her hair never grew again. Her first recollection of Charles was that he was a troublesome child because he was very active and smart; he was sent to school quite young—when six years old—to learn to talk; he could make noise, but could not talk; he used the word "ped" for "come" and the word "pail" for "quail;" his father punished him for it, but that made no difference. She thought he could not comprehend the difference. After his mother's death he lived a year or so with his grandfather, and then came back to his father. Witness was married in January, 1853, while Charles was living with his grandfather; subsequently when he was twelve years old, he lived with witness for a year in Chicago, where he went to school; she recollected nothing peculiar about him then except that he was very affectionate, and she was very much attached to him; then he went to his father, and subsequently, when he was seventeen years old, he came again to live with witness at Oak Park, near Chicago. He attended school at Commercial College, Chicago; and after that he went back to Freeport, and from there he went to Ann Arbor to attend school; she went to Ann Arbor to see him, as she had been informed that he was going on worse than her father had ever done; she found that he had abandoned his studies and was giving his whole time and attention to studying the Berean and the publications of the Oneida Community; she argued with him for a whole evening, appealing to him to go on quietly like other young men and to give up all that stuff. Her appeals had no effect upon him, however and she made up her mind that he was crazy; she told her uncle, who lived at Ann Arbor, to pay no more attention to him, but let him go his own way, as he was "clear gone daft." She afterward visited him at the Oneida Community, but could hardly have any conversation with him, as they were not left alone a moment together; she noticed that he acted like a person who had been bewildered, struck on the head or had partly lost his mind; she could not learn from him whether he wanted to leave the Oneida Community or stay there.

The prisoner.—" I had been there three years

at that time, and was right in the heart of their fanaticism."

Witness went on to relate the prisoner's history, including his admission to the bar (at which she was very much surprised), his marriage, and his separation from his wife, down to the time he visited her in Wisconsin, in 1875. She noticed then a great change in his personal appearance; he was also very hard to get along with, and he used to get in a "highfalutin" state; he seemed willing to do anything that he was told, but he got very much befogged and could not do it. She related the incident of his attacking her with an axe. She had given him no provocation, but had got out of patience with him; it was not the axe that frightened her so much as it was the look of his face; he looked like a wild animal; she retreated into the house and ran up to her daughter's room; then she called Olds, the hired man; she said, "Here, take this boy and put him off the place;" Olds took hold of him and brought him to the dining room.

At this stage of her testimony, which was given in a very low tone and with great rapidity of utterance so as to be almost unintelligible, the Court, at twenty minutes past one P. M., adjourned.

CHAPTER XIII.

The Prisoner's Sister, Mrs. Scoville, Again on the Witness Stand—Her Impressions as to Guiteau's Insanity—Other Witnesses think Him Crazy or a Fool—Guiteau's Brother John as a Witness—The Prisoner Sworn.

ON Monday morning, November 28, Mrs. Scoville resumed her testimony. Referring to the prisoner's visit to her house in Wisconsin, in the summer of 1875, she said she noticed only that he was wild in his ideas, and had visionary schemes, such as buying up the *Inter-Ocean*, etc. She then came to the visit in 1876, when the prisoner attacked her with an axe. Here a tilt occurred between counsel as to the character of the evidence in regard to a conversation with a third party, and the witness paused. Resuming her testimony, witness related her conversation with a lady in which she said she thought it high time that measures were taken to do something about her brother's case; that she would consult a physician and that if he thought proper she would have him put in an asylum. Her brother overheard that conversation and became very violent about it; he said among other things that if the witness were put away safely in a lunatic asylum it would be all right and everything would go along on the place smoothly; he became very violent and commenced gesticulating. If it had been any one else she would have said that he was abusive, but she did not think him abusive because she was sure he did not know what he was doing. She related the sail-boat incident, and said that her brother was very much frightened, and looked like a wild animal, jumping on the edge of the boat and making an effort to leap into the water until somebody caught hold of him. Then she described the incident of the prisoner's soaping the hickory trees, and insisting that if they were not apple trees they were certainly peach trees. He became very violent about it, but the witness was very much amused. The prisoner that summer spent most of his time reading the newspapers and a Testament which he kept in his pocket; he said he was preparing to go in with Moody and Sankey. Finally the witness' son Louis, would not stand any more nonsense from her brother and put him off the place without her knowledge. She was very much worried about him, but a day or two afterwards he rode past with a lady and tipped his hat to the witness, as if to say he was all right. On his return she sent him to the cottage kept by the hired man, where he spent a couple of days.

Witness was proceeding to detail a conversation between Mr. Scoville and herself, in order to show the reason that the prisoner had not been committed to an insane asylum, when Mr. Davidge interposed an objection.

Mr. Scoville stated that the object was to meet any averment that his relatives did not think it was necessary to put him in an insane asylum and to explain why this was not done. A lengthy argument on the admissibility of the evidence followed, when the witness broke in with the statement:

"The reason why was because he had a father and brother living, and we knew they ought to be consulted before putting him away quietly in Wisconsin on the certificate of two doctors. I wanted him taken to Chicago and tried by a jury and found insane, as I had no doubt he would be."

Q. What was your opinion in 1876 as to his insanity? A. I had no doubt whatever of his insanity; his mind was breaking up; he was losing his mind in addition to his insanity.

The witness testified that in the summer of 1877 her brother Charles was still interested in some big lecture scheme; witness thought he denounced everybody who did not believe as he did and said they were going to hell. He used to talk with one of her boarders at Beaver lake (Mr. Burrows), on the subject of the second coming of Christ until she told him he must not talk so to her boarders; she told Mr. Burrows that her brother was crazy and not worth spending breath upon; her brother never bore any malice; it was remarkable that he never laid up anything against anybody; no matter what was done to him he never tried to pay it back; in this respect she thought he was silly. Her brother had always been in dead earnest about everything; she never knew him to do as other young men in regard to games or swimming or anything of that kind; he was always by himself. In ladies society he was always very polite and pleasant.

Cross-examination was postponed to allow a witness to testify who desired to return to Chicago.

George T. Burrows was called to the stand. It was objected to by the District Attorney that he had remained in the room during the examination of the first witness in violation of the rule. He explained that he expected to be the witness who would be examined this morning and had, therefore, come into the room, and that he had remained because he did not wish to cause any confusion in trying to get out. The explanation being satisfactory, the witness proceeded with his testimony. He became acquainted with the prisoner at Mrs. Scoville's country place. The prisoner had often talked with him about his book on the second coming of Christ, till finally the witness stopped talking to him because the prisoner became violent. Witness also related an incident of the prisoner's at that time dropping a puppy dog out of an upstairs window, breaking the dog's leg, and the prisoner saying he did not think it would hurt the dog; he supposed the dog would strike on its feet just as a cat does; witness from all these circumstances and from the general conduct of the prisoner, had decided in his own mind that the prisoner was either a fool or crazy, and he thought he was not sane.

Nothing was elicited in a cross-examination of the witness. While waiting for another witness, the prisoner, who had been scanning the newspapers all the morning, suddenly broke out: "I desire to tell all these crank newspaper men that I appear here as my own counsel. That is my answer to all this silly stuff they have been delivering themselves of for some days past. Some of these newspapers have gone crazy. I appear here, in part, as my own counsel, as I have a right to under the law and constitution of all America."

Charles S. Jocelyn, of Lennox, N. Y., business manager of the Oneida Community, testified that he knew the prisoner when he was a member of that Community; he came there in 1860 and remained for nearly five years. Excessive egotism was his peculiar characteristic; he was the most egotistical man the witness ever knew, so much so as to be eccentric and different from other men. He was absorbed in himself and had such a high idea of himself as to think himself a superior being qualified to be a leader and manager of men. He never noticed any insincerity about him. He had a very strong religious bias towards exaltation and even fanaticism. He attempted to deliver lectures there, but they were mainly made up of ideas rehashed from former publications of the Oneida Community; there was nothing original in them; they were not a great success as works of art or literary productions.

John W. Guiteau, of Boston, the prisoner's brother, was the next witness. He went over the prisoner's history so far as known to him, and related a conversation in which he upraided him for not paying Mr. Scoville five or six hundred dollars that he owed him. The prisoner said that he had paid it long ago. That he had given Mr. Scoville his note a year ago, which note Mr. Scoville could get discounted in a bank in Chicago, but that he was too stubborn and ugly to do it; he insisted that that was a discharge of the debt, and the witness thought that he was a fool or crazy While witness was living in Brooklyn in 1871, the prisoner came to board in the same house and witness did not pay his board.

The prisoner.—" I paid it myself."

The District Attorney (to the witness).—" Why did you make the last statement?"

The witness.— 'I was under the impression that he would not pay his board."

The prisoner (excitedly).—" That was a false

impression. I have paid my board as often as you have paid yours, if the record was made up.

The witness (as an illustration of the prisoner's ignorance of law) told of his coming to him one day in Brooklyn to be shown how to fill up a chattel mortgage.

Witness saw his brother next in Boston, in 1879, and had since seen him several times in Washington, in court and in jail; had frequent conversations with him. He described the first conversation which he had with the prisoner in company with Mr. Scoville at the jail. The conversation was first carried on between Mr. Scoville and the prisoner, who insisted on the management of the case, and objected to several of Mr. Scoville's ideas as to witnesses; part of the time he was excited, part of the time he was very quiet. He said he would not have any witness put on the witness stand until he knew what he was going to swear to; witness supposed that the prisoner might be dangerous, and managed to keep him in front of him; he thought that possibly the prisoner might intend to harm him, as they had previously had some difficulty.

Mr. Davidge.—"Oh, we don't want that."

The witness.—"I managed to keep him in front of me; I do not think I was afraid of him; after a while I saw that he was perfectly harmless, so far as I was concerned and I soon entered into conversation with him; he said that the name of

Guiteau would get honor instead of dishonor; that it would be "Guiteau, the patriot," instead of "Guiteau, the assassin;" he spoke very loud, louder than in any exhibition here. I then said:

"I believe you are honest in your view." He said he had acted under an inspiration, and was willing to suffer or die for the principle of inspiration. I said:

"I believe you are honest in your conviction." He said—"Yes, I am."

I asked him—"Are you willing to be sacrificed for the principle as Christ was?" He said he was.

I said—"You know that there are two influences in this world, a God and a Satan, and a spirit of truth, which is Christ." He said—"Yes."

I said to him—"You know that the jury and the lawyers and the Court are more or less under the influences of God?" "Yes," he said.

I said—"You cannot expect that they will receive your views about God?" He said "No."

"And therefore you cannot expect that the jury will accept your interpretations and views in regard to inspiration?" "No."

"Now," I said, "are you willing to abide by the decision of the jury and suffer the penalty imposed by the Court if they fail to agree to your views?" He said—"I am."

I said—"Then are you willing to abide by it?" "I am," he said.

I said—"They say that you are afraid of your life." "That is not so," he answered; "I do not care a snap for my life."

"Now," I said, "I think you are telling me the truth. Which would you prefer, to be hanged by the verdict of the jury or shot by the mob?"

"I do not want either," he cried, and he flew as quick as a flash into the corner and got behind a table. When he saw the ludicrousness of it he laughed at his sudden emotion, and we all laughed. His eyes looked wild, I became satisfied from that conversation that he was sincere as to his reason for shooting the President, and thoroughly believed in the inspiration. I believe him insane.

The witness identified an old Bible handed to him by Mr. Scoville as the family Bible of Francis Guiteau, who was his father's father.

Mr. Scoville called attention to an entry of the birth and death of "Francis Guiteau the second," (1800—1829) and said that he would produce the records of the Bloomingdale Asylum to show that he died in that institution.

On cross-examination the witness stated that his opinion as to the sanity of his brother underwent a change last October, when he received from Freeport, Illinois, some of the prisoner's letters to his father. That changed opinion was confirmed by the interviews had with his brother since he came here.

Q. Before that time had you stated to various

persons publicly that you had no doubt of his sanity and responsibility? A. No, sir, as to his sanity, what I did state was published.

Q. Did you state in conversation with John H. Barron, of Concord, N. H., that the prisoner was sane? A. I did not.

Q. Did you state that the act was the result of "pure cussedness?" A. I do not think I did in the connection in which you use it. I believed my brother's case was one of demonism—that he was possessed of the devil.

Q. And you stated that substantially to Mr. Barron? A. Yes, sir.

Q. Did you attend a meeting presided over by Dr. Charles Collis, of Boston, about the 5th of July. A. I did.

The prisoner.—"I used to attend those meetings myself when I was in Boston."

Q. Did you there state that the prisoner was not insane, but was responsible? A. I stated that I believed him to be responsible, but not insane; I stated that constantly and always until about the receipt of those letters; I said that I believed that before God he was responsible for his act—morally responsible—because I believed that some time in his past life he made a choice to follow the path of evil rather than of good; that so far as regarded his responsibility before the law, I could not determine that, because the law dealt with a man's body. The interpretation of the law as to insanity I was not to judge.

Q. You could only judge of his responsibility before God? A. I had no question of that at the time.

Q. You stated then and before that and afterwards, that you had no doubt of his responsibility before God? A. I did.

Q. That he had deliberately chosen evil instead of good? A. I did.

The prisoner.—"I will state here that my brother and I were not in fellowship with each other for years. The last interview that I had with him was in Boston, a year and a half ago when he was offended with me, so that he does not come here with the ordinary affection of a brother."

Q. Did you state to C. B. Robbins, of Worcester, Massachusetts, while travelling with him last October, that the prisoner was not insane? A. No, sir; nor to any other person either.

Q. Did you state to him that the prisoner was responsible? A. I did, before God.

Q. And that he was possessed of the devil? A. That was the thought that I had.

The prisoner.—"My father ran me into the Oneida Community and my brother sympathized with my father."

Mr. Davidge (remonstrating).—"Come, come, Mr. Prisoner."—

The prisoner (to Mr. Davidge)—"You just be quiet, Judge. There was not, therefore, much fellowship between us for fifteen or twenty years. Mr. Scoville and my sister and their family sympathized with me in the Oneida Community business, but my brother sympathized with my father. That accounts for any disability on his part."

In response to questions on the subject of life insurance policies, the witness mentioned several that he had taken—the last in September or October, 1881—and admitted that he had replied in the negative to the usual question as to there being insanity, consumption or scrofula in the family; he also stated that he had helped to get the prisoner (when fifteen or sixteen years old) a situation in Davenport, Iowa.

Q. Did you think him then of unsound mind? A. Not in the sense of being crazy.

Q. In what sense did you think him of unsound mind? A. To use a common expression, "he did not have any sense."

Q. Is not that well nigh to being crazy? A. Probably it may be, but there is a difference between that phrase and the phrase "of unsound mind."

Q. On the occasion that you quarrelled with him about his not paying Mr. Scoville what he owed him, did you treat him as one brother would treat another whom he believed to be of unsound mind? A. No, sir; and I am very sorry that I did not. I reproach myself for it.

The prisoner.—" We were always at loggerheads on account of his sympathizing with my father for running me into the Oneida Community. That is the secret. I never liked him and he never liked me. I like him better now than I ever did."

The witness.—" I can say the same as to him. I never thought so much of him in all my life as I do now."

In reply to further questions, the witness expressed his ignorance of the prisoner being ever employed by any insurance company, and the prisoner himself denied that he ever had been so employed formally. The witness was then inquired of as to his putting the prisoner out of his office in Boston, and he related the circumstances. The prisoner called at the office and complained that the witness had told certain persons that the prisoner was worthless and would not pay his board bills. Witness told him that he had never meddled with him by making any voluntary statement, but that when any one came to inquire about him, he told the truth. My brother said (he continued) that I had no business to make any statement about him or nis indebtedness; that I was no better than he was; that I was in debt, which unfortunately was true, and we had some strong talk. At first I spoke kindly to him, and he to me; I told him that if he was honest in the publication of his book and in his method of life, he should not deceive people about his means of paying for his board, and that if he was meritorious he would find that people would be kind to him, even though he was unfortunate.

The prisoner.—"I never deceived people about my board bills."

The witness.—"He said that he wished to live as Christ did. That Jesus Christ went to a house and if the people received Him He blessed them. That he was working for God, and that he considered God and not himself responsible for his board; we had some further conversation and I drove him to the wall, as I always did in conversation; I entertained the same views of the Oneida Community as my father did. Then his spirit of antagonism came up, and he attempted to drive me to the wall by asserting that I was no better than he. He usually intimated that he was a fighting man and I said that I was not. At that time I told him he had better leave the office, and I caught hold of him and rushed him to the door; he was passing ahead of me and he said as he went along, that I was a thief and a scoundrel; I slapped him on the side of the neck with the back of my hand and he turned round and gave me one on the side of the face, for which I very much respected him."

The prisoner.—"He never struck me and I

never struck him, the rest of the statement is true."

The witness.—"I took him by the collar and hustled him out forcibly and harshly, I conducted myself as no man ought to who professed a Christian life."

The prisoner.—"I say the same too."

Mr. Davidge (to the witness).—"I am not trying you as a Christian man.

The witness.—"But I am glad to make the statement."

The prisoner.—"I never saw my brother from that time till I met him in the jail two weeks ago. That accounts for his poor opinion of me."

The witness in reply to further questions spoke very highly of his father's character, and repudiated the idea of ever regarding him as insane.

After recess J. W. Guiteau resumed the stand. He had heard that his uncle Abraham was insane. His uncle Francis Wilson Guiteau (mentioned in the family as "Francis Guiteau the second") died in an asylum. He understood that in early life Francis had fought a duel with a rival in love. Witness had understood that his uncle had killed the man, but the records of the asylum showed that his insanity had been caused by mortification at fighting a sham duel. Besides Abby Maynard, the daughter of his aunt Julia, and Augustus Parker, who was a cousin, witness had never heard of any other case of insanity in the family.

In redirect examination witness was asked: Q. What is your opinion now as to your father's sanity? A. I think he was sane.

Mr. Scoville.—"That is not taking into account the testimony of the witnesses, North and Amerling.

Mr. Davidge.—"Oh, no, I object."

The Court.—"The witness can only give his opinion on facts founded on his own observation."

Q. What do you mean by saying your brother was possessed of a demon or a devil? A. The religious theory is that there are two forces in the universe—one under Satan or the devil, and one under God or Jesus Christ. My father held to the view that there were living in the world those who were seized of the devil or Satan, and of Christ or God. He believed that these two forces were at war, one with the other, and that at present and since the fall of man, Satan had to a very great extent, dominion on the earth to possess himself of all those who were not absolute believers in the Lord Jesus Christ, as Saviour, and who had not been saved from the power of sin by a complete union with the Lord and Saviour Jesus Christ. That all evil, all disease, all deformity, all infirmity was the result of sin or the admission of those who had a free will that they were under the dominion of Satan or the evil spirit or of evil nature. That was my father's theological view, it was my brother's view, it was mine. And so I believe that at some time in my brother's life, as he had a free will to choose good or evil, he must have through his evil, through his wilfulness, through his stubbornness, through his perseverity of nature, allowed Satan to gain such a control over him that he was under the power of Satan. That idea is the one on which I based my opinion that my brother was morally responsible to God, but perhaps not responsible according to human or legal responsibility, being in one sense insane.

The prisoner.—"You have that thing wrong side up."

The witness.—"Perhaps I have."

The prisoner.—"That's very poor theology and a very poor position for you to take."

Coming back to the subject of his uncle, Abraham Guiteau, the witness stated that when he saw him last in 1867 he was "off his base very badly;" he was a "gassy blowhard" kind of a man. The witness would have said of him that "he was a little weak in his upper story." He remembered his brother in his infancy; he was so nervous that he could not keep still for five minutes. His father once offered him ten cents if he would do so, and he did not get the money. His mother had salt rheum very badly. That disease affected the witness and his sister. He never heard of it in the prisoner.

Mrs. Sarah W. Parker, of Chicago, was called.

She stated that she was the widow of Augustus, one of the sons of the prisoner's aunt Anna. Her husband died in the Insane Asylum at Elgin, Illinois. He had become insane from disappointment in not obtaining a piano agency which he expected. She visited him several times at the Asylum. He was then very violent, and he died after being there three years. Her husband was the prisoner's cousin. The prisoner and his wife came to her house in Chicago. Witness had then two children, a son and a daughter, twelve and thirteen years old. She had requested the prisoner to cease visiting at her house, because he had proposed to educate her daughter so as to marry her. This was in 1876, soon after her husband became insane. He seemed to have fallen very desperately in love with her little daughter, and to want to marry her. Witness went on to say that her little daughter complained to her that the prisoner used to follow her on the street, wanting to talk to her, and that she was afraid to go out on the street alone. Her daughter thought him crazy, and told her so. Witness formed an opinion at that time about the condition of the prisoner's mind. She thought him crazy, and thought so when she first saw him, ten or eleven years ago. She thought then his mind was cracked.

On cross-examination she said she had not forbidden him the house until he had paid those attentions to her daughter. She did not like to have him come at all.

The prisoner.—"They were very poor, and I used to go down there and give them money and they appreciated that very much. Incidentally I became pleased with the little girl, who was very smart. She was too young, however."

Fernando Jones, of Chicago was the next witness. He stated that in 1878 he had boarded at the same house with Guiteau in that city. For four years witness had been one of the Board of Trustees who had supervision over the Insane Asylum at Jacksonville. That was previous to the time he met Guiteau. He had formed an opinion as to Guiteau's mental condition, considering him to be of unsound mind, and what some authorities would call in a state of incipient insanity. At that time the prisoner was memorizing lectures on Mormonism and the second coming of Christ, and talked very incoherently.

On cross-examination witness stated that in 1878 he had paid several visits to Guiteau for the purpose of helping him out of a difficulty—something in regard to collecting money and not paying it over.

The prisoner.—"That part of the statement is incorrect. It is erroneous. I boarded some years ago in the same house with him. It was a high-toned place on Michigan Avenue, in Chicago, and I paid my board. Probably he and other people thought that I was very cranky at that time."

On redirect examination witness stated that later in 1878, he had seen Guiteau in New York, and he observed that his ideas had become exaggerated and that he was not in a sound state of mind.

THE PRISONER SWORN.

The examination of this witness having been completed, a buzz of expectancy ran through the assemblage as Mr. Scoville asked that the prisoner be sworn.

The prisoner nervously proceeded to the witness stand in the custody of two Deputy Marshals, and the oath was administered to him. He then whispered a few words to a policeman who was standing near the witness box, and immediately the three deputies ranged themselves, shoulder to shoulder, behind the prisoner, who, apparently more at ease, said inquiringly to the Court, "I can sit down?" "Yes," replied the Court, and the prisoner seated himself accordingly.

Mr. Scoville then stated he merely wished the prisoner to identify some letters.

The prisoner.—"I understand from Mr. Scoville that all I am to do is to identify some letters. I do not appear as a witness aside from that."

Mr. Scoville then presented a number of letters dating from 1857 to 1868, which were identified by the prisoner, who made running comments upon his penmanship: "This does not look like my present handwriting; there is a decided improvement shown here. This is better than I can do now. This is as fine as steel plate."

There were about twenty letters which had been written by the prisoner to his father, his sister (Mrs. Scoville) and his brother (J. W. Guiteau) and to Mr. Scoville.

The identification having been completed, the Court at three o'clock adjourned.

CHAPTER XIV.

Guiteau on the Witness Stand—His Own Account of His Life—His Efforts to Obtain Possession of the INTER-OCEAN Newspaper—His Experiences of the Oneida Community.

THE crowd which on Tuesday morning, November 29th, attempted to gain admission to the Court room was probably twice as large as on any previous day, in consequence of the fact that the prisoner was to take the stand. The proceedings were opened by Mr. Scoville who tendered the record of the Bloomingdale Insane Asylum to prove the admission and death in that institution of Francis W. Guiteau. The District Attorney admitted these facts. The prisoner was then directed to take the witness stand, and at once commenced a colloquy with his counsel, claiming that he was not feeling well and only expected to be asked to identify certain papers. Mr. Scoville attempted to effect an arrangement to that effect, but the prosecution insisted that the prisoner must either take the stand as a regular witness and be subject to cross-examination or be passed over, the Court ruling that no other proceeding could be allowed without the consent of counsel on both sides.

Mr. Scoville then proceeded to read the letters

identified by the prisoner yesterday. Those dated in 1857, merely acknowledged the receipt of money from the prisoner's father.

The first letter in which any theological theories were announced, was one directed to his sister Frances, in November, 1859, in which he eulogized the Oneida Community and stated his great admiration for Mr. Noyes.

The prisoner.—"That is the way my father used to talk about the Oneida Community. I was about seventeen years old when I wrote that letter, and considerable of a crank too."

In a subsequent letter to his sister the prisoner says:

"My eternal marriage to Jesus Christ and His people in this world, Hades and the resurrection world, is pre-eminently paramount to every other attraction."

In a letter written to Mr. Scoville from the Oneida Community in 1869, Guiteau says:

"I have forsaken everything for Christ—reputation, honor of man, riches, fame and worldly renown—all hankering after the things of this world have ceased, I hope forever. This association is the germ of the kingdom of God, and we expect, without wavering, by the steady, irresistible advance of this association, the conquest of the whole world."

In a letter written to his father in 1865, Guiteau expresses his desire to extend the sovereignty of Jesus Christ by placing at his disposal a powerful daily paper. This letter was read by Mr. Scoville in his opening remarks, and contained the claim of the writer that he was in the employ of Jesus

Christ & Co. The writer also asks his father to send him $100 or $200.

"Father didn't send the money," explained the prisoner; "he thought I was badly cranked."

In a letter written from Brooklyn, N Y., in 1868, Guiteau states that he wants to see the Oneida Community wiped out, and to that end he encloses an appeal.

The appeal was handed to the prisoner and identified by him. "I think that I issued it about that time," said he. "That is the way I felt about it. If I had any money or friends I should have had them cleaned out, sure. I recognize it as my work. It was like a retaliation for living at that hole."

The appeal which is addressed to all lovers of virtue, recites that the Oneida Community is among the most spiritual and social despotisms of the nineteenth century; that it constantly violated the sacred laws of God and man; that those innocent girls and women went through an experience easier imagined than described; * * * and calls upon all good people to frown upon such outrageous practices, upon merchants to refuse to deal with members of the Community, and upon the pulpit and the press to denounce them.

The prisoner.—"Some of the New York papers at that time sustained that appeal by editorial comments. I am very glad to say the Oneida Community is wiped out now, and has been for two or three years. I was a virtuous man all the time I was there."

The last letter was dated from the Cook County Jail, a circumstance which was explained by the prisoner by saying: "I had been arrested by an infernal little whelp for $20. I was on theology and law together at that time and did not attend to my business. The District Attorney released me. That is all there is to that."

GUITEAU'S DIRECT TESTIMONY.

The prisoner who had returned to his seat at counsel's table during the reading of the letters, now resumed the witness stand, closely guarded by police officers and was examined as follows, by Mr. Scoville:

Q. Tell the jury your earliest recollections of your mother, if you recollect her at all? A. Mother died when I was about seven years old; I do not recollect anything special about her. I have always felt that I never had a mother.

Q. Can you recollect her appearance? A. I recollect nothing about her at all, except she was an invalid and confined to her bed; that is the only recollection I have of her. It was probably during her last illness.

Q. After her death where did you live? A. At Freeport, with my father.

Q. Do you remember removing to Ulso, Wisconsin? A. Yes. About a year or two after my mother's death.

Q. Do you recollect when your father married the second time? A. Very distinctly.

Q. Were you in Freeport then? A. Yes, I was living with him. He was agent at Freeport for what is now the Northwestern Railroad Company.

Q. Do you recollect when your sister (Mrs. Scoville) was married? A. Very distinctly.

Q. Were you there then? A. I was.

Q. Do you know what year it was? A. My sister was married in January, 1853, and my father was married in September, 1853. I think I went to live with you some time during the spring after you were married.

Q. Where? A. In Chicago.

Q. What did you do there? A. I boarded at your house, and did chores and went to school. I was twelve years old then. I went to a private school. After several months I went back to Freeport, and lived with my father. He was married in September. I know that I was very indignant at his going off to get married without consultation with me. I was so indignant that I got on the cars that night and went back to your house in a great state of wrath. My father started in the afternoon for New York. He went to Cazenovia to get married. His wife had formerly lived at Freeport, where she was in business as a milliner. She had gone to New York on a visit and my father went off in the afternoon without consultation with me. He left word at the office that he had gone off to get married, and I was very indignant about it. I thought it a very strange way of doing business.

Q. Were you in Freeport when he returned with his wife? A. Yes; I think I was. (Correcting himself). No; I think I was at your house. The night that I left Freeport when my father went to get married, I had not a cent of money, but I told them on the railroad who I was, and they allowed me to pass to Chicago.

Q. Do you recollect how long you attended school from your mother's death till your fathers' second marriage? A. That was all I did at Freeport after I got old enough. I think I attended school every winter from the time I was seven till the time I was twelve.

Q. How old were you when your father married the second wife? A. I was twelve years old.

Q. How long did you attend school after that, before you went to Bell's Commercial College? A. I don't think I attended school at all. My impression is that I was writing in my father's office for a year or two. I think I got uneasy at that and wanted to get an education. I made up my mind to go to Chicago and attend Bell's College, that was when I was about sixteen years old. My father was always opposed to my getting an education. He thought the great thing for me to do was to save my soul, and that the only way to save my soul was to go to the Oneida Community; that was his theory. The only way to save my soul or his was to go into that stinking Oneida Community. It makes me mad to think of it; the greatest outrage ever perpetrated on a boy was the act of my father in running me into that; I have never been able to forget it from that day to this. I would have gone to school and college, and to a law school if my father had been out of the way.

Q. When did this idea come to you of going to the Oneida Community? A. I drank it in right from my mother's womb, not actually, but spiritually. My mother was dead and my father was both father and mother to me. I drank in the fanaticism under his influence at Freeport. He used to talk it by day and by night; to sleep over it, to dream over it. He could not see any way to save his soul or mine except by getting into the Oneida Community.

Q. How long did you attend Bell's Commercial College? A. One winter. Then I went back to Freeport and went to work in my father's office. He was Clerk of the Circuit Court and recorded all the deeds in the county.

Q. How long did you work there? A. I worked there until I made up my mind to go and get an education, against my father's will; all that time I was fighting my father because he was opposed to my getting an education. He was so thoroughly bedeviled by Noyes and the Oneida Community that he could see nothing outside of them.

Q. Did you consult him about your going off? A. Yes, and we had a terrible noise about it. I wanted an education, and he thought that his duty was to save my soul. He was all the time upon my soul.

Q. What argument did he use in regard to saving your soul? A. He said that if I got to be the greatest man whoever lived and was not saved, it would count for naught in the end, and he was correct in that; that was his way of saving my soul.

Q. How? A. Running me into the Oneida Community as he did and keeping me there a slave, practically, for seven years. There is the greatest sympathy between that Community and Mormonism, and I hope that the United States Government will wipe out Mormonism, now that the Oneida Community is gone.

Q. Did you ever go to Ann Arbor to school? A. Yes, in September, 1859, when I was eighteen years of age. I went there contrary to my father's advice; I remember distinctly that I got sixty dollars from him on a Saturday afternoon to go with and, hit or miss, I was determined to go. He did everything he could to prevent my going, but as my guardian (pronouncing it "gardeen") he had control of one thousand dollars which my grandfather left me, and he gave me sixty dollars to go to Ann Arbor. As soon as I got there he began to fire letters at me; he used to write me two or three letters a week, each of them three or four pages long, telling me about Noyes and the Community, and that education would not be any good to me if I did not go to the Saviour. I drank it all in. It was the first religion I had.

Q. Did you have any works of the Oneida Community with you at Ann Arbor? A. Yes, my father sent me all the Community works.

Q. What were they? A. A book called the *Berean*, written and published by Noyes; another book called *The Bible Argument*, in which they advocated their social theory, and a paper called *The Circular*. Father sent it regular to me every week; he dosed me with that kind of stuff.

Q. Did you go on with your studies at Ann Arbor? A. Yes, I went on with my studies and kept reading those Oneida Community books up to twelve or one o'clock at night; there is where I ruined my eyes, and they have been weak from that time to this.

Q. What was the result of your studying there? A. The result was that I went to the Oneida Community. I left Ann Arbor in June, 1860. There was a man there named John Lord, a silk agent, he left Ann Arbor and met me at Niagara Falls. We were there a few hours, and went to Oneida that night.

Q. You met him by appointment? A. Yes, it was all fixed; he had been a member from his boyhood.

Q. Did you go direct to the Community? A. Yes, sir.

Q. When did you pay in your money? A. I should say in a few months after I went there; my father sent nine hundred dollars which he had held as my guardian; he sent a draft to the Community, and that is the way they got hold of it.

Q. You say that your father was to blame for your going to the Community; how so? A. If my father had been out of the way, I never would have gotten under the fanaticism.

Q. What was the fanaticism. A. I look upon the whole thing as the most distressing fanaticism ever concocted by the brain of man. * * * I was practically a Shaker all the time I was there. They held the theory that if a man left the Community he would be damned; I made up my mind that I was in hell anyway, and resolved to go, but as a matter of fact I went clandestinely.

Q. Did you believe that you would be damned if you left the Community? A. More than I do that I am alive; I had that belief all the time that I was there, and after I left the Community I was haunted by that old Noyes and his stinking fanaticism. It had such an influence over me that it was all I could do to keep from going back; so you may know the spiritual pressure upon me. I felt haunted and depressed for fear that I had lost my eternal salvation by leaving the Community. After I went to New York I got acquainted with the Young Men's Christian Association and joined Beecher's church and came gradually under new influences; my mind was awakened to the fanaticism of that hole, and the scales fell from my eyes. That is the way I got out of the place.

Q. Did Noyes have the theory of inspiration? A. Most decidedly; he claimed that his Community was the beginning of the kingdom of God upon earth; that he was God's partner, and that there was no way to be saved except through him. He thought he was greater than the Lord Jesus Christ.

Q. Did you believe it? A. I believed it decidedly at that time, and therein came his power over those people—by the infusion of the idea that there was one God, and Noyes was His partner.

Q. To come back to your boyhood; was there a river near Freeport? A. There was a little stream in which the boys used to go swimming. I don't recollect whether I went; very likely.

Q. Do you remember getting a blow on your head when a boy? A. Yes, I have the scar now.

Q. State how that happened? A. I was going up the street when a little fellow struck me on the head with a stone; I thought I was dead and made a noise about it. I have a scar on my head in which I can put my little finger about half an inch.

Q. Did any other person besides your father exercise over you the care of a guardian? A. No, sir; he had full charge of me.

Q. Did you have counsel or advice from any person else? A. No, sir; my stepmother and I never got along well together; she never cared much for me and I never cared much for her.

Q. When do you first remember your father's peculiarities about religion? A. I remember as a boy he used to think it wicked to go to church and Sunday-school; he thought he was so holy and good that it was not necessary.

Q. Did he think that of you? A. I presume so; I remember distinctly that I used to go to Methodist and Presbyterian churches. Being naturally of a religious turn of mind he did not think it at all necessary, and wanted to run me right into the Community.

Q. Did he have family prayers? No; he used to think it wicked to pray in the ordinary way.

Q. What did he substitute for it then? A. When we took a meal we would gather around a table and he would say: "I confess Jesus Christ in food; I thank God for John H. Noyes and the Oneida Community," making Noyes a substitute for the Lord Jesus Christ; that is the short of it.

Q. Do you recollect any of his expressions of faith in Christ? A. He was religious—nothing else; he used to do his work in a mechanical sort of way. The rest of the time his mind was on religion and the Community; he used to dream over it day and night.

Q. Did you ever hear him say anything about joining the Community? A. Oh, yes; he was anxious to go there; he would have gone there except for his wife; my mother would not allow her daughter to go there, and that rather offended old Noyes, and he would not allow my father to come.

Q. His wife would not go? A. No.

Q. Was that the cause of the difficulty betwen them? A. Very decidedly; they were at loggerheads all the time, for my father's heart was in the Community for twenty-five years and his body was in Freeport.

Q. Had your father any peculiar ideas about healing diseases? A. Oh, yes; he was cranky, terribly cranky, upon that.

Q. What makes you call him a crank? That is a short way to say that a man is very badly insane.

Q. What was there about his ideas or conduct that was peculiar? A. He used to say that he was in such perfect accord with the Saviour and the Deity, through faith and through the Oneida Community, that diseases were something entirely irrelevant to health spiritual, and that if a man was sick it was because the devil had got the start of him, and he prepared to resist the devil by Jesus Christ; if a member of his family was sick, he would go to the bed to excommunicate the devil by talk, prayer and so forth.

Q. Did you ever see him do it? A. I think I can recall the cases stated by Mr. North.

Q. How, in reference to your father's conduct, did he put those ideas in use in practical life? A. Oh, yes; he believed with the Oneida Community in making everything common——common property; that is their doctrine; if a man goes there with $10,000, he is not counted any better than a man with ten cents; money does not count anything at all there.

Q. Did your father carry out those notions of his? A. I think in 1859 he bought a farm in Freeport, and proposed to establish a branch Community at Freeport, and he wrote to Noyes, and Noyes and Burt went out there to see the propriety of establishing a branch Community on my father's farm.

Q. How was your father as to sincerity? A. He was a very conscientious man and a very honest man.

Q. As to intensity of belief or conception? A. He was very intense; he could not bear any adverse talk about the Community.

Q. Did you ever have any controversy with him

on that subject? A. I did prior to my becoming religious; I do not think I had religious sensibility until I was about seventeen and a half; I went to Ann Harbor when I was eighteen; prior to that I used to think he was crazy; I did not believe in his religion or any religion prior to my conversion—"conversion" is the word they used; that conversion was some time in 1859; prior to that I had been rather worldly like most boys of my age.

Q. When did that conversion culminate? A. I was gradually lending myself to my father's spirit, and under the influence of that spirit I got into the Oneida Community.

Q. Did you ever adopt your father's belief as to healing diseases by the effect of faith? A. I did somewhat; I remember some of the time when I was in Oneida I was sick and had a headache; I used to say to the devil: "Go away from me old devil."

Q. Did you do that in fun? A. Dead earnest; you may be sure of that; dead earnest; many people do not believe in doctors; they (referring to the Oneida Communists) say a man is sick because he is possessed of the devil, and that if they excommunicate the devil, the man will be restored to health.

Q. Did you believe that? A. Decidedly.

Q. When did you get over that idea? A. By the time I got my eyes open from the other ideas; when I got under the influence of the Young Men's Christian Association and Beecher's Church; Beecher was supposed to be a virtuous man at that time; I do not know anything about him now, except what I said the other day.

At this point a recess was taken.

After recess the prisoner resumed his life history by stating that he left the Oneida Community in 1865 and went to New York, where he had paid five dollars a week for a room over a bakery. He had got thoroughly disgusted living in Oneida. He made up his mind he was in hell. and that if he ever got in another place he would have a respite. He had gradually become dissatisfied with the whole business—social, spiritually and everything else. He went to New York intending to establish a great theocratic paper. The letters which had been read indicated the condition of his mind very well. He consulted with printers and editors and reporters and those kind of people, and they had discouraged him. He proposed to call the paper *The Theocrat*, and one of those wise newspaper fellows thought that that was enough to damage the paper, so he gradually abandoned the idea. In August of the same year he went back to the Community. He was haunted day and night by the idea that perhaps he had missed his eternal salvation; he could not get any relief, and he went back to the Community.

Q. Did you get relief there? A. Yes, I could not get it in any other way.

The prisoner went on to relate, in reply to questions by Mr. Scoville, how he came to be admitted to the Bar. He said that he read law for three or four months in the office of Mr. R. Reynolds, in Milwaukee, and that then Mr. Reynolds told him to go and see Charlie Reed, the District Attorney of Chicago. He went to see Reed, who took up a sheet of paper and began to write something like this:

"We hereby certify that Charles J. Guiteau has been examined by us and we consider him qualified to practice law in the Supreme Court in the State of Illinois."

Then Reed said to him: "Take this paper to Judge Williams, the Judge of the District Court, and you will be admitted on your getting a certificate of good moral character." He went to Judge Williams, who signed the paper as a matter of course. "That is the way," added the prisoner, "that I was admitted to practice. I made three thousand dollars the first year in Chicago and two thousand dollars the second year."

Q. Did Mr. Reed ask you any questions? A. He asked three or four questions, and I think I answered all of them, possibly I may have missed one.

Q. When you opened your law office in Chicago, what did you do? A. I went around among business men—high-toned business men—and I got business from first class merchants. I would go up to a man and show him my card and references (I had always good references), and that is the way that I got business—on my references and my appearance. If a merchant said to me, "Call in again and I will look up my accounts," I would follow that man right up until I actually got his business. That is the way that I got business in New York and Chicago. The prisoner then related his experience in practising law in New York from 1871 to 1875, and said that if he had not been troubled with the *New York Herald* and had let theology alone he would have done well. He made one thousand five hundred dollars there the first year and two thousand five hundred the second year. Then he had that trouble with the *Herald* and had got run down and demoralized. He had gone to a hotel one rainy night and had been arrested by an impudent detective, who took him to the Police Station. He was in the Tombs about thirty days at that time, when Mr. Scoville went to District Attorney Phelps and got him off. He felt immensely relieved at getting out of that terrible place. He was five days in Jefferson Market and thirty days in the Tombs, and he was during that time deserted by all his supposed friends – lawyers who ought to be ashamed of themselves for their desertion of him; that was the unhappiest streak of luck he had ever struck in his life.

At Jefferson Market he was put in a miserable dark hole with three or four of the lowest class of New York bummers—fellows whom it would make one sick to look at. He thought that the keeper did it out of spite because he was a decent and well dressed man. After he was released from the Tombs he went and got some articles of attire and put himself for two hours in a bath-tub of boiling hot water.

A day or two after that he went to Chicago and opened a law office and did well. He always could do well at the law business if he stuck to it. That was about the 1st of February, 1875, and he settled right down at the law business and did well until the following September. Then he got the idea into his head of getting hold of the *Chicago Inter-Ocean* and he went to wrestling with the idea for two or three months. The stock of the *Inter-Ocean* was very low at that time. The proprietors had sunk all the money they could raise. He presumed that the paper had then cost them about $200,000 or $300,000, and he thought that the proprietors would be glad to get rid of it for $75,000. He consulted some of his wealthy friends (or supposed friends), but they thought it was not advisable to go into the newspaper business then. After exhausting himself three or four months on that he gave it up.

Q. What do you mean by exhausting yourself?
A. I stuck to it, as I always do to an idea, until

GUITEAU, THE ASSASSIN. 293

I got exhausted physically, morally, and financially. I had used my friends as far as I could, and had to go to work to make a new start in the law business in Chicago.

Q. What was your idea in buying the *Inter-Ocean?* A. I proposed to make it the great newspaper organ of the West; I proposed to put into it the advertising patronage of the *Chicago Tribune*, the Republicanism of Horace Greely and the enterprise and snap of James Gordon Bennett. I suggested it to some first class newspaper men and they said that it was a brilliant idea and they thought it feasible. If I had got hold of the money it would have been feasible.

Q. How much money did you want? A. I believe that seventy-five thousand dollars would have bought up the whole concern. I consulted several parties about it, and they all thought it a grand scheme, but would not put money into it, and so it fell through. Among others I applied to Mr. Adams, President of the Second National Bank of Freeport, supposed to be worth five-hundred thousand dollars.

Q. Did you offer him any inducement? A. Yes, I told him I would make him Governor of Illinois, and he said he did not want to be Governor. He had been State Senator and was a man of reputation and character, but he did not pan out very well after my interview with him.

Q. What do you mean by his not panning out?

A. He did not have any political aspirations. I wanted to get hold of those fellows who had both aspirations and money; they were the kind of fellows to help me. Adams did not have political aspirations; he did not seem to care anything about being Governor; he was a man about sixty years old, and he preferred his old simple way of living, and did not care to go into politics. I also consulted my old friend, Charles Reed on the subject; I believe that he put twenty-five dollars into it, which he has not got back yet. I went to theology after that, and that was worse than the newspaper business.

Q. Did you have at any time an idea of publishing the *New York Herald* simultaneously in Chicago? A. That was part of the *Inter-Ocean* scheme. Mr. Nixon was then proprietor of the *Inter-Ocean*, and my idea was, in starting the new concern, that Nixon was to be the manager and financier, and I was to be the editor. I gave him some ideas about duplicating the despatches of the *New York Herald* which I notice since he has realized.

Q. Did you take any steps for securing a building to carry on the new paper? A. Yes, I went to look at a building on Fifth Avenue which I thought would be a good one. I inquired who owned it, what it would rent for, etc.

Q. Did you take any steps to obtain printing presses? A. I consulted Hoe's agent at Chicago.

Q. How many presses did you arrange for? A. I cannot recollect the details; I went through all that business and worked it out in detail in my own mind. I went around among newspaper men, pressmen, etc.

Q. Did you arrange for telegraph despatches? A. I consulted the manager of the Western Union Telegraph Company and also the manager of the Atlantic and Pacific Telegraph Company. The Atlantic and Pacific was just starting at that time, and its manager was an active young fellow who wanted to get business. I said that I proposed to duplicate the *New York Herald* despatches, and he said he thought it an immense thing—and so it was.

Q. Did you have any plan in your mind for obtaining the *Herald* despatches? A. I wrote to James Gordon Bennett at the time. I got no answer, and I believe he was then in Europe.

Q. What inducements did you hold out to Mr. Bennett to furnish the despatches? A. Nothing very persuading. I think I told him that if he would help me out in the matter, I would consider the *Herald* suit at an end.

Q. Did you consider that a fair equivalent? A. Yes, because I had no doubt that I would recover ten or fifteen thousand dollars.

Q. After you gave up the newspaper enterprise in Chicago what did you next do? A. That brought me down to the winter and spring of 1876. I tried to pick up law business again, which I had neglected, but law business was scarce and I found it hard to get any. Then I went out to your place in Wisconsin. I worked around the house, studied theology and the New Testament, read the papers, soaped trees, and all that kind of thing.

Q. Do you remember the circumstances of your soaping trees? A. Yes, I remember my sister advising me to go down one morning and soap some fruit trees, but I could not tell fruit trees from other trees; I am not a horticulturist or farmer. I remember her laughing at the time.

In October, 1876, I was in Chicago during the Moody and Sankey meetings. I attended prayer meetings and services regularly day and night during the three months that Moody was there, from October to January; during all that time I was with Moody, and bore an active part.

Q. What did you do? A. I was an usher and helped around in a general way.

Q. Did you speak at prayer meetings? A. Yes, frequently.

Q. To what particular branch or subject of religion was your mind directed at that time? A. Some time in November, during the Moody work, I heard Dr. Kittredge, of Chicago, pastor of the Third Presbyterian Church, say in reference to the text: "If I will that he (meaning John) tarry till I come, what is that to thee?" Brethren, I have to confess, as a man of God, that I do not know what that means." At that time there was considerable expectation in the public mind that the Saviour might soon appear, and that idea has pervaded people's minds ever since; that set my brain awhirling, and I began to investigate it. I went to work in the Chicago Public Library and I dug out my lecture on the "Second Coming." As the result of that investigation I went to work and wrote my lecture. The idea of that lecture is briefly this: That the second coming of Christ occurred on the destruction of Jerusalem, in the clouds directly over Jerusalem, that it was an event in the spiritual world, and that the destruction of Jerusalem was the outward sign of His coming; I hold that for all these eighteen centuries the churches have all been in error in supposing the second coming of Christ to be in the future. That is the proposition on which my lecture was written, and that was the result of three or four years investigation on that subject. The witness then went on to relate his various failures in delivering his lecture in Chicago, Evanston, Racine, Kalamazoo, Ann Arbor, Detroit, Ypsilanti, Toledo, Cleveland, Buffalo, Washington, Rochester, Syracuse, Albany, Troy and elsewhere. He frequently laughed as he repeated some of the humorous incidents of his failures, the various times that he was put off railroad cars for not paying his fare, and arrested for not paying his board bills. At other times he grew excited in the assertion, that in all he did, he was, like St. Paul, engaged in the service of God, and that God was therefore responsible for his board bills. On this latter point he said: "I did not give up lecturing because of my repeated failures; I stuck to my work; my idea was that, as I was working for the Lord I would do my duty, and let Him take care of me as He felt disposed; I went into that whole business to serve the Lord, not to make money; success or failure was nothing to me; I considered that the Lord's affair; my duty was to continue with my work; Paul had no success, because he had new ideas on theology; I kept thinking of Paul all the time, and how he stuck to his theology all the time. On my way from Baltimore to Washington, I avoided the conductor who had ordered me to get off at the Relay House, and so managed to get on to Washington. The strangest thing about it was that after I had changed my seat, a man came alone to me and said: "My friend, are you going to Washington?" I said, "Yes;" he said, "Would you like a good boarding-house?" I said: "Yes;" and he said he could take me to one. Now I had been praying that I could get a boarding-house, as I did not want to go to a hotel, and I had no sooner got the prayer out than this man came along, and was just as free and easy with me as if he had known me twenty-years; now, that I call providence; I have had hundreds of that kind of experiences where the Lord, in direct anwers to prayer, has befriended me.

While the prisoner was giving his testimony he was watched most attentively by all the medical experts present, and with great curiosity and interest by every person in the crowded court room. At times he showed his exhaustion by a lowering of his voice, and it was in consequence of one of these signs that, some ten minutes before the usual time of adjournment, the Court, at the instance of the District Attorney, adjourned.

CHAPTER XV.

Guiteau Still on the Witness Stand—He Details his Applications for Office—His Book "Truth" and His Lectures on the "Second Coming"—His Aspirations for the Presidency of the United States.

THE crush on Wednesday, November 30th, fully equalled that of the previous day. The prisoner was brought into Court shortly after ten o'clock, and after the removal of his handcuffs led at once to the witness stand.

Mr. Scoville first called upon him to identify a blue advertising bill, announcing that Charles Guiteau would lecture on the "Second Coming of Christ," and the prisoner smiled pleasantly as he recognized it to be one which he had distributed in Evanston, in June, 1877. He also identified a handbill calling attention to his book "Truth." These papers were put in evidence, but were not read.

His regular examination was then proceeded with by Mr. Scoville, as follows:

Q. Was there any theory of belief in the Oneida Community as to inspiration? A. Most decidedly, that was the foundation of it. They claimed that no man could go into the Community unless he was specially sent there by the

Lord. If he endured the discipline, that was an indication that he was God's chosen man; if he left, they looked upon him as a child of the devil, and as forever cut off from salvation.

Q. Was there any theory of a special inspiration in any individual? A. Oh, yes. Noyes claimed inspiration in all that he taught and all that he spoke.

Q. State fully if there was any prevailing opinions at the Oneida Community as to the special inspiration of any individual, what that opinion was? A. They looked upon Noyes as God's Prophet on earth, and everything was under his active control in the Community. He ruled the body and soul and property of every man in the Community. He had absolute control in every department of life and thought.

Q. What was your belief on that subject when you first went there? A. I was entirely in sympathy with Noyes and the Community on that point. I drank it all in through my father. It was just about then that I began to get my first impression about a religious life. My father stood right behind me and pushed me into that belief.

Q. State what books you were in the habit of reading before you went to the Oneida Community? A. I used to read physiological works at that time, as Hall's "*Journal of Health*" and the writings of such reformers. I used to take it all in. Then I read theological works.

Q. What were you in the habit of reading at the Community? A. History, Theology and the Bible.

Q. What history? A. French history. I drank it all up. I used to read the *New York Tribune* and *Independent* and *Harper's Weekly*. My reading was promiscuous.

The prisoner seemed to be less precise and accurate about dates and more flurried generally, than on any previous day of the trial. Upon Mr. Scoville's calling his attention to the incident of his throwing a little dog down stairs while on his visit to Wisconsin, the prisoner stated that he was carrying the dog and that it slipped out of his hands and fell down stairs. That, said he, is all there is about it. But I had better go on and talk about my experience in Boston four years ago and where we left off last. I want to give a clear and graphic account of my career for four years. It takes in theology and politics and the cause for which I am now under trial."

He then proceeded to give an account of his lecturing tour through the country. He had gone to Boston in 1868—" I mean in 1878," he interjected; "I don't feel well to-day"—intending to lecture against Ingersoll. The latter was announced to lecture against "Hell," and drew an immense crowd. Many people were willing to pay fifty cents to hear that there were no hell, but did not like to hear that there was one. The witness advocated the existence of hell and heaven. That was his idea. He delivered his discourse with a good deal of energy, but there were only about a dozen persons present. In February, 1878, he went around the streets of Boston and sold his lecture. He then went to lecture in Worcester, Hartford, Newark and New Haven, but failed as usual. About the first of April he got thoroughly sick and tired and disgusted with the whole business, and he got his lectures printed in Philadelphia and started West. He used to go around among the merchants selling his lecture. If he could not sell a lecture he generally set them thinking that there was a heaven and a hell and that they were in danger of losing their souls. In 1873 he started a law office in Milwaukee, but he soon got restless and uneasy and went to St. Louis. He went about thinking that he was making a mistake. He felt haunted and oppressed with the feeling that he had to preach the Gospel as he understood it, and nobody went to hear him, and he had no money nor friends, and generally had a hard time. He then started lecturing again, but had no success, and detailed the story of his failure with a good deal of earnestness and humor. In Boston he got out his book, "*Truth, a Companion to the Bible.*"

Mr. Scoville produced a copy of the book, which was identified by the prisoner, who expressed his desire to read certain portions of it. To this, however, objection was made by the prosecution, but on Mr. Scoville stating that such paragraphs as were read by the prisoner, he would not read when the book was put in evidence, the objection was withdrawn. The witness read but one paragraph, relative to the trials and troubles of the Apostle Paul. And when he had concluded he compared his own misfortune to them, stating that the Apostle Paul had done the very thing that he had tried to do. I claimed, he said, that I had new light on theology. My views were offensive to Christian people, as Paul's were to the Jews. I travelled around the country on my own account, without money or friends, and had a hard time—about as hard a time as Paul had. He stated that he sent his book to leading ministers and advertised it extensively, and yet it fell perfectly flat and he did not sell fifty copies.

That brings us down to January 1st, 1880, continued the witness. I had no money but got on the best way I could, and made up my mind that I would go into politics. (At the word "politics" the audience, which had been listening in a listless way, became suddenly silent and paid the strictest attention as the prisoner rapidly and with a great deal of gesticulating related his subsequent history.)

I had a great interest in General Grant's nomination. The Chicago Convention came on and I watched the proceedings with great interest. Finally General Garfield was nominated. I was in Boston at that time, but decided that I would go to New York and offer my services to the National Committee and take an active part in the election of General Garfield. I left Boston on the 11th of June. I was on the Stonington when she struck the Narragansett and I thought my time had come then, but it haden't.

The witness at this point gave quite a graphic account of the collision, describing the relative positions of the two boats, the burning of the Narragansett and the wailings and prayers of her unfortunate passengers.

Continuing he said: I was in New York about two weeks. I had my speech, "Garfield Against Hancock," in manuscript.

Q. Where did you write that? A. It started out to be a speech on General Grant. I wrote it prior to the Chicago Convention, supposing that he would be nominated, and as a matter of fact I had to write it over to make it fit General Garfield. It was written in the State Library in Boston.

Q. How long were you at work upon that speech? A. A couple of days. The speech as originally prepared was quite a different affair, because things about General Grant would not be proper to put into a Garfield speech. I remodelled most of it in New York. I called upon

General Arthur at his house two or three times, but he was not at home. I called upon him at his office in relation to that speech and to my taking part in the campaign. That was five or six weeks before my speech was printed. I went to Poughkeepsie and advertised the speech, but it did not draw. I did not deliver it because no one came, on account of the rain I suppose. I went to Saratoga and tried to deliver it there, but no one came as usual. I came back and saw General Arthur and other prominent men at the Fifth Avenue Hotel. Of course they knew me and were glad to see me and all that. A conference was held on the 6th of August at the Fifth Avenue Hotel. It was a conference of the "Stalwart" element of the Republican party, though all were invited. Grant and Conkling and Arthur and that kind of men were in the convention. I sent my speech, which was printed on the 5th of August, to all men connected with the conferrence, also to the leading editors of New York.

Q. Did you get any assignment to speak? A. I was only actually assigned once, some time in August.

Q. What place was that? A. I think in Twenty-fifth Street, at a colored meeting.

Q. What was the result there? A. I delivered part of the speech and gave the newspaper men the rest. I did not exactly like the crowd; it was a hot, sultry night, but I did not thank them for putting me out doors. I was put on as the first speaker, but I only spoke a few minutes. There were no demonstrations, except that they applauded when they thought I made a good point. I was in and around the National Headquarters on Fifth Avenue almost every day and night, except Sunday (they close up on Sunday; they were religious men like myself) from the first of August to the first of November.

Q. Did you apply to any other committee? A. I consulted with Jewell and Arthur, and they were perfectly friendly. The trouble was simply this:—The committee wanted men of reputation, like General Grant and Senator Conkling; no matter how much brains a man had, unless he had reputation they would not choose him. My intercourse with those gentlemen was always friendly and delightful; they treated me well, and seemed to think I was a good fellow. I was, so to speak, on free and easy terms with them.

Q. What did you do with your speech? A. My zeal for the success of General Garfield was so strong that I printed it at my own expense and sent it to public men.

Q. Did you send a copy of it to General Garfield? A. Yes; at that time he attended a conference at the Fifth Avenue Hotel; he and General Logan, and General Arthur, and that sort of men; I afterwards saw them, and as soon as I mentioned my name they pricked up their ears and said, "Oh! yes, that is a very good speech of yours." That was their general comment. That is the only thing I had to recommend me to them, but they liked the ring and tone of that speech, and as soon as I called their attention to it they remembered it. After the October elections I wrote to General Garfield at Mentor and sent him my speech. I called his attention to the fact that probably I might marry a wealthy lady in New York some time during the ensuing spring, and that I thought we could represent the United States at Vienna with dignity and grace. I let that matter drop until the first of January, when I called his attention to it again. After Mr. Blaine was appointed Secretary of State I knew I had no chance of getting the Austrian mission, because it would go to a Blaine man and I was a Stalwart. I called on General Garfield on the first week after the inauguration. He was in conversation with several politicians. I especially remember Minister Morton, who knew me and cordially received me. As soon as General Garfield was at leisure I stepped up and gave him my speech. Of course he recognized me at once. I marked my name for the Paris Consulship at the end of it, and I told him I was an applicant for that position. That was the only interview with him on the subject. I wish to say emphatically on the threshold of my examination, that my getting office or not getting office had nothing to do with my attempt to remove the President. That was a political necessity under Divine pressure.

Q. When did you cease to make application for the Austrian mission? A. As soon as I ascertained that Mr. Blaine had been appointed Secretary of State. I was in good standing with Garfield and Blaine; both were very clever with me. My first interview with Mr. Blaine was in the elevator at the State Department; I gave him my speech. He knew my name better than he did my person; I knew there was no use in pressing my name until the deadlock in the Senate was broken.

The witness, after getting through with the subject of the Senate deadlock, was next inquired of as to his interview with Secretary Blaine. He said that he saw the Secretary personally five or six times and sent five or six notes on the subject. The Secretary generally gave a public reception at twelve o'clock to the fifty or seventy-five persons in waiting to see him, and would go from one to the other, with a private whisper to each. The witness took his turn and waited and waited, but sometimes he did not care to do that and would write a note telling the Secretary what he wanted. His last interview with Mr. Blaine occured about the twenty-fifth of April, when Mr. Blaine said to him rather abruptly :— ' Never speak to me again on the subject of the Paris Consulship." That hurt his feelings in view of Mr. Blaine's former kindness and pleasant attentions and pleasant talk. He (the witness) then said:—"I think I can get the President to remove Mr. Walker, and I am going to see the President about it."

"Well," said Mr. Blaine, "I do not think he will, but if he will—" as much as to say that if the President wants to remove Walker I will not interfere with him. That was the way he (the witness) understood it. He had no conversation with Mr. Blaine on the subject after that.

Q. After that did you make any further application to the President himself? A. Yes. I devoted my attention to the President for several days. I never had any personal interview with him after that. I called there frequently, and would find fifty or a hundred persons hanging around, so I used to write little notes to the President. I said in one of these notes: "Can I have the Paris Consulship?" I asked the doorkeeper who knew me from seeing me frequently, to take the note to the General, as we always called him, and after some twenty minutes he brought me back an answer from the Private Secretary, like this: "Mr. Guiteau, the President says it will be impossible for him to see you to-day." I understood by the word "to-day," that the President was entertaining the proposition to remove Walker, and that as soon as he got Walker out of the way gracefully, I would be given the office; that is the way the matter stood from that day to this. They never told me that I could not get the office, but so far as getting or not getting the Paris Consulship or any other office is concerned, it had nothing whatever to do with my inspiration. (Raising his voice and speaking excitedly as he thumped the railing in front of him.) That was purely a religious necessity, done under Divine pressure for the good of the American people.

Q. When did you cease to press the President in reference to the Paris Consulship? A. I should say abont the 1st of May.

Q. What next took your attention in connection with politics? A. The political situation kept getting bitterer and bitterer and I got worried.

Q. What worried you? A. The fact that the President and General Grant and Senator Conkling were at loggerheads over the Robertson matter and other matters. I kept reading the papers and reading the papers and feeling in great distress about the whole matter, I wrote several notes to the President, in which I told him he should do something to arrange things, and that if he did not the Republican Party would go to wreck and ruin, and there would be trouble in this country. He never answered the notes at all.

Q. Was that your real opinion? A. Most decidedly.

Q. After you gave up applying for the office, what employed your mind mostly? A. I was thinking about the political situation more than anything else. I kept reading the papers and kept being worried and perplexed and in a great state of mind about the future of the country. I think that that was the prevailing thought in my mind after I saw the President and General Grant and that kind of men who were wrestling and at loggerheads. I saw this nation was going to wreck, (emphasizing the sentence with a bang on the railing).

Q. Did you find anything to confirm that opinion? A. Yes. The papers talked a good deal about General Garfield at that time. The newspaper articles confirmed my impression and what I saw occurring between General Garfield and Mr. Blaine.

Q. You have spoken of inspiration. What do you mean by that? State when it came first to your mind and the circumstances connected with it? A. Inspiration, as I understand it, is where a man's mind is taken possession of by—by—by a superior power, and where he acts outside of his own natural—outside of himself.

Q. I wish to call your attention to the time and circumstances when this inspiration came to your mind. A. It came to me one Wednesday evening, the evening Senators Platt and Conkling resigned. At this time there was great excitement in the public mind in regard to the resignation, and I felt greatly perplexed and worried about it. I retired about eight o'clock that evening, greatly depressed in mind and spirit over the political situation. Before I went to sleep the impression came on my mind like a flash that if the President were out of the way the difficulty would be all solved. The next morning I had the same impression. I kept reading the papers and had my mind on the idea of the removal of the President. This idea kept working me and working me and grinding and oppressing me for about two weeks. All this time I was horrified and I kept throwing off the idea and did not want to give it any attention at all; in fact, I shook it off, but it kept growing on me and growing on me until at the end of two weeks my mind was thoroughly fixed as to the necessity of the President's removal. As to the Divinity of the inspiration (excitedly) I had not the slightest doubt about the Divinity of the inspiration from the 1st of June to the present moment. I felt just as confident as to the Divinity of the inspiration as I do now.

Q. After the idea took full possession of your mind about the 1st of June, what did you do with reference to that subject? A. I kept praying about and praying about and praying about.

Q. What was the substance of your prayer? A. The substance of my prayer was that if it was the Lord's will I should not remove the President, He should in some way by his providence interrupt it; that is always the way I have found the Lord. When I feel a pressure upon me to do anything and when I feel doubt about it, I keep praying to the Deity that He may show it in some way if I am wrong.

Q. Did you get any information from the Deity as to whether you were right or wrong, in answer to your prayer? A. (in a loud voice and excited manner)—I never had the slightest shadow of doubt on my mind as to the divinity of the act and as to the necessity of it to the great American people (with a bang on the railing).

Q. Wherein did it seem to you necessary for the good of the American people? A. To unite the factions of the Republican Party, which were then in a most bitter and deplorable state.

Q. Did you consider that necessary to the good of the American people? A. Most decidedly.

Q. Why? A. Because in the way that things were going last spring another war was going to break out.

Q. How would that result be reached? A. It would be reached by the destruction of the Republican Party.

Q. State how it was necessary in order to avoid war that the breach in the Republican Party should be healed. A. I stated that very clearly in the *Herald* interview. The idea was if the disruption of the Republican Party was to continue as it was going on last spring the Democrats would have taken entire possession of the Government and by the mismanagement of finances would precipitate the country into another war. That was the central idea that was talked of in the National Republican Committee and on the stump, and by all the leading Republican papers in the canvass, that the safety of the Republic depended upon the Republican Party continuing in control. That the Democratic Party and the Rebel element were not yet sufficiently civilized to take possession of the national finances. That main idea was put into all the stump speeches and into all the newspapers.

Q. Did you believe it? A. Most emphatically. More than I believe that I am alive. That is the point made in my speech, "Garfield against Hancock," and in all Republican speeches on the stump, that the perpetuity of the Republic depended on the Republican Party keeping control of the Government.

Q. How did you occupy your time mostly from the 1st of June to the 2d of July last? A. I was making my preparations to attempt the removal of the President by preparing a revised edition of my book. I was reading the newspapers and having my inspiration confirmed almost every day by the way that the newspapers were denouncing the President.

Q. Where did you live during that time? A. I lived in a first-class boarding-house in Washington; I had good clothes, too, and was in very easy circumstances. There was no anxiety about money or circumstances. I spent my time at the Arlington, the Riggs House and the Treasury Department, reading the newspapers, praying about the matter, praying the Lord if the inspiration was not from Him, or if there was any mistake about the inspiration to stop it by His providence. That was the burden on my mind all the time—the six weeks after I conceived the idea.

Q. Did you have conversation with any one on other subjects during that time? A. Not much. I am not in the habit of talking about my business to any one. I keep my mouth very tight. My only thought was (again growing excited) to execute the Divine will; after making sure that it was the Divine will, that was the only burden on my mind.

The prisoner was then inquired of in regard to his interviews in the jail with medical experts, detectives and the District Attorney and his stenographer, who represented himself as a *Herald* reporter. As he was showing signs of fatigue, and said he was not well, having had too much Thanksgiving, and that he always felt better after dinner, a recess for an hour was taken.

After the recess, the prisoner again took the stand, and was questioned by Mr. Scoville as to his experience with special providences.

The witness.—"I have always believed in special providences; there are four distinct times in my life when I claim special inspiration—first, when I went to the Oneida Community; second, when I left the Community to go to New York to establish a theocratic paper to be the organ of the Deity in this world; third, when I left a good law business in Chicago to go out lecturing and working for the Lord; the fourth time, I claim special Divine authority when I attempted to remove the President. These are the four distinct times when I claim inspiration."

Q. I mean a special Providence for your protection? A. I had abundant evidence of the Lord's protection all the time I was on theology lecturing around the country. Two or three times I came near meeting serious accidents, but the Lord spared me. Since I have been in jail I have been shot at three times and missed.

Q. On what special occasion before you were arrested were you protected by special Providence? A. I think the preservation of my life at Newark was one, when I jumped from the train which was going thirty-five miles an hour; another, was when I was on the Stonington, when we were all in momentary expectation of going down. I remember praying to the Lord that He might spare my life, but I felt perfectly willing to leave it to the Lord. I felt happy that I had been a faithful servant of His by trying to preach the Gospel.

I remember that I thought that if my time had come I could go with a good heart. Since my arrest it has been my constant feeling all the way through. When I was shot at and missed, and when last summer, a mob was howling for me, I had no anxiety for myself and (excitedly) I have no anxiety as to the result of this trial. (To Mr. Scoville, who attempted to interrupt him)—Don't interrupt me. I feel that the whole matter is with the Lord and I am willing to leave it with Him.

Q. When you talk about a mob to what time do you refer? A. Last summer at one time everybody wanted to shoot me or hang me; it didn't disturb my equilibrium any. I thought that the Government and the Lord would take care of me. I want to say right here that my idea is this: the first thing is that the Deity will protect me; my idea is that He is using these men—soldiers, jury, experts, counsel and Court—to serve Him and protect me; that is my theory about Divine protection. The Lord is no fool, and when He has anything to do He uses the best means He can to carry out His purpose. I say He is using all these men to serve Him and protect me.

During all this speech the prisoner showed much excitement, and pounded the rail of the witness stand vigorously with his hand, while he spoke with great rapidity of utterance.

Q. What was the first instance of Divine interposition after you went to jail? A. When that keeper attempted to shoot me and put his pistol within eight inches of my head; he denied the whole thing, but I am satisfied that I am right. General Crocker said it was all a mistake and he hushed it up. I do not care to discuss it, but the fact is that man came into my cell deliberately to shoot me, and the only reason he did not is that I happened to be awake.

The witness here described in detail the manner in which he had seized the keeper and pinioned his arms. The special Providence here was that the man had ten or twelve seconds in which to fire but that the Lord stopped him.

Q. What was the next interposition? A. I claim a certain interposition when Mason fired at me. Witness then described this incident at length; he was standing in a cramped position; if he had been standing up the ball would have gone through his heart, just what Mason aimed for.

Q. Do you consider any thing providential in that? A. Decidedly providential that I was in a cramped position at that moment.

Q. Has there been any special providence since? A. I think Jones' failure to shoot me was providential. I was standing directly behind the driver of the van; I was in a quiet happy frame of mind; I had a fine jury and was pleased with the Court, and I was pleased with the way everything was going; I was praising the Lord for all this. Just as we got to the Capitol I saw a flash, and in a moment I saw another, and then the horses began to run away. I thought that my guard was killed and that the horses were running away. I said to my guard, "Ed, are you shot?" "No," said he, "are you?" The Providence was that the ball struck me here (pointing to his torn coat sleeve). It did not strike my arm, but the concussion made my arm sore. If it had gone two or three inches to the right it would have gone through my heart; it was a good shot, considering the fact that the van was going and that he was moving, I should say it was an exceedingly good shot; the Lord saved me from that. I would say in relation to this whole business that the Lord inspired the removal of the President; that he has taken care of me so far and He will continue to do so. If I had not the absolute certainty that the Deity inspired the act, I never should have shot the President.

Q. Had you any ill feeling against the President? A. Decidedly not. I considered him as my political and personal friend. I never had the slightest ill towards General Garfield in any shape. I simply executed what I considered the Divine will for the good of the American people, to unite the two factions of the Republican Party and thus prevent another war. (This speech was delivered in a rapid and wild manner, the prisoner pounding excitedly on the rail of the witness stand, and raising his voice as he proceeded.) My opinion, he contined, has never changed as to the necessity of the act. I undertake to say that the people of this country, when they know that another war has been prevented, instead of saying "Guiteau, the assassin," will some day say "Guiteau, the patriot."

Q. Were you easy in your mind? A. I was under a great pressure, and that is why I looked gaunt and thin. I could not eat well; I was ground and ground, and pressed and pressed, and I could get no relief until it was actually done. I felt greatly relieved when the thing was over; I felt happy, I had not been so happy for weeks, as I did when I was in the cell on the 2d of July, and I thanked God that it was all over.

Q. When you sent your first letter to General Garfield in regard to the Austrian mission, did you send any recommendation? A. No, sir, I never filed any formal application for the Austrian mission.

Q. Did you expect to get it without recommendation? A. I had an idea that I was in pretty good standing with Garfield and Blaine and Logan and that sort of men, and I expected to get it on account of my personal standing. These offices are distributed more on account of personal relations with the President and Secretary of State than on recommendations. If you had a bushel of recommendations and were not in with these men you would not get it. They were perfectly free and easy with me. If I had been a Governor or Senator or ex-President they could not have treated me better than they did. I used to address them with the utmost freedom.

Q. Have you supposed since you have been in jail that you have influence with President Arthur? A. I have not had any occasion to test it. He was my friend last spring and fall.

Q. Have you written any letter to him? A. I have addressed several letters to him. I don't know whether they were delivered or not. From the way I have been treated in other matters, I suppose not.

Q. Do you recollect a conversation with me in the jail about a month ago in which the subject came up of the removal of the District Attorney here?

The District Attorney.—"I recognize the fact Your Honor, that it is extremely difficult to keep this examination within legal and proper bounds, but this man is a witness in his own case, and is entitled to the same consideration as any other witness and to no more. There is no rule of evidence that will allow him to repeat a conversation he may have had with his attorney in the jail.

The Court.—"I think not."

The witness (breaking in).—"I presume Arthur is my friend, but I have never asked any favor of him since I got into this trouble, though I made him through my inspiration.

Q. How? A. (apparently amazed). Why my inspiration made him.

The District Attorney.—"This kind of interrogatory is very objectionable."

The witness.—"I have nothing more to say on this subject, but I wanted to define my position, that I have not asked any favors from President Arthur and probably shall not."

HIS PRESIDENTIAL ASPIRATIONS.

Q. Had you any political reasons for not pressing your suit against the *Herald?* A. Yes, but they are rather remote. I have had an idea in my head for twenty years that I should be President of the United States. I suppose people think that I have been badly cranked about that. I had the idea in the Oneida Community. I went to Boston with the distinct feeling that I was on the way to the White House, and I shall make it yet.

A laugh spread through the audience at this prediction, but to judge from the prisoner's manner and tone, he was decidedly earnest in his belief. "If I am ever President," continued the witness, "it will be by the act of God. I shall get the nomination as Lincoln and Garfield did, and I shall be elected as they were. I anticipate a decided change of public opinon as regards me."

The Court.—"Mr. Scoville, confine the witness to the narrative, if you please."

Q. Did your abandoning the claim against the *Herald* have anything to do with political inspiration? A. The idea has been in my head for twenty years that I would be President, and I didn't want to get the *Herald* down on me. That is one of the reasons I did not press my suit against it. The *Herald* had always been mad at me, and it might do harm to my candidacy for the Presidency. I did not want to get it down on me, so I let the matter drop. I don't care now a snap of my fingers about being President. I don't care anything about it. I don't know that I should take it now if I were actually nominated and elected, but I have had the idea in my head, all the same, for twenty years.

Q. Had you any purpose or object in selling your book in connection with the removal of the President. A. No, sir, no sir.

Q. Did you offer your revised edition of "*The Truth*" for publication in the *New York Herald*? A. Yes, sir; the object was to get my views before the American people. There is no money in that business in any way, shape or manner, and never has been. When Colonel Corkhill came to me in July and talked of some great lot of money and about some great men backing me with money, and all that kind of nonsense, I told him about my circumstances and convinced him that I had no money.

This closed the prisoner's direct testimony.

THE CROSS-EXAMINATION.

Judge Porter, with great solemnity of manner then commenced his cross-examination as follows:

Q. Mr. Guiteau, I think you are about forty years of age? A. Forty on the 8th of September last, Judge.

Q. Are you conscious of being a man of considerable ability? A. I would not express my opinion on that, Judge.

Q. Have you not expressed opinions on that subject? A. I think not.

Q. Have you an opinion on it? A. (repeating) Have I an opinion on it, well, I decline to answer.

Q. Are you a man of truth? A. Most decidedly, Judge, I am in dead earnest in anything I do.

Q. I think you were converted at the age of seventeen or thereabouts? A. Yes, sir.

Q. From that time on you have been a man of truth, have you not? A. Yes, sir.

Q. And, as you believe, a Christian man? A. I hope so, Judge.

Q. You have hated all shams? A. Most decidedly.

Q. And you do now? A. I do.

Q. You have had no bad habits? A. I think not.

Q. Did you pass through the ordeal of the

Oneida Community and maintain your virtue? A. Well, not absolutely.

Q. I thought you said yesterday that you did? A. I said, or intended to say, although misreported, that I had been mostly a strictly virtuous man. They left out the word "mostly; that is what I intended to say.

Q. Did you believe in the doctrines of the Oneida Community while you were there? A. I did. I thought that the Community was the commencement of God's kingdom on earth.

The prisoner was then cross-examined in regard to his business as a lawyer in Chicago and New York, the result of it all being that he only had some collection cases in Chicago and a similar kind of business in New York, mixed up with some stray jobs in connection with getting prisoners out of Ludlow Street Jail, for which jobs he paid a commission to a prisoner in the jail, who was a big talker and who would recommend him to other prisoners. He admitted that he was behind in his office rent in New York, and perhaps in some of his collections, but thought that one thousand dollars would pay all those debts, together with his board bills.

After this subject was disposed of, the cross-examination proceeded as follows:

Q. You have always been a very persistent and persevering man? A. Yes.

Q. Have you been a man of a good deal of force

of will and determination? A. (With a laugh) Some people think so.

Q. That has been a characteristic of yours from boyhood, has it not? A. I have been very earnest in what I undertook.

Q. You determined to kill General Garfield, did you not? A. I decline to answer that. That is a very strong way to put it (with some excitement). I consider myself the agent of the Deity in the matter; I had no personal volition in the matter.

Q. Did General Logan say to you that he would indorse your application for the Paris Consulship? A. I understood him to say so.

Q. Did he say so? A. Yes, he did say so.

Q. Then when General Logan swore he did not say he would recommend you, he did not tell the truth? A. I would not like to say that. One evening at the boarding-house I asked him to sign my application, and he said he had no pen just there to do it with, but told me to come up to his room next morning and he would do it. Next morning he had changed his mind. I do not want to make any reflections upon General Logan, but that is the way all these politicians do.

Q. Did Secretary Blaine promise you the Paris Consulship if General Logan would recommend you? A. No, sir, he did not.

Q. Did you say to Officer Scott on leaving the depot after the murder of the President; "General

Arthur is now President?" A. I decline to answer that.

Q. Why do you object to answering that? A. I suppose I did say that. (Then he added excitedly) I want it distinctly understood that I did not do that of my own personal volition, but on the inspiration of the Deity. I never would have shot the President on my own personal account.

Q. Who bought the pistol, the Deity or you? A. I said the Deity inspired the act and the Deity would take care of it.

Mr. Porter.—"The question is, who bought the pistol?"

The prisoner.—"The Deity furnished the money with which I bought the pistol. I was agent."

Mr. Porter.—"I thought it was somebody else who furnished the money?"

The prisoner.—"It was the Deity who furnished the money with which I bought the pistol."

Mr. Porter.—"He furnished you all the money you ever had on earth, did he?"

The prisoner.—"I think so."

Q. From whose hand was it that you were furnished the money with which you bought that murderous weapon? A. It is of no consequence (somewhat flurried and excited), Mr. Maynard swore he loaned me fifteen dollars.

Q. Did he? A. Yes, he loaned me money.

Q. What did you do with that money? A. I used it for several purposes.

Q. What were they? A. I have no objection to stating frankly that I got fifteen dollars from Maynard and that I used ten dollars of it to buy that pistol with.

Q. Did you deny when he was on the stand that that was the money with which you bought the pistol? A. No, sir, I never denied it because that is the truth, but it is of no consequence whether I got the money from Maynard or whether I pawned my coat for it.

Q. Were you inspired to borrow fifteen dollars from Maynard? A. No, sir. Mr. Maynard did not know what I wanted the money for.

Q. Were you inspired to buy that British bulldog? A. I do not pretend that I was inspired to do that specific act, but I claim that the Deity inspired me to remove the President, and that I had to resort to my own means to accomplish the Deity's will.

Q. The only inspiration you had was to use the pistol on the President? A. The inspiration consisted in trying to remove the President for the good of the American people, and (impatiently) all these details are nothing to the case.

Q. Were you inspired to remove him by murder? A. I was inspired to execute the Divine will by murder, so-called.

Q. You did not succeed in executing the Divine will? A. I think the doctors finished the work.

Q. The Deity tried and you tried and you both

failed, but the doctors succeeded? A. The Deity confirmed my act by letting the President down as gently as he did.

Q. Do you think it was letting him down gently to let him suffer that torture, over which you profess to feel so much solicitude, during those long months? A. The whole matter was in the hands of the Deity, and (impatiently) I do not want to discuss it any further; I appreciate the fact of the President's long sickness as much as any person in the world; but that is a very narrow view to take of the matter.

Q. What time did Senator Conkling resign? A. About the 15th of May, I should judge.

Q. That was Monday, and you had no inspiration on that day? A. No, sir.

Q. Had you any inspiration on Tuesday? A. No, sir.

Q. On Wednesday night you went to bed at eight o'clock, and then came the inspiration? A. It came between eight and nine o'clock.

Q. Did you believe that it was the will of God that you should murder the President? A. I believed that it was His will that he should be removed and I was the appointed agent to do it.

Q. Did He give you a commission in writing? A. No, sir.

Q. Did He give it in an audible tone of voice? A. He gave it to me by His pressure on me.

Q. Did He give it to you audibly? A. No.

Q. He did not come to you as a "vision of the night?" A. I do not get my inspirations in that way.

Q. It occurred to you as you were lying in your bed that if President Garfield were dead it would solve the whole difficulty? A. Yes.

Q. Did it occur to you that you were the very man to kill him? A. Not at that time; my mind was unsettled.

Q. Who did you think, then, was the man to kill him? A. I had no thought on the subject. The mere impression came on my mind that if the President were removed everything would be well.

Q. Did you contemplate his removal otherwise than by murder? A. No, sir, (petulantly) I do not like the word "murder."

Mr. Porter.—"I know you do not like the word "murder," it is a hard word, but it is there.

The prisoner.—"I do not recollect the actual facts in the matter. (Excitedly.) If I had shot the President of the United States on my own personal account no punishment would be too severe or too quick for me, but acting as the agent of the Deity, that puts an entirely different construction on the act, and that is what I want to put to the Court and jury and to the opposing counsel. I say that the removal of the President was an act of necessity from the situation and for the good of the American people. That is the idea that I want you to entertain, and not to settle down on the cold blooded idea of murder, because I never had the first conception of murder in the matter."

Q. Do you feel under great obligation to the American people? A. I think the American people may some time consider themselves under great obligations to me.

Mr. Porter.—"My question was whether you felt under great obligation to them?"

The prisoner.—"I do not know why I should be."

Q. Were you under great obligation to the Republican Party? A. Not that I know of.

Q. Did the Republican party ever give you any office? A. I never held any kind of political office in my life.

Q. And never desired one? A. I had some thought about the Paris Consulship. That is the only office I ever had the slightest thought about.

Q. That was the one that resulted in the inspiration of murder? A. No, sir, my getting it or not getting it never had the slightest effect upon my mind in attempting to remove the President. That was purely a political necessity. If the political necessity had not existed, the President would not have been removed by me.

Q. You never desired the removal of Mr. Blaine? A. No, sir.

Q. And never suggested it to anybody? A. No, sir.

Mr. Porter.—"Allow me to read to you your letter written on the 23d of May—four days according to your account after you made up your mind to remove the President. Let me refresh your recollection as to whether you desired at that time to remove Mr. Blaine also."

The prisoner.—"I never had the slightest thought of removing Mr. Blaine: I had not made up my mind to remove the President on the 23d of May, nor until the 1st of June. For two weeks after I got the conception I was shaking it off; my natural feelings were all against it, but the pressure continued, pressing me and pressing me, so that at the end of two weeks and about the 1st of June I had made up my mind as to the inspiration of the act and as to the necessity for it."

Mr. Porter.—"That reminds me of another very deliberate utterance of yours made on the 16th of June, the day on which you intended to murder the President."

The prisoner.—"I intended to remove him under Divine pressure, never to murder him."

Mr. Porter.—"Divine pressure? I understand you?"

The prisoner.—"Then state it in proper language."

Mr. Porter.—"Oh, certainly. On the 16th of

June, in an address to the American people, which you intended should be found on your person after you had shot him, you said, "I conceived the idea of removing the President, four weeks ago." Was that a lie?"

The prisoner.—"I conceived it, but my mind was not fully settled on it. There is a difference between conceiving a thing and actually fixing it in your mind. You may conceive the idea of going to Europe in a month and yet you may not go. That is no point at all."

Mr. Porter.—"I will proceed with your address. You say, 'I conceived the idea myself.'"

The prisoner.—"That is correct."

Mr. Porter.—"Why did you conceal it? Why did you keep it yourself?"

The prisoner.—"Why should I go and tell it? That is no point."

Mr. Porter.—"Had you made up your mind whether or not it would be murder?"

The prisoner.—"I had not made up my mind to do the act until about the 1st of June; I was resisting it with all my might and strength and prayer. I prayed that if wrong the Deity would stop me by His Providence. Just please take that in."

Mr. Porter.—"Let me return to the subject of Mr. Blaine. You say in your letter to the President: 'Mr. Blaine is a wicked man, and you ought to demand his immediate resignation.

Otherwise you and the Republican Party will come to grief.'"

The prisoner.—"Political grief, not physical grief; every intelligent man will see that I meant political grief."

Mr. Porter.—"Was that after Wednesday night, when you conceived the idea of removing the President?"

The prisoner.—"That was a mere flash which had not taken shape or form in my mind and did not take shape or form for over two weeks; all that time I was resisting the idea."

Mr. Porter.—"Then there was no inspiration in May?"

The prisoner.—"No, it was a mere flash, an embryo inspiration, a mere impression which came into my mind that possibly it would have to be done; my mind was fully made up about the 1st of June."

Mr. Porter.—"You say 'about the 1st of June.' Was it on the 1st of June?"

The prisoner.—"I say in about two weeks from the 16th of May; during that time I was resisting it with all my might, all my strength, and all my prayers; at the end of that time my mind was fully fixed in regard to the necessity and divinity of the act."

Mr. Porter.—"Then the question was not whether you should obey the inspiration, but whether it was an actual necessity?"

The prisoner.—"I was finding out during those two weeks whether it was God's will or not; at the end of the two weeks I made up my mind that it was His will, and that it was for the best interests of the American people. That is the way that I get inspirations."

Mr. Porter.—"Your making up your mind was not His act?"

The prisoner.—"Yes, it was."

Mr. Porter.—"While you were praying and professing to be in doubt, were you in doubt?"

The prisoner.—"For two weeks I was in doubt, but I never had any doubt since that time."

Mr. Porter.—"What occasioned the doubt?"

The prisoner.—"Because I wanted to know whether it was the Deity that inspired me; I kept praying that the Deity should not let me make any mistake about it, and the Deity has not made any mistake about it."

Mr. Porter.—"Why did you have doubts about it?"

The prisoner.—"Because all my natural feelings were opposed to the act."

Mr. Porter.—"You regarded it as murder, then?"

The prisoner.—"So-called, yes; it was not murder for me; all my natural feelings were against it."

Mr. Porter.—"Were you aware that it was against human law?"

The prisoner.—"I felt that the Deity would take care of me; I never entertained the idea of murder in the whole matter; I never had any conception of the matter as murder; my mind is perfectly blank on that subject, and has been."

Mr. Porter.—"Why were your natural feelings against murder?"

The prisoner.—"I cannot make myself better understood than I have done."

At this period of the cross-examination, which the prisoner bore with considerable self-possession, although he occasionally got flurried and excited, the Court at three o'clock adjourned.

CHAPTER XVI.

Judge Porter Cross-Examines the Prisoner Closely—A Terrible Ordeal for the Shifty Scoundrel—Guiteau Claims all His Acts to be Inspired and all Attacks on Him Mere Human Crimes.

THURSDAY the 1st of December, found another large crowd clamoring for admittance to the Court House. The prisoner appeared nervous and excited and as soon as he reached the witness stand, claimed the attention of the audience while he made an appeal for money to be used in his defence. He presumed he had some friends who were interested in the cause of justice, and they could send any sum from five dollars to a thousand to Mr. Scoville. Mr. Porter then took the witness again and resumed his merciless cross-examination.

Q. You mentioned the other day to the jury that you have never struck a man in your life. Was that true? A. I do not recall ever striking a man. I have always been a peace man. Naturally I am cowardly. I always have kept away from any physical danger.

Q. But morally brave and determined? A. I presume so, especially when I am sure the Deity is back of me.

Q. When did you become sure of that? A. In

this case I became sure about the 1st of June, as far as this case is concerned.

Q. Before that you did not think the Deity was back of you. Who did you think was back of you in the suggestion of murder? A. (violently) There was no suggestion of murder.

Q. The suggestion of killing? A. The suggestion was to remove the President.

Q. When did you first think that it was the Deity that was back of you? A. It was the Deity who made the original suggestion. I was entertaining the proposition for two weeks.

Q. But you say the Deity did not make the suggestion? A. (With great violence and pounding the witness rail with forcible blows of the fist) I say He did about the middle of May. I was entertaining the proposition for two weeks preceding. About the first of June I made up my mind it was His will.

Q. Whose will did you think it was? A. It was His.

Q. But you were in doubt? A. I was not in doubt.

Q. Not even for the two weeks? A. I had no doubt of the inspiration for the act being from the Deity. As to the feasibility of the act I was in doubt.

Q. You differed in opinion from the Deity? A. I was testing the feasibility of the act, whether it would be feasible or not.

Q. Did you suppose the Supreme Ruler would order you to do a thing not feasible? A. No, sir; everything the Deity does is always right. He desired me to remove the President for the good of the American people.

Q. Did the Deity use the word "remove?" A. It is the way it came to my mind; if two men quarrel, and one kills the other, and there is malice, this is murder. I say the doctors killed the President, not I; that was homicide.

Q. Were they guilty of murder? A. In my opinion they were.

Q. Was Mason guilty of a murderous assault? A. Most decidedly.

Q. Was Jones? A. Most decidedly.

Q. Do you think it was wrong? A. Without they can show they acted as the agents of the Deity, it was wrong; if they can show that it was right; anything the Deity does is always right.

Q. How do you know they did not act as agents of the Deity? A. I have no knowledge of it

Q. But if you knew they did? A. I know nothing about them and care nothing about them.

Q. But you did care about them yesterday. A. I never saw the men; I care nothing about them; I have no doubt they should be punished. I expect the Court and the American people demand that they should be punished.

Q. Why should they be punished? A. Because they made an assault on a citizen of the

Republic without it was the action of the Deity.

Q. You do not know whether it was or not? A. Without they can show that they acted as agents of the Deity they ought to be punished; but if they were executing the Divine will they should be set free.

Q. Why should they be punished? A. I told you at the time. If you cannot understand it I will not repeat it.

Q. Why do you think they should be punished for shooting at you? A. Because they have no right unless they can show it was the act of the Deity. The Deity's action supersedes man's law.

Q. What law did they violate if they shot at you? A. (Impatiently and impertinently) What law did they violate if they shot at you?

Q. That's what I ask you? A. I ask you.

Q. (Persistently) What law did they violate? A. They violated the law on the statute book of this District; the only way they can mitigate that violation is showing that they acted as agents of the Deity; the Deity's law supersedes any man's law.

Mr. Porter.—"You said yesterday that if the Deity did not inspire that act of yours, no punishment could be too severe or too quick for you?"

The prisoner.—"That is my position exactly."

Mr. Porter.—"Do you think it was wrong for Mason to shoot at you?"

The prisoner (angrily.)—"I am not an expert,

and I decline to answer any more questions on that point. I am not afraid of you Judge Porter; I know bigger men than you; I have seen you shake your finger before in New York; I am not afraid of you."

Mr. Porter.—" If Mason shot at you with intention to take your life without trial would he have done wrong?"

The prisoner.—" I decline to answer."

Mr. Porter.—" Are you afraid that your answer would criminate you?"

The prisoner.—" I decline to give an opinion about Mason or Jones; they are in the hands of the law, and let the law take its course; let these men defend themselves in the best way they can. I don't know anything about them and care nothing about them. I expect the dignity of the law to be vindicated in their case. I have no wish, however, about it."

Q. Do you believe in the ten commandments?
A. Yes.

Q. Have you higher evidence that the Supreme Ruler of the universe said to you, " Thou shalt kill," than you have that He said, "Thou shalt not kill?"

The prisoner (excitedly). " I do not entertain the idea that there was any murder in the matter; no more murder in removing General Garfield than it was to kill a man during the war, and who would contend that the shooting of a man during the war was either murder or homicide? I do not want to discuss this matter with you; it is altogether too sacred a matter to make light of it and I will not have it. Now you know my position just as well as if I had been talking six weeks about it. I do not wish to discuss it in this foolish kind of way. I will not discuss this matter with you any further."

Mr. Porter.—"Your friend, Thomas North, swears that in 1859, when you were eighteen years of age, you struck your father from behind his back. Is that true?"

The prisoner.—"I do not recollect anything of the kind."

Mr. Porter.—"Your sister swears that in 1876, when you were thirty-five years old, you raised an axe against her life. Is that true?"

The prisoner.—"I have no recollection of it."

Mr. Porter.—"Your brother swears that you called him a thief and a scoundrel. Did you believe that he was a thief?"

The prisoner.—"Under some circumstances I did, and under some circumstances I did not; it was true in a certain sense. I will explain that. My brother had been the general agent of a prominent life insurance company, and he defaulted for some $3,700; he afterwards paid the money back. Mr. Scoville was his surety."

Q. You had no ill will against your brother on the occasion he swore to? A. No.

Q. Nor against your sister when you raised the axe against her? A. No.

Q. Nor against the President? A. No. If there is anybody in the world that I have got ill will to it is the man Noyes; he did my father harm, and he did me and my family harm.

Mr. Porter —" Your associate counsel, Mr. Amerling, swears that when you heard of his using insulting language towards your father in connection with the Oneida Community, you told him his life should be taken, but the Almighty ordered it otherwise. Is that true?"

The prisoner.—" I never said anything of the kind."

Mr. Porter continued his cross-examination in this style, contrasting the testimony of witnesses with the various statements of the prisoner, in order to involve him in contradictions, but the prisoner generally managed to maintain his position. Referring to the prisoner's statements to a police officer, that he had shot the President, Mr. Porter asked him: "Had you then forgotten that the Deity was the One who shot him, and that He commanded you to do it?"

The prisoner replied angrily: "I do not want to discuss that matter with you any further, Judge Porter; I want you to know that when I speak of myself I always associate myself with the Deity; there is no use splitting hairs on that point."

Witness was closely questioned with regard to the different boarding-houses at which he had lived while in Washington, and became very uneasy at the bad showing he was making by his own evidence, in respect to honest dealings with his landladies. His restlessness soon found expression as follows:

"I decline to go into this boarding-house business. It has no bearing on this case. I suppose I owe $150 in Washington to these genteel ladies, and some time or other I expect to pay them. When I have money," he continued angrily, "I pay my debts, and when I have not I can't pay them; that's all there is in it."

Mr. Porter.—"Perhaps the Judge will think differently."

The prisoner (turning with a smile and a nod of satisfaction to Judge Cox).—"Your Honor will see how irrelevant all this talk is."

Judge Cox.—"You were allowed great latitude, prisoner, in making your statement; you will reply to the questions."

The witness was readily driven from one position to another till confronted with the evidence of his witnesses, when he would unhesitatingly pronounce their evidence false. Once he emphasized his contradiction by saying: "Anything that I swear to, Judge, is true; you can put that down as a fixed fact." Being pressed as to how he proposed to raise the funds which he had said

he was expecting to receive, the prisoner replied
" I intended to borrow it from some of my friends,"
and added: " I'll tell you, Judge, how I borrow
money. It may be of service to you when you
want to borrow for yourself. I don't lie or sneak,
but go right up to a man and ask him for what I
want, and if he has got it, perhaps, on the impulse
of the moment, he will give it to me; if not, that's
all there is to it."

Witness was closely questioned about the purchase of the pistol, and was asked why he bought the one with an ivory handle instead of a plain one. He replied: "Because I thought it worth a dollar more."

Judge Porter.—" Did you not say that it would look better in the Patent Office?"

Witness admitted that he might have believed or thought that the pistol would some time be placed in the State Department. Shortly afterwards Guiteau became very indignant at Judge Porter's use of the word "murder," and shouted fiercely: " You seem to delight in the use of the words 'kill and murder.' There's no use in your whining in that way. The mere outward fact of how I removed the President has nothing whatever to do with this case."

Mr. Porter.—" After you bought the revolver, being unused to fire-arms, did you practice with it?" A. I went down to Seventeenth Street and fired it off over the river.

Q. Why did you go there? A. Because the man in the store told me I would have to go outside the city limits to fire.

Q. Did you take the box of cartridges with you? A. I think so; I fired it off two rounds, ten cartridges.

Q. What did you shoot at? A. I shot at a sapling.

Q. Why did you want to shoot at a sapling; you had no divine command for that? A. I wanted (and here the witness hesitated for some time) to fire it two or three times; I know nothing about a weapon; I expected to have to use it and familiarize myself with the outward use of the weapon.

Q. You did not know how to fire a pistol, but this was the work of the Deity? A. (Apparently in a violent passion and gesticulating wildly.) There is no use of whining in this kind of way; you might as well rest; you are making entirely too much talk about the outward act of the Deity; I say you have to go back and look at the motive.

Q. The motive was to kill——. A. (Interrupting excitedly.) To remove the President for the good of the American people; the outward fact which you desire is irrelevant matter; there's no use whining.

Q. You practiced repeatedly? A. Never repeatedly. I fired it off twice on two different occasions, just to get used to the outward act of handling it. I knew no more about it than a baby. When I went to buy it I looked at it and it kinder scared me; I went back after two or three days and bought it; the man in the store loaded it and I put it in my pocket.

Q. Were you afraid it might go off? A. I knew nothing about handling a weapon; I was as innocent as a baby; I do not know that I had any especial fear, but I kept the point away from me pretty well.

Q. When did you practice the first time? A. I think I bought the revolver in the middle of the week and went down Seventeenth Street Saturday evening about seven o'clock. The first time I fired it off it nearly knocked me over and scared me.

Q. Did you hit the sapling? A. I hit it the first time and not the other time.

Q. Did the sapling go very nearly as Garfield went? A. I don't know.

Q. Have you had occasion to speak of it that he went down as that sapling? A. I never used that expression in the world.

Q. When did you try it again? A. I went down a week or two after that and fired it again; when I had finished I put the pistol in my pocket and went back to my room, wiped it and laid it in my drawer, and there it remained a couple of weeks.

Q. Did you have it with you the day you intended to kill President Garfield—the 16th of June? A. It was the 18th.

Q. Did you have the pistol with you? A. Yes.

Q. During all this time were you on the lookout for General Garfield's movements? A. I was looking out for him somewhat.

Q. Did you go to the White House? A. I never was in that neighborhood.

Q. When did he go to Long Branch? A. About the third week in June.

Q. Among those scraps which you preserved were there any saying when he would go and return from Long Branch? A. I think that was mentioned.

Q. You kept that for the purpose of keeping an eye on his movements? A. I was watching his movements.

Q. When did you begin watching the President's movements? A. About the time he and Mrs. Garfield went to Long Branch.

Q. Did you not go to the White House grounds to see when he went out? A. I did not go near the White House grounds, or if I did it was in the latter part of June. I used to sit in the park opposite the White House.

Q. For the purpose of observing him and watching your chance? A. I wanted to execute the Divine will, and to obviate all this loose talk, I will state that I would have removed the President any time from the middle of June until I shot him, if I had had an opportunity. At any time I would have executed the Divine will from the middle of June until the time I actually did shoot him.

Q. I thought your mind was clear from the 1st of June. A. It was, but I was not actually ready to do the act until the middle of June.

Q. And had not practised with your pistol? A. That is not the point—what do you want to put that in for? I had a good deal to do until the middle of June; I went to work to revise my book, "*Truth;*" I knew that there would be some demand for that; I did also several other matters —personal matters; as a matter of fact, at any time after the middle of June I should have shot him if I had an opportunity during those two weeks; any time I should have executed the Divine will, so that disposes of all that loose talk about the outward act; the entire responsibility of this thing is on the Deity; it is His act, and He can take care of it; He has taken care of it thus far, and He will continue to take care of it.

Q. Then what was the necessity that you should be a witness in the case? A. The Deity uses certain men to serve him; He is using this honorable Court, and this jury, and these police, and these troops to serve Him and protect me; I don't want any more talk on this subject; if you go on to other subjects I will discuss them.

Q. Where were you on the morning of June 16th, when you wrote your address to the American people? A. That was prepared at the Arlington.

Q. In this address you say: "I conceived the idea of removing the President four weeks ago?" A. (Impatiently.) Oh! that is the great point you tried to make yesterday; I meant that the first impression came upon me about the 16th of May, and in about four weeks it became a fixed necessity to remove him; I went to work after the first of June to prepare myself, in an orderly way, to do the act; that is all there is in the whole case.

Q. (Reading from the address.) "Not a soul knows of my purpose?" A. That is correct.

Q. Then you did "purpose" it for four weeks before? A. That is not literally true.

Q (Reading) "I killed the President because he proved a traitor to the men that made him, and thereby imperilled the life of the Republic?" A. That was the idea; that was the cause under Divine pressure.

Q. You do not speak of Divine pressure? A. I did in a letter later than that, and I did in the close of that letter say that I would leave the responsibility with God and the American people.

Q. Did you hold the American people responsible for the act of God? A. No, sir.

Q. But you left your vindication to the American people? A. I leave my justification to God and the American people—principally to God and second to the American people. I never shot the President on my own account. I want the American people to undersand that.

Q. Did the Deity tell you what the President had been a traitor to? A. That was in my own judgment.

Q. You say "owing to his misconduct and his Secretary of State he could hardly carry ten Northern States?" A. That was true.

Q. What was the misconduct? A. He had gone back on Grant and Conkling and Arthur, the very men who carried New York, and put himself under the influence of Mr. Blaine.

Q. Suppose he had appointed Mr. Conkling as Secretary of State would you have killed him? A. That is a supposition I don't care to discuss.

Q. Have you any objection to telling the jury? A. The Republican Party would not have got in any such snarl if Conkling had been Secretary of State.

Q. How do you think Mr. Blaine would have liked Mr. Conkling being Secretary of State? A. He would have disliked it.

Q. Would it have prevented the disunion of the Republican Party to have had Mr. Conkling Secretary of State? A. General Garfield never would have been elected in the world except for Grant and Conkling. This whole subject of political disruption is going to be developed here so that the Court and jury will see the necessity for the Divine inspiration.

Q. If Conkling had been Secretary of State still you would have killed Garfield? A. That is a proposition that did not exist, and I decline to discuss it.

The witness was then asked whether if he had been appointed Consul to Paris he would have killed the President, and in reply repeated his answer of yesterday that he would not have accepted the Paris Consulate if it were offered him after June 1st.

Q. If General Garfield had sent your name to the Senate you would have laid in wait and murdered him? A. I would have sent it right back after the 1st of June. My whole heart and mind and inspiration were in removing him.

Q. Did you have any malice? A. (Interrupting) I repudiate you for making that allusion; you know as well as I do that I never had any malice; he was my personal and political friend.

Witness then explained that his personal friendship with President Garfield consisted in speaking with him once, and his political of belonging to the same political party. He did not consider it necessary to be a man's bedfellow to be his friend.

Q. (Dramatically, and modulating his tone at the close of the question) And you had no ill-will? A. (Imitating and mockingly) I had no ill-will against him.

Q. And no ill-will against your sister when you raised an axe against her? A. I never raised an axe against her.

Q. You had no ill-will against your brother when you struck him? A. I never struck him.

Q. You think that General Garfield was to blame in appointing Mr. Blaine Secretary of State? A. I think most decidedly that it was a very unwise thing. I say that was an open insult to General Grant and Conkling for General Garfield to appoint their worst enemy. I think that that caused all the harm (with a bang on the railing). It made it so bitter for Grant and Conkling and Arthur that they would not go to the White House. I say that (with more banging of his fist on the railing) to the American people and to the jury and to the Court.

Q. Is this what you said in your note to Mr. Blaine, "I am very glad personally that the President selected you for his Premier?" A. I said that.

Q. Was that true? A. It was true then.

Q. You were glad? A. I was glad. (After a pause) That needs modification however.

Q. What modification does it need? A. The modification is that at that time General Garfield had not insulted Grant and Conkling by Robertson's appointment and Merritt's withdrawal.

Q. Then you were a Blaine man until that time? A. Under the circumstances I was. I thought Blaine a good fellow, and was glad to see him promoted. I thought, and so did other Stalwarts that Garfield was disposed to do the fair thing by the Stalwarts, but after he appointed Blaine and got under the Blaine influence he studied wickedly to slaughter Grant and Conkling and to pave the way for Garfield's nomination in 1884.

Q. You say in the same note: "I have got the President and General Logan worked up about it so that they are willing to leave it to you?" Was that true?

The witness then related how he met General Logan in New York and Washington, and told of his final interview with Mr. Blaine on the Paris Consulship, as stated on the direct examination. He was asked whether at the time of his last interview with Secretary Blaine he gave the latter to understand that he would support him for the Presidency. He replied in the negative. Upon Judge Porter's reading, however, a paragraph from a letter of Guiteau to Secretary Blaine, saying that he (Guiteau) hoped to get back from Paris in time to be of service to him (Mr. Blaine) in the Republican Convention of 1884, the witness modified his previous answer, and admitted he had some such idea.

About this time the prisoner, who had been speaking very rapidly, showed signs of considerable exhaustion, and Mr. Porter had got tired of standing and was occupying a seat. At the suggestion of the District Attorney the Court, therefore, took a recess for an hour.

After the recess the prisoner was again conducted to the witness stand, looking very haggard and worn, and his cross-examination proceeded.

Q. Had you a purpose in telling Mr. Blaine that? A. I had no special purpose about it. I simply made the suggestion to him that, in case he assisted me in getting the Paris Consulship, I should feel bound, in case he was a candidate at the National Convention, to assist him. That is the way they do in politics, Judge; understand that; that is the way politicians get on—"You tickle me, I tickle you."

Q. Did you try to tickle President Garfield? A. I do not think I did. I may have made similar suggestions to President Garfield at the time I was pressing my application in March and April.

The witness then said that he and all the Stalwarts were deeply interested in General Garfield after his inauguration, and that there was perfect harmony until he began to make war on the Stalwarts in the matter of patronage, then there was a decided reaction.

Q. Did you write to President Garfield on the 8th of April a letter marked "Private," in which you said: "I intend to express my sympathy for you on account of the pressure that has been on you since you came to the city?" A. Yes; I wrote that letter. My idea was just this: to express my personal regard for General Garfield, on account of the pressure on him for office, and that is what I meant by saying that I considered him my personal friend. I sympathize with any President who has this enormous horde of office-seekers at his throat.

Q. Did you intend, as you said in that letter, to remain in Washington until you got your commission as Consul to Paris? A. At that time I did. I was pressing my application for the Paris Consulship during the months of March and April. You ought to make a broad distinction in the position between the time prior to the 1st of May and the time after that.

Q. On the 29th of April did you write to the President that Mr. Conkling had worked himself up to a white heat of opposition. A. I remember using that phrase.

Q. Had you ever spoken with Senator Conkling from the time you came to Washington on the 6th of March until you wrote that letter? A. I think I had met Senator Conkling several times, and we had exchanged "How do you do, Senator?" and "How do you do, sir?"

Q. Did you speak with him on the street? A. Yes, decidedly.

Q. How many times? A. I met him once on the street, I remember distinctly. He was exceedingly cordial, and he bowed and said: "How do you do, Mr. Guiteau?" That was near the Patent Office, some time in March, or April. I was on good relations with all those men during March and April.

Q. Did Senator Conkling ever promise to support your application for the Paris Consulship? A. I never suggested it to him. My expectation about the Paris Consulship was that I would get it through my personal influence with the President, Mr. Blaine, and Mr. Logan, and that when my nomination went to the Senate, Senator Conkling and that sort of men would see it through. But I do not think it necessary to discuss this matter of the Paris Consulship; I went over it all yesterday, and I decline to discuss it further. There is no use in wasting the time of this honorable Court on it in going over it again. If you do not know the facts about it you had better read this morning's papers and you will find them.

Q. Did you write on the 7th of May to President Garfield, whom you afterwards shot: "I am sorry you and Senator Conkling are apart, but I stand by you?" A. I wrote that; that was the time I was trying to bring these men together; I was acting the part of a peacemaker.

Q. And you stood by President Garfield? A. I tell you I did; but after Robertson was nominated, and when the public announcement was made that any Senator who would decline to vote for Robertson's confirmation would need a letter of introduction to the President, then I stood by Mr. Conkling and the Stalwarts. That was the occasion of the break between the President and the Stalwarts.

Q. Did you write to President Garfield on the 10th of May: " I have got a new idea about 1884. If you work your position for all it is worth you can be nominated and elected in 1884. Your opponents will probably be Gen. Grant and Mr. Blaine. General Grant will never be so strong again as he was just after his trip around the world. Too many people are dead set against a third term and I do not think he can be nominated, much less elected. Two National Conventions have slaughtered Mr. Blaine on account of his railroad record. The Republican Party is afraid to nominate him. This leaves the course open to you. Run the Presidency on your own account. Strike out right and left. The American people like pluck, and in 1884 we will put you in again?" A. I wrote that letter.

Q. Did it express your then opinion and intention? A. It expressed my opinion; I had no no special intention about it.

Q. You added a postscript: "I will see you about the Paris Consulship to-morrow unless you happen to send in my name to-day?" A. That is the way I felt and talked, but that was long before this political disruption.

Q. Did you think that President Garfield, after reading this letter would give you the Paris Consulship? A. I had no special thought on the subject.

Q. Yet you had the Paris Consulship much at heart?

The prisoner (angrily).—"I did have the Paris Consulship at heart, and I told you so, but after the disruption of the Republican Party I never thought of it any more. If you cannot get that into your head I refuse to discuss the subject any more. I have told you a hundred times that my getting or not getting the Paris Consulship had nothing to do with my removing the President."

Q. After that, on the 16th of May, did you write to President Garfield a letter marked "private," saying: "Until Saturday I supposed Mr. Blaine was my friend in the matter of the Paris Consulship, but after his tone on Saturday, I judge he is trying to run the State Department in the interest of the Blaine element?"

The prisoner (with a violent bang on the railing). "Yes, and that is the truth about it. I hit him square there, and that is the reason why Blaine went back on me; because I was a Grant man, and he thought he would put a Blaine man in the Paris Consulship."

Q. Were you ever inspired with the idea that

President Garfield would be re-elected? A. I did not have any inspiration on that subject at all. It was a mere casual thought of my own. I did not need inspirations for that kind of work.

Q. How came you to write to Mr. Garfield on the 13th of May: "The idea of 1884 flashed upon me like an inspiration, and I believe it will come true?" A. All these letters were written prior to General Garfield's disrupting the Republican Party, and it is mean and unfair in you to distort my letter. After he disrupted the Republican Party by bringing Grant and Conkling down on him there was a very different condition of affairs. Now, I protest against this kind of work. It is not fair or manly in you.

Q. You said in this letter that the idea of 1884 flashed through you like an inspiration? A. But Mr. Garfield killed the idea by his disruption of the Republican Party.

Q. Did you then believe in the inspiration? A. (resolutely) I decline to discuss this matter any further. You have gone over it two or three times, and I decline to discuss it any more. If your idea were correct about my having malice in the matter, Blaine was the man for me to have shot. What possible ill will could I have had against Garfield? Blaine was the man to have been shot according to your theory; my not getting the office had nothing to do with it whatever. It only shows how absurd and nonsensical your theory is. If General Garfield had paid respect to these letters it would have been all right. But what did he do? He went and sold himself soul and body to Mr. Blaine. He did not appreciate the sentiment and kindness of those letters, and threw himself into Blaine's hands and allowed Blaine to use the Presidency to destroy Conkling and Grant.

Q. Did you say to General Garfield in a letter written on the 23d of May that Blaine was a vindictive politician and was his evil genius? A. I did, and that was my opinion of Mr. Blaine when I saw him take full possession of General Garfield and use the Presidency to destroy Conkling and Grant and the men who made him.

Q. Did you say that he would have no peace until he got rid of him? A. Yes, and that was the way the Stalwart and liberal papers all over the country talked; that was the way the *Washington Republican* and Gorham and that kind of people talked.

Q. Did you say that Mr. Blaine was a wicked man? A. Yes; because he was using President Garfield, who was a good man and a kind man, but a weak politician. Garfield just sold himself body and soul to Blaine; that was what General Grant himself said in his letter denouncing Garfield for selling himself out to Blaine.

Q. Was your motive for demanding Mr. Blaine's resignation because he had said to you on the

Saturday proceeding never to speak to him again on the Paris Consulship? A. (excitedly) I told you that it had nothing to do with the Paris Consulate. I want to ram that into you and put it down deep. I am talking now about the National politics and not about a miserable office, and if you would try to get your brains to take that in it would be better. I am not a disappointed office-seeker.

Q. On the 2d of July you wrote a letter to "The White House People." Whom did you mean by the White House People? A. I meant all the inmates of the White House.

Q. Including Mrs. Garfield? A. Of course— the entire White House family.

Q. You stated in that letter that the President's tragical death was a sad necesity? A. Certainly —a political necessity.

Q. Did the Deity tell you that? A. That did not require any telling.

Q. You say: "I will unite the Republican Party." Who told you that? A. It did not require any telling (with excitement), and that is exactly what it did do, too; that shows that the inspiration was correct.

Q. Who told you it would save the Republic? A. My own judgment told me and it proved to be correct.

Q. You say that Mason fired at you while under the protection of the law. Did you esteem that to be a crime? A. Of course that was a crime.

Q. Did it occur to you, then, in the language of your letter to Mrs. Garfield and the White House people, that "life is a fleeting dream, and it matters little when one goes?" A. Those are my sentiments.

Q. Does it matter much to you when you go? A. (coolly) I have got no great fear of death; you are liable to die in five minutes, and so is every one in this Court House. The only question is whether you are ready to die.

Q. Did you say in your letter to the White House people: "I presume the President was a Christian, and he will be happier in paradise than here?" A. I did, and I am sure the President is a great deal happier at this very moment than any man on earth.

Q. You have no doubt that when you killed him he went direct to paradise? A. I believed him to be a good Christian man.

Mr. Porter (solemnly).—"And you believe that the Supreme Being who holds the gates of life and death wanted to send him to paradise for breaking the unity of the Republican Party, and for ingratitude to General Grant and Senator Conkling?"

The prisoner.—"His Christianity had nothing to do with his political character. His political record was very poor, but his Christian character was good, because he was a good man as far as I know, although they did tell very hard stories about him in connection with the Credit Mobilier and such things.

In the course of his further cross-examination the prisoner said in relation to the time of the murder: "The Deity seemed to be on my side and everybody else against me. But there is a great deal better feeling towards me now than there was some three or four weeks ago. Some of these bitter crank papers have been toning down wonderfully for the last three or four weeks. What they want is change of heart. They want conversion. They want new ideas about the President's removal. Nothing but a change of heart will satisfy their diabolical thirst for blood. It is not likely that the Deity will gratify them in their thirst for blood. They begin to see it too, and they will see it more and more.

In reply to a question why it required a special inspiration to shoot General Garfield, he said: "It required special directions from the Deity to me. I suppose there were a thousand men in the Republican Party who would have shot General Garfield if they had the chance and had got the nerve, and the brains, and the opportunity to do the work."

Q. Did it occur to you that there was a commandment, "Thou shalt not kill?" A. The Divine authority overcame the written law.

Q. Was there any higher Divine law than that spoken on Sinai? A. Indeed there was.

Q. When you pointed that pistol at General Garfield and sent that ball into his backbone, you believed it was not you but God that pulled the trigger? A. That I was simply executing the Divine will. He used me as the agent in pulling the trigger; I had no option in the matter; I would have done it if I knew I was to be shot dead the next moment. The pressure was so enormous I could not resist it: put that down.

Q. Did you walk back and forth in the depot watching for him? A. Yes, I was working myself up, for I knew the hour had come.

Q. Working yourself up. Was it necessary to do that to obey God? A. It was all I could possibly do to do the act any way, and I had to work myself up to it. I had to obey the God Almighty if I died the next second.

The prisoner was then questioned with regard to the events which immediately preceded the shooting, and was asked whether he was afraid of personal violence. He replied that he was not, but admitted that he did want protection until the people cooled off. In conclusion he declared that the Deity had protected him from that day to this.

Q. How do you know that. A. I know it was the Deity more than I knew I was alive.

Q. It depends on whether the jury believe you.

A. That is exactly what the jury is here to pass upon—whether the Deity and I did the act; or whether I did it on my personal account. And I tell you further that I expect that there will be an act of God to protect me, if it is necessary, from any kind of violence, either hanging or shooting.

Mr. Porter read an extract from one of Guiteau's letters, where he alluded to his leaving the Oneida Community as a "devilish delusion," but the prisoner repudiated that expression, and then said irritably: "That's just the way you jump from one thing to another without any sense."

Mr. Porter then asked if the prisoner had written a letter stating that he would have killed the President on June 18, if it had not been that Mrs. Garfield was with him, leaning tenderly on his arm. The prisoner stated that that was correct, and thought it spoke well for his heart. 'My heart would not allow me to remove him in the presence of Mrs. Garfield."

Q. What objection would she have? A. A decided objection. She was a sick lady, and the shock might have killed her. That was my reason for not doing it. I only had authority to remove the President.

Q. And did not intend to kill Mrs. Garfield? A. Decidedly not. I felt very sorry for her; remarkably sorry for his children, and for everybody; I was grieved that it was necessary to save the Republic from another war, and it has saved the country from another war.

Q. There would have been a war now but for you? A. I do not pretend that the war was immediate, but I do say emphatically (and here the prisoner began to declaim in a dramatic manner and in the style of a stump speaker) that the bitterness in the Republican Party was deepening hour by hour, and that by two or three years at least the nation would have been in a flame of war. In the presence of death all hearts were hushed, dissension ceased. For weeks and weeks the hearts and brains of the nation centered on the sick man at the White House. At last (and here the speaker lowered his voice so as to be almost unintelligible) he went the way of all flesh, and the nation was in mourning. That is a paragraph from the speech I wanted to make two weeks ago, he continued, resuming his natural tone and apparently well satisfied with his effort. It comes very pertinent here and I am glad I had a chance to deliver it.

Mr. Porter then went into a searching examination of the letters written by the prisoner before the shooting to show that in none of them had he alluded to the act as being the act of the Deity. Many of the questions the witness declined to answer, suggesting that it would be much more sensible to have the letters read in full.

Counsel then branched off and asked the prisoner the necessity of requesting General Sherman to send troops to the jail to protect him for having obeyed the Deity? A. I would have been shot and hung a hundred times if it had not been for the troops at the jail.

Q. Any harm in that? A. That is a matter for the law to pass upon. (Impatiently) I will not have any more conversation with you on this sacred subject; you are making light of a serious matter, and I will not talk about it.

Q. Did you think it wrong to remove Garfield without a trial? A. I decline to discuss the matter.

Q. Did God tell you that he ought to be murdered? A. That he ought to be removed.

Q. When did he tell you so? A. I decline to discuss that.

Q. Would it criminate you? A. I don't know whether it would or not.

Going back to the letters Mr. Porter read that in which the prisoner stated that Garfield's nomination, election and "removal" were acts of God, and then asked: "Who nominated him?" A. The Chicago Convention.

Q. Was that inspired?

The prisoner hesitated and seemed about to dodge the question, when Mr. Porter stopped him with an impatient "Now, now, now,"

A. (mockingly) Now, now, now; I thought that Grant or Blaine would be nominated, and when Garfield was nominated on the thirty-sixth ballot it was an act of God; the facts surroundin his election would sustain the position that it was an act of God, and the facts surrounding his removal would sustain the same position.

Q. Was the Chicago Convention inspired? A. In a certain sense it was.

Q. In the same sense that you were? A. No, sir; I had a positive and direct inspiration.

At this point of the testimony the prisoner complained of being fatigued, saying that he was not used to speaking five hours at a time, and the Court, at a quarter to three, adjourned.

CHAPTER XVII.

Cross-examination of the Prisoner Concluded—He Deliberately Recounts the Circumstances of the Assassination—The Redirect Examination.

ON Friday morning, December 2d, as soon as the Court was opened, the prisoner, on resuming the stand, at once addressed Counsel as follows: "I desire to say to you, Judge, and to this honorable Court, that I decline to answer any more questions by a repetition of what we have already had. If you have anything new I am ready to answer, otherwise not, unless by special direction of the Court."

The Cross-examination was then continued.

Q. Was it one of your purposes in killing the President to create a demand for your book? A. One of the objects was to preach the Gospel as set forth in my book.

Mr. Porter repeated the question and was answered with a sullen, "I have answered it," from the prisoner. The question being repeated once more, the prisoner appealed to the Court as to whether he had not already answered.

The Court having held that the question must be answered more specifically, the prisoner replied in the affirmative.

Q. You regard your book as the Gospel? A. As an important explanation of the Bible, I claim that it is a collateral Gospel; I undertake to say that the book is the Bible brought down to the present day; in so far as there is any truth in any book it comes from the Deity, and I claim that it contains important truth.

Q. Have you read a good deal about Napoleon? A. No.

Q. When you wrote "The President's nomination was an act of God; his election was an act of God; his removal was an act of God," did you have Napoleon's bulletins in your mind? A. That is the way I express myself—sharp, pointed, sententious. If you would like to see a specimen of that kind of style look through my book.

Mr. Porter.—"I think you have remarkable power of brain, and whatever your brother-in-law may think, I appreciate your ability."

The prisoner (highly pleased).—"I thank you, Judge, for your good opinion."

Mr. Porter (significantly).—"I think that is the opinion of every juror."

The prisoner (excitedly).—"I take my chance before this Court and the jury on the fact that the Deity inspired the act. I am not a fool, and the Deity never employed a fool to do His work. He put it into my brain and heart, and left me to work it out in my own way."

Q. And you did? A. Under the sanction of the Deity.

Q. He did not give you an after sanction? A. The pressure on me commenced about six weeks before the actual shooting. I was the predestined man from the foundation of the world to do this act, and I had to do it.

Q. You believe in the doctrines of predestination? A. Most decidedly; I claim that I am a man of destiny. You spoke of Napoleon; he thought he was a man of destiny though he had different work from me. I am a man of destiny as much as the Saviour, or Paul, or Martin Luther or any of those religious men.

Q. And your destiny was to kill Garfield? A. It was my destiny to obey the Divine will, and let Him take care of it; I put up my life and I have not been hung or shot yet.

Q. And you did not expect to be? A. I had no expectation except to do the Divine will and let Him take care of me; I am satisfied with the Deity's conduct of this case up to the present moment.

Q. When were you first inspired? A. I decline to discuss the matter with you any further. I have gone over the whole ground several times before, and the papers are full of it this morning; if you want any more ideas on that subject I refer you to the papers; I will not be annoyed in this way any more; the Court and jury and the country understand it. Now, if you have got anything new I will entertain you, otherwise not.

Q. Was it the same sort of inspiration that caused you to join the Oneida Community which inspired you to kill Garfield? A. It was from the same Deity.

Q. And communicated in the same way? A. (with excitement) My inspirations always come upon me as the result of pressure. I do not believe in Spiritualism or anything of that kind. I have communication with the Deity as the result of pressure. Sometimes pressure comes upon my brain, my spirit and my heart. That is the way I got into the Oneida Community.

Q. Did the Deity inspire you to leave there? A. I decline to answer; I have gone over that several times; I refer you to the newspapers.

Q. But the jury is not permitted to read the papers. A. They have heard my statement on that point several times and that ought to satisfy any gentleman.

Q. Then the Deity inspired you to leave the Oneida Community and to establish a theocratic paper that turned out to be a failure? A. I did not actually start the paper, although I consulted about it. I do not consider that the time has come to establish that kind of a paper.

Mr. Porter went on to cross-examine the prisoner, with the object of showing that the pretended inspiration in regard to a theocratic daily, to the book called "*Truth*," to the lecture on the second coming of Christ, etc., were merely borrowed from the ideas of Noyes, and that portions of the book and lecture were plagiarisms from the book called "*The Berean.*" In connection with the prisoner's leaving the Oneida Community Mr. Porter put in evidence a letter written by the prisoner in April, 1865, in which he says that he is leaving in obedience to an irresistible conviction that if he did not do it woe would be upon him. That he must obey the will of God. That God and his conscience were driving him to the battle and that he dared not draw back. A package of manuscript tied together was shown to the prisoner and admitted to be his writing, although he said it appeared to be mutilated, having neither head nor tail.

The District Attorney then proceeded to read the document from a printed slip, and the prisoner cautioned Mr. Scoville to follow the reading with the original, because he was " afraid to trust those men." The document was then read. It was a paper written by Guiteau to the Oneida Community at the time of his leaving it, and is principally devoted to advocating his theory of establishing a great theocratic paper. The substance of it had already been published. The prisoner listened attentively to the reading, interrupting now and then to make some explanation.

"That's a very strong idea," he commented

when the idea of establishing a number of theocratic papers was mentioned. The idea was to make the world an entire community. It was a grand conception, but not at all feasible the way this world is run. There are too many bad people in this world."

A note was also read which had been written to the Community by Guiteau and in which he confessed his love for and his subordination to Mr. Noyes, and withdrew all charges previously made against him. The prisoner's comment on this was in a conversational tone.

"You want," he said "to imagine yourselves in hell, ladies and gentlemen, and you will get some idea of my feeling in the Oneida Community."

A letter addressed by Guiteau to a member of the Community was also introduced in evidence. In this he says: "When in the world I had a programme of my own, but God smashed that and hurled me into the Community." He also refers to himself as a creature of predestination, but states that, having God's work to do, he would not abandon it for the wealth of the Rothschilds or the fame of Napoleon. "That is so now," murmured the prisoner.

The letter written by Guiteau asking to be received back into the Community was next read. He states that he gave up his project of establishing a theocratic paper because he was not up to the "tricks of the newspaper trade," and further, that the project was a "devilish delusion."

The prisoner.—" It was no devilish delusion; it was an inspired idea, but not feasible."

The cross-examination was then resumed.

Q. Do you not think that you ever had a devilish delusion? A. No, sir, I do not have devilish delusions; Noyes believes in devilish delusions; the devil and the Almighty are fighting it out, according to him. I believe in a personal devil. There is an article in my little book about it. It is good reading, Judge.

Mr. Porter.—" I have read it with a good deal of pleasure."

The prisoner.—" There are good ideas in it. It has not been published yet, Judge."

Q. Do you believe the devil tempts men? A. Most decidedly; he tempts them to do evil, and that is the reason, when pressed to do a thing, I first question whether it is the devil or the Deity.

Q. And that was so when the question came up about killing the President? A. For two or three weeks I entertained the proposition, praying the Deity not to let me make any mistake; and the confirmation of the idea came to me in the fact that the newspapers were denouncing Garfield and I saw the necessity of his removal for the good of the American people; if the political situation had not existed, then I should have said that it was the inspiration of the devil. But the political situation required the removal of the President for the good of the American people, and that is the way I knew it was the Deity and not the devil.

Q. And it was in view of the political situation that you made up your mind to murder—

The prisoner (interrupting excitedly).—"Don't use that word 'murder;' you are entirely too free with that word."

Mr. Porter.—"Are you not on trial for murder?"

The prisoner.—"So it is said; can't you use the proper word, 'removed?'"

Mr. Porter.—"I can use the word 'remove,' but it is as repulsive to me as 'murder' is to you."

The prisoner (insultingly).—"I presume you have a big fee for this, Judge. You are working on conditions I see."

Mr. Porter.—"You are a practical man in your notions of law?"

The prisoner.—"I decline to answer. Go back to theology."

Q. What is your theory of your defence? A. I stated it very frequently; if you have not the comprehension to see it by this time, I will not attempt to enlighten you.

Q. Your defence is that you are legally insane and not in fact insane, is it? A. The defence is that it is the Deity's act and not mine.

Q. Are you insane at all? A. A good many

people think I am badly insane. The Oneida people thought so, my father thought so, and my relatives thought so and still think so.

Q. You told the jury you were not insane? A. I am not an expert, let the experts and the jury decide whether I am insane.

Q. Did you expect at the time you shot the President to be tried for it? A. I had no expectation about it. My only thought was to execute the Divine will and let Him take care of me. I would not have been deterred from the act if I had known I should be shot in five minutes. I decline to discuss the subject any further with you. If you want any light read the newspapers. I am unwilling to have the time of the honorable Court and jury and country absorbed any more than necessary.

The prisoner was then inquired of as to the night he followed Mr. Garfield to Mr. Blaine's house, but declined to answer any more questions on that point without positive directions from the Court.

The Court (to the prisoner).—"You ought to answer. Your refusal to answer will operate against you."

The prisoner.—"I have stated the matter repeatedly, and will state it again if necessary. (To Mr. Porter) ask your question again."

Q. Did you lurk in an alley that night while the President was at Mr. Blaine's house? A. I saw General Garfield one evening come out of the White House about seven o'clock. I was in the park opposite the White House. He passed along the end of the park, crossed down the street, passed Wormley's Hotel and went to Mr. Blaine's house. I was several yards behind him.

Q. Walking after him? A. I walked along on the opposite side of the street.

Q. Was the pistol loaded? A. It was loaded.

Q. Did you intend to kill him? A. I intended to remove him.

Q. That night? A. No sir.

Q. Why did you follow him if you did not intend to remove him? A. I walked down that way as I had a perfect right to do.

Q. Then it was merely in the assertion of your right as a free citizen that you walked dogging the President? A. Possibly.

Q. Did you take out your pistol? A. Yes; I took it out.

Q. Did you point it at him? A. (Imitating Mr. Porter's tones, and grinning maliciously) No, sir, I did not point it at him.

Q. When he came out of Mr. Blaine's house, was he alone? A. Mr. Blaine was with him. I am glad you have given me a chance of telling about it. (To Mr. Porter who was about putting another question.) Now wait a moment. General Garfield and Mr. Blaine came out arm in arm, and passed down on the opposite side of the street.

It was about seven o'clock on the evening of the 1st of July.

Q. Did you hear them talk? A. Now wait a moment. I want to tell you some news. They were in a most delightful and cosy fellowship, just as hilarious as two young school girls; they had their heads together this way (making a motion). Blaine was striking the air like this (imitating) and Garfield was listening very attentively. Their fellowship was perfectly delightful (with a horrible facial expression and a wolf-like exhibition of teeth), it proved what the Stalwart and liberal papers were saying—to wit: that Garfield had sold himself, soul and body to Blaine, and that Blaine was using Garfield to destroy the Stalwart element of the nation. That was the first occult (hesitating and correcting himself) eye evidence that I had of their exceeding intimacy, and it confirmed what I had been reading for weeks in the newspapers.

Q. Then you did not believe until that night in July that there was any such public necessity for the removal of the President? A. I did believe it all along. This was a positive eye confirmation of what the newspapers were saying—to wit: that Garfield was entirely under Blaine's control. Blaine is a bold, wicked, vindictive man, and I tell him so to his face. I say furthermore, that Mr. Blaine is morally responsible for Mr. Garfield's death. If it had not been for Blaine's influence over Garfield, Garfield would have been alive to-day. He would not have disrupted the Republican Party and imperilled the Republic. There would have been no necessity for his removal, and hence there would have been no necessity for the inspiration of his removal. But enough of that.

Q. Had you ever before tried to kill Mr. Garfield? A. (Again imitating Mr. Porter's tones and snarling at him) No, I had never before tried to kill Mr. Garfield.

Mr. Porter then led the prisoner through all the circumstances of his going to the church which Mr. Garfield attended seeing him in his pew, afterwards examining the pew through the window from the outside and thinking whether that would not be a good place to remove him. On being further pressed as to the inspiration, he refused in an angry tone to discuss the subject any further. He did not think it necessary to irritate the public and to irritate the Court and jury with any more of such talk.

Here the District Attorney interposed with the suggestion that as the prisoner was tired, the Court should now take a recess, which was accordingly done.

After the recess Mr. Porter questioned the prisoner as to his visit to the jail made prior to the day of the shooting. The prisoner stated that that visit had been made after the inspiration had first seized him, and that its purpose was to see where he would go under human law. The examination was then addressed to the occurrences of the night before the shooting when the prisoner followed the President and Mr. Blaine. The prisoner stated that he had not shot that night because it was hot and sultry.

Q. And you were afraid you would make Mr. Blaine sweat? A. No, sir.

Q. Did you think it would make you hotter to pull that trigger? Inquired Mr. Porter, raising his arm and making a motion as if shooting with a pistol.

The prisoner (contemptuously).—"Oh, don't put on so much style with the trigger."

Q. Did you think so? A. (imitating) No, sir, I did not think so. It was extremely hot and I did not feel like it at that particular time.

Q. You felt like it when you did shoot? A. Under extraordinary resolution and pressure I did it. I had to do it.

Q. There was a remonstrance against the murder in you all the time? A. No, sir; I never had a conception of it as a murder. I have no idea of it as a murder. (Impatiently) You have gone over this two or three times.

Q. You never had a remonstrance after the 1st of June? A. Never.

Q. In your own conscience? A. In my own conscience. It was simply a question of opportunity.

Q. Did the Deity tell you that? A. The Deity told me to remove him whenever an opportunity occurred.

Q. That was His language? A. In substance it was.

Mr. Porter having again questioned the prisoner as to his pistol practice prior to the shooting, the latter turned to the Court and said: "If your Honor please, I want to know if it is necessary for Judge Porter to go through this business again. I do not see the pertinence of this kind of talk and I ask the protection of the Court. If you have any new question, I am willing to solve it. I object to going over this ground again. If you have any new ideas you want to show and elucidate I will assist you."

Mr. Porter then called the prisoner's attention to the fact that he had made arrangements to go to the jail, and inquired why he had done so.

The prisoner replied that he was afraid of being mobbed before he could explain his views to the people. They would say that he was a disappointed office seeker, and would hang him up. That was the only possible motive they could concoct for the act.

Mr. Porter then put some questions as to the occurrence of the 18th of June, when the prisoner refrained from shooting the President on account of Mrs. Garfield's presence, and finally asked, if Mrs. Garfield had been with the President on the

2d of July, would you have shot him? A. No, I should not have shot him in her presence. I did not know what the effect might be on her.

Q. Then it depended entirely on your will? A. It depended on whether I had a suitable opportunity.

Mr. Porter inquired why he would not have shot in Mrs. Garfield's presence.

The prisoner.—"If your head is so thick that you can't get the idea in, I won't try to pound it in. Don't ask your questions in a mean, sickly sort of way." He then settled himself back in his chair and adjusting his glasses began to read a newspaper.

After one or two insolent replies, and the interposition of Mr. Scoville, who supported the prisoner's views that counsel was going over old ground, the prisoner again lapsed into sullen silence.

Judge Porter then shifted his examination and asked: "I suppose you have no objection to answering what you did on the day that you killed him?" The prisoner then gave an account of his actions on the morning of July 2d. He had slept the previous night at the Riggs House, had risen early and sat in Lafayette Park some time before breakfast. After breakfast he went to his room and put his revolver in his pocket. A little before nine o'clock he went to the depot, and had his boots blacked.

Mr. Porter.—"Did you want to be in full dress when you killed him?

The prisoner (drawling).—"No. I didn't want to be in full dress. I don't want to be interrupted."

Mr. Porter.—"And I don't want to be interrupted."

The prisoner.—"Then keep quiet."

THE ASSASSIN DESCRIBES THE DEED.

The prisoner then proceeded with his story. Blaine and the President drove up in a single horse carriage, and not in the White House carriage, which showed how much the President was under Blaine's influence; Blaine was blowing and blowing, and the President was listening; they were on the most intimate relations; Blaine got out of one side of the carriage, and Garfield out of the other; they walked into the depot and passed within a few feet of the prisoner, who drew his weapon and fired twice and hit him once.

Q. You shot him in the back? A. I did not fire at any particular place.

Q. Did you not fire for the hollow of his back? A. My intention was to shoot him in the back.

Q. Did you think that if he got two balls in his back it would remove him? A. I thought so.

Q. And you intended to put them there. A. I did.

Q. (In a solemn manner) And from that hour to this you have never felt regret or remorse? A. I regret giving pain or trouble to any one, but I have no doubt as to the necessity of the act or the divinity of the act.

Q. You have never hinted at any remorse? A. My mind is a perfect blank on that subject.

Q. Do you feel any more remorse about rendering his wife a widow and her children fatherless, than about breaking the leg of that puppy dog? A. I have no conception of it as murder or killing.

Q. And you feel no remorse? A. (In a low and almost inaudible tone) Of course, I feel remorse, so far as my personal feelings are concerned; I feel remorse as much as any man, and regret the necessity of the act, but (raising his voice)—

Mr. Porter.—"Cross-examination is closed."

"But" continued the prisoner, excitedly, "my duty to the Lord and the American people overcame my personal feelings. If the Lord had not inspired that act it would not have been done."

Mr. Scoville then proceeded with the redirect examination of the prisoner, as follows:

Q. Is your feeling at present, or has it been at any time since the 2d of July last, any different from what it was at the time of the shooting in that respect? A. No difference whatever; I have been just as clear as to the divinity of the act, and as to the necessity for it for the good of the American people since the 1st of June, as a man can be on anything.

Q. Did you have before the shooting any feeling such as we would call a human or humane feeling on account of the suffering which might be produced by your act? A. From the middle of May to about the 1st of June all my natural feelings were against the act; that was the period when my natural feelings were excited, but since that time I have not had the slightest doubt as to the necessity for the act, and the divinity of it, not the slightest doubt that the whole thing was inspired by the Deity, and that he would take care of it.

Q. Did the matter present itself to your mind in the ordinary view of humanity, as to whether it would cause personal suffering or not? A. No; I never had any conception of it in that way at all; my mind was a perfect blank on it.

Q. Do you recollect the interviews which I had with you in the jail two days after the shooting? A. Yes; Colonel Corkhill and his stenographer, Mr. Bailey, were present, and I want to say here what I have not said before--I told Mr. Scoville and Colonel Corkhill that I did not think the President would recover, because the Lord did not wish him to recover.

After answering a few questions by Mr. Scoville and Mr. Davidge in reference to the Oneida

Community, and his scheme in regard to the *Inter-Ocean* newspaper, the examination of the prisoner was closed, and leaving the stand, he resumed his seat by the side of his counsel.

Dr. Alexander McNeil, of Columbus, Ohio, was then called by Mr. Scoville. Witness had seen the prisoner at Columbus three or four years ago, when he was attempting to lecture on theology, and sell an inspired volume of his own authorship. There was nothing of importance in the testimony, and Emory A. Storrs, Chas. B. Farwell, and others failing to respond when called for, the Court at 2.30 P. M., adjourned.

CHAPTER XVIII.

Emory A. Storrs Gives His Views About the Prisoner—Considers That He is "Off His Nut"—The Ponderous Form of David Davis on the Witness Stand—The Senator's Views About Matters in General.

ON Saturday, December 3d, the examination of witnesses for the defence was resumed.

J. O. P. Burnside, of the Post-Office Department, testified that he lived in Freeport, Illinois, in 1841. Lived there six years before, and fifteen years after. Knew the family of L. W. Guiteau. Mrs. Guiteau was quite unrivalled, and always wore a white cap.

Charles C. Allen, United States Marshal for the Western District of Missouri, testified that he lived in Freeport, Illinois, from 1839 to 1850. Knew the family of L. W. Guiteau. Mrs. Guiteau was a confirmed invalid the summer before the birth of the prisoner. Witness never saw her on the street afterwards, but she always wore a white cap.

Emory A. Storrs, of Chicago, was the next witness. He testified that he had known the prisoner eight or ten years, and had seen him frequently in Chicago, New York and Washington. Saw him during the political campaign in the rooms of the Republican National Committee in New York.

In reply to further questions witness said: "I met the prisoner in New York on August 5th, 1880, when there was a large gathering of Republicans to meet General Garfield. He was exultant in manner and gave me several copies of his speech which I was surprised to find appearing as if printed under the auspices of the National Committee. He had rendered no services to the party and did not claim to have done so. I met him again in April, 1881, at the Riggs House, in Washington.

"I observed nothing peculiar in his dress; his manner might be called one of exaltation. My recollection is that he told me he was going to have the Austrian mission, though it might have been the Paris consulship. I suggested that the position was a very important one. He then referred to his speech as being an important factor in the campaign. I said that this was in Blaine's department, and that he was a politician, and an able one. I think his language in reply was that he was 'solid with Blaine.' I don't think he asked me to see Mr. Blaine, but seeing that the conversation was tending to that point, and as I did not wish to see Mr. Blaine on that business or any other relative to appointment to office, I rather forestalled what he had on his mind by saying that my hostility to Mr. Blaine was so active politically, that I thought that any advocacy of mine would be a serious damage to him. That I apprehended if Mr. Blaine knew of my promoting his claims, it would be a sure way of defeating him, and that on the whole I thought Blaine had better not know that I had any views in his favor. All I know about it is that from that time he never spoke to me, he seemed rather discouraged."

In reply to further questions as to his opinion on the sanity of the prisoner, Mr. Storrs said: "I am not an expert on the subject of insanity or any other medical topic. I have stated about all I have seen; I cannot express an opinion as to his sanity or insanity. I shall express no opinion whatever as to his sanity or insanity, or as to the degree of any mental difficulty under which he may have been laboring. My impression was that he had an illy-balanced judgment and an illy-balanced mind, and did not have what the average man would call good common sense."

Witness further stated that while cognizant of disagreements in the Republican Party, he would not admit that they amounted to a breach, and claimed that the good sense of that party was sufficient, in the rank and file, to prevent a disruption.

On cross-examination, by Mr. Davidge, witness said: "I have never seen anything in Guiteau which led me to believe that he could not distinguish between right and wrong." Mr. Scoville made several objections which were overruled and exceptions were noted during the cross-examination. In re-direct examination witness admitted having said to Mr. Scoville in Chicago that he thought Guiteau was "off his nut."

Edward A. Daniels, of Virginia, testified that he had met the prisoner at the Young Men's Christian Association, and thought his conversation and movements peculiar.

Senator David Davis, of Illinois, was next sworn. In reply to Mr. Scoville he stated his official position, and that he was not connected with either of the political parties of the country.

Q. Did you know of the breach in the Republican Party growing out of the difficulties last summer between President Garfield and Senator Conkling? A. I had no personal knowledge of it, not going into a caucus with either association. I know that there were factions in the Republican Party.

Q. From your knowledge of the political difficulties which grew up at that time, and from your knowledge of the American people, what, in your opinion, was the probability of those difficulties disrupting and destroying the Republican Party? A. That is a far-reaching question. The Republican Party has not been destroyed, and yet there have been breaches in it. There is only one way in which the Republican Party can ever be destroyed.

Q. What way is that? A. The disruption of the Democratic Party would destroy it.

Q. Is it your honest opinion that the difficulties between branches or factions of the Republican Party have been or are in danger of absolutely disrupting the Republican Party? A. That is a mere matter of opinion. I cannot understand this line of examination. The Republican Party is an extraordinary organization. I do not believe it will die until the Democratic Party is dead.

Q. What is your opinion on this position; whether the success of the Democratic Party at this time or at the next Presidential election would imperil the existence of the Republic? A. I do not think that the success of any political party would imperil the Republic. I do not believe that at all.

Q. Do you believe that the success of the Democratic Party would tend in any degree to bring on another civil war? A. No, I do not. I think that the Southern people are the last people in the world to desire to go into any war. If there be any war it will come from somewhere else than the South.

The witness then left the stand remarking that he had never seen the prisoner before, and knew nothing of the matter. Mr. Scoville replied that the reason for the summons would be shown in the argument later.

Edward A. Bailey, a stenographer, was the next witness. He testified that he accompanied the District Attorney to the jail on the 3d of July and subsequent days and took shorthand notes of the prisoner's statements. He was asked to produce his notes, but he said that he had destroyed them because their substance had been embodied in a transcript which he had handed to the District Attorney. Mr. Scoville called upon the District Attorney to produce this transcript, which Mr. Corkhill declined doing, on the ground that it was got up for his private information.

The prisoner then read a list of names of persons he wanted subpœnaed, to show the political condition of the country last spring. The names were President Arthur, General Grant, ex-Senators Conkling and Platt, Messrs. Jewell, Robertson and Dorsey and Senators Jones and Logan; also Mr. Reid, of the *Tribune*, Mr. Jones of *The Times*, Mr. Dana, of *The Sun*, and Mr. Hurlburt, of *The World*, Mr. Gorham, of the *Washington Republican*, Mr. Hutchins, of the *Washington Post*, and Mr. Nixon, of the *Chicago Inter-Ocean*.

Mr. Scoville said that he had issued a subpœna for President Arthur, but he did not care to have him summoned until he had seen him personally, and had directed the Marshal to that effect. The case then at ten minutes past twelve, went over until Monday.

CHAPTER XIX.

The Expert Testimony Commenced—Remarkable Hypothetical Questioning to Obtain Presumption of Insanity—Guiteau makes a Speech and Gives Advice to President Arthur.

MONDAY, December 5th, was the commencement of the fourth week of the trial, and initiated the tedious and reiterated examination of expert witnesses. The prisoner again opened the proceedings by a statement that he would submit the point upon which he wished the experts to pass. This assumption of the right to conduct and regulate the trial produced laughter, but Guiteau looked solemn and said: "When a man claims that he is compelled to do an illegal act from a power beyond him which he cannot control, where his moral agency is dominated, I want these experts to say whether that is insanity or sanity.

The Court.—"They will be heard on that subject."

James P. Kiernan was called. He testified that he had been a practicing physician for eight years; was managing Editor of the *Chicago Medical Review* and lectured on mental diseases in the Chicago Medical College; had made a study of mental diseases since 1874.

Q. Assuming it to be a fact that there was a strong hereditary taint of insanity in the blood of the prisoner at the bar; also that at about the age of thirty-five years his own mind was so much deranged that he was a fit subject to be sent to an insane asylum; also that at different times after that date during the next succeeding five years, he manifested such decided symptoms of insanity, without simulation, that many different persons conversing with him and observing his conduct believed him to be insane; also that in or about the month of June, 1881, at or about the expiration of said term of five years, he became demented by the idea that he was inspired of God to remove by death the President of the United States; also that he acted on what he believed to be such inspiration, and as he believed to be in accordance with the Divine will in the preparation for and in the accomplishment of such a purpose; also that he committed the act of shooting the President under what he believed to be a Divine command which he was not at liberty to disobey and which belief made out a conviction which controlled his conscience and overpowered his will as to that act so that he could not resist the mental pressure upon him; also that immediately after the shooting he appeared calm and as if relieved by the performance of a great duty; also that there was no other adequate motive for the act than the conviction that he was executing the Divine will for the good of his country—assuming all of these propositions to be true, state whether in your opinion, the prisoner was sane or insane at the time of shooting President Garfield? A. Assuming these propositions to be true, I should say that the prisoner was insane.

The witness was then cross-examined by Mr. Davidge, and stated that he did not believe in a future state of rewards and punishments. Witness gave a resume of his career after graduating from the University of New York City. Had been connected with a department for the insane on Ward's Island, New York, and acted as assistant physician. Had been apothecary for the infirm from 1875 to 1878, and was dismissed for refusing to sign a paper in a case of violence, and for discussing a medical subject.

The testimony in reference to some of the prisoner's relatives having been summarized, the witness was asked whether in his judgment that evidence made out a strong hereditary taint of insanity in the blood of the prisoner. His answer was taking all that into consideration, I should certainly say the case was one of hereditary insanity. Witness further stated that he believed in moral insanity and that when the moral nature is diseased, the mind is diseased.

Witness was inquired of in connection with the testimony of Dr. Rice, that he had once recommended the prisoner to be sent to an insane asylum, and the witness stated that he should think that if the prisoner had then been sent to a lunatic asylum, he would not have been discharged. Witness was not influenced in his opinion by the common idea that the prisoner was insane. His opinion was based, first, upon the strong hereditary tendency; second, upon the testimony of Dr. Rice as to the impairment of the prisoner's judgment and his moral excitement, and third, upon the prisoner's strong conviction that he had a mission from God to fulfill in the removal of the President.

Q. And on these elements alone you would give the opinion that the prisoner was insane? A. I should.

Witness had come into contact with patients laboring under delusions of having missions from the Deity. He gave one instance of an insane man in Chicago who had a Divine revelation that his wife was unfaithful to him and should be removed, and yet that man instead of killing his wife, set to work to remove her by divorce. This was an illustration of the proposition that insane men often act as sane men. He instanced another case of a patient on Ward's Island, named Williams, who used to claim that he was inspired by God to do certain things. Witness did not think that a man believing himself commissioned by God would bear himself very differently from a sane man. He would be governed in a general way by his own specific characteristics. It would not depend upon the fixity of the belief.

The prisoner.—"The Lord injects an inspiration into my brain and leaves me to work it out in my own way. That is the way I get my inspiration. God does not employ fools to do His work. He gets the best brains he can find."

Q. Suppose a man told you that he had a grand inspiration—say to slay a ruler—and suppose you watched his conduct and behavior and it turned out to be that of a vulgar criminal all the way through, what would you think of his statement that he had a Divine commission?

The prisoner.—"There is no vulgar criminal in this case; please leave the 'vulgar' out."

Mr. Scoville objected to the question, because the witness' opinion of what was "vulgar" might differ from the counsel's.

The prisoner.—"Nothing vulgar about this case. It is all high-toned."

Mr. Davidge (to the witness).—"Assume that a man says to you, 'I am commissioned by God to slay a ruler,' and you follow the conduct and behavior and operations of that man for six weeks and find them to be those of an ordinary sane man, what weight would you give to his declaration?

The witness.—"If I am to assume the condition of things which you state, I have to answer I would not have given any weight to his declaration.

Witness went on to state that while an insane man might reason logically from false premises, or seem to do so, he would not undertake to say that these conditions prevail in a majority of cases.

Mr. Scoville asked the witness to explain his answer as to a non-belief in a hereafter, and the witness replied, that, "like many other scientfic men, he was simply an agnostic on that subject; he had no evidence upon it."

Mr. Davidge.—" If a man thinks that he is excuting a Divine command, has he any wear and tear of conscience?"

The witness.—" There is wear and tear very often where a man is dominated by a delusion. Strong delusions very often have a great physical effect on the frame of a man; every one knows that there are sane men who would have such a murderous design for five or six weeks and yet not show the slightest physical change."

The witness in the course of a discussion on the various forms and types of insanity, spoke of progressive paresis of the insane as one of those forms that produce physical changes.

The prisoner.—" What is the English of that, Doctor? We are all common folks here and cannot understand that scientific language."

The witness having first obtained from the Court permission to answer, replied that it was a form of insanity attended by very strongly marked physical and mental symptoms. For instance, a man who was penurious would suddenly become extravagant and spend his money lavishly. It was also attended by a strong tendency to believe himself immensely wealthy or immensely strong, or something of that kind; at the same time his walk would become tremulous and he would have frequent disturbance of gait and a tendency to eat. The witness instanced Wemyss Jobson, formerly of New York, as one so affected; he also spoke of an inequality in the two sides of the head as an evidence of hereditary insanity.

"That hits my case exactly," the prisoner broke in, "one side of my head is larger than the other. Doctors examined me the other night. (To the witness.) When hereditary nimbus exists in a man, does it not have to show itself, sooner or later, on sufficient cause?"

The witness.—"Yes, it has to show itself, sooner or later, on sufficient cause."

The prisoner.—"My case. That is all."

The witness, in reply to a question by Mr. Scoville, said that perhaps one-fourth of the cases of insanity that came under his observation were of this form, and it would be classed as hereditary insanity. Insanity of this character manifests itself after puberty; after death certain conditions of the brain are found in such persons which must have existed from birth—a decided deficiency; a person so affected may be more excitable at times and more quiet at times. That kind of insanity is not curable. The line between sanity and insanity is not easily determined. It is much easier to determine whether a man is simulating insanity than it is to determine whether he is sane or insane. Insanity always follows an abnormal brain.

Mr. Davidge.—"What is the proportion of insane people to sane people in the world?"

The witness.—"I have not any exact statistics; probably out of every twenty-five persons in ordinary life, five are insane, and sooner or later they become inmates of insane asylums. I mean to say if I talk with twenty-five ordinary business men I would probably find five of them insane."

Mr. Davidge.—"Even among business men?"

The witness.—"Yes, among business men."

Mr. Davidge.—"And of course among the floating, idle people who have no settled occupation the proportion would be still larger?"

The witness.—"I am taking all that into account."

Mr. Davidge.—"And one in five is insane. Well, at least two of the jurors are doomed."

Mr. Scoville.—"Perhaps some of the lawyers may take their places."

The witness, in describing the border line between sanity and insanity, said that there were a large number of men who, while not positively insane, are deficient in judgment, and cannot be classed with properly well balanced men.

Q. Do you mean that as a general thing men of that class become fit subjects for insane asylums? A. Not all of them, but many of them do; there are three times as many persons outside of asylums as there are inside who are proper subjects for insane asylums.

Richard J. Hinton, a Washington newspaper man, was called. He testified to having seen the prisoner frequently last summer at the rooms of the National Republican Committee in New York; he had also read his speech of Garfield *vs.* Hancock, but not until after the assassination; he thought it ill-jointed and utterly inconsequential.

Dr. Charles H. Nicholls, of New York, was called. He testified that he was Superintendent of the Bloomingdale Asylum for the Insane; has been connected with insane asylums since 1844, and had during all that time made a study of mental diseases; was first connected with the New York State Lunatic Asylum at Utica, then with the Bloomingdale Asylum, then with the Government Hospital for the Insane for the District of Columbia, and lastly with the Bloomingdale Asylum. The propositions in the hypothetical question were read to the witness, and he was asked whether, in his opinion, the prisoner was sane or insane when he shot President Garfield.

Witness replied: "Taking that hypothetical

case to be true, I should think the person described in it was insane."

Mr. Davidge started to cross-examine, but Mr. Scoville objected to the form of the question put, and Mr. Davidge said the witness might stand aside, and he would be called afterwards for the prosecution.

Dr. Charles Folsom, of Boston; *Dr. Samuel Worcester*, of Salem, Massachusetts; *Dr. William W. Golding*, Superintendent of the Government Hospital for the Insane at Washington, D. C.; *Dr. James H. McBride*, of the Insane Asylum at Milwaukee; *Dr. Walter Channing*, of Brookline, Massachusetts; and *Dr. Theodore W. Fisher*, of Boston, were then severally called. The questions and replies in each case were very similar, the mode of examination being as follows: The proposition laid down in the hypothetical question was read to the witness, and he was asked: "leaving out of view your own opinions or anything that you may draw from anywhere else, and taking the facts as stated in the hypothetical question as proved to be true, what, in your opinion, was the mental condition of the prisoner at the time of his shooting President Garfield?"

Witnesses replied: "On the assumption that those facts are true in the same way as I use language I should say he was unquestionably insane."

In the case of Dr. Worcester, the witness

insisted on a definite interpretation of the word "inspiration," which was used by Mr. Scoville, and that gentleman (with some asperity) replied "If the witness did not understand the question he could stand aside." In the case of Dr. Fisher, the witness intimated that he objected to be confined to the hypothetical state of facts, and the prosecution stated that he would be called by them at a later period.

Mr. Scoville stated that he had no other witnesses present; he had but three or four other witnesses to examine before closing. He had expected to have President Arthur present, but that gentleman was engaged on the Message to Congress.

The prisoner then broke into a long harangue, and was allowed to have full swing, as follows: "I want to say here that I want to have here as witnesses General Grant, Senators Conkling and Platt, Governor Jewell and those other men who were doing politics last spring. I appear here as my own counsel, and I want an order signed by the Court to have those gentlemen here. I do not want to have my case compromised by Mr. Scoville. I want to show by General Grant the personal feeling that he had towards President Garfield last spring, when he wrote his letter to Senator Jones, showing a very bitter spirit towards the President. I want to show that neither Grant nor Conkling nor Jewell would go to the White House; I was on friendly re.ations with these men. The inspiration which came to me for President Garfield's removal arose from the political situation, and I want to keep thumping that into the ears of the civilized world; of course, it is very important for me to have these men examined in this defence. Mr. Scoville has altogether too narrow a view of this matter. Scoville is a good man, but he is no politician, and he is no criminal lawyer; he has done remarkably well considering, but he is not an expert."

Mr. Scoville.—"I presume that President Arthur will be willing to attend, and I suppose his testimony will be sufficient."

The prisoner.—"I do not think so. I want Grant, Conkling and Platt and Jewell, all those men here. I am going to have an order prepared (beginning to write), and I will ask the Court to sign it and have subpœnas issued for these men (After a short pause he broke out again.) Mr. Storrs, of Chicago, one of the most brilliant members of the American Bar, says that I have got the true theory of this defense. He does not take any stock in Scoville's theory that I am a fool. He says also, that I am the ablest lawyer in this case, and I shall not quarrel with him for his opinion. I should be highly pleased if President Arthur would recognize Mr. Storrs' services, and make him Attorney General. He is a man of brains and a true blooded Republican, and would do honor to the nation in that position. I make one suggestion publicly to President Arthur. I have not asked him for any favors, and probably shall not; but I feel authorized to make this suggestion about Mr. Storrs, and unless the President has made other arrangements I hope he will act on this suggestion.

Mr. Scoville proceeded to read the book called "*Truth*," and he continued to read until three o'clock, when the Court adjourned.

CHAPTER XX.

The Prisoner Insists in Having all His Distinguished Friends Put upon the Stand—The Evidence for the Defence Practically Closed.

AS soon as the Court convened on Tuesday, December 6th, Guiteau, with unusual moderation said, "may it please your Honor, I have prepared an order for the witnesses suggested last evening. I will hand it to your Honor." Judge Cox took the paper but made no comment.

Charles B. Farwell, a member of Congress, from Chicago, was the first witness to take the stand.

Mr. Scoville called the witness' attention to the dissensions in the Republican Party last spring, and then inquired whether, in witness' opinion, those dissensions did not contain the disruption of the Republican Party. To this question, Mr. Davidge objected and the Court held that the question was too leading; a decision which Guiteau supplemented by remarking, "It is a rather abrupt way of putting it. You want to smooth the way, Mr. Scoville, with preliminary questions. That was the trouble you had with Mr. Davis. You ought to ask preliminary questions, and not get up to the point at once."

Mr. Porter said that the prosecution had allowed the defence to go into this question of the political situation, but they must not forget that this was a Court of Justice and a prisoner on trial for crime. "Yes," said Guiteau, "that's the very point I want to discuss this morning."

Mr. Porter.—"If the Republican Party was in a state of disruption, it could not be sustained by the opinion of witnesses, sane or insane. If there is any purpose in this line of inquiry, it is to show that the prisoner acted on the reasonable conviction of actual facts, and is not insane. If, on the other hand counsel propose to prove, even by the opinions of witnesses, that the Republican Party was not in danger of disruption, and that it was not needful to save the Republic, we will save all trouble by admitting that fact in behalf of the Government. Under that view of the case, your Honor will I think, waste no more time in this irrelevant and wild inquiry."

Mr. Scoville.—"If the gentleman had made that speech two or three days ago we might have saved the time he talks about. I understand now that the prosecution admits that the differences in the Republican Party did not threaten its existence or integrity. If that is admitted that is all I ask."

Mr. Porter.—"I have made an admission in terms intelligible to every gentleman in the Court room. I do not propose to adopt the terms my friend proposes. The Republican Party was not in danger of disruption. It was not needful for the purpose of saving the American Republic, that its President should be murdered. While we admit these facts, however, we by no means admit that there were not those so vile and revolutionary in spirit and so desirous of notoriety that they entertained a different view—not from insanity, but depravity and desire of self-advancement.

This put the prisoner in a towering rage. He shouted violently: " That is false. I will tell you that to your face. I say that the Republican Party was heating up. It was red hot about the 1st of June; redder hot about the 1st of July, and there was no telling what might have resulted. My inspiration was to remove the President. I do not pretend there was going to be a war, but it would have come in two or three years. Everything was tending in that direction."

On further examination the witness related the incidents of his first acquaintance with the prisoner, who introduced himself, exhibited a roll of papers and wished to borrow $200,000 to start a newspaper, promising in return to make witness President of the United States. On cross-examination by Mr. Davidge, after many interruptions by the prisoner, and objections to questions by Mr. Scoville, it was elicited from witness that he thought the prisoner knew the difference between right and wrong.

The prisoner.—"That was about three months before the alleged shooting; this whole business rests on the simple question whether the Deity inspired the act."

The Court (severely).—"What is the necessity of your making that statement so often. Keep quiet."

The prisoner.—"It saves a good deal of foolish talk."

The Court.—"No; it does not."

Mr. George C. Gorham, editor of *Washington National Republican*, then took the stand. He stated that he had never read the speech of the prisoner, entitled "Garfield against Hancock." A copy was handed to him by Mr. Scoville, with the request that he should read it. At this point Mr. Porter interposed and demanded that the trial should proceed. Mr. Scoville sneeringly replied, and then requested the prisoner to read extracts from his book "*Truth.*" After further trifling and by-play of this kind, varied by spats between counsel, and interruptions by the prisoner, who claimed that the speech had been approved by the best men in the country, the witness was again asked his opinion of the speech. He pronounced it "a pretty well endorsed statement of the situation as viewed by a good many people; neither remarkable on the one hand, nor ridiculous on the other." Guiteau then endeavored to examine the witness as to the tone of certain editorials in the

Republican, and finally announced that he should ask for an order to have the files produced. After a pause, Guiteau turned to the Court and said: "I would like to know if your Honor has signed that order?"

The Court.—"I have not looked at it."

The prisoner (excitedly).—"What has become of that order? (To Mr. Scoville)—I suppose you have suppressed it. It looks as if you were sitting down upon it. I would like to ask the clerk of the Court if he has an order to issue subpœnas for General Grant, Collector Robertson, Mr. Jewell and those kind of men."

Mr. Scoville here stated that he had issued a subpœna for President Arthur, and had expected him to be in Court, but he proposed that the President's testimony might be taken at any convenient time. Mr. Davidge asked what it was intended to prove by the President.

Mr. Scoville replied: "I expect to prove by him that the prisoner, some time in October last, after I came here, wrote to the President a letter, which was sent to him, addressing him in very familiar terms, and requesting him, as one equal might request another, to do certain things of a public character. I expect to prove that the prisoner in this letter applied to the President, apparently with perfect confidence that the President would heed his requests and comply with them, and I expect to show by the President that he had never given the prisoner any ground for supposing that he even knew him."

The prisoner here, in an excited harangue claimed that he was on the most friendly terms with Grant, Arthur, Conkling, Jewell and "all that kind of men."

Mr. Scoville.—"I propose to show by President Arthur that all that the prisoner is now saying is false, and that the prisoner had never any reasonable grounds, any such grounds as a sane man would act upon—to apply to President Arthur for any favor or position whatever. These are some of the facts which I expect to show by the President. I do not expect to question the President as to public affairs or as to his public or private relations, but simply as to those personal matters connected with the prisoner as to which President Arthur is informed, and which I cannot show by any other person."

The prisoner (contemptuously to Mr. Scoville). —"You had never anything to do with those high-toned men. You do not know how to act with them. You had been always away down in the dirt. You have got no political record. You ought to have stayed in Chicago and not come into this case. You have no capacity for this kind of business. What do you know about it? You will not 'sit down on me' any more."

Mr. Porter suggested that this Court, a branch of the judiciary department of the Government, had no right to compel the attendance of the President, summoning him from the discharge of his duties to the nation to serve the purpose of a criminal, and he proposed that interrogatories in writing should be submitted to the President and his answers to them received in evidence.

Guiteau broke in again and excitedly exclaimed, that he did not want Scoville to compromise his case; he wanted a first-class artist on it.

Mr. Scoville said he would accept the offer of Mr. Porter, and propound the questions. The President might know a fact maintained by the defence and the prisoner was entitled to the benefit of it from President or laborer.

The Court.—" Reduce your interrogatories to writing, and if the ruling of the Court is wanted I will rule upon them."

Mr. Scoville.—"I am willing to do that. I only want to get at this matter in the best way it can be done. I have stated fairly and candidly what I proposed to show by the President, and I do not propose to go any further. But I cannot reduce my interrogatories in writing now and here."

The Court.—"It can be done this afternoon."

The prisoner.—"I wish to know whether Your Honor considers the defence as now closed. I want the chance to subpœna those prominent men whose names I have given to Your Honor, and I want a ruling on that."

Judge Cox.—"I will look into that matter."

The prisoner.—"I thank Your Honor. I want justice and nothing more than justice in the matter. We will be allowed to introduce these prominent gentlemen whenever we can get access to them. I wanted them subpœnaed several days ago, but Mr. Scoville and I do not agree on the theory of this defence. If Mr. Storrs were defending this case he and I would be in perfect harmony. He is an abler man than Scoville in every way. I am very sorry that I could not get Storrs into the case. Storrs is a politician and one of the most brilliant men at the American Bar. Scoville is doing well enough on his theory, but his theory is too narrow on this kind of business. That is all the trouble with him. It requires a first-class artist to do this fine work."

Mr. John W. Guiteau was recalled to give the date at which he began to change his mind as to his brother's mental condition. He dated the change from the receipt of a bundle of his letters from his sister Flora after the 21st day of October last.

Mr. Scoville then proceeded to read some posters and handbills advertising the book called "*Truth,*" and the prisoner's lecture on the second coming of Christ. In the course of the reading the prisoner occasionally broke out with remarks, among them the following: "The people are beginning to understand that the Deity inspired this act, and they say: 'Well, if the Deity inspired it let it go.'"

The prisoner.—"I want a ruling on my application for subpœnas for these prominent men."

The Court.—"I do not think it necessary

The prisoner.—"Then the reporter will note an exception. Let the record show that I applied in person for subpœnas for certain persons to show the political conditions last spring and to show my connection with these prominent persons— Conkling, Grant, Arthur, Jewell and that class of men. I want to show my relation with them personally and politically and the Court refuses to allow it. Note an exception on that point."

Mr. Davidge asked Mr. Scoville what he proposed to do as to the portions of the book "*Truth*" to which he intended to call the attention of the jury.

Mr. Scoville replied that he proposed to mark and refer to them. On objection being made to this, he said he should be compelled to read the whole book and began to do so. The prisoner interrupted with, "Do not read it like a school boy, read it with more spirit," and then proposed to read the book himself. This was agreed to and for three quarters of an hour he occupied the time of the Court until the District Attorney consented that Mr. Scoville should mark certain passages, and thus stopped the farce.

Then, at twelve o'clock, at the suggestion of the District Attorney, the Court adjourned.

CHAPTER XXI.

Another Cranky Speech—Rebuttal Testimony to Prove the Sanity of the Guiteau Family—If They were Insane, Nobody Knew it—The Prisoner Compliments President Arthur's Message.

THE Court had barely been called to order on Wednesday, December 7, when the prisoner addressed Judge Cox:

"May it please Your Honor," he said, "the American people don't desire that this case shall be tried again, and I don't desire it. I say, with the utmost respect to this Court and jury and my counsel, Mr. Scoville, that I am not satisfied with the political situation as developed in this case. That is the gist of this alleged offense. The President of the United States would never have been shot if it had not been for the political situation as it existed last May and June, and I say I have a right, as a matter of law, appearing as my own counsel, to ask your Honor that General Grant, Senators Conkling and Platt and President Arthur, and those kind of men, who were so down upon Garfield that they would not speak to him on the street and would not go to the White House; I have a right to show that; I have a right to show my personal relations to those gentlemen; that I was on fiiendly terms with them; that I was cordially received, well dressed and well fed at the Fifth Avenue Hotel, by the National Committee; I want to show my supposed personal relations to those men; I don't want to take exception to your Honor's ruling, but I shall be obliged to do so; I have no doubt that the Court in banc will give me a new trial.'

The Court.—"Your exceptions have already been noted."

The prisoner.—"I intend to make the closing speech in this case, after Mr. Scoville has had his say. He is doing splendidly, according to his theory; but his theory is altogether too narrow in my judgment. That is all I have against Mr. Scoville."

Mr. Scoville stated that in accordance with the agreement entered into yesterday, he had drawn up six interrogatories and sent them to the President yesterday afternoon, asking him as to his knowledge of the prisoner, the relations between them and generally as to those matters. He had requested an answer to be returned last evening, or by nine o'clock this morning, but had not yet received it.

Mr. Porter said the prosecution expected that the interrogatories would be submitted to them, but Mr. Scoville explained that in view of the President's engagements, he had sought to save time by submitting them direct. He continued: "I want to have the testimony of the President, either by his answers to my interrogatories or by his personal attendance in Court."

The Court.—"If the answers to the interrogatories are produced you can have the benefit of them at any time."

Mr. Scoville then called *Dr. Spitzka*, of New York, and *Nettie G. Rood*, of Chicago, but neither responded, and counsel asked for attachments against them, which the Court granted. A long discussion here ensued between Mr. Scoville and the District Attorney as to the admission of Dr. Spitzka's testimony at a later date, which was terminated by the Court informing Mr. Scoville that he could have his attachments, and the other questions could be disposed of when Dr. Spitzka appeared. The Court added: "You will not be prejudiced, of course."

Mr. Scoville.—"I have glanced over this book "*Truth*," and find that its general character is the same as in those portions of it which have been read in Court. I shall probably only have to call the attention of the jury to the alterations in the book made in writing."

The prisoner.—"When I come to address the jury I propose to show the substratum of thought and the new ideas running through that book. Mr. Scoville may do what he has a mind in his talk—"

Mr. Scoville.—"That is all."

THE PROSECUTION'S REBUTTAL TESTIMONY.

General William T. Sherman, General of the Army, was then called as the first witness for rebuttal. Witness identified the letter of the prisoner, which was handed to him at five minutes to twelve A. M. on the 2d of July, at his office in the War Department. The prisoner suggested that the letter should be read, but no attention was paid to him. In response to a question by the District Attorney, the witness stated that the four companies of artillery, which then constituted the garrison of Washington, were called out by him on the first intimation to him that the President had been shot; the shooting of the President under the circumstances, as reported to him, had given rise to an apprehension that it was part and parcel of a conspiracy pervading the country, and therefore he had promptly called out the troops in order to check it.

Q. Did you make an examination to ascertain the facts? A. I did; I went to the depot and saw the Secretaries of State and War, and learned from them and others the principal facts; I then sent Colonel Kidball to the depot with troops; I then went to the War Department and there received the letter which I hold in my hand.

Q. After you ascertained that there was no conspiracy did the army still remain in charge of the jail? A. The army did not take charge, but assisted the civil authorities in the execution of their duties; a guard was sent to the jail at the request of Major Brock.

Cross-examination by Mr. Scoville:

Q. You said something about a conspiracy? A. I said that when I first learned that General Garfield had been shot down in the depot my mind jumped to the conclusion that it must have other connection resulting from a conspiracy.

The prisoner.—"Resulting, General, from the political situation; wait a moment" (as General Sherman was about to leave the stand).

Mr. Scoville.—"Did you have any other foundation for that opinion than your own suspicion?

The witness.—"None."

In response to further questions, witness said he had investigated the matter and arrived at the conclusion that it was the act of one man, and one man alone. Guiteau politely remarked: "I am much obliged to you General, for sending troops to my protection at that time. I should not have been here if it had not been for you and General Crocker and Major Brock."

Edward P. Barton, a lawyer of Freeport, Illinois, testified to having known Luther W. Guiteau very well from 1856 until the day of his death. He had the character of a very reliable, honest, clear headed, straightforward business man. He was intelligent to an unusual degree, and kept posted in the current literature and politics of the day. His mind was a peculiarly logical one.

A further question as to whether witness had heard of L. W. Guiteau's sanity being questioned was ruled out, and the witness then stated that he had known other members of the family and believed them to be sane.

On cross-examination, witness admitted conversations with L. W. Guiteau in which the idea had been brought forward that a person living a pure life, such as was required by the New Testament, possibly might not die. Some similar ideas had been advanced by the prisoner.

A. T. Greene, a collector, of Freeport, Illinois, testified his belief in the sanity of the whole Guiteau family, and the cross-examination failed to shake his testimony.

Gardner W. Tandy, a boot and shoe dealer, of Freeport, Illinois, also testified to the sanity of such members of the Guiteau family as he had any knowledge of.

Benjamin T. Buckley, a practicing physician, of Freeport, Illinois, was the next witness. For some years he had been the doctor of L. W. Guiteau's family. Had always regarded Mr. Guiteau as a man of fine intellect, with a clear, logical mind. He was a public spirited man, a man of benevolence, always interested in the cause of education and temperance. Witness never saw the slightest indication of mental trouble in the man.

The witness was asked by Mr. Scoville if he did not know the fact that Flora, the prisoner's half sister, was sent to St. Louis to undergo treatment for insanity, and gave a negative reply.

As this witness left the stand, Mr. J. W. Guiteau indignantly repudiated the slur cast on his sister, and after an angry colloquy between counsel, the witness in reply to the District Attorney said, that Miss Flora was a girl of remarkable ability and of high standing in the community. Guiteau added: " I am sorry my half-sister Flora's name was mentioned in this case. I know she is a high toned lady and stands well in Freeport. I send her my greeting."

Smith D. Atkins, editor of the Freeport *Republican*, was the next witness, and testified to the sanity of the Guiteau family. He was questioned as to the character of Messrs. North and Amerling, witnesses for the defence, and stated that North had been excluded from the Methodist Church for lascivious conduct, and that Amerling was such a man as Luther W. Guiteau would not associate with.

The prisoner.—"I never heard any Oneida believers in Freeport ever charged with lascivious conduct."

The Court then at half-past twelve took a recess for one hour.

J. S. Cochran, a lawyer of Freeport, Illinois, was the first witness after recess. He testified that he had resided in Lockport since 1858; knew Luther W. Guiteau intimately up to to the time of his death; never saw in him any indication of mental disturbance, however slight; knew also Abram Guiteau; never saw any evidence of insanity in him; never had any reason to suppose that any of the family were of unsound mind.

The cross-examination elicited no important facts, and the witness was about to step down when the prisoner stopped him and asked: "Don't you know that my father had an active interest in the Oneida Community? Have you not heard him discuss free-lovism and Noyesism in Freeport, and did you not know he was the laughing stock there for twenty-five years? Did not everybody look upon him as cranky? (To Mr. Scoville, who was attempting to repress him) I am doing this."

The District Attorney stated that the witness might answer the prisoner's question, as he was acting as his own counsel.

The official stenographer read the questions and the witness replied, that he had never heard of L. W. Guiteau being a believer in the Oneida Community or being at all cranky.

The prisoner.—" All these witnesses, it will be observed, knew about my father's business affairs. They know nothing about his social and religious character.

George W. Oiler, a justice of the peace of Freeport, Illinois, was the next witness, and testified as to the sanity of the Guiteaus. He was then questioned by the District Attorney as to Mr. Amerling, and stated that he had received a letter from that gentleman before the trial, asking him to look up the eccentricities of the Guiteau family; he thought that the letter was written for the purpose of getting him to manufacture—

The District Attorney.—" So I thought."

Mr. Scoville started up angrily.

The District Attorney.—" That is irregular, I admit it."

Mr. Scoville.—"Then don't do it. You first do it, and then admit it."

Mr. Scoville also bitterly complained of the slurring manner in which the District Attorney alluded to Messrs. North and Amerling, instancing the fact that he had asked one witness whether he knew a "supposed lawyer named Amerling."

The witness admitted on cross-examination that he knew nothing of L. W. Guiteau's religious views.

Anson A. Babcock, a farmer of Freeport, Illinois, testified that he had lived there forty years; never saw anything in L. W. Guiteau or his family indicating insanity. On cross-examination he stated that he knew nothing of Guiteau's private actions.

While waiting for the next witness, the prisoner looked up from the paper which he had been reading for some time and stated his opinion of the President's Annual Message. "I am very glad," he said, "that General Arthur has rapped those miserable Mormons, and I hope he will do it again. I want him to make it a specialty of his administration to destroy Mormonism. The Message shows that he is a very fine man in his administration. I expect he will give us the best administration we have ever had. The Message has the true ring to it."

David H. Sunderland, State Senator from the county in which Freeport is situated, and formerly a schoolmaster of the prisoner, then took the stand. He had never seen any symptoms of insanity in the Guiteau family. On cross-examination he stated that when the prisoner went to school to him he was six years old, and had great difficulty in articulating and giving the right pronunciation to words. L. W. Guiteau had taken great interest in education and his name was inscribed upon one of the public schools in Freeport.

Horace Tarbox, capitalist, of Freeport, testified to the sanity of the Guiteaus, and stated that L. W. Guiteau was the third smartest man in the county. He mentioned the names of men who were smarter, upon which the prisoner smilingly said that those two men were dead, and so the father must have been head of the county.

The witness stated that Abram Guiteau was a drinking man, whereupon the prisoner stated that he was the only Guiteau who ever drank. "They were all high-toned folks."

The District Attorney inquired whether witness had ever heard of there being insanity in the Guiteau family before the assassination?

The witness.—"No."

The prisoner (to the District Attorney).— "That would not have been, Colonel, if I could have got out of it. It is the only bad thing the family ever did."

The witness stated to Mr. Scoville that the

smartest man in the county was M. P. Sweet, and Mr. Scoville was about to ask in what that smartness consisted, when he was interrupted by the prisoner, who resented Mr. Scoville's attempt to silence him with an angry "Don't punch me under the table when I am talking. Sweet was an Oneida Community crank, and father got his fanaticism from him."

Subsequently he interrupted his counsel with the remark that he (Scoville) had got to abandon his theory; that was all there was about it."

The Court then at three P. M. adjourned.

CHAPTER XXII.

The Rebuttal Testimony Continued—The Answers of President Arthur to the Interrogations—Some Further Chapters out of The Prisoner's Life.

ON Thursday, December 8th, Guiteau opened the proceedings by denying that he had any acquaintance with a "crank" in Chicago who had claimed to have conversed with him on this matter. As usual he was allowed to talk and the Court listened in a perfunctory manner.

Mrs. Julia W. Wilson, of Leadville, Colorado, was the first witness called by Colonel Corkhill. She testified that she was a niece of L. W. Guiteau and a cousin of the prisoner. The only point in her evidence was that her mother Mrs. Julia Maynard died in 1856. She spoke in terms of deep affection and testified that she had never noticed a trace of flightness in that dear mother's conduct. She admitted that her sister Abby had been a bright child, until about nine or ten years of age when she came under the influence of a professed teacher of Animal Magnetism and Clairvoyance, etc. After that she became eccentric and is now in the State Asylum for the insane. On cross-examination by Mr. Scoville, the witness admitted that her father died insane. During the testimony of this witness there was much confusion in consequence of discussions between Mr. Scoville, J. Wilson Guiteau and the prisoner, the two latter strenuously endeavoring to make it appear that the insanity in Abby's case was inherited from the father, in which theory they were, of course, ably supported by the District Attorney. Mr. Scoville on the other hand claimed to trace the insanity back into the Guiteau family.

George C. Maynard, of Washington, was the next witness. He was the gentleman from whom Guiteau borrowed the money to buy the pistol, and had previously testified in the case. His evidence now was simply to the effect that he was a cousin of the last witness; that he knew her mother intimately and that he had never seen any signs of mental disturbance, on the contrary she was even tempered and of very superior ability. He also knew Abby and considered her bright and intelligent. He never knew of any signs of weakness in her father, who was a man of great prominence in Ann Harbor. At the close of this testimony Mr. John W. Guiteau wished to make a personal explanation but was restrained by the Court and the customary side dialogue took place between the prisoner and some of the counsel, till the Court took a recess.

Frank Bartlett, of Chicago, was next called. He knew Mr. and Mrs. Scoville, and had met the prisoner in 1878. Never saw any signs of insanity.

Florence L. Bartlett, wife of the last witness gave similar testimony, with the addition of a story about the prisoner throwing a small dog down stairs. The testimony was unimportant and was fitly closed by the prisoner's remark: " We've had enough of the dog business."

Howard C. Dunham, Acting Secretary of the Peace Society, at Boston, was the next witness. He testified that in 1879, in the month of November, the prisoner secured desk room in the office of the Society. After a few weeks the prisoner remarked that theology did not pay and that he was after money. Witness did not see the prisoner after April, 1880, but received a letter from him on the 9th of June, 1881. After some discussion the letter was admitted and read. It was dated from the Riggs House, Washington, and simply asked Mr. Dunham to forward a copy of the prisoner's book "*Truth.*" Witness testified that from his observation and knowledge of the prisoner he had no suspicion that he was insane. Witness also stated, on redirect examination, that about the beginning of last November, J. Wilson Guiteau told him that there was not a well established case of insanity in the family. The prisoner here broke in again and claimed to be the only exception. He proceeded to denounce his brother, and concluded by remarking: "It has been shown that two of my cousins are in lunatic asylums. Probably I will be there soon."

The District Attorney here sent up to Judge Cox a communication received by him from the President of the United States. The Judge, after reading it, sent it down to Mr. Scoville with the remark that the paper contained the President's answers to his (Scoville's) interrogatories.

The prisoner.—"I had sent the President a note this afternoon requesting him not to appear in this case, and saying that I did not want his answers to the interrogatories. I presume he sent them before he got my note."

The next witness was *John Palmer*, proprietor of the Circular Street House, Saratoga Springs. The substance of his testimony was that the prisoner spent a week at his house in July, 1880, and left without paying his bill.

PRESIDENT ARTHUR'S TESTIMONY.

Mr. Scoville read to the Court the answers of President Arthur to the interrogatories. To the first and second questions whether he knew the prisoner, and how often he had seen him, the President replied that he knew him; that he had seen him at least ten times, and possibly twenty times. To the question as to whether he had ever conversed with him he replied; "Never, excepting to return the ordinary salutations of the day and once or twice in answer to his request to be employed in the campaign as a speaker by the Republican State Committee, of which I was chairman." To the question what political services the prisoner had rendered to the Republican Party during the last Presidential campaign, the answer was "None that I know of." The fifth question was: "Whether there was anything in the prisoner's relations to himself or to General Grant or to Senator Conkling or any other leader of the Republican Party, socially or politically, to furnish him with any ground for supposing that he would receive any political preferment." The answer was "No."

The prisoner.—"That is a matter of opinion."

The last question was: "Did you ever give him any reason to think he could have any political or personal influence with you?" The answer was, "I never did."

The prisoner.—"He never had occasion to."

The President added to his answers the following: "I have been requested by counsel for the defence to produce a letter written by the prisoner since his indictment. That letter was received by me in October last and was not preserved. I do not recollect its contents particularly, excepting that it contained some claims of his having rendered some important services to the Republican Party during the Presidential campaign, and an appeal for the postponement of his trial to give him time to prepare for his defence."

The prisoner.—"That is all that there was to it."

Rev. R. S. Mac Arthur, pastor of the Calvary Baptist Church of New York, was then called. As soon as he was sworn the prisoner remarked: "I know Dr. Mac Arthur very well. He is a nice, fine fellow—very high-toned in every way. I owe him ninety-five dollars."

In answer to the question when, where and under what circumstances he had known the prisoner, the witness said: "In the latter part of June or the early part of July, 1872, the prisoner introduced himself and his wife to me at the close of one of the Sunday morning services. He presented at the same time a letter of dismission from the First Baptist Church, of Chicago, of which Rev. W. W. Evarts was then pastor. This letter dismissed him and his wife honorably from that church and recommended them heartily to the watchful care and fellowship of the Calvary Baptist Church, of which I was then and am now pastor; with the letter was also his business card—Charles J. Guiteau, Attorney and Counsellor-at-law, at such a number, Broadway. He stated to me at that time that in Chicago he had had a lucrative practice of law, but that owing to the disasters following the fire, his practice had entirely or in good part gone, and that now he and his wife had come to New York to start life afresh. He was gentlemanly in his manner and was neatly, I might say elegantly dressed; his deportment, if not specially prepossessing, was certainly not noticeably unprepossessing. My heart went out to him kindly. He and his wife had struggled with adverse fortune and had come to try life over again in the great city of New York. I received him with cordiality: I think I may say that the church of which I have the honor to be pastor has a reputation for treating strangers cordially and for extending help towards the worthy. I introduced him and his wife to men of prominence in society and in church relations, and know that I was of service to him. The letter which he brought was referred, as our custom is, to a committee; the chairman of that committee was a gentleman of very high standing, at one time an Indian Commissioner under the U. S. Government, and who took an interest—"

Here the witness was interrupted by Mr. Scoville, who remarked that all this was very interesting, but entirely irrelevant. He did not want this whole history.

The District Attorney.—"But I do want the whole history connected with the prisoner."

The prisoner.—"It is all interesting and important. Dr. Mac Arthur was a very nice gentleman. I owe him ninety-five dollars and I am sorry I cannot pay him now."

Mr. Scoville remarked that he objected to the witness stating the qualifications of some chairman of a committee not knowing how far he might go in that history.

The witness then continued: I was simply about to say that this gentleman after an interview with the prisoner and his wife, heartily recommended them to the fellowship of the church; owing to the fact that the church was closed during a portion of the summer we were not able to act on the letter, but at our first regular business meeting in September, 1872, the prisoner and his wife were received into the fellowship of our church. In the meantime I had been of some service to him, introducing him to some gentlemen of the legal profession and to other gentlemen of some standing. His wife came to me one Saturday, late in July or early in August, with a letter from her husband stating that he was in great distress for money; I have looked for the letter, but have not found it; it stated that a case was then in Court on which a decision was expected on the following Monday, and that a large fee would be received and the money returned. The letter enclosed a promissory note to me, the amount being one hundred dollars.

Mr. Scoville.—"Have you got that promissory note?"

The witness.—"No, I did not think it negotiable and have not preserved it. The money was most urgently asked for by the wife; they were to be turned out on the sidewalk if the money was not given. When my heart goes out kindly towards a man believed to be worthy, my hand goes out in helpfulness, and so I gave the money. Afterwards letters were received from the prisoner expressing his regret that he could not pay me as promised, and so the time passed on. That fall we were entering on a political campaign. During the early part of the fall the prisoner used to attend our meetings and to participate in our prayers and remarks. He was always welcome; there was nothing noticeable either in the direction of superior excellence or in the direction of peculiar unfitness in his remarks. He received that hearty welcome which a kind-hearted church would extend to a man believed to be worthy. During the campaign he was not seen at our meetings so often, and the reason assigned by him was that he had gone to some degree into politics and that he expected an office as the result of these political excitements.

The prisoner.—"I took some interest in Horace Greeley in 1872."

The District Attorney.—"Do you recollect the office that he expected."

The witness.—"My impression is that the office was Minister to Chili."

The prisoner.—"Nothing of that kind. I think it possible I may have mentioned to you the Swiss mission. It was that which I had in my mind at that time. I never had any idea of the Chilian mission. I think that I had some idea that if Horace Greeley were elected he would let me have the

Swiss mission. It is only a small affair any way —only five thousand dollars a year."

The witness continued.—"During the year 1872 and the early part of 1873 we saw him at the meetings less frequently. Now and then there were remarks made in newspapers reflecting somewhat on his character in the management of some business affairs, but in conversation with me he gave what he deemed a satisfactory explanation, and there seemed to be no sure ground on which proceedings of discipline could be instituted against him, and so the matter went along until the spring of 1875. I remember that he was arrested and thrown into Jefferson Market jail because of some difficulty with a hotel, and that from the jail he wrote to me, saying that I was the only one to whom he could apply and that he was absolutely helpless. I put myself out very considerably to go to the jail to see him. I saw the Judge, and the Judge kindly offered to attach importance to any suggestion that I might make to him. I informed him, however, that I wished the law to take its course. I then saw the prisoner in the corridor of the jail, and although besought very piteously by him to intercede in his behalf and to procure bail for him if possible, I shut out the natural promptings of my heart and told him that I feared he was a bad man and that he must allow the law to take its course. I saw him led away by the proper officer and go into the cell. In the meantime it came to the knowledge of the officers of the church that he had been guilty of gross immorality, and about the 13th of April, 1875, he was summoned to appear before the Advisory Committee to answer to the charge of gross immorality. I was chairman of that committee. There were three counts to the charge; the first was that he took money which his wife had earned by working in a hotel in the country and which was remitted to him to assist in supporting him, and spent it in improper relations with other women. The second and third counts charged that he had been guilty by frequent acts of violation of his marriage vows. These charges were recited to the prisoner by myself in the presence of the committee."

The prisoner who had twice previously, insolently contradicted the witness, here shouted out: "That is erroneous. I beg to differ from you."

The Court (severely).—"Keep quiet. Let the witness go on."

The District Attorney (to the witness).—"Pay no attention to him."

The witness continued: "I recited those charges to the prisoner, and he acknowledged the truth of every one of them; he was pressed to know whether he felt a sense of guilt; whether there was any consciousness of remorse, or of repentance for the past, or any promise of reformation for the future. The church was disposed to deal fairly; the gentlemen on that committee were gentlemen who were above anything like unfairness towards any person."

The prisoner (in spite of all Mr. Scoville's efforts to repress him).—"I remember this. I take back my contradiction to what the doctor said, because upon thinking it over, I find it is correct. The men on that committee said that they had been in the same boat themselves, and for that reason they felt sympathetic. They thought that if a man had been unfortunately married he had a right to get out of it."

Mr. Scoville said he had he had not objected to any legitimate evidence, but did object to this irrelevant testimony. The Court sustained the objection.

The District Attorney.—"We present this testimony, because we want to show that what the defence calls insanity, is nothing more than devilish depravity."

This remark elicited applause, and the Marshal removed one of the audience. When order was restored, the witness continued: "There was at that time on the part of the prisoner, no evidence of repentance for the past. There was very great solicitude when the Church proceeded against him. The prisoner applied to me in that room to use my influence with the committee not to proceed against him, and not to exclude him from the Church, because such exclusion would injure him in his business relations and professional position. My reply to that was that we should do fairly to him, but for other considerations than those he named; he was cited to appear before the church at the next regular meeting, on April 23, 1875; he failed to respond; the motion was put by myself, after asking whether he was present to answer."

Mr. Scoville.—"You need not tell what was done if he was not present."

The District Attorney.—"We have a right to show he was expelled."

The Court.—"No."

Q. Has he any relations with your church now? A. No.

Q. Did he have after that meeting? A. No.

Q. Did he retire creditably?

Mr. Scoville objected. Objection sustained.

The District Attorney (to the witness).— "From your observation and from your conversations with him, did you ever consider him in any sense an insane man? A. It never occurred to me for a moment that he was other than sane.

The prisoner.—"You thought I was totally depraved because I owed you ninety-five dollars, and could not pay you. Pretty good theology; wasn't it Doctor?"

Mr. Scoville then proceeded with the cross-examination, questioning the witness more especially as to the fact of his receiving the promissory note for one hundred dollars from Guiteau. The prisoner throughout the examination on this point kept up a running discussion with witness, counsel and Court. The Court repeatedly ordered him to be quiet, and to allow the witness to speak, but he continued in his denunciation of the prosecution for its "impertinence in raking up my record." Mr. Scoville also became indignant and angry at the prisoner's outbreaks, which prevented him finishing his questions, and several times declared to him, "I will clear out if you don't stop. You must be still." But neither Court nor counsel could repress the prisoner, who had been nervous and excited all day, and he continued to the adjournment in his running comments upon the witness' veracity.

When the cross-examination was closed, the prisoner, looking up at the clock, announced that it was three o'clock and time to go home. He also inquired: "How many more witnesses like that have you got, Corkhill? I think it is an outrage on the public. If you had to pay some of that money yourself you would go slow."

The Court then adjourned.

CHAPTER XXIII.

Testimony that the Guiteau Family Have Denied Insanity in Insurance Policies—Guiteau's Threats Years ago to Imitate Wilkes Booth—His Pawning a Brass Watch for Gold.

WHEN the Court opened on Friday, December 9th, Rev. Dr. MacArthur, of New York, again took the witness stand. Mr. Scoville interposed with an objection to the range which the examination of this witness had already taken, and claimed that the defence being insanity, it was not competent for the prosecution to offer evidence as to acts which had no relation to the prisoner's state of mind. In reply, the District Attorney said that Mr. MacArthur detailed to the jury the opportunities he had to observe this man's conduct, very properly, so as to know how much weight to give to the evidence of the sanity or insanity of the prisoner.

The Court stated that under general circumstances, Mr. Scoville's objection would be a sound one, but in view of the line taken by the defence, the testimony would be admitted.

The prisoner broke in with a statement about having been virtuous, and giving a list of his debts, but was severely checked by the Court.

The redirect examination was then resumed.

The witness stated that in the various conversations he had with the prisoner he did not see any indications of an unsound mind; that the amount of money asked for in Guiteau's letter and mentioned in the promissory note was one hundred dollars, but by recollection over it he was inclined to believe the amount actually paid was ninety-five dollars; it was given in three installments, and he had to put himself about very considerably to get it at all.

The prisoner.—"And I appreciate it. You are a good fellow. You drew the money out of your salary. I am sorry I can't pay the money, but I gave you my note, payable on demand."

The District Attorney rose to stop the prisoner, who again broke forth; "If your record was dug up, Colonel, it would stink worse than mine. I understand you are booked for removal. You had better go slow. The President is only waiting to get this thing off his mind before you get your ticket of leave. I want the absolute truth about this."

The Court.—"Keep quiet and let the truth come out by degrees."

The witness had very few interviews with him alone, except those he named: had conversations with him on the subject of religion in the vestibule of the church, perhaps half a dozen times.

The witness identified at the District Attorney's request, the minutes of the meetings of his church, together with the rules of faith and order followed by its members, also a volume of church letters received from other churches.

W. S. Caldwell, of Freeport, Illinois, testified that he was a physician; that he attended the prisoner's father during his last illness; saw no indications of unsoundness of mind; the patient was incoherent and towards the last had stupor, but that was from blood poisoning, caused by inaction of the liver.

George W. Plummer, of Chicago, testified that he was a lawyer; that the prisoner obtained desk room in his office and got out cards on which he described himself as "late of New York City." Witness did not think the *Inter-Ocean* negotiations were irrational considering the first-class men whom the prisoner mentioned as backing him. Guiteau blurted out "I owe Plummer twenty dollars and it will cost the Government one hundred dollars to prove that."

Granville P. Hawes, one of the Judges of the Marine Court of New York, testified that in 1874, the prisoner had a desk in the outer room of his office. Witness had never seen anything indicating unsoundness of mind in the prisoner.

Stephen English, of New York, was then called. He testified that he was editor and proprietor of the *Insurance Times*. He detailed the circumstances connected with the prisoner's procuring bail for him while he was in Ludlow Street Jail on a charge of libel. He was interrupted at every step of his narrative by the prisoner, who applied most abusive epithets to the witness.

In reply to the question whether he had had any doubt as to the sanity of the prisoner, the witness said: "Never; on the contrary he appeared to be a man of remarkable keenness of intellect, because he completely outwitted me. He was a shrewd, active, intelligent lawyer."

Warren C. Brown, of New York, testified that he was a lawyer. He became acquainted with the prisoner from the fact of being retained in December, 1873, by his wife to get a divorce from him; in conversation on the subject he seemed to be perfectly sane and treated the matter as most people would under the circumstances.

Thomas Darlington, of New York, a lawyer, testified that he had acted for Stephen English in perfecting his bail, and in procuring from the Court of Common Pleas an order for the arrest of the prisoner for cheating English.

The District Attorney, in reply to an objection to the testimony, stated that the object was to show the prisoner's capacity.

After a recess, Mr. Corkhill proceeded to read in evidence some of the legal papers in the case of English and Guiteau. After the reading of one of them the prisoner exclaimed: "That is a square transaction, Colonel. That knocks your 'total depravity' theory on the head."

Charles H. Wehle, a lawyer of New York City, was then called to the stand. He was acquainted with the prisoner, and had first met him in 1873; saw him twice, once in prisoner's office, once in his own; on those occasions the purpose was to get money from him which he had collected from witness' client and not paid over. "That is not true," was the prisoner's comment, and Mr. Scoville objected to the evidence and it was stricken out.

Witness presented a book showing the contract which he had with Guiteau to collect money and read a number of claims which were to be collected for Mr. Emil Haas, one of witness' clients. The items collected amounted to $585.12.

A stormy scene ensued, the prisoner interrupting the witness at every sentence, but the latter managed to give a detailed account of the transactions, when Mr. Scoville objected. The objection having been overruled, he noted an exception.

The District Attorney.—" From those interviews with him was there anything in his actions or conversation to indicate that he was a man of unsound mind?"

The witness.—" Nothing, on the contrary I considered him very sharp and keen and as rational as you or I."

The prisoner here broke into a passionate harangue but was sternly repressed by the Court. His conduct however was so violent, especially toward his sister, that Mr. Scoville was obliged to change seats with her, for her protection.

On cross-examination, the witness stated that he had come to Washington in consequence of a telegram from Col. Corkhill. He believed it was his duty in the interest of justice to let the prosecution know anything he was acquainted with about the prisoner. The witness was sneeringly handled by Mr. Scoville, and the prisoner incessantly insulted him, by calling him a miserable Jew.

Benjamin Harrison, U. S. Senator from Indiana, was next called. He testified that he had met the prisoner a few times in Washington last spring. Some time after the inauguration of President Garfield, the prisoner called to see him at the Riggs House, and sent him several copies of the speech, "Garfield *vs.* Hancock." He saw him several times in the office or reading room of the Riggs House in the course of six weeks, and had several brief conversations with him. The prisoner applied to the witness for some assistance in connection with his application for office. The witness responded that he was already overloaded with similar applications from his own State and could not interfere in his behalf. In several other conversations the prisoner spoke about the deadlock in the Senate and said that his name had not yet been sent to the Senate, but that he thought it would be as soon as the deadlock was broken. Witness saw nothing in the conduct or conversation of the prisoner that raised in his mind any question of a man's sanity.

Isaac F. Lloyd, of New York, testified that he was Secretary of the Mutual Life Insurance Company. He presented applications for insurance, four from John W. Guiteau, two from the prisoner and one from the prisoner's father, the point being that those applications contained negative answers to the question whether there was insanity in the family. Objection being made by Mr. Scoville, the applications of John W. Guiteau were excluded and those of the prisoner admitted.

Walter R. Gillette, of New York, testified that he was a physician and medical examiner of the Mutual Life Insurance Company. He stated that the prisoner came to his office in the fall of 1880, introduced himself by name, and said that he was a lawyer by profession; that he had some leisure time which he proposed to devote to the soliciting of life insurance, and that he wanted to make the acquaintance of the witness as an officer of the company. Witness saw nothing in him to indicate him a man of unsound mind.

Charles H. Raymond, General Agent of the Mutual Life Insurance Company of New York, testified that the prisoner called upon him in September, 1880, and told him that he was about to engage in soliciting applications for insurance, and in the course of the winter he brought in six applications. He borrowed thirty dollars from the witness.

Dr. McLean Shaw, of New York, lawyer, was then called. As he stepped to the witness stand the prisoner exclaimed: "I have not seen Shaw since 1874. He is a good fellow. I officed with him for several months. I owe him fifty dollars for office rent. (To the District Attorney) That is a very important part of your evidence, Colonel."

The witness testified as the prisoner renting an office room from him at No. 59 Liberty Street in 1872. The prisoner told him that he had been practising law in Chicago, where he had lost his library and everything in the fire. That he was a member of the church and had letters of commendation from the church in Chicago; that he had joined the Young Men's Christian Association, and had the honor of an acquaintance with General Jones and others. Witness did not approve of the way he did business, and asked him to get an office elsewhere. Witness related the incident of the prisoner burnishing up an oriode watch and saying that he was going to fix up somebody with it. The prisoner went out and came back shortly afterwards in great glee, saying that he had stuck a Jew for twenty-five dollars on that watch. Witness asked him how he did it, and the prisoner related how he went into a pawnbroker's office, handed the pawnbroker his business card and told him that he was a little short of money to-day, and wanted him to advance some money on his watch. The Jew asked him how much he wanted, and he said: "Well, twenty-five dollars will do me to-day." The Jew took the watch and gave him the money. Witness said: "I think you would be ashamed to do that. He has got your card and will come back on you." "Oh, no," said the prisoner, "I took my card back again."

The prisoner.—"The fact is that the watch was worth fifty dollars, so you are short in your story, Shaw."

The District Attorney.—"Did the prisoner say anything about getting any money from Dr. Mac Arthur?"

The witness.—"He said he was going to get some money from Dr. Mac Arthur, and he mentioned one hundred dollars. I advised him not to and told him he ought not to borrow money from his friends unless he was going to pay it back. "Well," said he "I must have the money anyway."

The prisoner.—"I owed Shaw fifty dollar for office rent, and he could not see any good in me after that. He is a man who likes money too well."

The District Attorney.—"Did the prisoner say in substance that he intended to become notorious before he died?"

The witness.—"He did."

Mr. Scoville objected to question and answer. The Court sustained the objection.

The District Attorney.—"State any conversation that you had with the prisoner bearing on his intentions in life."

The witness.—"From the first time that I knew him, I knew that he was vain and egotistical, and that he had a great desire for publicity. He said to me once that he was bound to be notorious before he died."

The prisoner.—"I never said so."

The witness.—"I asked him what he meant by that, and he said that if he could not get notoriety for good he would get it for evil. Of course that surprised me, and I asked him what he meant. He said he would shoot some of our big men."

The prisoner.—"That is a lie. I never thought so, and never said so."

Mr. Scoville.—"I want it distinctly understood that all this evidence is excepted to."

The witness.—"He said he would imitate Wilkes Booth. Said I, 'And get hanged for it?' 'Well,' said he, 'that is an after consideration.' I did not carry that conversation any further."

The prisoner in excited tones denied the whole of this and wound up by denouncing the witness as a low dirty liar; a sneaking liar.

The District Attorney.—"Have you given the whole conversation on that occasion?"

The witness.—"So far as I recollect."

The District Attorney.—" Where did that conversation occur in which he said he intended to imitate Wilkes Booth and to become notorious?"

The witness.—" In my office; of course I cannot fix the date."

The prisoner (snarling at the witness).—" No, of course you cannot fix the date, you miserable, lying whelp. I never said nor thought so."

The witness.—" The moment I heard of the shooting of President Garfield—"

Mr. Scoville (interrupting).—" Wait, sir. How long have you been a lawyer?"

The prisoner.—" He is no lawyer; he is a pettifogger."

The District Attorney.—" From your observation of the man and from your conversations with him had you any question but that he was a sane man?"

The witness.—" I never had any doubt of his sanity."

The District Attorney.—" How did you regard him mentally?"

The witness.—" I did not think much of him mentally at that time."

The prisoner threatened to " show up" the witness, and shouted: " You are a low, dirty lived puppy, to come here and lie about me in that way."

The Court (severely to the prisoner).—"Silence!"

The District Attorney.—" What was his reply to your remark as to his being hanged?"

The witness.—"He said that would be an after consideration, and that he would get notoriety anyhow."

The prisoner.—"I do not care a snap about notoriety. I have told you three or four times that you lie. That settles you. I will not condescend to notice you again."

The District Attorney.—"In your conversation with him about the watch, did he say anything to you about his being bound to get a living?"

The witness.—"Yes; he said that he was bound to get a living anyhow, that the world owed him a living and he would get it. I am not sure whether that conversation was in regard to the watch, or in regard to his borrowing money from Dr. MacArthur.

Q. After he borrowed money from Dr. MacArthur, did he make any remark to you about that? A. I remember his saying something about that.

The cross-examination developed nothing new, and did not shake the evidence-in-chief. The prisoner, however, used it as a means of working in more vituperation of the witness, whom he termed "a consummate jackass and liar and villain in every way."

With the consent of the District Attorney, Mr. Scoville called to the stand *Judge Granville P. Hawes,* who had been occupying a seat beside Judge Cox. He did not recollect whether the prisoner had come into his office on Mr. Shaw's recommendation or not. His managing clerk, H. T. Ketcham, could tell that.

The Court then, at the instance of District Attorney Corkhill, adjourned until eleven o'clock Monday.

CHAPTER XXIV.

An Expert Who is Convinced that the Prisoner is Insane—Dr. Spitzka's Remarkable Statements—He Objects to Veterinary Allusions—Guiteau in a Great Rage.

ON Monday, December 12, Mr. Scoville obtained the consent of the prosecution, and called to the stand his trump card for the defence, an expert who was fully prepared to declare the prisoner insane.

Dr. E. C. Spitzka, of New York City, was then sworn. He testified that he had followed the medical profession for eight years, and for six of those he had made a specialty of nervous and mental diseases; he had studied in Vienna and this country; he had been called as expert in insanity cases twenty-five or twenty-six times; he had written articles upon the subject, and had received the International competitive prize in 1878 for an essay on insanity.

In reply to a series of questions, witness stated that he had examined the prisoner at the jail on the previous day; had never seen him before. The result of the examination was that witness found the prisoner to be insane; had no doubt on this point; examined the background of his eye by an instrument, known as an ophthalmoscope; I examined the pulse with an instrument which magnifies the pulsations called the sysgimograph; found both normal and he.lthy.

Q. State somewhat further the particular phase or character of the insanity in this case, as observed by you? A. That would be very difficult to render clear to a jury not composed of experts; I simply say that the marked feature of this man's insanity is a tendency to delusive or insane opinions, and to the creation of morbid and fantastical projects; there is a marked element of imbecility of judgment, and, while I had no other evidence than the expression of his face for this, I have no doubt that he is a moral imbecile, or rather a moral monstrosity.

Q. Will you state whether you observed any indication of insanity from the general appearance of his eyes? A. That was to my mind the most conclusive evidence of his insanity; I concluded that I had an insane man to deal with before I asked any question or said anything to him. He had an insane manner as well marked as I ever saw it in an asylum.

Q. From your knowledge of the insane, is it or not an indication of insanity that a man has an acute retentive memory? A. It is consistent with some forms and inconsistent with others.

Q. Is it consistent with a condition of in anity that a man has a quick perception? A. The same answer would apply to that question.

Mr. Scoville then propounded a long hypothetical question similar to a great extent to that which he had already asked the other expert witnesses, ending with the interrogatory as to whether Guiteau was insane on the 2d of July.

The witness.—"I decline to answer any hypothetical questions in a case where I have examined the prisoner himself, that would not incorporate the result of that examination."

Q. Then include in that hypothetical question your own conclusion of his mental examination. A. I should say that the prisoner whom I examined had been more or less of a morbid mental state throughout his life, and that he was probably insane at the time that you mention.

The witness was then cross-examined by Mr. Davidge.

Q. What do you mean by insanity? A. That is a question which I never attempt to answer. I can give you an approximate definition. Any profound deterioration from a normal standard of human thought and action excluding the ordinary phenomenon of the common nervous disease, and excluding acute intoxication and febrile delirum.

Q. There are very many degrees of insanity, are there not? A. Certainly. There is every degree.

Q. There may be degrees involving want of discrimination between right and wrong, and there may be other degrees which do not involve want of discernment? A. That is so, and it varies in the history of the same person.

Q. You have had submitted to you quite a long hypothetical case. Suppose every element of that case to be removed except the single one that the prisoner was dominated by the delusion that in putting the President to death he was carrying out the Divine will and that he had not capacity to resist the force of that delusion, would not that postulate alone have led you to the conclusion that he was insane? A. Is it an insane delusion that you refer to?

Q. It is an insane delusion. A. A person who has an insane delusion is insane even if it is a single delusion.

Q. Then if you can assume that postulate to be true the rest of the question amounts to nothing? A. I do not see how that follows.

Q. If the fact that the prisoner was dominated by an insane delusion alone led you to the conclusion that he was insane, do you attach any importance to the other postulates in the hypothetcal case? A. The greatest as strong confirmatory evidence.

Q. If the first postulate was sufficient to lead you to the conclusion of his insanity, did you want any confirmatory evidence? A. I should feel very much more positive if I had it than if I had not it; as medicine is not an exact science, we strengthen our diagnosis by taking every available point.

Q. You are not making a diagnosis here, but answering a hypothetical case, and one fixed fact in that hypothetical case is tantamount to a proof that this man is insane. Now I want to know why you need any corroboration of his insanity? A. I think you misunderstood me. As a witness on this stand I needed nothing further than that single postulate.

Q. Where did you graduate? A. At the Medical Department of the University of the City of New York.

In reply to further questions the witness said that he had never had charge of an insane asylum, but that he had applied or made inquiries looking to application for such employment to the asylums at Blackwell's Island, New York, Oshkosh, Wisconsin, and Danville, Pennsylvania. The application for the asylum on Ward's Island, was made at the instance of Dr. McDonald, its superintendent. These applications were not gratified for reasons he would like to state. He had never made such application to the Bloomingdale Asylum. He had never been professor in a medical school, but was Professor of Comparative Anatomy at the Columbia Veterinary College.

Q. What sort of a college is that? A. A college where physicians are instructed in the art of treating the lower animals.

Q. Horse, mainly, I suppose? A. Yes, the branch which I treat of is the branch pursued by such men as Thomas Huxley, Baron Huget, Heckel and others of our most eminent scientists. I have no reason to be ashamed of it.

Mr. Davidge.—"I do not mean that you should be."

The witness.—"The same question has been asked me before on suggestion from a special quarter, and I know that it comes from the same quarter. I expected it; it is done with the intention of casting a reflection on the witness."

Mr. Davidge.—"All these doctors, and the doctors belonging to this college are called 'horse doctors,' are they not?"

The witness.—"I never have treated any lower animal, except the ass, and that animal had two legs—I therefore cannot consider myself a veterinary surgeon."

Q. But you are a veterinary surgeon, are you not? A. In the sense that I treat asses who ask me stupid questions, I am."

In reply to several other questions, the witness declined to admit that he was an expert in the sense that he was willing to testify simply for pay.

The witness was then examined as to the circumstances of his visit to the prisoner yesterday in the jail. He had gone into the cell behind other visitors, so as to take the prisoner unawares. He had gone to the jail with Mr. Scoville and spent about an hour and a half with the prisoner; he did not examine the prisoner physically at first;

that was done at the same time that he examined him mentally. Witness represented himself as a professor of phrenology—Professor Brown, of Fowler & Wells; in that way he was enabled to induce the prisoner to allow him to put aconite in his eyes so as to dilate them in order that he might examine them; as a phrenological dodge he first examined the shape of his head, and asked him to give him his psychological condition at the time he shot the President; the prisoner repeated the word "psychological" and said "*psychos*," mind, soul; witness then asked him what objection he had to the President; the prisoner said he had not any; witness asked him why he had not removed Mr. Blaine, instead of the President, he said: "Because that would not have done any good. There would have been just such another man as Blaine to step into his shoes, and Arthur would not have been President."

Then the prisoner became wildly excited about the trial, and yelled forth about the way the prosecution was attacking him, bringing up (as he said) lying witnesses. He yelled out loudly declaiming and shouting the insane manner very perfectly. The witness told him to keep cool, but it was difficult to restrain him. Witness asked him why he interrupted the Court if (as he said) God had got the thing in His hand and would bring it to a successful conclusion, so far as he was concerned. He made a quotation from Scripture about Jesus Christ sending the lying to utter damnation, and he said: "May I not do the same thing? Am I not in the position of Jesus Christ? Am I not a martyr? Have I not sacrificed myself for the American people?"

The witness went on to state that he found the prisoner's physical condition, so far as he noticed it, good, his memory good, and his legal attainments (in conversing with Mr. Scoville about his trial) those of a third class shyster. He displayed a certain amount of judgment, parried questions which he did not want to answer, and went to subjects which developed something flattering to his self-love.

Q. Did you form the opinion that this man did not know the difference between right and wrong? A. That would depend on the interpretation given to the question; if you ask me whether he knew the full consequences of his act, I should say without any hesitation, that (at least since he has been a lawyer) he has always known the ordinary legal consequences of criminal acts.

Q. You have no doubt of that? A. Not the slightest, but that is not my interpretation of insanity; it is outside the idea of right and wrong.

Q. You reached the conclusion first that he did not know the difference between right and wrong? A. I did not say that.

Mr. Davidge.—"I understood you to say that."

The witness.—"I am positive I stated that this

man ever since he was a lawyer always knew the legal consequences of criminal acts."

Mr. Davidge.—"I understood you to say distinctly that you had no doubt he did know the difference between right and wrong."

The witness.—"I would not like to answer anything under the construction of a foreign mind; I want this answer to stand as I gave it—that this man, since he was a lawyer, always knew the ordinary consequences attaching to criminal acts; but I again wish to add that that is not my test of right."

Mr. Davidge.—"But it will be that of the Court. On these postulates you base the opinion that his mind tended to insane delusion. You did not find any insane delusion, but a tendency to insane delusion."

The witness.—"I found a tendency toward insane delusion and I found delusive opinions."

Q. What do you mean by a tendency to insane delusion? A. A phenomena frequently exhibited by those having an insane constitution, a tendency to misinterpret the real affairs of life, especially of those of a complex nature.

Q. You found in him a tendency to morbid opinions? A. To the formation of morbid projects.

Q. What made you think that he had a tendency to the formation of morbid projects? A. Because he told me as positively and sincerely as a man could, that when he got out of jail (feeling firmly convinced that the American people would not allow him to die a disgraceful death after what he had done for them), he would go to Europe for three or four months to keep out of the way, and then come back and lecture, and that he expected to make a great success. That was a morbid project in the future. I became convinced that the crime for which he is indicted was the result of a morbid project rather than of a delusion, strictly speaking.

Q. You found that he shot President Garfield not so much in consequence of an insane delusion, as on account of the formation of a morbid project? A. Based on a delusive opinion.

Q. You concluded that the shooting of the President was not the result of an insane delusion, but rather of a tendency of the mind to the formation of morbid projects? A. That is the main motor.

Q. Do you not think that every murder originates in some such tendency? A. On the contrary, I think it is the great exception.

Q. Could any man who does not indulge in morbid projects commit a murder? A. Most murders are not committed from morbid projects, but from sane motives, criminal motives.

Q. The murderer as a general thing is in a healthy state of mind, and his projects are not morbid? A. I did not say that; I only say negatively that the ordinary murderer is not insane; I do not say that he is in a typical good condition of bodily health.

Q. Is not a man who murders another a creature of a morbid project? A. Positively, no.

Witness further stated that he found no fixed delusion, illusion nor hallucination.

Q. You attributed this crime to the formation of a morbid project? A. A morbid project growing out of a diseased condition of the mind.

Q. Was there any instance (except the remark about lecturing) that showed the formation of a morbid project? A. He gave me an account of the shooting of the President, which I considered another morbid project.

Q. You do not undertake to give an opinion as to his condition at the time of the shooting? A. Only so far as I would say that this man has always been of a morbid mind. If I were to be very accurate, I should draw a line between the disease which attacks the brain after it has been developed, and the improper development of the brain; I should rather say he was a brain monstrosity—a congenital malformation of the brain.

Q. As to his project to go to Europe for a time, and then to return and lecture, was that a morbid project or a depraved one? A. Depravity enters as an element, but it is a morbid project.

Q. You thought that the scheme was so revolting that it could not originate in depravity, but was the result of a morbid disease? A. Yes.

Q. Would not that depend upon a degree of depravity? A. I suppose if there was an extreme degree of depravity it might co-exist in the scheme: the idea that the American people would be so grateful that they would flock to his lectures, which could only be based on an insane conception.

Q. Might not that be the outcome of a depraved heart? A. No; it could not.

The Court then at half-past twelve took a recess for one hour.

As the manacles were being placed upon the prisoner he broke forth with a denunciation of the prosecution for the use of the word "depravity." With the exception of committing adultery to get rid of his wife and of owing some debts, he had always been a Christian man. "And," he concluded, violently: "I am not afraid to go to the gallows if the Lord Almighty wishes me to go there. I expect an act of God that will blow this Court and the jury out of the window to protect me, if necessary. I want to thunder that in the ears of the American people.

The afternoon session was opened as usual by the prisoner, who, thumping the table with his fist, cried: "There are a good many poodle dogs in the newspaper business, and I want to express my utter contempt for some of those poodle dogs. I am glad to notice that the high-toned conscientious papers are saying almost with one voice that it would be a stain on the American name for the jury to hang a man in my condition on the 2d of July, when I was precipitated upon the President."

Hardly had he ceased speaking, when a voice from the most crowded corner of the Court room, exclaimed: "Shoot him now!" The prisoner glared around in a frightened manner, while there was a good deal of suppressed commotion among the spectators. The Deputy Marshal endeavored to discover the offender, but was unsuccessful in his search.

The cross-examination was resumed.

Q. The appearance of his face indicated moral insanity? A. I made the general proposition that this man's facial expression agreed with that which we know as the usual manner, and that without having some other evidence, I would have concluded that he suffered from moral imbecility or moral monstrosity.

Q. What do you mean by a moral monstrosity? A. By a moral monster, I mean a person who is born with a nervous and defective organization, one altogether deprived of that moral sense which is an integral and essential constituent of the normal human mind, being analogous in this sense to a congenital cripple who is born speechless or with one leg shorter than the other.

Q. From that brief interview with this man you conclude that he was born a cripple in respect of his moral sense? A. Yes.

Q. What means had you to attribute his crippled mental condition to a congenital cause and not to natural causes? A. The shape of his head and his face and certain physical evidences of imperfect brain development which I found, these being a defective innervation of the facial muscles, asymmetry of the face and a pronounced deviation of the tongue to the left. I found that he was born with a brain whose two sides are not equal, or so much unequal as to constitute a diseased brain. The end of his tongue deviated one-half or three-quarters of an inch from the medium line. I do not wish it to be understood that on any of the evidences singly I would call a man insane.

Witness further stated that the insanity of two cousins from causes foreign to their ancestry would not prove anything in the prisoner's case, but in regard to Abby Maynard who had been a bright child until subjected to mesmeric influences, witness further said it threw the strongest light on the congenital insanity of the prisoner. No one could become insane or of feeble mind from mesmeric experiments who was not already tainted with insanity. Witness added: "She was susceptible because she was predisposed. I could probably mesmerize one out of thirty of the persons in this Court room one hundred times without affecting their health, unless they were of an imperfect mental organization. But no person can be mesmerized frequently without being injured."

Q. The degree of damage would depend upon the organization of the subject? A. Certainly; I consider those experiments inexcusable. I doubt not that ordinary persons in ordinary conditions of health become insane or feeble minded from such experiments.

Q. Suppose that the idea of hereditary insanity had been removed, would you still have reached the conclusion you did from the formation of the prisoner's head, his facial muscles and the deviation of his tongue? A. It would amount to no more than a strong suspicion; the fact that the head is larger on one side than the other is not the most pronounced anomaly; there is a peculiar ascent of the back part of the head, as if it were cut off suddenly, and a sort of keel-like prolongation in the middle line extending along down the back of the head; that is what we call *rhombo-cephalic*.

Q. What is the keel? A. A ridge in the middle line.

Q. Have you examined any more monsters? A. They are not so frequent that any one can examine any large number. I do not think I have seen a case exactly like this, and I have not seen more than half a dozen that would belong to it.

Mr. Davidge then went into an exhaustive examination as to the exact difference between the prisoner's head and the heads of normal persons, the extent of the deviation of the tongue and the effect of the facial muscles to which the witness had referred. The witness detailed the peculiarities—stating that none of them taken singly could be looked upon as evidence of congenital insanity, but that being grouped and taken in connection with the fact of hereditary insanity, was strong evidence.

Q. You base your opinion as to his moral monstrosity on the shape of his head? A. Only incidentally; I base it upon his expression taken in connection with the abnormal shape of his head. It proves the congenital character of the trouble. If the man only had the mean face he has, I should say he might be a depraved man; but when I add to that the defective shape of his skull, I am strongly of the belief—as strongly as science permits us to come to a conclusion—that he is a congenital monstrosity.

Q. You refer to the shape of the head and the inequality of the facial muscles and the deviation of the tongue to the left as indicating that the lack of moral sense is congenital and not acquired? A. Yes; among the other physical evidences I noticed was a defect in his speech.

Q. What do you mean by an unequal facial development? A. One side of the facial folds, when he was laughing, rose higher than the other.

Q. His smile was a one-sided smile? A. A lop-sided smile.

Q. In your practice have you met with many lop-sided smiles? A. It is the characteristic of those insane whom we term "primary monomaniacs."

Q. Taken alone what would it amount to? A. Absolutely nothing.

Q. When he put out his tongue it went to the left side? A. Yes; over half an inch.

Q. And that was another proof of congenital monstrosity? A. I never said anything remotely leading to that conclusion.

Q. How common is it for tongues of people to deviate? A. In a perfectly healthy person the tongue will not deviate.

Q. Is it uncommon for the tongues of sane people to deviate? A. In the experience of physicians it is one of the common evidences of other diseases than insanity.

Witness further said this deviation only threw light on insanity as an accessory fact; he believed there were cases of moral insanity, but doubted if he could always distinguish between moral monstrosity and depravity.

Q. Did you discover any defect in his reasoning faculties? A. I did; the man based his conclusions on insane and erroneous assumptions throughout.

Q. I want to know whether between the assumption and the conclusion, you discovered a lack of reasoning power? A. Taking his assumption to be correct his conclusion was logical.

Q. For instance, you asked why he did not remove Mr. Blaine, and he said: "Because another just as bad would get in his place." A. That was logical from his point of view.

Q. He said his act would cement the Republican Party? A. From his point of view, and perhaps from the point of view of many politicians that are not insane, that is correct.

Q. What experience have you had with men under trial for heinous crimes? A. Within the last three months I have examined three criminals whose attorneys claimed insanity for them, and I found them all to be sane; one of them was shamming and two of them were not shamming.

Q. As a sensible man do you mean to say that you can base any opinion on such an experience as that? A. Certainly; I am one of those who believe that the careful analysis of one case is worth more than a slipshod examination of a thousand cases.

In answer to further questions, witness said he found the prisoner's memory and perceptive faculties good, and admitted that he had the abilities of a third-class shyster. He had low cunning, leading to unscrupulous actions, but witness attributed this to disease.

Q. Have you had any experience of men who professed to believe that that they were instruments in the hands of Divine Providence? A. With insane men, yes, quite a number: it is a common symptom of the insane that they consider themselves the instruments of a higher power, and according to their degree of education they would make it more or less plausible.

As Mr. Davidge concluded his cross-examination it was taken up by the District Attorney, who endeavored to show an inconsistency in the witness expressing to-day a disinclination to reveal a professional communication, and his having written a letter published in the *New York Times* on the 2d of November, stating that he had declined to appear as an expert for the Government. The witness explained that what he meant was, that he would not make the statement on the stand lest it might prejudice the case. He drew a broad distinction between that and his letter in the *Times*. He also admitted having written a paper which was published in the *New York Medical Record*, of October 20 (ten days before Mr. Porter called on him), in which he said that there was not a scintilla of doubt in his mind that Guiteau was insane, and that he would be admitted into any insane asylum as a proper subject for sequestration. He added, "That was my opinion then, and is my opinion now." The District Attorney recited the points in this article on which the witness had based his opinion, and the witness stated that they were all correct. An allusion being made in this article to a certain writer on insanity, who would turn over in his grave if Guiteau was hanged, the District Attorney asked him if that were true. The witness replied with considerable asperity of manner: "That is an absurd question. You know that was intended figuratively. I am not here to give you instructions on the use of metaphors."

The District Attorney.—"Is that one of the metaphors upon which you based your opinion?"

The witness.—"That is nonsense."

The prisoner (to the District Attorney).—"The Doctor gives you trouble, Corkhill. I am sorry to see you heated up so. You had better cool off and let us go home."

The District Attorney.—"You state in this article that Mr. Blaine, Senator Logan and the President recognized the insanity of the prisoner. Is that true?"

The witness.—"It was so stated in the papers of the day. An interviewer in the *New York Herald* made a very exhaustive statement of an alleged interview with Mr. Blaine, and gave the unqualified opinion of Mr. Blaine that the man was insane, and I know, furthermore, that there was a telegram from the Cabinet to the American Ministers in Europe stating that there was no conspiracy, but the assassination was the act of an insane man."

The prisoner (tauntingly to the District Attorney).—"That settles you, Colonel."

The District Attorney then got into an unpleasant colloquy with the witness in reference to the Gosling case, and significantly asked, if the witness had not taken a fee on both sides. The witness appealed to the Court for protection against insult.

The District Attorney.—"I understand that this witness, over a month ago, wrote an opinion upon the subject of this prisoner's insanity and criticized the whole case. I want to show that he did not come here with unformed opinion."

The witness.—"Nor did I claim to do so."

The Court.—"There is nothing wrong in that."

The District Attorney.—"Did you say in this article that it would be a matter of regret if the Guiteau case ever came before a jury?"

The witness.—"I said it then and I say it now."

The District Attorney.—Did you say that a narrow minded official conducting this trial would find experts who would be only too willing to chime in with the public prejudice."

The witness.—"I said that decidedly."

The District Attorney.—"To what official did you refer?"

The witness.—"I referred to you."

The District Attorney.—"Did you say that it

was to be feared that the conviction of Guiteau would be nothing more than a form of lynch process, which would reflect great discredit on American medical jurisprudence?"

The witness.—"Yes; I said that."

The District Attorney.—"Did you say that the insanity of the assassin was recognized by many of the journals, but that the organ of the officers of asylums expressed itself adversely, and that several superintendents of asylums pretended that Guiteau was sane?"

The witness.—"I said that."

The District Attorney.—"So that when you came into this case you had not only expressed your opinion as to the sanity or insanity of the prisoner, but you had criticized the law officer in charge of the case, and said that it would be disgraceful to hang the prisoner, and that the case ought never to go to a jury. Now do you pretend to say that you came here an unbiased witness?"

The witness.--"I mean to say that I am an honest, scientific, unprejudiced witness, and if you will say—(restraining himself). I will not go any further."

The District Attorney.—"Do not hesitate to go as far as you want to."

The prisoner.—"Let us go home, Colonel; it is three o'clock. You are in bad repute, Corkhill, with every member of this Bar, and I tell President Arthur publicly that he ought to remove you at once. You are an unmitigated nuisance in this case. If President Arthur has any respect for his administration, he cannot do a better th'ng than to give this man Corkhill the go at once."

The Court (reprovingly).—"You have said that once already."

The prisoner.—"I want the President to act upon it, too. Corkhill is an unmitigated nuisance and has been from the start. He lied to me all the summer. He has shown himself to be a man of low tastes and of no conscience. The administration ought to kick him out at once."

Without concluding the cross-examination of the witness, the Court at three o'clock adjourned.

CHAPTER XXV.

Dr. Spitzka Declines to State Whether he Believes in a God—He Gives His Views upon Experts in General and Lawyers in Particular—Dr. Fordyce Barker, Expert on the Prosecution Side.

ON Tuesday, December 13th, the cross-examination of Dr. E. C. Spitzka was resumed by Col. Corkhill. After requesting the witness to make diagrams of heads illustrating deviations, etc., the District Attorney suddenly asked.

"You believe in God?"

The witness.—"If the Court does not declare that the question is irrelevant I will answer."

The Court.—"You are not obliged to answer that question."

The witness.—"On principle I decline to answer it."

The prisoner.—"Do you believe in a God, Corkhill? I have been digging up your record, and it stinks worse than a mackerel."

The District Attorney (to the witness).—"Then you decline to answer."

The witness.—"I decline to answer on principle. It is, to my point of view, an impertinent question in a country that guarantees civil and religious liberty."

Mr. Davidge.—"But not irreligious liberty."

The District Attorney.—"As you decline to answer that question, I do not think I have any further questions to ask you."

On re-direct examination, witness stated that he had met with several cases of simulated insanity, but detected no evidence of simulation in this case.

Mr. Scoville then summarized all the evidences of insanity, which, according to the witness for the defence, had existed in the prisoner's family, and asked the witness whether if those facts were proven, they constituted a proper claim for a hereditary taint of insanity in the prisoner.

The witness.—"I would say that the family was strongly drenched with hereditary taint and that the prisoner might or might not have inherited the taint. But I would have to exclude a good many things you said from that opinion. For instance, the belief (held by Luther W. Guiteau) that a sick man might be cured by prayer is not a sign of insanity, though it may be a sign of weakness of judgment. As to the belief of Mr. Abram Guiteau that he would never die, did you mean spiritually."

Mr. Scoville.—" No, bodily?"

The witness.—" That would be a strong evidence of insanity."

A long and unimportant colloquy ensued between witness and the District Attorney, the latter desiring to pin the witness down to the authorship of certain articles in medical journals in which the trial had been commented upon. Finally the District Attorney asked: "And your sentiment is that these medical witnesses are here to swear to what they do not believe?"

The witness.—" I did not say that; all that I intended to imply was that the habit of a lawyer, who is not an expert in insanity, prejuding the case of a prisoner and then sending for experts, looks involuntarily to the selection of such experts as will meet his view; and as there are in our profession, men who are weak and bad, you may get such men to sell their opinions in cases where the United States Treasury is behind them."

The District Attorney.—" That is not the question. I ask you whether you believe that the gentlemen subpœnaed on this trial as medical experts are going to perjure themselves?"

The Court.—" We have not got to that point."

The District Attorney.—" This gentleman appears here as an "involuntary" witness under an extraordinary process of the Court, which did not reach him until he got here. There is no process of the Court, however, which could have compelled him to examine the prisoner or do anything but make a cursory statement. Long before this trial began, this witness had been writing about the character of the trial, not only criticizing the law officers, but throwing his filth on the medical professors of the country."

The Court.—"I have not heard anything emanating from this witness reflecting on the medical gentlemen summoned for the prosecution."

The District Attorney read a paragraph from the article in question, calling attention to the spectacle of a prosecuting attorney graduating into an expert on insanity, and then sending for experts favoring that view, and stating that only such experts had been summoned in this case as would pronounce Guiteau sane.

The witness, after an attempt to evade the question, admitted that he had originated the paragraph, but not with intent to publish it.

Dr. Fordyce Barker, physician and surgeon of New York, was next called as an expert witness on behalf of the prosecution. He was examined by Mr. Porter. He stated his professional experience, and that he had carefully investigated and studied the subject of insanity; he defined insanity to be a disease characterized by an alteration of the mental faculties and a perversion of the normal actions of the individual. In cases of insanity, either a change of substance (and that wrought by disease), or a change in the healthy performance and functions and duties that belong to some part of the body is always found, either one or both.

Q. Is insanity a hereditary disease? A. There is no such disease known to medical science as hereditary insanity; there can be no hereditary insanity; there is undoubtedly a hereditary tendency to insanity—that is, men are born with a temperament or nervous organization which renders them more liable to become insane under the influence of a specific cause, less than would produce insanity in other persons.

On further examination the witness stated substantially that insanity in a remote generation does not prove an especial liability to inherit the disease. That the term "moral insanity," is not found in medical science but is a term loosely used to excuse or palliate conduct otherwise undefinable. That the habit of falsely boasting of intimacy with important personages does not indicate disease, but merely vice and vanity. That an inconsistent claim of belief in Divine inspiration is not necessarily evidence of insane delusion.

Q. Assuming it to be in proof that a person charged with crime and claiming to have a delusion has in repeated instances controlled himself and voluntarily refrained from the act on which he professes to have a command from God, would you call that evidence of uncontrollable impulse?
A. It would show that the individual had not lost his power of will or his self control under the influence of his delusion.

Q. If it be assumed that in repeated instances the party thus accused avowed that he had personal motives for his act, would that in your judgment as a scientist show that the act was or was not committed under the influence of uncontrollable impulse? A. I should say it was a proof it was not. When persons are acting under an insane delusion they have a steadfast, unflinching, unyielding, abiding faith in that delusion. That faith governs and controls their act; they are not influenced for or against the performance of the act by mental process. If one is so governed it shows that the delusion does not control the will.

Q. Are eccentricities evidence of insanity? A. Eccentricities are exhibitions of character, in language, dress, modes of expression, or conduct, different from the ordinary standard of the world, and are usually the result of vanity or self love. Witness further stated that he had not made personal examination of the prisoner, not having been requested to do so.

On cross-examination the witness stated that he had delivered frequent lectures in the Bellevue Medical College and in the New York Medical College on certain forms of insanity. He had never lectured on the general subject of insanity. He was largely engaged in connection with the obstetric business, but more than half of his time was consumed in consultations in regards to all forms of medical disease, exclusive of surgery.

Q. Is it not true that there can be no insanity unless the brain is diseased in some form? A. There can be no insanity unless the action of the brain is disturbed.

The Court.—"State to what class of subjects insane delusions generally relate."

The witness.—"Insane delusions are false beliefs as to facts; absurd and extravagant opinions are governed by differences in the intellectual powers of different individuals; some are buoyed up by extravagant hope and confident belief in success, while others are depressed and inclined to take a dark view of every question."

The Court.—"Is an insane delusion ever the result of a process of reasoning?"

The witness.—"No."

The Court.—"You have described a state of things in which a party has no delusion and yet in which there is some perversion by which his will does not control his action, and you stated that that is not moral insanity. State the difference between that and moral insanity and between that and irresistible impulse?"

The witness.—"Those cases that I spoke of where there are no delusions are perversions of the morals and instincts of the individual to such a degree as to produce conduct entirely different from that person's ordinary conduct."

The Court.—"What is the difference between that and moral insanity?"

The witness.—"I do not think there is any such thing as moral insanity. I have no faith in its existence whatever; moral insanity is simply wickedness."

The Court.—"Is there any difference between that case and the case of irresistible impulse?"

The witness.—"Decidedly."

The Court.—"What is the difference?"

The witness.—"Irresistible impulse is where the functions and the emotions are so perverted as to destroy the person's power of acting otherwise. Uncontrollable impulse may exist in a perfectly sane person, as the result of bad habits or passions. If a man who is in the habit of using tobacco or opium is not able to break off, that habit is an uncontrollable impulse. But that is not insanity—it is a vice."

The prisoner.—"Where a man does an apparently illegal act from an irresistible pressure, is that insanity or sanity, Doctor?"

The witness.—"That fact shows insanity."

In reply to further questions from Mr. Scoville, the witness said that insane people may be very wicked and are responsible for such wickedness as they can restrain themselves from doing: if they can find a motive for doing or not doing an act of wickedness, it shows that their insanity has not destroyed their power of will.

At this point, Mrs. Scoville, unexpectedly, even to her husband, took part in the examination, and elicited an admission from the doctor that a person with a malconstructed brain may be more liable than others to insanity. She expressed her thanks and satisfaction in regard to the reply.

L. S. Goble, of Newark, New Jersey, was the first witness after recess. He testified that he was agent for a life insurance company and had lent money to the prisoner.

William P. Copeland, a Washington journalist, was then called to indicate the newspapers from which the various scraps found on the prisoner had been cut.

H. T. Ketchum, of Brooklyn, attorney-at-law, testified that he had lent the prisoner small sums of money. In reply to several questions, the witness indicated that while he never saw any indications of unsoundness of mind, he had the general impression that the prisoner was a person of little sense, a statement which considerably angered Guiteau, and led to an attack upon Mr. Scoville, whom he accused of getting cranked and being worse than Corkhill.

Henry Wood was then called. As soon as he came to the witness stand the prisoner exclaimed: "That is the man who knew my wife before I did." The witness testified that he is a resident of Philadelphia and a railway manager; he first met the prisoner in 1872. The prisoner called at his house at that time to thank his family for some friendliness they had shown to his wife. He had subsequently seen him several times in connection with his divorce proceedings; the last time he saw him was when the prisoner attempted to deliver a lecture in the Presbyterian Church in Philadelphia on the "Second Coming of Christ." The prisoner spoke for about fifteen or twenty minutes and then stopped, saying that his book would soon be out, and that everybody could then see what he thought on the subject; he then passed around his hat for a collection.

The prisoner.—"I got fifty cents, and twenty-five cents of it came from the witness."

To the question whether the witness had seen anything in the prisoner to indicate unsoundness of mind, the witness replied: "I did not; quite the contrary; he always appeared to me as a man of more than ordinary intelligence, but wholly wanting in principle."

On cross-examination the witness said that he had not known the prisoner's wife before her marriage.

Simon D. Phelps, broker, of New York, was the next witness. His testimony was mainly in reference to conversations with the prisoner about the *Chicago Inter-Ocean* scheme.

On cross-examination he was asked whether the prisoner was a man of ordinary prudence and judgment. His reply was, "Of extraordinary prudence and judgment, of the Colonel Sellers stripe."

Mr. Scoville.—"Explain yourself."

The witness.—"Colonel Sellers is the type of a character who has more or less egotism, and who is constantly getting up schemes that are to make great fortunes for himself and friends—a genial, good-natured fellow, differing, however, from this man, who, instead of being genial and good-natured, has the most unbounded selfish disposition that I have ever met."

The prisoner (contemptuously).—"That is the best you can do; is it? That indicates your brain."

The witness further stated on cross-examination that he had expressed the opinion that the prisoner ought to be hanged.

Without concluding the cross-examination the Court at three o'clock adjourned.

CHAPTER XXVI.

A Short Session in Consequence of Juror's Illness—Several Witnesses who did not Admire the Prisoner's Character and One who Thought he Ought to be Hung.

WEDNESDAY, Dec. 14th, was destined to be a short session, Mr. Gates, one of the jurors who had been ailing for some days, being compelled to suspend his duties.

John L. Withrow, of Boston, was the first witness. His profession was stated by the prisoner as "the honorable pastor of the Park Street Church, in Boston—the church I used to attend there. He is a very fine man." The witness stated that in 1877 or 1878 the prisoner had commended himself to witness as being a co-worker with Moody. He asked witness if he could lecture in witness' church—a reply to Ingersoll. Witness told him "No," because he was not in that line of business. He had spoken with great earnestness, but with nothing more than earnestness, of the importance of having Ingersoll answered. At the weekly prayer meetings held at the church, the prisoner was constantly taking part. Witness never introduced him to anybody, and he never asked to be introduced. He was always to witness' mind an ill-natured man.

Witness then stated that he lost sight of the prisoner until the winter of 1879-80, when he met him and was told that he had opened a law office.

Q. Did you ever see anything to indicate that he was an insane man or a man of unsound mind? A. Oh! never, not the least.

Q. What was your impression of his character in that respect? A. I should have taken him to be a very shrewd man. I should say a very cute man, nstead of shrewd.

The prisoner.—" What's the difference?"

The witness.—" One is sharper than the other."

The District Attorney.—" And shorter."

The prisoner.—" He did not say that. You put that in, Corkhill. You must have slept well last night."

The cross-examination elicited nothing important, the witness stating that the prisoner's conversation would signify that he was critical and accusative rather than kind and consenting.

On re-direct examination the witness stated that the prisoner had given him a copy of " *Truth.*" He thought it was a book indicating careless composition and thoughtless, unverified opinion.

At this point juror Gates, who had been suffering all the morning, asked permission of the Court to get fresh air for a brief period. This was granted and the opportunity was eagerly seized upon by Guiteau to work in one of his rambling speeches.

"While in Boston," he said, "I attended Dr. Withrop's church regularly. I was around the Christian Association regularly and the Christian Union regularly, and I associated with high-toned Christian people. I say this for Corkhill's benefit, on the ground of total depravity. I always have associated with high-toned people. I don't know any dead beats or disreputable characters of either sex" (After a pause.) 'The object of this kind of examination is to settle this question—whether I knew I was doing wrong. My answer is, that I don't care whether I knew I was doing wrong or not. My free agency was destroyed, and I hadn't any choice; and I will take my chance with this Court and this jury and the Lord on that point. The question is not whether I was insane five years ago, but whether I was a free agent at the time I killed the President. That kills your theory. That is the question for the Court to pass upon. It is not a question of right or wrong, but of a free agency. I am not here to save my neck from the gallows. I am here for right, for justice, for vindication. That is all I have got for that. When I go before the jury I am going to talk to them on that. This is simply an incidental speech to put in the time."

The juror having returned, the trial was resumed.

Charles A. Bryan was called, and testified that he was City Clerk of the Equitable Life Insurance Company, of New York. He first saw the prisoner in February, 1881, when he called to inquire what commission would be allowed for obtaining applications for insurance; he brought in an application and asked for a loan or advance, which he did not get; he came in the next day and pressed his claim for a loan or advance, but the witness did not entertain the proposition; he handed the witness a copy of his speech, "Garfield against Hancock," and spoke of his familiarity with "Jim" Blaine and other leading men of the Republican Party.

The prisoner interrupted and insisted that he had always said Mr. Blaine or Secretary Blaine. He further claimed that witness had given him fifteen dollars, and repaid himself out of commissions earned.

The witness went on to say that the prisoner became importunate for a loan; witness had in the meantime investigated the proposed risk and advanced him five dollars; the prisoner said he was a prominent applicant for the position of Consul to Paris, and that he would soon go to Washington to obtain his appointment; be came into the office on the 5th of March, and pleaded very hard for another advance; the witness was surprised to see him, as he thought he had gone to Washington to look after his appointment, but the prisoner said he had not the money to go to Washington; the witness then gave him ten dollars with the understanding that when the matter was consummated he should receive the difference.

The prisoner.—"The commission amounted to ninety dollars; Bryan got fifty dollars of it, and I got forty dollars.

The witness produced two letters written to him by the prisoner from Washington, and said that he had received quite an avalanche of letters from him. He had never seen anything in the prisoner indicative of unsoundness of mind, but thought him a pretty shrewd sort of a fellow.

On cross-examination the witness said that the commission in the case brought into the office amounted to ninety dollars.

Q. Have you ever expressed an opinion as to the guilt or innocence of the prisoner? A. I was not aware that there was any question about his guilt.

Q. Have you expressed an opinion as to whether he ought to be hung or not? A. If I have expressed an opinion about it, it was that he ought to be hung. That is my opinion now.

Mr. Scoville.—"And you can come here for the purpose of doing your share towards hanging him?"

The witness.—"Not at all. The idea of coming here was very repulsive to me."

Henry M. Collyer was the next witness, and as soon as he had taken the stand the prisoner as usual proceeded to introduce him to the Court and audience. "Oh, I remember you as the man that put up that *Herald* job on me! This is the man who represented Reese Bros. & Co., of Chicago, at the time I was tried before Judge Donohue. Judge Donohue said that I had a right to retain the money, and then the *Herald* came out with its sensational editorial."

The witness stated that Reese Bros. & Co. had given him a claim upon the prisoner, who had collected money and not paid it over. Witness had asked the prisoner if he had collected the money. Prisoner acknowledged that he had collected one hundred and seventy-five dollars through his attorney at Meridian. Witness had asked as to the balance (the claim was for two hundred and seventy-five dollars). He said he had instructed his attorney to bring suit for the balance. The witness asked him whether it was not true that he had surrendered the notes of indebtedness and compromise for one hundred and seventy-five dollars, and the prisoner replied that it was not true. He said that he was entitled to fifty per cent. of the full amount of the claim, that he had got his half and that when he got the other half he would settle with Reese Bros. & Co.

Witness produced several of Guiteau's letters corroborating his statement, and in the further course of his examination said that he told the prisoner that he was a thief and a scoundrel.

The prisoner.—"You never said that, or I would have knocked you down at the time, though I wouldn't do it now. I am not in that business."

At this point it was intimated to the Court that Mr. Gates, the sick juror, was suffering to such an extent as to be wholly unable to concentrate his attention on the proceedings. Judge Cox suggested that he might feel relieved after a recess, but Mr. Davidge at once said: "I do not think that any good would be accomplished by a recess. We are deeply interested in the preservation of the health of the jury. I value the time of the Court as much as any one, but it appears to me the proper course in view of the evident condition of the juror, is to adjourn."

Accordingly, at half-past eleven, the Court adjourned.

CHAPTER XXVII.

Guiteau's Divorced Wife on the Witness Stand but Withdrawn—Another Egotistical Address to the American Public—Some lively Scenes in Court.

WHEN the jury came into Court on Friday, December 15th, the juror Gates was among them and looked as though he had recovered from his temporary indisposition. There was a large attendance of interested spectators, including Representatives Le Fevre, of Ohio, and Spear, of Georgia, ex-Sergeant-at-Arms Thompson, Senator Hawley, of Connecticut, and Hon. R. T. Merrick. Hon. Charkson Potter, of New York, Judge Paxson, of Pennsylvania, and Judge Courtland Parker, of New Jersey, sat on the bench with Judge Cox. Secretary Folger also came in about 11.30 o'clock, and took a seat beside the Judge, by invitation. In the course of the day Representatives William Mutchler, of Pennsylvania, Hendee, of Vermont, Tucker, of Virginia, McCook, of New York, and Holman, of Indiana, were also spectators.

As soon as the Court was opened, the prisoner said: "If your honor please, I want to make a little speech. It is very important that the health of this juror should be cared for, and we don't want this thing to slip. It is a very fine jury in every way—good, honest, intelligent men. I suggest to the Marshal that they be allowed to take a walk of four or five miles every day. Some of them are not used to good food, I understand, and it disagrees with their digestion."

The Court remarked that the Marshal would look after that.

Henry M. Collier was then recalled. When Mr. Scoville got the witness, Guiteau began a fire of interruptions, and when counsel asked of witness if he had ever expressed an opinion as to the prisoner's guilt—

"I object to that," said Guiteau. "You are about as stupid as you can be, Scoville. You haven't got sense enough to know better than to quiz a man of his character."

Witness replied that he might have expressed an opinion but did not think he had ever said that the prisoner ought to be hung.

Upon re-direct examination the witness said he thought that at the time he knew the prisoner (1873) he was perfectly competent to judge between right and wrong.

Mr. Scoville excepted to the evidence.

J. M. Justice, a lawyer of Logansport, Indiana, the next witness, testified that about June, 1878, he met the prisoner in Logansport. The prisoner stopped at Wm. Jones' boarding house, about a square and a half from the witness' residence.

Witness saw the prisoner daily for about three weeks. The prisoner was selling a life of Moody. Guiteau at once began to insult the witness grossly and finally called him a liar.

The prisoner was sane and knew the difference between right and wrong. He remarked that the prisoner's appearance had changed, and that he now exhibited a suppressed expression. In reply to Mr. Scoville, witness said it seemed to indicate fear in the Court room.

The prisoner in an excited manner denied that he was fearful.

Rev. Rush R. Shippen, pastor of All Souls Unitarian Church, in Washington, testified to meeting with Guiteau at Mrs. Grant's boarding house. The prisoner was a little peculiar but there was nothing indicating insanity.

The District Attorney here instructed the Marshal to call Mrs. Dunmire—and the name produced a buzz of excitement.

GUITEAU'S DIVORCED WIFE.

Mrs. Ann Dunmire, the ex-wife of Guiteau, the witness wanted by Mr. Corkhill, was escorted in from the witness' room by one of the bailiffs. She took a seat on the stand and talked so low that only those near the stand could hear her. During her brief examination, Guiteau never looked up from a paper he pretended to read.

"I first met him in Chicago, in 1868," the witness said: "when I was employed in the library of the Young Men's Christian Association."

"Were you ever married to him?" asked the District Attorney.

"I was married to him on the 10th of July, 1869, in Chicago."

"If the Court please," said Mr. Scoville, rising, "I object to any further testimony from the witness. She states that she was his wife in 1869, and there is nothing to show that she is not his wife now. She is, as it stands, incompetent as a witness."

"Have you been divorced from the prisoner?" asked the District Attorney.

"Wait a minute," exclaimed Guiteau, "that's not the way to do it: you must produce the record evidence."

The Court sustaining this view, the District Attorney asked for the record of the divorce, and the witness produced a paper. Mr. Scoville objected that it was merely a copy of the divorce.

The Court, having been satisfied that it was merely a copy, and not an authenticated record, said that it could not be introduced as evidence.

"Very well, we'll withdraw her," said the District Attorney, "and send for the rest of the record."

Dr. Noble Young, the attending physician at the jail, was next examined. He saw the prisoner the day he was brought to the jail; did not remember any special conversation. He had seen him nearly every day since, and conversed with him regarding his health. A few days after Guiteau was brought to the jail, in a conversation with the witness he said he was inspired to do the act, and that if the President should die, he would be confirmed in his belief of inspiration. He asked him once why he should lay the blame of the death upon the doctors. His answer was that things must take their natural course. After the question of insanity began to be mooted, the witness' examination of the prisoner was directed to that point.

The District Attorney asked the witness what his opinion was as to the prisoner's sanity or insanity.

"A perfectly sane man, sir," said the witness, "as bright and intelligent a man as you will see on a summer's day." The witness never saw anything about Guiteau that indicated insanity.

Upon cross-examination, the witness being asked as to Guiteau's statement in jail that if the President died it would confirm his belief that he was inspired, the prisoner, interrupting, said: "I said if the President recovered it would show that the Lord had countermanded his order, just as he did in the case of Abraham. He commanded him to kill his son, and then countermanded the order. The Lord has taken care of it, too, gentlemen. I am entirely satisfied with the way the Deity has taken care of this case so far."

Mr. Scoville asked if it would be possible to administer digitalis to the prisoner in his coffee without his knowing it.

The witness said if any one wanted to do it he might.

"They don't do it there, Scoville," said the prisoner. "They think I am a great man at the jail."

At this point Mrs. Scoville desired to ask some questions, but was snubbed by the prisoner, and advised by the Court to ask them through her husband. As Mr. Scoville continued to ask questions, which the prisoner thought ill-judged, Guiteau heaped abuse upon his long-suffering counsel, and turning patronizingly to the witness, said: "That's all, Doctor, I am much obliged to you. You can go."

Gen. Joseph S. Reynolds, of Ravenswood, Illinois, who practised law in Chicago, was next called to the stand. Guiteau, he testified, came to his office in Chicago in 1868, and applied for admission as a law student. The witness described at some length the prisoner's *Inter-Ocean* project and other schemes, giving about the same facts as were given by the witness' former law partner, Mr. Phelps, who was examined Tuesday. The witness said he thought Guiteau would have made a very successful lawyer, if he had stuck to it industriously. After Guiteau left Chicago, he saw him in 1879, and next saw him in jail here on July 14th, last. After leaving the jail he made memoranda of the conversation.

"I want you to state what he said regarding the murder," said Mr. Corkhill.

The witness then detailed the conversation with the prisoner in jail. He asked the witness when General Logan would come; expressed his Stalwart views, and stated that the *Herald* was publishing several columns of his biography every day.

"That was what I understood," interrupted the prisoner, "but it was false. That was one of Corkhill's lies."

General Reynold said the prisoner referred to the murder as an assassination, and said: "When I assassinated the President."

"I never said so, General," interrupted the prisoner, "I always spoke of it as a removal."

The witness, continuing, said the prisoner told him that he expected Conkling and others to befriend him when there was a reaction in the public feeling. He said also that Mr. Corkhill had promised to put off the trial until the feeling had changed in favor of the prisoner."

"That's what Corkhill said, but he lied about it," shouted the prisoner. "I have found him out now. He's a first-class fraud."

He made no reference to inspiration in that

conversation said the witness: the subject of the cause or motive of the act was not alluded to.

"I want to ask the General if he was in the employ of Mr. Corkhill at the time?" said the prisoner. "He pretended to be my friend. If he came in the guise of a detective I want that fact shown up before the American people."

The witness said that at an interview with the prisoner the next day, the latter referred to an article that had been printed in the *National Republican* to the effect that General Garfield had sounded the death knell of the Republican Party.

The witness testified that the prisoner said there was no malice in the crime, that his act had been a patriotic one. On the 18th, the witness told him that the President would recover, and the prisoner seemed much disappointed. He showed him papers giving the sentiments uttered by prominent Stalwart leaders regarding the crime, and the prisoner seemed much stupified; he said he thought these men would defend him. He was astounded that they should look at this act merely as a bloody assassination, as they had been denouncing General Garfield and making him out a monster.

"I want to say," interrupted the prisoner, "that General Reynolds was the first man to open my eyes about Corkhill. Why, he says he's just as bitter as gall on you. The whole thing was a gigantic lie from beginning to end. If you expect to succeed by lying, Corkhill, you will find out you can't do it. God Almighty will strike you dead just as He did Ananias and Sapphira." The witness said that at the interview on the 18th, the prisoner wrote his address "To the American People." This paper was produced by the witness, and read to the jury by Judge Porter, as follows:

GUITEAU'S ADDRESS.

TO THE AMERICAN PEOPLE.

I have just discovered that all the papers setting forth my motives in attempting the President's removal have been suppressed. I was almost stupified when I discovered the fact. I have not been permitted to see a single paper since I came here. I have been most outrageously deceived. A young man who said his name was Nordhoff, and that he was sent to me by Mr. Connery, the managing editor of "New York Herald," came to my cell the Sunday afternoon following the attempted removal of the President. He was accompanied by District Attorney Corkhill, and he introduced Nordhoff to me as a special "Herald" reporter, and said if I wished to make any statement to the American people the reporter could take it. They spent two hours in my cell. I spoke with great earnestness and feeling, and the reporter took it down. He assured me, positively, that he was a special reporter for the "New York Herald," and I have had in all six or eight interviews with him, supposing him to be a "Herald" reporter. I have just discovered that he is a fraud, and that not a word I gave him has appeared in any paper. Whereas, in fact, he told me distinctly that he had sent his report to the "New York Hearld," and that it had appeared in all the papers. I gave him a full account of all my life, which he said would be published in the "Herald." I sent a letter to the "Herald" last Monday, and he told me positively that the letter had been mailed. I am just informed that not a newspaper in America, and that not a man, woman or child has spoken in my defenee. I claim that the reason the people feel as they do is because I have had no defence. I now wish to state distinctly why I attempted to remove the President. I had read the newspapers for and against the administration very carefully for two months before I conceived the idea of removing him. Gradually, as the result of reading the newspapers, the idea settled on me that if the President was removed, it would unite the two factions of the Republican Party, and thereby save the Government from going into the hands of the ex-rebels and their northern allies. These papers were the mouthpiece of the Stalwarts, the Administration and the Democratic Party. The idea of removing the President pressed upon me for several weeks, and finally I attempted to execute it. I had none but the best of feelings for the President personally. I had no malice and no murderous intent. I acted solely for the good of the American people. I appreciate all the religious sentiment and horror connected with the attempted removal of the President. No one can surpass me in this; but I put away all sentiment and did my duty to God and the American people. I claim to be a gentleman and a Christian, and do not dissipate in any way. All my papers have been suppressed, and the public mind sees nothing but the fact of the assassination, and this is why there is such a terrible cry against me. I claim my attempt to remove the President was a patriotic act, and demand a full hearing.

Very sincerely, CHARLES GUITEAU.

UNITED STATES JAIL, WASHINGTON, D. C., July 18, 1881.

P. S.—Not a soul in the universe knew of my purpose to remove the President. It was my own conception and execution, and whether right or wrong I take the entire responsibility of it.

CHARLES GUITEAU.

P. S.—I demand as a matter of right the immediate publication in the papers of the story of my life, which includes all the facts and circumstances connected with the President's assassination, Mr. Nordhoff, the supposed "Herald" reporter, has the entire story of my life, and I insist that it be published as my defence in this matter. CHARLES GUITEAU.

During the reading of the paper, Guiteau kept making interruptions, saying: "That's a manly document," and using other phrases.

When Judge Porter concluded the reading at 12.25 P. M., a recess of half an hour was taken.

When the Court was reconvened at 1 o'clock, the prisoner opened the session with a speech.

After an allusion to his autographs and Mr. Scoville's lecture, he added: "I want to say, also, that there are certain office holders in this city who are benefitted by my inspiration. They now hold nice, fat offices, and they would never have gotten them had it not been for me. I ask them as men of conscience, to respond. We want money. If they don't take the hint I am going to call their names. The rich men of New York gave Mrs. Garfield and her family, two hundred thousand dollars or three hundred thousand dollars. It was a splendid thing—a noble thing. I want them now to do something for me. I don't want anything for the defence, but Mr. Scoville and his family are poor. These fellows who have been benefited by the inspiration and are ashamed to give their names can send it on the sly and we won't give their names."

The examination of General Reynolds was then resumed. He identified as being in Guiteau's handwriting the answers to the interrogatories in the two applications for insurance heretofore introduced in evidence. The witness also identified Guiteau's handwriting on other documents in evidence.

The District Attorney then read the first application of insurance, which was for twenty-five hundred dollars for the benefit of his wife. This application was indorsed by Guiteau to the effect that the family was subject to no mental derangement. This indorsement, however, was not admitted as evidence.

General Reynolds then continued his narration of his interview of July 18th with the prisoner. The prisoner wrote the statement while he was present and very rapidly. He requested witness to take the paper to Mr. Gorham, of the *National Republican*, and insist that it should be published. Witness said, if he made anything public, he would violate the privileges accorded to him by the officers.

The witness' fourth visit to the prisoner was made on the morning of July 19th. He repeated to witness what he proposed to say in an address to the public; he copied it for the witness. The witness, though calm, seemed dispirited and dejected. He said that whenever his mind would turn from the subject he would read the papers, and that brought his mind back to it.

Colonel Corkhill then read from and commented on the address to the public, and Judge Porter remarked "that the inspiration idea originated on the 19th of July." This precipitated a dispute among counsel. Mr. Scoville demanding that this remark be withdrawn.

"I shall," said Judge Porter, solemnly, withdraw no utterance I have made during the progress of this trial."

The Court remarked that Judge Porter's words were premature.

During the altercation, Guiteau kept up a continual clamor. "The mills of the gods grind slow," he said, "but they grind sure. They will grind you down to atoms, Corkhill."

The District Attorney read the various letters identified by General Reynolds as being in the handwriting of the prisoner. One was from the prisoner to the District Attorney, and had a portion cut out. The prisoner accused the District Attorney of having cut out a part of the letter. None of the letters were important. Most of the letters were requests made to various people for loans. In the midst of abusive interruptions on the part of the prisoner and without concluding the examination, the Court adjourned.

CHAPTER XXVIII.

The Prisoner's Ex-Wife Again upon the Stand—She never Considered Guiteau Insane—More Medical Expert Testimony to Establish the Prisoner's Sanity.

ON the opening of Court on Friday, December 16th, the District Attorney stated that he desired to interrupt the cross-examination of General Reynolds for the present, and called to the stand, George D. Bernard, Deputy Clerk of the Supreme Court of Kings County, New York. He produced the original record in the case of Anna Guiteau against Charles J. Guiteau, application for divorce.

Mr. Scoville objected, but the objection was overruled and the decree admitted in evidence. The District Attorney then proceeded to read the record, which shows that in 1874, a decree of divorce was granted to Anna Guiteau on the ground of her husband's adultery.

General J. S. Reynolds, was then recalled to the stand and cross-examined by Scoville.

Q. You received from the prisoner the address to the American people. What did you promise to do with it? A. I said I would keep it.

The prisoner broke in with a statement that the witness promised to give it to the press, and had lied every time. He said it was all Corkhill's doing, but the Lord Almighty would get even with him for persecuting a righteous man.

Mr. Scoville read a letter written by the witness to the prisoner on the 25th of July, 1881, stating that no paper in the country had mentioned his (the witness) visits to the prisoner in jail, and adding, "Anything you write to me will be sacred from the public, unless it be some communication which you desire to reach the public." He asked the witness whether the disclosures made by him yesterday could be called as "kept sacred from the public."

The witness replied that he had not testified to anything occurring since the date of that letter.

The witness stated in response to a question by the District Attorney, that besides the personal motive of curiosity his reason for visiting the jail was to ascertain whether there was any socialistic plot in the assassination, and he was satisfied that there was not and that the prisoner had no associate.

The witness on being pressed by Mr. Scoville to state why he had made memoranda of his visits to the jail if he had not expected to make use of them, replied that it was to give correct information to the Attorney General, and that after each interview he recited to the Attorney General and the District Attorney what had occurred, using his memoranda for the purpose.

The District Attorney proceeded to read newspaper extracts which the last witness had brought to the jail and read to the prisoner. They comprised telegraphic despatches from Senator Conkling expressing abhorrence of the prisoner's act; also reports of interviews with Fred. Grant, Senator Logan and others; also editorials on the assassination. The reading of them by the District Attorney was interrupted by exclamations from the prisoner, of which the following are types: "That is false; General Grant was always very kind and polite to me. He liked the ring of my speech." "That is what Fred. Grant says. He is a nice youth, is he not? He is too lazy to get a decent living. He is a dead beat, not I." "I used to be a member of Beecher's church. He was supposed to be a virtuous man then, and perhaps he is now." "I used to go up to Logan, pat him on the back, and say, 'How are you, General?' and he would say, 'How are you, Guiteau?' He thought I was a good fellow." "Then they all turned against me, just as Peter did when he denied the Saviour, when he was on the cross and in trouble. But they have got over it now and they are coming up like proper men. My life would have been snuffed out at the depot that morning if God Almighty had not protected me. I was thinking about it this morning when I awoke, and it seemed to me that that act was the most audacious thing a man could do—to shoot down the President, surrounded by Cabinet officers and the police. I would not do it again for one million dollars. But I was in such a desperate state of mind under the pressure upon me that I could not have resisted it if I were to be shot down the next moment. My free agency was destroyed." In reference to another newspaper extract speaking of Guiteau's boast that if he got the Austrian Mission, he would fill the position with proper dignity, he said, "That part is true."

Mrs. Ella C. Grant, of Fourteenth Street, Washington, was called. She testified that the prisoner had boarded in her house forty-one days, leaving on the last day of June. "That was," said the District Attorney, "two days before the murder of the President."

"The doctors did that," said the prisoner; I simply shot at him."

The witness stated in response to questions by the District Attorney, that she never noticed in the prisoner anything indicating unsoundness of mind. She had considered him as intelligent as any one in her house. She had noticed nothing peculiar about him.

Mrs. Anna Dunmire, the prisoner's ex-wife, as he terms her, was then recalled by the District Attorney.

Mr. Scoville objected to the examination of the witness on the ground that any communications between her and the prisoner while living together as man and wife were privileged.

The Court overruled the objection until the point of privileged communication should be raised.

The prisoner.—" This lady is married and has children, and it is an outrage for Corkhill to be permitted to call her and dig up her reputation, which I will have to do if she attempts to do me any harm. I ask the Court to stop this man Corkhill. He is an old hog. He has no conscience or character or sense, and he is using his official position to traduce this lady. If I was President of the United States I would kick that man out of office in two hours. I want to make a speech to President Arthur. There are scores of first-class lawyers in New York City whom he knows, high-toned, Christian, conscientious men, any one of whom would be a hundred thousand times better than Corkhill. I ask President Arthur as a personal favor, and in the name of the Republican Party, to kick this man out of office at once. I made General Arthur President, and I have a right to make this personal request of him. If he is the man I take him for he will act upon it."

The District Attorney waited quietly until the prisoner had finished his abusive talk, and then proceeded to interrogate the witness. She stated she was married to the prisoner on the 3d of July, 1869, in Chicago, and that Mr. and Mrs. Scoville were present at the marriage; they lived together in Chicago until the fall of 1871, her husband being engaged in the law business; then they went to New York; she could not recollect at how many places they lived in New York, but probably they had lived at fifteen or twenty places.

"Probably six or seven," said the prisoner, "and I paid my board bills too."

In New York her husband followed law and politics; he was engaged in the Greely campaign, and expected as a reward for his services to be appointed as Minister to Chili.

"I thought I might get the Swiss Mission," said the prisoner; "I never thought of Chili."

Mr. Scoville asked the witness whether she knew that from what the prisoner had told her, and when she replied in the affirmative, he objected to the admission of the testimony.

Then the prisoner broke out in a protest against the whole examination, and said: "All the question here is, whether my free agency was or was not destroyed at the time I fired the shot. All this collateral evidence about my circumstances and about what I did or said or did not do or say during the last forty years has no bearing whatever on the point; and with all due respect to the Court, I do not think that the Court in banc would admit it."

The District Attorney asked the witness whether, in her association with the prisoner, she had ever noticed any insanity, and her reply was, "I never did."

The District Attorney said to Mr. Scoville, "You may take the witness."

"Thank you, Mr. Corkhill," said the prisoner (ironically), "that is the decentest thing you have done on this trial. I suppose that Porter insisted on it, as he is supposed to be a decent man, and so is Mr. Davidge." Then turning to Mr. Scoville, he said: "Cut your cross-examination short, Scoville, and let us get to something else."

Mr. Scoville asked the witness whether she had stated since the 2d of July last, that she had considered the prisoner of unsound mind when she lived with him. Her reply was: "No; I never have said so."

Mr. Scoville was about to cross-examine, when the prisoner broke into a torrent of abuse of his counsel, and called him, among other things, "a consummate jackass." Mr. Scoville asked a few questions, of an unimportant bearing, and then said: "I will not ask this witness any more questions."

The prisoner himself expressed approval of this and said: "I know nothing against this lady's Christian character, except that I know her to be a high-toned Christian lady. I know her well and have much respect for her."

A recess of one hour was then taken by the Court.

Dr. Francis D. Loring, of Washington, a physician, was then called as an expert by the prosecution. He testified that he had made a specialty of diseases of the eye and ear. He has been in the habit of examining the eyes of patients for the purpose of determining whether or not the appearance of the eye gives indication of disease of the brain; he examined the prisoner's eyes at the jail on the 30th of November and 5th of December, and had found nothing in them indicating an affection of the brain; the pupils of both eyes contracted and expanded naturally; there was some inequality in the strength of the muscles moving the eyes, which, after constant reading, sometimes produced something like a squint, but that had no connection with disease of the brain.

Dr. Allan McLane Hamilton, of New York, a physician, was the next witness. He testified that for the past nine years he had made a special study of mental and nervous diseases, and had written extensively on the subject. He had made three personal examinations of the prisoner and proceeded to state the points. He found no apparent physical deformity, nor anything whatever indicating any congenital defect. There was an appearance of flatness on the top of the head, but that was owing to the cutting of the hair. There was no irregularity of contour of the head. It was a fair sized head, etc.

In reply to a series of questions by the District

Attorney, witness stated in effect, that he did not find any external evidence of mental or physical disease; as to traits of character, he found the prisoner was eccentric and probably ill-tempered, but he believed the prisoner to be sane, to be able to distinguish between right and wrong, and to know the consequences of his acts.

After the cross-examination had gone on for a little while, the prisoner exclaimed: "With all respect to the Court and jury, and to the witness, I do not think that this kind of testimony amounts to a snap." (To the witness.) "How are you going to tell whether my free agency was or was not destroyed; I swear that my free agency was destroyed by the Deity, and how is the prosecution going to prove that it was not? That is all the point that the Court and jury have to pass upon."

In the course of a protracted cross-examination the witness was asked whether, in cases of congenital insanity, there were always external indications of it. His reply was: "Not always, but usually. It is not a uniform rule."

The witness was asked whether the prisoner's scheme in regard to the *Inter-Ocean* newspaper did not prove a defect of the prisoner's reasoning power.

The reply was that it proved bad judgment on his part, but there are many men in the world who are schemers and visionaries and who have, nevertheless, capacity to reason. That was not necessarily an evidence of insanity.

Mr. Scoville represented to the Court that he was not prepared to finish the cross-examination to-day, having relied upon Mr. Reed to conduct the cross-examination of the expert witnesses; and therefore, the Court at twenty minutes to three P. M. adjourned until Monday.

CHAPTER XXIX.

Death of the Wife of Juror Hobbs—The Court Adjourns until Wednesday without Further Action—Guiteau Expresses Confidence in the Jury.

ON Monday morning, December 19th, although it was quite generally known that one of the jurors, Mr. Hobbs, had suffered a severe bereavement in the death of his wife, an eager throng pressed into the Court room.

At ten o'clock, Deputy Marshal Williams, stepping into the witness stand, rapped the crowd to order, and said: "I am authorized by Judge Cox to say that there will be no session of the Court to-day. There will be no trial. Those who wish to leave will have an opportunity to do so. The jury will be called, but I don't know whether the prisoner will be brought into Court or not."

About twenty minutes later, eleven jurors filed into the Court room and were seated, leaving one chair in the jury box—the one occupied by Mr. Hobbs—vacant.

At ten minutes to 11 o'clock, the afflicted juror, Mr. Hobbs, was brought into Court. He gave visible evidence of his grief, and sinking into his chair buried his face in his hands which held a pocket handkerchief.

GUITEAU, THE ASSASSIN. 521

A few minutes later the Court was called to order. The prisoner was then brought in and unmanacled.

When the roll of jurors had been called, Mr. Hobbs, at the request of the Judge, left the jury box and coming up on the bench, held a whispered conversation with the Judge. When Mr. Hobbs returned to his seat, the District Attorney had a whispered talk with the Judge. Returning to his place, the District Attorney addressing the Court, said that one of the sad afflictions of life common to humanity had befallen one of the members of the jury. "The situation," he said, "is one of difficulty, still the instincts of humanity demand that some steps be taken to allow the juryman to render his last duties to his dead wife." With the concurrence of the defence, he would like some order made that would allow the juror to perform his duty to the memory of his deceased wife.

Mr. Scoville, rising, said the defence concurred in the suggestion. He not only concurred, but it was his wish that the juror should have such privileges as he desired without being encumbered by the attendance of a Deputy Marshal. He thought it proper that the Court should call the attention of the jury to the matter of communications from outside.

The Court remarked that the bailiffs had full instruction on that point.

"I have entire confidence," said the prisoner, "in the personal honor of every member of the jury."

After reminding the jury of the impropriety of receiving any communication in regard to the case, Judge Cox then directed the clerk to make the necessary order permitting Mr. Hobbs to leave his associates, in company with a bailiff.

Mr. Corkhill having stated that he had no further business to present to the Court, the Court was adjourned to Wednesday morning.

CHAPTER XXX.

Another Day with the Experts—Testimony Bearing Strongly against the Irresponsible Theory—Guiteau again in Several of his Raging Moods.

ON Wednesday, December 21st, the trial was resumed. All the jurors being in their seats at 10 o'clock, A. M., Mr. Scoville at once asked for an order, or rule, excluding the expert witnesses from the Court room while other experts were being examined. This was opposed by counsel for the prosecution, and the prisoner either from sheer perverseness or a desire to conciliate somebody or something, announced that he was perfectly willing that all should remain as he had perfect confidence in their honor and integrity. Mr. Davidge sarcastically agreed with this view of the case, and the Court refused to grant the rule.

Dr. Hamilton was then cross-examined by Mr. Scoville. After some preliminary questions as to the training and experience of the witness, a series of questions, which were mere variations, were propounded. The following are salient examples:

Q. Do you understand what is meant by inspiration as commonly understood by persons of various denominations? A. Inspiration is a "drawing in." I believe that the word "inspiration" is used in a very disorderly and irregular way by a variety of persons conveying a variety of ideas.

Q. On what do you found that belief? A. On what I have heard in this Court room for instance; a good deal has been said here about insanity, and I have heard it used by insane people for years.

Q. When you heard it used by insane people, what has been the connection in which it was used? A. The cases in which I heard it used by insane people were usually when the individual imagined himself to be the Saviour or somebody else. I had a patient three or four months ago who imagined that she was the bride of the Saviour; I had a patient in Dr. Macdonald's asylum who thought he was the Saviour. It is a very common thing to find insane people believing themselves members of the Trinity and believing themselves inspired. There are a number of people who say that they are inspired, that they are pleasing God in building churches or doing certain other things. In Utah people believe themselves inspired to take three or four wives.

Q. Is that an inspiration to each particular man? A. No, it is an inspiration that is divided up.

Q. What do you mean by that? A. I mean an inspiration which a number of people believe in and take to themselves. I do not suppose that every man has his own inspiration, but their faith in the tenets of their creed goes so far as to make them believe that they are doing a good act and complying with the Divine will when they take a certain number of wives.

Q. Do you not know that that is merely an article of their creed, and that the question of personal inspiration has nothing whatever to do with that pratice? A. It is my impression that there is a personal inspiration, that they believe themselves inspired. I may be wrong, I am not an expert in Mormonism.

Mr. Davidge made objection to the range which the cross-examination was taking and Mr. Scoville took up the direct disease theory again.

Q. Whenever any disease in the nervous system in any of its divisions has so far advanced that the power of will is insufficient to control physical impulse all the impressions of the mind are so rapid that to compare ideas and to determine with consistency is impossible, what would you consider the state of mind of a person so circumstanced? A. I will answer that by saying that the will does not control physical impulse. If a man has sufficient nervous disease to destroy intellectual pressure and prevent his exercising control of his will he is insane.

Q. What controls the will? A. Other mental processes.

The prisoner.—"The will is controlled by spirits—not by intellectual process. You had better drop this, gentlemen, and put Clark Mills on the stand. He is a better man for you. Dry that thing up. Clark Mills took a bust of my face. He thought that some one hereafter would be interested in it. He thought I was a great man. He was the man that did Jackson, opposite the White House. He thinks I am a greater man than Jackson, though Jackson has been President and I haven't been President yet. Mills wanted to immoratlize his name by getting it on my bust, so I took off my beard for his benefit. He is a great deal better man for you than this one. He said that one side of my head was badly deficient."

The witness further stated that insanity manifests itself in various ways in the same patient. He admitted that experienced people are sometimes deceived and that patients are frequently discharged, as cured, when they are not so.

In reply to questions as to the acquaintance of witness with the views of writers on insanity, the witness stated that he did not agree with the theory of moral insanity.

Q. Do you ever find such acts committed by inmates of insane asylums? A. I do: by men who have intellectual insanity as well as moral insanity. I believe that there are moral expressions of intellectual insanity.

Q. But you do not believe that acts of such persons, apparently prompted by ugliness or viciousness, are evidences of insanity? A. Not of themselves.

Witness believed that if insane persons knew the nature and consequences of their acts they should be punished like other people. He admitted, however, that they were not so punished in asylums.

A number of questions of an unimportant character were propounded and finally the witness said there were a great many eccentric people who never became insane. The phrase, "on the verge," implied the danger of falling over. He admitted that in the cases described there was a decided predisposition to mental disease.

Mr. Davidge then took the witness in hand and elicited his opinions to the effect that sanity and insanity are divided by a very vague line and that one may become gradually shaded into the other, that many people may be medically insane and yet know perfectly well the difference between right and wrong, and know when they are doing wrong.

The prisoner interjected his theory about an overpowering force but was silenced by Mr. Davidge.

The witness was called upon to explain the diagrams of the prisoner's head, which he had produced last Friday. The prisoner interrupted this part of the examination by saying: "Clark Mills will tell you all about my head. You had better get that point settled by him and not spend any more time on this kind of business."

Dr. Worcester, of Boston, whose examination on the part of the defence was commenced some weeks ago, and closed abruptly, because he insisted on Mr. Scoville defining what he meant, in one of his questions, by the word "inspiration" was called to the witness stand on the part of the prosecution. He stated in reply to questions by the District Attorney, that he had examined the prisoner at the jail, and that he had been also in daily attendance at the Court room for several weeks past, and had carefully watched the prisoner's conduct during that time, and heard what he said. He thought he was sane.

The District Attorney then proceded to put to the witness a long hypothetical question, embracing the history of the prisoner's life and the facts that have appeared in the case, and asked whether assuming these propositions to be true, the prisoner was sane or insane on the 2d of July last? Witness replied: "In my opinion he was sane."

The District Attorney read an additional hypothetical question, reciting many of the discreditable incidents in the prisoner's life, in which he was constantly interrupted by the prisoner exclaiming, "That is false; that is absolutely false.

That is one of Shaw's lies. I have disposed of him." At the close of the hypothetical questions, the witness was asked whether, assuming these propositions to be true, the prisoner was sane or insane at the time of the shooting of President Garfield. The witnes sreplied, "In my opinion, the prisoner was sane."

After recess, Mr. Scoville proceeded with his cross-examination of the witness, his questions being principally directed to the point of showing that the witness had not an extended medical experience. He also questioned him as to his motive in writing a letter to him inquiring whether he could be of any service to the prisoner. His reply was that he did so because at the time he believed the prisoner to be insane. He was asked what had changed his opinion as to the sanity or insanity of the prisoner, and his reply was: "Mainly his own testimony and my interview with him in the jail, supported by the evidence which I heard."

Mr. Scoville.—"What were the grounds of your opinion that the man was insane before you left Salem to come to Washington?"

The witness.—"I formed my opinion from statements which I had seen that he was **actuated at** the time he shot the President by an insane delusion, and that he was under the influence of an irresistible pressure which was the outgrowth of that insane delusion."

Mr. Scoville.—"If any one of the propositions contained in the hypothetical case put to you by the District Attorney were left out would your opinion still be the same that the prisoner was sane?"

The prisoner, who had been incessantly interrupting, now broke into a great rage, and exclaimed: "You are stupid, Scoville, as the witness is. You are just compromising my case every time on cross-examination. You are no more fit to manage this case than a ten-year-old school boy. You have no ability in examining witnesses. Your business is in examining titles. You had no business to come here at all and compromise me with your blunderbuss way."

The witness (in answer to the question).—"I should reply sane to any one of those propositions taken separately, without modifying circumstances."

Mr. Scoville.—"And you would answer sane to all the propositions taken together?"

The witness.—"Yes, sir."

After the witness had admitted that he believed it was possible for a person's mind to become so dominated or controlled by a religious emotion or delusion as to lose the power to control his own actions by his own mind, Mr. Scoville presented a postal card which the witness admitted having written, dated Salem, Massachusetts, November 24th, saying: "Accept my congratulations on the manner in which you have conducted the defence. It may not be popular, but it is right and just." The witness added that he saw no reason to take it back, at the time it was written.

Some further conversation took place about a letter which the witness had written to Mr. Scoville, and it was agreed that the letter itself, if Mr. Scoville could find it, should be put in evidence.

Guiteau broke out with a statement that Scoville was compromising his case, and he would rather, even at this late hour, take his chances with Charlie Reed, than with this idiot. "Between Corkhill and him," said Guiteau, "I have a pretty hard time of it."

In reply to Mr. Davidge, witness said his first impressions had been formed on newspaper reports and conversations, but that his opinion had been changed by examination and observation. He had communicated that change to Mr. Scoville to a certain extent personally, and to the full extent to Mr. Reed, prior to being put on the stand, in fact, on the evening of December 4. The witness went on to state the circumstances connected with a meeting of the experts, who had been summoned for the defence; there were nine or ten experts at that meeting. Mr. Reed was there and asked each expert his opinion; the witness, when it came to his turn, expressed his opinion. Mr. Reed said, in summing up the opinion of the experts: "You seem to have the prisoner on the border line of insanity, and a little more testimony will carry him over." The impression of the witness was that he told Mr. Reed that he considered the prisoner responsible.

The District Attorney.—"What do you understand by the word 'pressure,' as used in this case?"

The witness.—"I understand it as simply another form for the conflict going on in a man who is subjected to the temptation to do evil."

The prisoner.—"Scoville, you should have let the man go two hours ago. If I were indicted for manslaughter and Scoville defended me I would be hanged for murder. If you had let this man go two hours ago it would have been better for the defence." (To the Court.) "I tell him to get out of the case. He is ruining my case. He is not fit to try it."

Mr. Scoville.—"No one realizes that more than myself."

The prisoner.—"Then get out of the case, you consummate idiot. You have got no more brains for this kind of work than a fool. You compromise my case in every move you take. If you had let that man go at one o'clock he would have done me no harm."

Mr. Scoville.—"If the Court please, I have no more questions to ask the witness."

The prisoner.—"You had better get off the

GUITEAU, THE ASSASSIN. 533

case. I expect that the Almighty, notwithstanding Scoville's asinine character, will see that I am protected. I expect that it will take a special act of God to do it."

Mrs. Dunmire, the divorced wife of the prisoner, identified two photographs of him taken some years ago, and denied having said to Mrs. Scoville anything about the prisoner being insane.

Mr. Justice, of Logansport, Indiana, a former witness, produced a volume of Moody's life, which he said the prisoner had been peddling in Logansport, and in which he claimed the prisoner's name was legible, though it required to be looked at in a strong light. The prisoner himself denied that there was any such writing in the book.

The Court then at three o'clock adjourned.

CHAPTER XXXI.

Another Tiresome Day with Expert Testimony—Guiteau Doing a Good Deal of Talking and Roundly Abusing the Witness Shaw.

ON Thursday, December 22d, the prisoner, instead of his usual address to the audience held a stormy private discussion with Mr. Scoville and Col. Charles Reed, of Chicago, who had taken his seat at the counsel table apparently with the intention of coming into the case.

Dr. Theodore Dimon, of Auburn, New York, was the first witness. He testified that for two years up to last year, he had been Superintendent of the asylum for insane criminals at Auburn. He had made a personal examination of the prisoner, had noticed the prisoner in Court and heard his testimony. He considered the prisoner sane.

The District Attorney then propounded to the witness a hypothetical question, assuming to be true all the evidence brought forward by the prosecution, and asked the opinion of the witness as to the sanity of the prisoner at the time of the shooting of President Garfield.

The witness.—"It is my opinion that he was sane."

The cross-examination was long, mainly pointless, and wearisome in the extreme—the only break in the tiresome monotony being the interruptions of the prisoner. The following are some of the more important portions of it. In reply to questions, the witness stated that he had examined the prisoner twice for two hours upon one day, and for one hour the next day. The prisoner did not attempt to conceal anything, he appeared open, frank and sincere in his statements. Witness had no reason to suppose that he was feigning. The prisoner was stripped of everything except his pantaloons, and witness examined his person above the waist in the ordinary way of making an auscultatory examination. He examined the tongue particularly, but did not feel the head.

Q. What is your opinion as to whether he has been playing a part in the Court room? A. I do not think he has—a part in simulating insanity. He has been acting a part natural to his circumstances and character.

Q. Does egotism appear as one of the manifestations of insanity? A. I think that is a feature; the excessive idea of the importance of everything that concerns themselves and an absence of ideas of whatever injurious effect their conduct might have on others.

Q. Does the moral sense appear to be blunted? A. Blunted, yes; perverted, yes.

Mr. Scoville then recounted to the witness the circumstances attending the prisoner's attempt to establish the *Theocrat,* and asked, assuming all the facts stated to be true, what would they indicate as to his mental soundness or unsoundness? A. I do not think that by itself that would be sufficient to determine the question whether it was fanaticism or insanity.

Q. Are insane people ever fanatics? A. I never saw one.

Mr. Scoville then took up the hypothetical case stated by the District Attorney and questioned the witness closely on each separate circumstance mentioned therein, obtaining in reply the admission that there was nothing there to show that the person described might not afterward become insane. Mr. Scoville further stated the circumstances attending the prisoner's attempt to lecture and his habit of leaving the stage in a great hurry, and inquired whether that was not an indication of his unsoundness of mind. A. It might, or it might not be an indication of intoxication.

In reply to further questions, witness said it took a good deal of experience to make a competent observer on insanity. He did not know enough himself of it to be always able to judge between sane an insane people.

Mr. Scoville then alluded to the first letter written by the prisoner to President Garfield applying for the Austrian Mission, and the witnesss stated that it might be an evidence of insanity, but could not say positively, as he did not know sufficiently the ways of office seekers.

Q. Do not insane persons frequently write rational letters? A. Yes.

The prisoner here broke into an harangue about the contents of his mail, until stopped by the Court.

After some further unimportant testimony the Court, at half past twelve, took a recess for half an hour.

The cross-examination of Dr. Dimon was resumed after recess. Mr. Scoville again called the witness' attention to Mr. Corkhill's hypothetical question, and he, while contending that though the facts tended to show that the prisoner was sane, admitted that many of them taken individually were not inconsistent with the existence of an unsound mind. He said that many insane persons had good memories and were capable of laying and following plans of action.

Q. Is there anything in this hypothetical question of an immoral or vicious character attributed to the person there that might not be exhibited in ordinary cases of unsoundness of mind? A. Distributing them through a number of cases you find these peculiarities existing in some one or other through them all.

Witness admitted that a fixed conviction of duty urging a person to commit an act that his will was not able to resist was characteristic of epileptic mania.

Q. Suppose a person acts under what he considered a divine command, and in obedience to that command he should kill the President, and suppose he honestly believed that the people of the United States, as soon as they were informed of his motive, would not only excuse him but applaud him for the act, in your opinion would that be any indication of unsoundness of mind? A. I think it would—an honest belief, a sincere belief; the domination of his will by that belief is what I mean by this answer.

Q. Did you ever believe in personal divine inspiration in this age of the world? A. Not specially.

The prisoner.—"Well, Doctor, if the Lord could inspire a man two thousand years ago, why can't he do it to-day? Is there anything in human nature different now from what it was then? What is your idea on that?"

The witness.—"If the Lord did inspire anybody two thousand years ago, he can now if he choose."

The prisoner.—"That is my idea on that. He not only can, but he did in this particular case."

In the course of the examination Mr. Scoville questioned the witness on the subject of hereditary insanity, and received the information that whereas in England fifty per cent. of the insanity was hereditary, in witness' asylum only four or five per cent. was.

Mr. Scoville then propounded a hypothetical question, taking as his strongest point the averment that the prisoner believed firmly in his inspiration to shoot the President, and inquired whether, if that averment were true, the man was insane at that time.

The witness.—"I don't think that that is a question for an expert; any one can answer that; there is only one answer to that question; suppose a man to be insane, is he insane?"

Mr. Scoville then proceeded to question the witness as to his opinions on the works of certain writers on insanity, but Judge Porter objected on the ground that the jury, after a trial of Guiteau for six weeks, did not care to pass to the merits of certain authors. The Court sustained the objection.

On re-direct examination the witness was asked the reason for his conclusion that the prisoner was sane. Mr. Scoville objected, but the Court overruled the objection, and the witness stated that his conclusion was based upon his examination of the prisoner and from his testimony. Witness saw nothing in the prisoner that was not the result of his natural character, early training and the life he had led.

The Court.—"You have been asked whether a man might be impelled to the commission of an act he knew to be wrong by an insane delusion; could he be so impelled without an insane delusion, by an irresistible impulse to do what was wrong?"

The witness.—"I suppose that takes place in a fit of passion, where there is no deliberation, and where up to the moment of the act the person knew what was right and wrong."

Q. Can there be any sane irresistible impulse in the absence of a delusion? A. In the absence of an express delusion there may be, but my own belief is that there exists an unexpressed delusion in the mind of the actor.

The prisoner.—"These experts, allow me to say, are high-toned. High-toned, respectable men, but with all respect I say that they hang as many men as the doctors kill. There is no question about General Garfield being alive to-day, whatever my motive had been, if the doctors had not killed him, but the Lord allowed the doctors to finish the work I began, because He wanted him to go; and he did not go before his time any way. We have all got to go. It is a question of time."

Owing to the absence of Mr. Davidge and to the fact that the hour of three o'clock was approaching, the District Attorney suggested an adjournment, but yielded to Mr. Scoville's request to be allowed to recall at the present time D. McLean Shaw, the witness who testified to the conversation in which Guiteau stated that he would imitate Wilkes Booth. The witness was greeted by the prisoner with: "This is the man who told the lie about Booth. We have your record, Shaw, over there in New Jersey, where you were indicted for perjury. You only got off on a technical quibble."

The witness Shaw then in reply to questions, admitted that he had been indicted for perjury in reference to the payment of a note for one thousand dollars. He had been tried and acquitted on that charge. He was tried by his own desire to clear up the case. Finally the Court remarked, "I think we have had enough of this." Guiteau in an excited, but contemptuous tone, shouted "Shaw's statement about Booth is the most extraordinary statement that ever came from a human mouth. There is not one word of truth in it, and you know it, too. God Almighty will curse you for it. I never talked to you about Booth in my life; you are marked for life; it is the most extraordinary lie that ever was concocted. I never mentioned the subject of Booth to Shaw; it is not likely I would wait ten years to kill some great man. It is the most outrageous thing ever concocted by a human being: it is a lie on its face, and any intelligent man would say so."

The District Attorney then stated that he would call a witness who would testify to a somewhat similar conversation with the prisoner.

Mr. Scoville.—"Is it that man Foster? I

thought you would leave him to the last so that we could not look into his record."

The witness to whom the District Attorney alluded was not in attendance. He was not, so the District Attorney stated, Mr. Foster, but one who had heard the prisoner make the statement in Washington. But he (Corkhill) did not intend to bother the jury with any of those witnesses.

The Court then at three o'clock, adjourned.

CHAPTER XXXII.

Mr. Reed Comes into the Case as Counsel for the Defence—The Wilkes Booth Imitation Threat Confirmed—More Expert Testimony and more of Guiteau's Insolence.

ON Friday, December 23d, the prisoner resumed his pastime of opening Court with an address, and was hardly in the room before he broke out. Addressing nobody in particular, he remarked : " It is said that I have been abusing Mr. Scoville. Now the fact of the matter is I want to make a speech about that. Mr. Scoville is doing very well in this case considering his theory, but he is not a criminal lawyer. He is a fine examiner of titles. He can tell you all about your abstracts of titles. He is a good fellow and a first-class examiner of titles, but I cannot have Mr. Scoville here compromising my case. There is no lawyer in this Court room but knows that he has asked questions for the defence which have been a positive injury to the defence. I cannot sit here when my life is at stake and have him compromise my case in this way. My friend, Charles H. Reed, who was for twelve years District Attorney at Chicago, and a first-class lawyer, has very kindly consented to assume the charge of this case, and I introduce him to your

Honor, the jury and the American people. He is a good fellow. Scoville is a good fellow, too, and I want him to continue in this case and help in every way. I have not talked on this case and will not talk on it any more than is absolutely necessary for truth and justice. I am not going to sit here and allow witnesses to tell that which is absolutely false even if I have to interrupt the Court and jury and to seem indecorous. I claim to be a gentleman, and I want this trial to be conducted in a proper spirit. But I have been greatly excited on account of certain witnesses and on account of Mr. Scoville's inexperience. I expected to have three or four first-class lawyers here—Mr. John D. Townsend, of New York, Judge Magruder, of Maryland, and others who know all about this criminal business. But they have not come, and my opinion is that Mr. Scoville elbowed them off."

Mr. Scoville stated that he had endeavored, as the Court knew, to obtain such assistance in the case as would be appropriate. He had had an intimation that Mr. Townsend, of New York, would assist after the case had been in progress two or three weeks. On the Monday evening after he received that information, he telegraphed to Mr. Townsend, and Mr. Townsend sent a reply by telegram the same evening, saying he would come on Wednesday. That reply, however, for some reason or other, was not delivered until

Thursday noon, and he had therefore applied to Mr. Reed to assist him in the expert part of the case. Mr. Reed kindly consented to do so, and the same evening met with the experts.

Mr. Scoville stated that Mr. Reed would therefore appear openly in the case if the Court did not consider it inconsistent with the fact that he had been a witness. Messrs. Porter and Davidge objected to the Court being called upon to pass upon such a point, but stated that the prosecution would raise no objection to Mr. Reed appearing as counsel.

After a short wrangle as to whether Mr. Reed had not privately been acting as counsel all through, Mr. Scoville intimated that it would perhaps be better for the Court to assign him to the case. Judge Cox declined to do this but stated that he saw no impropriety in Mr. Reed taking part in the case. He assented however, to the view of counsel for the prosecution that they had a right to criticize if they thought fit.

This question having been disposed of, and it being understood that Mr. Reed was henceforth to be recognized as one of the counsel for the defence, the letter which was written by Dr. Samuel Worcester, of Salem, Massachusetts, to Mr. Scoville (and the substance of which was given in Dr. Worcester's testimony a few days ago), was read by Mr. Scoville, as follows:

SALEM, Massachusetts, November 2, 1881.

DEAR SIR—I am prompted to write to you, not from any love of notoriety nor for pecuniary reward, but simply in the hope that I may help to save the American people from the disgrace of hanging an insane man merely because the person murdered was our President. No one reprobates the crime more than I. But I believe also in justice, and justice tells me that it is not right to put to death an insane man for an act caused by a disease which took away his power of will and judgment. I believe that Guiteau should be kept securely in an insane asylum as long as he lives, for recovery from insanity with homicidal tendencies is never permanent. If half of what is said of Guiteau is true he is insane, and not fully responsible. I have made a special study of insanity since January, 1867.

* * * * You can judge better than I whether any views or opinions of mine can be of service.

Mr. Scoville then called attention to the letter from Dr. Spitzka, to which the prisoner alluded yesterday. It was but just to say that the letter was addressed to him (Scoville) and not to the prisoner.

Mr. Davidge objected to having the Court and jury regaled every day with explanations, and another little wrangle was precipitated.

Mr. Scoville then objected to some previous testimony and cited from 12 N. Y. (The People vs. Lake) the first citation made in the case, but the objection was overruled and an exception taken. After another interruption by the prisoner and the reading of a letter from Dr. Spitzka, the examination of witnesses was proceeded with.

William A. Edwards, of Brooklyn, was called. His evidence went to substantiate the statement of Mr. Shaw, in whose office he had been a clerk, that Guiteau had said he would some day kill some big man as Booth had done. Witness said the remark made but little impression upon him at the time, as he then thought the prisoner was the last man in the world who would do an act involving personal danger to himself.

Dr. Spencer H. Talbot, Medical Superintendent of the Homœopathic Asylum for the Insane at Middletown, New York, stated that he had closely observed the prisoner, and listened to his testimony on the stand. Witness believed that Guiteau was sane, and that he was so on the 2d of July. The prisoner interrupted the witness, by asking him how much he expected to get for his opinion, and was ordered by the Court to keep silence. He replied, "All right, your Honor, I'll be quiet now." Mr. Davidge remarked, "Your Honor will note that the free agency quoted by the prisoner operates all right now, as he can keep quiet when he wants to." The prisoner interrupted the statement. "I do not pretend to say that I am insane now any more than you are, but on the second day of July, and for thirty days prior, I was insane. That's the issue." The cross-examination of this witness was continued till the hour of recess, and he stated that "inspiration was merely in such cases an insane delusion, and there was no evidence that the prisoner labored under an insane delusion." After recess the cross-examination was continued, and witness said he had no reason to believe the prisoner was playing a part when visited in jail, but he thought that in Court he was exaggerating his tendencies to egotism, vanity and ingratitude. He did not consider these tendencies peculiar either to the sane or the insane. They may be seen in either case.

Dr. Henry P. Stearns, of Hartford, Connecticut, Superintendent of the Hartford Retreat for the Insane was the next witness. From eight hundred to one thousand cases of insanity had come under his supervision during the eight years he had been connected with the "Retreat."

Witness had made four examinations of the prisoner at the jail, directed to his physical and mental condition.

Guiteau interrupted, saying: "You came to me, doctor, as a friend, and I, supposing you were going to testify for the defense, talked very freely with you about my religious feelings and all about myself, but Corkhill's money was too much for you. I want to say here that I don't pretend that I am any more insane at this minute than Davidge. I won't say Corkhill, for I think he is cracked. But I rest my case right on this claim that I was insane on the 2d of July, when my inspiration and the state of my mind impelled me upon the President. To make it very short, that's all there is to it. I don't care what these experts say about my sanity, now that's got nothing to do with it."

Witness detailed at great length the results of his examinations and interviews with Guiteau.

Mr. Scoville recited the facts as to the members of Guiteau's family that had shown unsoundness of mind, and asked whether all these facts put together were any evidence of hereditary disposition to insanity in the family.

The witness in reply, said he would have to eliminate from the question the religious peculiarities of Guiteau's father, and the mental weakness of his cousin Maynard (produced as it was by mesmerism), also the dissipation of his uncle, but he admitted that there were in the Guiteau family more than the ordinary proportion of cases of insanity.

The cross-examination was continued at great length, and was rather tedious. Mr. Scoville propounded some questions as to witness' belief in irresistible impulses, when the prisoner burst forth again. "When you get in the domain of spiritology, you are in the dark, doctor. You can't tell what kind of a spirit will take possession of a man's mind and impel him to an act. I don't care about your head or antecedents. The whole thing rests on the spirit that gets into you. A man may be perfectly insane at the time of the commission of an act and an hour after be sane. (After a pause.) I wouldn't go to the depot again and shoot at President Garfield for a million dollars from the mind I have on me now and an hour after the act was committed, and yet for thirty days prior I would have shot him at any time I could. If I knew I was to be shot dead the next minute I could not have resisted it. That is all there's to it. I have said it about fifty times."

The Court (severely).—"Then don't say it again."

The prisoner.—"I say it because the whole theory of the prosecution is ridiculous."

The Court then, pending further cross-examination, adjourned.

CHAPTER XXXIII.

A Weary Court and Jury—Guiteau's Abominable Interruptions and Insolence Leads to a Threat of his Removal to the Dock—His Anticipations of a "Happy Christmas."

ON Saturday, December 24, the fatigue of the jury, and to a certain extent of the Court and counsel was painfully evident. Although the bright, clear day, with its golden sunshine, was so different in its effect from the gloom of yesterday, the jury did not appear very acute. They were undoubtedly tired and almost worn out, looking as if they had been spending sleepless nights. Several of the jurors held their heads down, and all gave more or less evidence of the great demand being made upon their physical system by this long trial. Ralph Wormley, the colored juror, who had been afflicted with some ailment, retained around his head and over his left eye, the greasy, faded, silk handkerchief which had served as a bandage for two weeks or more. Occasionally he would look up, and there was a muscular movement about his forehead that gave him a comical appearance. Mr. Hobbs, suffering from his recent bereavement, seemed to be absorbed in his own feelings, and seldom raised his head. It was not yet a week since he stood beside a new made grave, and heard the rumbling clods of earth that fell upon the coffin of his wife.

Guiteau, after examining his mail and consulting with his counsel, busied himself for a time with his newspapers.

Dr. Henry P. Stearns resumed the stand, and was further cross-examined by Mr. Scoville. He testified that in almost all forms of insanity, memory was the first faculty to show impairment. He also stated that there have been cases of undoubted insanity when, upon examination of the brain, no distinct disease had been found. In the course of this examination a dispute arose between Messrs. Porter and Scoville, which became very acrimonious, and in which the prisoner repeatedly took part. Mr. Reed then continued the examination, and the prisoner's interruptions became so annoying that Mr. Porter finally appealed to the Court to have him placed in the dock. This was also urged by the District Attorney, and the Court stated that the question had already suggested itself to his mind. The prisoner still continued defiant, and claimed to be acting as counsel, but was ultimately ordered by Judge Cox to remain silent.

Dr. James Strong, Superintendent of the Insane Asylum at Cleveland, Ohio, testified that he had examined the prisoner in the jail and found his bodily condition good. He stated that, as a rule, insanity is usually associated with the condition of bodily health. Guiteau broke in with the statement: "I will save you trouble, Doctor. I am in excellent health and am not insane." The prisoner continued his insolent interruptions, and compelled a renewal of the application to have him placed in the dock, and he was again severely admonished by the Court.

Then the witness proceeded with his narration of the results of his examination of the prisoner. The prisoner, he said, thought quickly and consecutively. The evidence which struck the witness with the greatest force was the prisoner's power of attention. This showed that he had control of his mind, because a man cannot fix his attention on a given subject without exercising his will power. He could fix his attention on a given subject and then turn it to another subject, and that implied brain power. So the witessn was thoroughly convinced that the prisoner's mental organization was thoroughly intact and that all his mental processes worked smoothly and harmoniously. He was sound in his perceptions, his sensations, his thoughts, his will. Such a condition he looked upon as entirely incompatible with insanity. The power of attention was there, the power of consecutive thought, as well as coherency. The power of order and command, the power to check a movement, the power to force a retreat, were there, all indicating very clearly that the prisoner's mental organism was sound and healthy.

Another wrangle between counsel ensued in consequence of the witness declining to answer directly the hypothetical case of the defense. Finally, he admitted that the position cited would indicate or point toward insanity. *Dr. Abram M. Shew*, Superintendent of the Middletown (Connecticut) Hospital for the Insane, and *Dr. Orpheus Evarts*, of College Hill, Ohio, medical superintendent of the Sanitarium, were also examined, and their testimony was to the effect of sustaining the sanity of the prisoner, not only now, but on the 2d of July. The latter witness said in his opinion the prisoner had been exaggerating his own peculiarities, which were egotism, sharpness, smartness, vulgarity and ingratitude. In consequence of illness in the family which would compel Mrs. Scoville to leave Washington, she was called to the stand to testify to the insanity of Mrs. William S. Maynard, but Mr. Davidge objected to this testimony, and the objection was sustained. Mr. Scoville put in evidence a letter written by L. W. Guiteau in 1875, in which he stated his belief in his son's insanity. The Court then at 2.45 adjourned until Tuesday. As the handcuffs were being placed upon the prisoner he broke out with: "To-morrow is Christmas. I wish the Court, the jury and the American people aud everybody else a happy Christmas. I am happy."

CHAPTER XXXIV.

After the Christmas Holidays the Dreary Farce Resumed—Guiteau Claims to Belong to the Abraham School of Insanity—He Sneers at Experts and Expects to Go to a Lunatic Asylum.

AFTER an adjournment over Christmas the Court reconvened on Tuesday, December 27. Judge Cox being engaged with the Grand Jury was late in taking his seat, and it was beyond half-past ten o'clock when the crier called "Order." On being brought in Guiteau, addressing the audience, said: "I had a nice Christmas. I hope everybody else did. I had a nice Christmas dinner, fruits, flowers, candies, etc., and plenty of lady visitors and gentlemen."

Dr. A. E. McDonald, Superintendent of the Ward's Island, New York, Insane Asylum, testified that he had treated some six thousand cases of insanity and had given special attention to its study. He described the difference between delusions and insane delusions, and upon the subject of inspiration said: "Inspiration always overrides all fear of bodily pain or injury, and renders the person who believes he is acting under inspiration wholly oblivious to such considerations." Witness was asked if such persons usually planned with deliberation, and replied: "On the contrary, their acts are sudden in both conception and execution as a rule, and they seldom attempt to avoid the consequences in any way." In reply to other questions, the witness said he did not believe in what was called temporary insanity, in which the act committed is the only evidence of insanity, and where the person is to all appearances perfectly sane in other respects both before and after the act. He had never seen an instance of it. In reply to questions as to the proportion of the sane to the insane, witness said: "As a matter of fact, statistics show that in the whole United States the proportion of the insane to the sane is one to every thousand; in New York State one to eight hundred; in New York City one to five hundred; and in England one to three hundred persons."

The prisoner made several interruptions, but no notice was taken of him. The most important portion of this witness' testimony had reference to visiting the prisoner in his cell. He had remained with the prisoner two hours, and made the usual mental examination in such cases. He talked over with the prisoner all the main incidents of his life up to and including the shooting of the President. The prisoner always spoke of the act as my "conception" and "soon after I conceived the removal of the President." Witness asked the prisoner why, if the act was the Almighty's and he was simply the agent, he was so particular as to practice his aim, and why he did not trust the details to the Almighty? And the prisoner, hesitated, flushed a little, and said: "The Almighty often trusts the details to his agents." Witness talked at considerable length with the prisoner in regard to the crime, and asked him what plans or expectations he had for the future, and his reply was to the effect that while he did not consider himself insane, he had studied up the question of insanity, and believed he would be found by a jury to be legally insane at the time of the commission of the act, and would be acquitted. He was asked: "What do you suppose will be done with you?" and replied: "I will be sent to an insane asylum, and I find, under the law, I can, after a few months, have a commission of lunacy to pass upon my case, and of course they will find me sane, and I will be discharged." Witness believed from his examination and observations of the prisoner in Court that he is a perfectly sane man.

Witness then proceeded at some length to give the reasons for his opinion, using the expression: "I have frequently noticed that his most violent interruptions have been made when the weight of evidence was against him." Several objections were made by the defence, but they were overruled and exceptions were noted. In further replies to the modified first hypothetical question of the prosecution, the witness said: "I believe the person to have been sane." After recess the witness in reply to the second hypothetical question said: "Assuming the facts set forth to be true, and adding that statement to the others, it strengthens my opinion that the man was sane on the 2d of July." Exceptions to questions and answers were noted by the defence.

In a long cross-examination by Colonel Reed and Mr. Scoville, witness admitted that insane persons were more liable to be adjudged sane than the reverse. He also admitted that overwork, care and anxiety might produce dyspepsia, which with other causes might lead to disease of the brain, and that in its turn would stimulate insanity. In reply to the question, "Is it not a fact that you learn that the brain is diseased from the evidence of unsoundness of mind?" Witness said: "From that and from physical indications also." Pending the cross-examination the Court at three o'clock adjourned.

ANOTHER ADDRESS.

Guiteau prepared and delivered to the press during the holidays a long document, which he termed, "A Christmas Address to the People of America." It was merely a labored and amplified embodiment of his statements before and during the trial, in which the inspiration theory was strongly dealt upon, and bitter denunciations were fulminated against any men who should kill him judicially or otherwise.

CHAPTER XXXV.

The Prisoner Placed in the Dock after an Exciting Contest between Counsel—The Assassin from this Time Forward to be Recognized as an Alleged Criminal.

ON Wednesday, December 28th, on the opening of the Court, Dr. McDonald again took the stand, and was cross-examined by Mr. Scoville. In answer to a question as to whether he had ever met with an instance of temporary insanity, witness said, "Yes, sir. I knew of a man who was insane for twenty-four hours." Mr. Scoville eagerly asked, "And then he got well?" Witness replied, " No, sir; he died." In further answers, witness stated that he believed that Guiteau was feigning what was intended for insanity, and with that idea had been acting a part. Considerable time was occupied by discussions between counsel in reference to questions put to the witness.

Dr. Randolph Barksdale, Superintendent of the Central Lunatic Asylum, near Richmond, Virginia, testified substantially that he had visited the prisoner in jail on November 30th, and had observed him in Court. Witness believed that Guiteau was feigning in Court; that he was sane now and on July 2d. On cross-examination, witness denied having ever said that he believed the prisoner to be insane.

Dr. John H. Callender, of Nashville, Tennessee, Superintendent of the Tennessee State Asylum for the Insane, gave similar testimony, and in reply to the hypothetical questions read by Colonel Corkhill, said he believed, taking the facts set forth to be true, that the prisoner was undoubtedly sane. Exceptions to questions and answers were noted.

The cross-examination was conducted by Mr. Scoville, who went into a dissection of the hypothetical questions of the prosecution.

Mr. Scoville admitted that in answering those questions, he had not taken into consideration the statement that the mother of the person described therein had been ill with inflammation of the brain for six months before his birth, nor had he assumed the father to have had any but a sound mind. Witness did not think that an enthusiastic and honest belief that the Oneida Community was the beginning of God's Kingdom on earth, was an evidence of insanity.

The Court then, at half-past twelve, took half an hour's recess.

After the recess, Mr. Scoville said that in order to be accurate, the defence had had a plaster cast of the prisoner's head taken by Clark Mills, the sculptor, and he would like to call that gentleman to identify it. The prosecution, however, objected to that course. While the discussion was in progress, the prisoner with a gratified smile, examined the cast.

The cross-examination was then resumed by Mr. Scoville.

Q. Suppose the person described in the prosecution's hypothetical question believed that he was in partnership with Jesus Christ & Co. in the establishment of the *Theocrat*; that Jesus Christ was with him as a co-partner in the business, and that it would be made a success through that means and that he was inspired to start the paper by a direct command from the Almighty, would that make any material difference in your answer?

Mr. Porter (solemnly).—"I object to that question as irreverent and blasphemous."

Mr. Scoville.—"I don't understand that the objection is under rules of law, but it is brought in under the province of Divinity. The only objection that Mr. Porter makes is that the question is irreverent and blasphemous. If the prisoner's belief that he was inspired is irreverent and blasphemous, and the Court rejects it on that ground, there is an end of the case, because we are not allowed any defence."

Mr. Porter.—"It is a question which purports to be justified by the proof in this case, and which your Honor is asked to countenance in the presence of this jury. There is no evidence even by the oath of the criminal, that he believed the Redeemer of mankind to be his partner in business, and when the learned counsel for the prisoner puts such a question in a Christian Court and a Federal tribunal, I hold (whatever your Honor may hold) that it is time to rebuke both him and his client. It is a hypothesis that no man who believes that God was our Creator should be permitted for one moment to present in a Court of justice and before this audience. If it had been presented to your Honor in your private chamber you would do in regard to the counsel what you have done in regard to the prisoner. The time has come when, in behalf of the American Government, I protest against these blasphemous utterances. The counsel can predicate his question on facts which have been proved, but not on those which assume that we make no difference between the Redeemer of mankind and ourselves."

The prisoner.—"How about Christ and Paul? Paul was in partnership with the Saviour. Have not I just as much right as Paul?"

Mr. Porter.—"I must insist, your Honor, in behalf of the Government and to vindicate it, that this criminal shall be remanded to the dock."

The prisoner.—"You had better mind your own business, Porter."

Mr. Porter.—"That is my business to-day. My motion is in abeyance and on the question of blasphemy, when this Court has been filled with it from the first day until now. It should not be heard coming from the counsel table. There is not that man at the American Bar who would not have been disgraced and silenced by coercion if he had uttered what this man, under the false pretense of being counsel in this case, has uttered from time to time. To your Honor I should say here that it was only the interruption of the prisoner which induced us to disturb the order in which Mr. Davidge desired to present this question. But on a question which touches the hearts and consciences of the people of this nation, I now invoke your Honor's action, not only in regard to the decision of this question, but in reference to the disposition to be made of the prisoner."

The prisoner (excitedly).—"The American people are with me more and more, and that is the reason you are mad about it. I appear as my own counsel, and his Honor has no discretion in the matter."

Mr. Scoville (to Mr. Porter).—"This case is not on trial before the American people."

Mr. Porter.—"Then why do you, and your client with your advice, address them?"

Mr. Reed.—"That is not true, Mr. Porter, and you know it is not true."

Mr. Porter.—"I only answer that it is true."

The Court called the counsel to order, and asked whether it was desired that the proceedings should be suspended for action on Mr. Porter's motion.

The District Attorney.—"We are ready to enter on that question, your Honor."

Mr. Davidge then rose and said he would briefly present the views of the prosecution. "Yesterday," he said, "was the commencement of the seventh week of this trial; the trial of the prisoner for the assassination of the ruler of fifty millions of people. From the inception of the trial to the present time (with the exception of yesterday), not a single day has passed without being characterized by aspersions on the part of the prisoner in contempt of the majesty of the law, in contempt of the authority of this Court, and imposing obstacles to the administration of justice. We have understood from the beginning that your Honor not only desired to accord to this prisoner the full measure of his constitutional rights, but that you wished furthermore not even to appear to impinge on those rights. We have supposed that not only were those rights to be respected in their integrity, but that any error on the part of the Court should be an error in the direction of mercy in respect to the prisoner. If not acquiescing in, at least respecting views of that sort (for we have not fully subscribed to the idea that those constitutional rights may not be lost by the conduct of the prisoner at the bar), we have allowed day after day to pass without making any application for judicial coercion. The prisoner has proclaimed himself to be sane to this

Court and to the world. The last theory of this case is that it presents an instance of what is called "transitory insanity;" that there was a particular segment of time during which he was deprived of reason, but within an hour after the crime recovered that reason, and has had it from that time to the present. Your Honor, in addition to the consideration I have referred to, has doubtless been strongly controlled by the consideration that here was a man on trial for his life whose sanity was one of the issues involved in the trial. I simply now assert that at this stage of the trial nobody can question the fact that he is sane in respect at least of his conduct and behavior in this Court. I think that your Honor cannot deny that a man who, as he says, is here as his own counsel, is at least to be treated as sane as to decency in conduct and behavior. Now I want to call your Honor's attention to the motion made by Mr. Porter on Saturday. That motion was to remand this prisoner to the dock, where he belongs. Your Honor and myself have tried many cases in this Court where men were under indictment. The old practice was, that a man indicted for crime should always be in the dock, no matter who or what he should be; we know that perfectly well, and we know that the relaxation has been for the benefit of counsel, and not for the benefit of the prisoner. We saw yesterday the salutary effect of this motion on the part of Mr.

Porter. We experienced then, for the first time, a day of quiet and order, as contrasted with the disorder and blackguardism of former days. That was the experience of your Honor in regard to the making of that motion. It seems to me, therefore, that the time has come for the Court to act. It seems to me that not to act is to encourage in the future what has transpired in the past, and hence I ask that your Honor will take up and decide the motion submitted on Saturday."

The prisoner.—"I am quiet, when I am treated decently, not otherwise. It is all caused by the mean, dirty way in which the prosecution have conducted themselves. If they had conducted themselves as high-toned lawyers there would have been no trouble. It has been all caused by Corkhill and Porter."

Mr. Reed.—"I do not know what the practice has been in this Court as to the place the accused should occupy."

Mr. Davidge.—"I will state to you as a fact known to all old practitioners that the place of the criminal is in the dock. General Sickles sat in the dock, and the Court refused to relax the rule, notwithstanding he was a lawyer in good standing, and at that time a member of the House of Representatives. I ought to have added to the remarks I made, that our intention was not to press the motion, except in the event of some expression on the part of the prisoner requiring, in our judgment, judicial action. His outrageous scandalous insults to my senior (alluding to Mr. Porter) furnish the necessity for calling for judicial decision on this motion."

The prisoner.—"I am quiet enough when I am treated properly, but not when I am abused. No decent man would be. Sickles did not appear as his own counsel, and that is the difference between Sickles and me."

Mr. Reed then proceeded to argue that under modern practice everywhere, the prisoner was allowed to sit beside his counsel, and instanced that such was the case in New York, where Mr. Porter practiced. It was also the case in the Chicago Courts. He denied that the conduct of the prisoner in Court had proved sanity, but the reverse, and appealed for kindly treatment of a diseased, deluded man.

Mr. Scoville said this was not a motion calling for any display of feeling, and he objected to the incessant use of the term "criminal."

The prisoner interjected: "I am here as my own counsel. I am no criminal."

Mr. Davidge.—"We think him a most extraordinary criminal."

The prisoner.—"More than you can manage, evidently. That is the reason you are excited about it. You see you have no case."

The District Attorney.—"The time has come for action in the interest and for the vindication of justice itself. There has been some public criticism with regard to the digraceful conduct of the man here on trial, because his conduct was an affront to the dignity of the Court, offensive to good order and against decency. Your Honor has borne with it very quietly, and I am here now to say, I think very judiciously. At the opening of this trial we were met with but one issue, as to whether the man was sane or insane. There have been brought here by the Government the most eminent men in their profession, for no other purpose than to honestly determine whether the man was in his right mind or not. One of the points in settling this matter was the conduct of the prisoner in Court. It was desired that the man should be allowed the free use of any conduct he might be pleased to exhibit. So, on the first day of the trial, when interruptions were abusive to myself, it was not proper then to state publicly what I do now, that the course of your Honor has been the best in the interest of determining the facts that could possibly have been adopted. But there has come a time when justice has been vindicated. It may be said now the prisoner has had every indulgence which justice requires. This man has unquestionably murdered the President of the United States. He is entitled to the same rights, privileges and protection that would be guaranteed to the humblest citizen of the Republic. But your Honor has thrown around him additional guards. It is not supposed that we can quiet interruption. He may abuse me and these distinguished gentlemen, but these utterances must come hereafter from the dock. He has around him policemen who do not belong to the official body of this Court. The President has appointed a Marshal, and the law imposes on him the safety and care of the prisoner. I want the Marshal to take him and sit him in the dock and take care of him. I want no more special guards. I want him to stand here on trial as any other man would stand."

The prisoner (violently).—"You cannot convict me and you want to shoot me. That is the confession of weakness. You want me to be shot; but I don't believe the Lord will allow it."

The District Attorney.—"Hereafter the responsibility of his conduct must be with him and him alone. We are not responsible for what may occur or happen to him. He shall be tried hereafter as any other criminal, but not, with our concurrence, with any other treatment. I want the Marshal to take the man to the dock. He is responsible if he escapes. Let the other officers who are responsible for the protection of private citizens, return to their beats, I am tired of this. The time has come when we must have action. We want no admonition to keep him quiet. Your Honor may not keep him quiet, but he can, under the order of your Honor, march to that dock and sit where criminals belong, and sit there till a jury of his countrymen declare him guilty or not."

The prisoner (violently).—"The American people will have something to say if you put me in that dock and I get shot, and God Almighty will curse you, Corkhill, you wretch, and any other man who attempts to do me violence."

Mr. Scoville rose, and in indignant and excited tone said: "I made no objection to the motion; but when I hear the prosecuting attorney stand up and give notice beforehand that the prisoner is to be placed by authority in a place where he can be shot, and virtually invites assassins to step into this Court room and shoot him, I disdain further concurrence in the motion. I supposed that if the prisoner was to be placed in the dock, that he would be protected by the officers of the law. There is not one man or woman within hearing of Mr. Corkhill's voice but understood it to be an invitation for an assassin to step up and shoot that man when put in the dock."

Mr. Porter (laying his hand dramatically on Mr. Corkhill's shoulder and speaking slowly).— "That imputation against this gentleman, just as vile as the obscene charges of the prisoner, calls for vindication. From the beginning of this trial the District Attorney has observed a spirit of fairness, of honor, of clemency, of forbearance toward the prisoner unexampled in any State trial reported in Christian history. He has shown a fidelity to his public duties, the fruits of which will come when your Honor shall deliver your charge, and the American people as represented by that jury shall have an opportunity to render a verdict. The prisoner, with an audacity and effrontry which spares neither man nor God, has chosen to put himself in the position of controlling his own trial, defying that authority to which he will soon learn to submit. In regard to the position taken by Mr. Corkhill, I entirely concur with him whatever the consequences to the prisoner. If he had in his hand that bull-dog pistol from which he sent the bullet which assassinated the President when your Honor pronounces your decision, his practice at the river would enable him to aim at your heart and you would be in the agonies of death. Once publicly when one of us was bowed down by an affliction such as comes to us rarely in life, the other members of this jury were menaced by this man. One of these jurors was threatened with a new inspiration by which he should die before this case came to an end."

The prisoner.—"You don't know but the Lord will do it."

"It may be in the province of God," returned Mr. Porter solemnly, "but not in the province of Guiteau. The assassin of the President will assassinate no more forever, and the voice which is not silenced now will be as dumb as that of his victim when the end of the law is reached. No man, sane or insane, is permitted to say that the arm of the law in his presence is nerveless. I have approved—I say it in view of the condemnation of the American people as represented by their papers, because they did not understand the situation as we did I have approved and vindicated your Honor's course down to the time that this prisoner proclaimed, with the acquiescence of his counsel, that he had been sane from an hour after he executed this foul, diabolical and infamous murder. When I made this motion I felt that the time had come when it was due to the majesty of the law, to the vindication of the American Government, and above all to the vindication of the judiciary, that the step should be taken which I now indicate. You suspended your decision in the hope that you might be able to extend to this sane criminal and homicide still further clemency. But if it be extended it will be at some peril— peril to the name of American jurisprudence— peril in respect of the indefinite continuation of the trial, which without the interposition of the prisoner would have terminated three weeks ago. The time has now come when the law must make its appearance in this Court room, and when a man who pretends to be a maniac shall no longer sit at the counsel table and exercise privileges which you would accord to no member of the American Bar."

JUDGE COX'S DECISION.

The Court then rendered his decision. It was hardly necessary to say that the conduct of the prisoner had been in persistent violation of order and decorum. In the beginning, the only methods suggested which could be resorted to to suppress this disorder were such as must infringe the constitutional rights of the prisoner, and that was conclusive argument against them. Until Saturday last, no other method had been proposed. Then this proposition (which he had already had in mind) was submitted. It had hitherto been an impression shared by the Court and counsel, that the prisoner's conduct and language in Court would afford the best indication of his mental and moral character, and contribute largely to the enlightment of Court and jury on the question of his responsibility. It was therefore on the express desire of the District Attorney, that the Court had allowed such latitude of conduct in order to furnish the experts an opportunity of diagnosing the prisoner's case. As it now appeared, the opinions of the experts had been largely founded on the exhibitions which had taken place on the trial, and if they had contributed to enable those experts to reach their conclusions, it would be a complete vindication of the view of the District Attorney as to the proper course to be pursued. At this stage of the trial, however, this object seemed to have been accomplished. The trial was now approaching its close. The experts had had ample opportunity to make up their judgments and pronounce them before Court and jury. It was incumbent on the Court now to impose such restraint as the circumstances of the case admitted, and which would conduce to the orderly conduct of the case. The prisoner had a right to hear the testimony of witnesses. He could not be gagged or sent out of Court. The proper place for a prisoner on trial for felony was the dock. He could only come within the bar to be arraigned and receive sentence. If the Court granted him the privilege of sitting beside his counsel, it was a privilege which could be withdrawn summarily. While the prisoner had the undoubted right to act as his own counsel, or to appear by counsel, he could not exercise both rights simultaneously. Having accepted counsel, the prisoner had waived his right to appear as such in person. On consideration of all the circumstances, the Court thought that the motion would have to be granted, and that the prisoner should be placed in the dock, but he did not mean that the prisoner should be exposed to any danger. He should have the fullest protection.

The prisoner (speaking quietly and as though he dreaded being placed in the dock, which was filled at the time with spectators).—"To settle the matter I will sit quietly here. Will it not be satisfactory if I keep quiet and stay here? If I sit in the dock I may be worse."

The Court directed the Marshal to clear the dock and place the prisoner there. During the confusion and noise incident to this movement the prisoner exclaimed in a subdued tone: "I have no objection to going to the dock if your Honor says so."

The Court.—"I say so, simply in hopes of keeping you quiet."

The prisoner.—"I move that the Court room be cleared if I am going into the dock; I want the Court room cleared."

The prisoner having been placed in the dock and quiet having been restored, Mr. Porter said: "It is to be borne in mind that the chimera which seems to haunt the prisoner has no foundation. He is in no danger, except from the hangman's rope; and so long as an officer of the law stands beside him, no man will imperil that officer in the discharge of his public duty by firing a shot at the prisoner."

The Court directed the Marshal to place the prisoner where he could have a full view of the witness.

The prisoner.—"I am doing very well here, if your Honor please. It is only a confession of the prosecution's weakness. I would not be afraid to go all over Washington alone, or New York, or Boston. Thunder that broadcast. God

Almighty will curse the prosecution. Take time on this, Corkhill. You are having your way for a few minutes, but God grinds slow but sure."

The District Attorney in reply to Mr. Scoville's speech, stated that he had been always opposed to having any extra guards around the prisoner. He believed in allowing him to stand his trial like any other man. No violence would come to him any more than to a criminal charged with a smaller offence. He did not wish any special protection around the prisoner nor did he think it necessary. It was an indication that he was in danger. He (Corkhill) never thought he was in danger.

Mr. Scoville (sneeringly).—"You must think that everybody is going to miss like Bill Jones."

The prisoner here broke in with an expression of satisfaction with his present position and thanking his Honor for moving him there.

The cross-examination was then resumed, and Mr. Porter's objection to Mr. Scoville's question on the ground of its being irreverent and blasphemous, was overruled by the Court.

Mr. Porter.—"As this case will be historical, as our exceptions are utterly unavailing, as we can in no case appeal in behalf of the American Government and those they represent, I protest against this decision passing into a precedent."

The prisoner.—"Sit down, Porter, and rest for the afternoon."

Mr. Reed.—"There is evidence to sustain Mr. Scoville's question produced by Judge Porter in a letter, which Judge Porter himself read to the jury, written by the prisoner in 1865 and addressed to the Oneida Community. The prisoner made a claim that he was in the employ of Jesus Christ & Co."

Mr. Porter.—"Neither introduced nor read by me."

The witness then replied that he should not consider it an insane delusion for a man to profess himself as "a member of the firm of Jesus Christ & Co." unless there were other evidences of disease.

On redirect examination, the witness stated that he did not think the prisoner had been feigning insanity in the Court room. He had merely been exaggerating his characteristics of self-deceit, impudence, audacity and insolence.

The prisoner.—"In other words, when I am assaulted, I talk back. Porter expects to get five thousand dollars for hanging me. He sees his money slipping away because the American people don't want me hanged, and he is mad at me."

The Court then at three o'clock, adjourned. The prisoner as he was passing his counsel, expressed his contentment with his position in the dock as affording him more pure air.

CHAPTER XXXVI.

Guiteau Again in the Dock—Some Expert Testimony on "Heads"—
The Prisoner Interpolates some Anxious Remarks About his
Own Safety—He Dreads Cranks.

ON Thursday morning, December 29th, when the prisoner was brought into the Court room, he was taken directly to the dock, a railed enclosure on the south side of the room, about eight feet long by four feet wide, furnished with two cane-seated chairs for the bailiffs, and a wooden seated one for the prisoner. Being close to a large window, usually open for ventilation, the occupants were far more exposed to attack than were those at the counsel table, a point which it was remarked did not escape the quick eye of this particular criminal. As soon as Guiteau was unmanacled, he made his regulation speech, this time in the form of a complaint. In an injured tone, he said: "Coming up in the van this morning I noticed that the usual policemen were withdrawn. I want to say emphatically that if I was turned out to-morrow I could take care of myself, but as long as I am in custody of the Court, the Court must take care of me. The greatest danger of being shot is in coming from the van to the Court house. I want your Honor to order that I have the usual number of policemen coming up in the van. The cranks are not all dead yet, though they have been dying recently. I got fifty letters yesterday, most of them sympathetic, asking for my autograph. There were only two or three cranks in the whole lot. But one crank could do the business if he had the nerve. I am most unprotected coming from the van to the Court house. If you turn me out loose I will take care of myself, but so long as I am in custody of this Court, the Court must take care of me. Some of these experts testified that in jail I am very quiet. So I am. I have the reputation there of being a perfect gentleman. They think I am a great man and a good fellow, but when I come into Court, I am abused and villified. Human nature can't stand it and I won't stand it. When I am attacked I defend myself. If people treat me well, I treat them well."

Judge Cox.—"In reference to the question of guards for the prisoner, it was remarked yesterday that the Court had surrounded the prisoner with unusual guards. That statement was made from a misapprehension of the fact. The Court had nothing in the world to do with it. The prisoner is in charge of the Marshal, and all the guards are under the direction of the Marshal and of his assistants, not of the Court."

"Suppose the marshal don't do his duty, is this Court going to allow me to be unprotected?"

asked the prisoner. "A crank might shoot at me. He wouldn't hit me though. He's liable to shoot at me and hit somebody else."

Mr. Scoville said what he had objected to yesterday was the fact that counsel had gone outside of his legitimate province to demand that guards be removed.

"I want the same protection as I have had before," broke in the prisoner.

Mr. Corkhill said he was not here to be lectured by counsel. He had merely said that this prisoner was not entitled to any more privilges or protection than other prisoners. He did not think there was any danger.

"There would be none if there were no cranks, your Honor," said the prisoner.

Mr. Scoville said that he and his associates had concluded to ask the Court to permit the jury to separate and go home, leaving it to their own honor not to communicate with any one regarding this case. He spoke of the hardships entailed upon the jurors, and said that if he had known how long the trial was to last, he would have made the motion, or suggestion, at first.

"I will consider that, Mr. Scoville," remarked Judge Cox.

The prisoner here chimed in, saying: "If your Honor please, there is all together too much draught coming into this window. A draught coming on me and the captain."

The officers upon this speech closed the windows behind the prisoner.

Dr. Callendar, of Nashville, resumed the stand and Mr. Scoville propounded a long hypothetical question, which included a letter the prisoner wrote to Senator Don Cameron. The prisoner interrupted Mr. Scoville and said the letter was a private one, asking for a loan of five hundred dollars, which he gave his brother to give to Mr. Cameron, and it had no business in the case. He took occasion to say that he was no longer associated with his brother or other members of his family, but with Mr. Moody, Mr. Pentecost, General Grant and Mr. Conkling. Mr. Davidge objected to the letter being read, but the Court did not sustain him. After Mr. Scoville had received a severe raking from the prisoner, the letter was read as follows:

"DEAR SIR.—I am on trial for my life, and I need money. I am a Stalwart of the Stalwarts; and so are you. You think a good deal of General Arthur, and so do I. My inspiration made him President, and I am going to ask you to let me have five hundred dollars. If I get out of this I will return it, if not, charge it to the Stalwarts. Yours for our cause, and very cordially,
CHARLES GUITEAU.
IN COURT, WASHINGTON, D. C., DECEMBER 19th, 1881."

"P. S.—Please give your check to my brother, John W. Guiteau, of Boston, and make it payable to my order."

Dr. Walter Kempster, of Winnebago, Wisconsin, Superintendent of the Wisconsin Hospital for the Insane, was then called to the stand. After answering the usual preliminary questions, the witness was given the cast of Guiteau's head.

The witness pronounced it "a very well shaped head. A head that compared very favorably with the majority of the heads in the community."

To illustrate his reply, the witness produced a number of charts or diagrams, taken from the heads of different individuals with a conformator. The witness said he had given his word to the gentlemen that their names should not be divulged. At first he was allowed to explain the characteristics of the head without giving names, but afterwards the Court, at the suggestion of the prosecution, required him to mention the names, saying that the Court thereby took the responsibility for the breach of confidence.

The first chart exibited by name was that of Treasurer Gillfillan.

The next was that of Robert G. Ingersoll, "You will see," observed the witness, "that while flat on one side, it bulges on the other."

"Bulges on the wrong side, don't it doctor?" inquired Mr. Davidge.

"In the estimation of some people," remarked the witness.

"That shows that Ingersoll and I are badly cranked," said the prisoner.

The witness then exhibited charts of the heads of N. J. Sibley, a resident of Washington, John P. Foley, a journalist, and Col. Corkhill.

"That's a crank's head," said the prisoner, when the latter was exhibited. "I suppose you could put your foot in the side of his head."

"Colonel Corkhill," said the witness, "has a very marked prominence on one side and is flat on the other. The prominence is greater than in the prisoner's head."

"That shows you are a worse crank than I am, Corkhill," called out the prisoner, laughing.

The other head diagrams exhibited, were those of Rev. L. A. Wilson, Mr. Isaac Johnson, Colonel Wyman, Governor Claflin, Den. Thompson, L. Hoffman, John Wilson, J. H. Boffinger, Mr. Jennison, Mr. Slocum, William Syphax, John C. Gossman and Judge Carter.

"Of all that I have shown you," said the witness, "there has not been a single symmetrical head."

The witness said the shape of the head did not indicate anything of the sanity or insanity of the individual, unless it deviated grossly from what they call a typical head.

Dr. Kempster's testimony as to the nature of insanity, the definition of various terms, etc., was similar in purport to that given by his predecessors on the stand.

Counsel afterwards became engaged in a controversy, and just before recess the witness, in reply to the hypothetical question of the prosecution, said: "Taking the facts set forth to be true, in my opinion the prisoner was sane." After recess, Dr. Kempster took the stand again, and related the circumstances of his interview with the prisoner in the jail. Guiteau had told him that he was not what experts would call insane, but he was legally insane. That is, if he could get the jury to believe he was acting under an inspiration when he shot the President, that would be all he wanted, and would acquit him. The District Attorney having alluded to a previous witness as a horse doctor, a somewhat acrimonious colloquy ensued between counsel, and the Court ruled that such allusions were improper. During the cross-examination by Colonel Reed, considerable bitterness was also shown between counsel, until the Court admonished them that the trial must proceed without consuming so much time in discussing immaterial disputes. This gave the prisoner another chance to interrupt, which he did by denouncing the conduct of Judge Porter and Colonel Corkhill as contemptible meanness. The cross-examination was continued by Mr. Scoville—with an occasional outburst on the part of the prisoner—until adjournment. "He came here," said Guiteau, "as an expert for the defence; that's what he said when he was in my cell, but the good living at Willard's and Corkhill's money have been too much for him." The Court then adjourned.

CHAPTER XXXVII.

Guiteau puts Himself in Nomination for the Presidency—A Suggestion that the Jury Separate for a Rest is Promptly Negatived by that Body—Another Lively Day.

ON Friday morning, December 30th, the rush for admittance to the Court room was greater than ever. Lawyers, reporters and others having actual business in Court had the utmost difficulty to obtain ingress, some being compelled to resort to climbing in at the windows. The destruction of ladies finery was almost as appalling as the language of some of the too utterly disappointed roughs on the outside. The Court was called to order promptly at ten o'clock, and Guiteau was at once brought in and placed in the dock. As soon as he had arranged his papers, he saluted the Court, saying: "S me of the leading people in America consider me a very fine fellow. Last night at eight o'clock, I received a telegraphic dispatch from Boston, which I will read for the edification of this Court and jury and the American people. It is as follows:

Mr. Chas. J. Guiteau, Washington, D. C.: Old Boston sympathizes with you. You are yet to be President. (Signed) A HOST OF ADMIRERS.

"I don't know but two men in America," continued the prisoner, "who want me hung. One is Judge Porter, who expects to get five thousand dollars for it. The other is Corkhill. Corkhill is booked to be removed anyway. He wants to get even with me, beause he thinks I am the man that did it."

The prisoner stopped awhile and then catching a new idea, continued to talk, saying: "It is said I am too severe in my talk. I have something to say on that. What do you think of this: Woe unto you, ye hypocrites, scribes and Pharisees! How can you escape damnation in hell? Ye generation of vipers! How can you escape the damnation of hell? Who said that? Who uses that language? The meekly and lowly Jesus. I put my ideas in sharp language, and have the example of the Saviour for it. He called things by their right names. When anyone struck at Him, He struck back. He did not lie down like a craven, and I don't."

A few minutes later, the prisoner announced excitedly: "I refer my nomination to the Republican Convention for 1884. I think I will be there. I don't think this jury is going into the hanging business, to enable Mr. Porter to get five thousand dollars. The American people don't want me hung."

Mr. Scoville then resumed the cross-examination of Dr. Kempster. Witness stated in reply to Mr. Scoville's questions, that he did not believe in temporary insanity in the sense that a person could be insane and wholly recover from it in an hour. He believed that Sickles was sane when he shot Key, and that Coles, who shot Hiscock at Albany, was undoubtedly insane. At the close of this examination, District Attorney Corkhill stated that he had but one more witness to introduce, and desired to know from Mr. Scoville how much time he would want to consume in surrebuttal. Mr. Scoville said the defence had witnesses whose names had been presented since they closed, and would ask the Court for permission to have them sworn, on the ground of newly-discovered evidence relative to the state of the prisoner's mind just before the shooting. For surrebuttal they would require several days, probably all the next week. Mr. Davidge replied: "We must object, your Honor, to the reopening of this case." Mr. Scoville declared that they did not want to delay the trial, but did not propose to be cut short in the matter of time. He would renew his proposition that the jury be allowed to separate and go to their homes, relying upon their honor and integrity. Guiteau again interrupted, and Judge Porter intimated that if these outbursts were to continue, he should move that the dock be placed in the further corner of the room, where the prisoner could not disturb the jury. After some further discussion, the foreman of the jury stated that they did not care to separate provided they could have a reasonable opportunity for exercise and fresh air.

Colonel Corkhill, after remarking that the jury were more anxious for the termination of the trial than for a separation, replied to counsel's aspersions upon the medical witnesses for the prosecution, and said the prisoner himself had woven the meshes which were fast enclosing him, while only two men, who would not even acknowledge that they believed in a God, had been found who would under oath declare their belief in the prisoner's insanity. Mr. Scoville replied in an impressive speech, vindicating the conduct of the defence, and rebuking the course of the District Attorney.

Dr. John P. Gray, Medical Superintendent of the New York State Lunatic Asylum, then testified that he had made a study of insanity since 1850, and had treated or investigated twelve thousand cases. He had never seen a case where the only indication of insanity was an exhibition of immorality or wickedness, and did not believe in what had been called moral insanity. After recess the witness gave a long account of his examination of the prisoner in the jail, and the conversation had with him. Witness had asked the prisoner: "Suppose the President had offered you the Paris Consulship while you was reflecting upon the subject of removing him, would you still have shot him." The reply was: "Well, that would have settled the matter. I should have taken the position and left." As to the alleged inspiration, the prisoner said it was in the form of a pressure constantly upon him to commit the act. Guiteau, who had repeatedly interrupted the witness, here remarked: "That is all there is in the case—short and to the point. You can talk about it six years if you want to." Dr. Gray continued the story of his interviews with Guiteau, with occasional comments by the latter of assent or dissent, but not to the extent of an annoying interruption, until the hour of adjournment.

CHAPTER XXXVIII.

The Last Day of the Old Year Consumed in a Wearisome though Careful and Critical Analysis of Guiteau and his Character by an Expert.

SATURDAY, December 31, the last day of the seventh week of the trial, the last day of the year 1881, found the last witness for the prosecution still on the stand. When the Court opened the absence of Judge Porter and of Mr. Reed was remarked, perhaps with a feeling of relief, since the personal antagonism of those gentleman precipitated many of the stormy scenes which had become disagreeably monotonous. Guiteau came in muffled up, shivering and complaining of the cold, for the despicable wretch, callous to the suffering of all others, was keenly alive to the slightest inconvenience which affected him. In this sense he has admirably maintained the consistency of his inferentially claimed position as "the only true and original Guiteau."

Dr. Gray, Superintendent of the Utica Lunatic Asylum, was recalled to the stand, and his examination-in-chief was procceded with. Being asked by the District Attorney to give the reasons on which he had previously stated his opinion of the prisoner's sanity at the time of his examination in the jail, he said: "In looking over the history of the prisoner as given to me by himself, and considering his physical state through life, I could see no evidence anywhere through his life when he had been insane or had any symptoms of insanity. (Objected to by Mr. Scoville and objection overruled) Coming down to the period of his arrival in Washington on the 5th of March, I found that the prisoner was then in good health; he came here for the purpose of applying for an office; from that time down to the killing of the President he continued in good health. He said that he had not even had a heachache, or any evidence whatever of any physical disturbance. He followed up his effort to obtain an office persistently, and in the manner which he himself thought best to secure it by personal application. He claimed no inspiration and no insanity of any kind. I took into consideration, in forming my opinion, his statement that the inspiration which he claimed, or the press of Deity, did not come to him at the time of the inception of the act, but not until after he had fully made up his mind to do the act. I also took into consideration the fact that while he was considering the question he held in abeyance his own act, his own intention. He controlled his own will, his own thought, reflection and intention to do the act pending the obtaining of the consulship. The presence in him of judgment, reflection, self-control, in regard to his acts, was a controlling matter in the forming of my opinion; also, the fact that he controlled himself as to the time in which he should do this act. All which, in the light of my experience with insane persons, who have the delusion that they are controlled or directed or commanded or inspired by the Almighty, would be entirely inconsistent with insanity; such self-control, self-direction and self-guidance is antagonistic to anything that I have ever seen in my personal experience with the insane having such delusions. I took into consideration also in forming my opinion the fact of his preparing carefully for his own self-safety and protection. In cases of insanity there would be no preparation for personal safety. He further stated to me that he had looked up the subject of insanity and had considered it in connection with his defence. That would not be consistent with anything in the nature of insanity I have observed. Persons who have the insane delusion that they are inspired by God have been in every case the most profoundly insane persons, independent of the delusion. The delusion itself is a symptom of the profound insanity pervading the whole nature of the man. I took into consideration also the deliberation with which he proceeded, as well as the change of purpose which from time to time he manifested.

The prisoner who had interrupted the witness at the close of every sentence with contradictions or simply downright insolence, had evidently noted with his usual keenness the absence of Judge Porter, and his consequent comparative immunity from reproof, here made a remark which proved not only his legal shrewdness but the reason for the license he was taking. He said: "Dr. Gray is arguing the case for the prosecution, which no expert has a right to do. Let him confine himself to facts and not to argument. Porter will do that business—Judge Porter, I mean."

The witness then stated that during the past ten years, three hundred cases of homicidal insanity had come under his care at the Utica Asylum and that of three hundred persons, only three claimed inspiration. They had all been insane before the offence at the time, and for a long time afterwards.

Being asked as to whether he regarded intense religious convictions as an evidence of insanity, witness replied, that in his judgment, religious delusion was the highest possible evidence of insanity.

Q. Suppose a man should state that he had murdered another man; that he conceived the idea himself; that he executed it himself; that no power in the universe knew of its conception; that his inspiration was only to do the act, and that the details were left to his own judgment, would you consider that any evidence of insanity? A. No; it would indicate wickedness.

Mr. Scoville excepted to the reception of this question and answer.

Witness stated his disbelief in hereditary insanity, but admitted that a susceptibility to the disease might be transmitted.

After further evidence of an unimportant nature, the witness was turned over to Mr. Scoville for cross-examination. In the course of this, the witness stated that he had believed in "moral insanity" but changed his views after going to the Utica Asylum. The rest of the day was consumed in wearisome cross-examination, Mr. Scoville himself seeming to be indifferent as to the replies made by the witness to the questions propounded to him and which took a wide range. The prisoner though paying attention to the evidence, did so in a listless way, and interrupted less frequently than usual, while the audience impatiently awaited the hour of three o'clock when they could escape from the chilling atmosphere of the Court room. When the hour had at length arrived, the prisoner called Mr. Scoville's attention to the fact, and then continued: "To-morrow is New Year's Day, 1882. I receive my calls this year in jail. Anybody can come that can get in. I will be glad to see anybody that can get in. I wish everybody a Happy New Year."

The Court then adjourned until Tuesday.

CHAPTER XXXIX.

The Prosecution Closed at Last—Sur-Rebuttal Testimony Offered—Counsel on both Sides Getting Ready For the Closing Arguments.

ON Tuesday, January 3d, 1882, the weary trial was resumed. When the Court opened and Guiteau was placed in the dock, he saluted the spectators by saying: "I had a very Happy New Year. I hope every one else did. I had plenty of visitors, high-toned, middle-toned and low-toned people, taking in the whole crowd, showing that public opinion is in my favor. They were very glad to see me and expressed the opinion without one dissenting voice that I would be acquitted."

Dr. John P. Gray, the Utica expert, was then called to the stand and his cross-examination was continued by Mr. Scoville. Witness stated that in giving his opinion on direct examination that the prisoner was sane, he had not taken into account the evidence of the prisoner himself, but taking that element into account, his opinion would still be the same, that the prisoner is sane, and was sane on the 2d of July. After several questions by Mr. Scoville, and interruptions by the prisoner, Dr. Gray stated that he did not believe in what is termed by some writers "emotional insanity" or "moral insanity." "Kleptomania" he considered simply thieving, "dipsomania" drunkenness, and "pyromania" incendiarism. Their designations were simply convenient terms which had been invented to cover certain crimes. "Insanity," said witness, "is never transmitted any more than cancer. I never knew any one to be born with a cancer. A susceptibility to insanity is undoubtedly transmitted from parents to children, but insanity does not necessarily follow, except from some profound physical disturbance."

After recess, Dr. Gray was asked a few more questions by Mr. Scoville, and then the District Attorney announced the conclusion of the evidence on the part of the Government. Mr. Scoville expressed his surprise at this action, and finally stated that the defence would inform the Court to-morrow morning as to their course. He complained that several witnesses named by the prosecution had not been called. Dr. Barker, of Kansas City, then took the stand for the defence, and testified to a conversation with Mrs. Dunmire at Leadville, Colorado, in which she had expressed some doubts as to the prisoner's mental condition at the time of the divorce. Clark Wells, the sculptor, was called to identify the cast of Guiteau's head, but Mr. Davidge objected, and was sustained by the Court. Guiteau then attempted to read a letter, but was ordered by Judge

Cox to be silent, and was ultimately suppressed by the Marshal and his deputy. John W. Guiteau was again called, but objection was made, and the witness was withdrawn. After further argument on the question of introducing new testimony, it was agreed that the defence should submit reasons in writing, with affidavits the next morning and the Court adjourned.

CHAPTER XL.

All the Evidence In—Mr. Scoville Presents His Affidavit—The Prosecution Submit Their "Prayer for Instructions."

ON Wednesday, January 4th, the feeling that the case was rapidly drawing to a close had the effect of fairly packing the Court by half-past nine o'clock. As soon as the Court was called to order, Guiteau remarked; "It is a good time to make a speech, but I promised the Marshal I would keep quiet to-day. I guess I'll try and do it." There was a suspicion among the audience that the presence of Perry Carson, a huge colored employee of the Court, and evidently under special instructions to station himself close by the prisoner, had something to do with this unusual modesty. Mr. Scoville then stated that he had prepared the affidavit of which he spoke yesterday, and he read the following:

In the Supreme Court of the District of Columbia, holding a Criminal Term.

THE UNITED STATES vs. CHARLES J. GUITEAU.

No. 14,056.

INDICTMENT FOR MURDER.

George Scoville, being duly sworn, deposes that he was sole counsel for the defendant in this case, in preparation for trial thereof, as to summoning witnesses and obtaining evidence on behalf of the defence; that upon the issue of insanity raised in this case, the defendant himself has not been in a mental condition to afford any aid to this affiant in obtaining the names of witnesses, or in giving him any information as to evidence material for the defence ; that since the case for the defence was closed, to wit: since the 15th day of December, A. D., 1881, this affiant has learned of the existence and names of certain material witnesses for the defendant upon the issue of insanity, and whose testimony it is very important on behalf of the defence should be given in this case ; that such additional evidence is material for the most part in view of the fact that it relates to the condition of mind of the prisoner at times nearer the date of commission of the alleged offence in this case than any other evidence produced for the defence, and goes to show his insanity at that date with greater certainty than any evidence within the knowledge of this affiant up to the time this case was announced closed for the defence. That the names of the witnesses whose existence and names have recently come to the knowledge of this affiant, as aforesaid, are T. Bragdon, Marshall Green, James Brooks, Thomas Rathbone, Katie Collins Geo. W. McElfresh, Manville A. Austin, and Andrew MacFarland. That this affiant is advised and believes it to be true that he can prove by said Bragdon, Green, Katie Collins and Edward Austin, that they and each of them frequently saw the defendant in the park opposite the White House during the latter part of the month of June, A. D., 1881, and observed his singular and strange conduct, showing every indication of insanity, so much so that said witnesses were thoroughly convinced that he was of unsound mind, and that fact was freely commented on between them. That affiant expects to prove by said Brooks and Rathbone, that they had an interview with the prisoner in jail on the 3d of July, 1881, or possibly on the 2d, in which the prisoner said: "I wish you people would let me alone, I have some rights ;" that it was some time before said Brooks and Rathbone could induce him to talk to them, and when he did talk, he said to them at that interview that he had contemplated the removal of the President for six weeks, and was forced to do it by an inspiration from God, or words to that effect, and that he had no fear of punishment and no fear that he would not be liberated ; that the prisoner in such conversation was apparently cool and unconscious of any risk or danger to himself from trial for his act, and showed to said witnesses by his words and manner, unmistakeable evidences of insanity.

Affiant further expects to prove by said McElfresh and M. A. Austin that they rode to the jail with the prisoner as officers in charge of him, immediately after the shooting on the 2d day of July last, and that all the actions and words of the prisoner on that occasion were indicative of an insane man.

That affiant expects to prove by said Andrew MacFarland, that he has been connected with insane asylums, and has had almost constant care and oversight of insane people for nearly thirty-seven years past, being many years in charge of the Illinois State Asylum for the Insane at Jacksonville, in that State, where he now resides and which position he now holds; that he knew Luther W. Guiteau in his life time, and had an opportunity for a week, during which time said Guiteau was his guest at Jacksonville, of scientific observations of the mental condition of said Luther W. Guiteau in or about the year 1864, and came to the conclusion that said Guiteau was insane on the subject of religion, and that is the present opinion of said MacFarland; and that from the circumstances and facts developed in the evidence in this case thus far, said MacFarland is of opinion that the prisoner is now insane. Affiant further says that he has been misled by the course of the prosecution, giving the name of said McElfresh to the defendant as a witness for the prosecution in this case and then in not calling him as such witness, and that he would otherwise have been called by the defence; that he is a detective, as also are said Brooks, Rathbone and M. A. Austin, as this affiant is informed and believes, and all in Government employ and subject to the call of the prosecution in this case at any time.

GEORGE SCOVILLE.

Subscribed and Sworn to before me, Fourth Day of January, 1882.

R. J. MEIGS, Clerk.

By W. G. WILLIAMS, Assistant Clerk.

The affidavit was passed to Judge Cox, who spent some time carefully studying it, and then asked Mr. Corkhill if he wished to be heard on the subject.

Mr. Corkhill replied that he did not think the question required argument.

Mr. Scoville said he believed that Dr. McFarland was of opinion from what he had read that the prisoner was insane.

"The jury have rather an advantage over the doctor," said Judge Porter. "They have heard the testimony."

Mr. Reed, speaking of the motion embraced in the affidavit, said he admitted that it was entirely within the discretion of the Court whether the motion should be granted, and he believed that discretion would be conscientiously exercised. The admission of such evidence at such a time, he held, was not without authority or precedent. He cited a case before Judge Blodgett, in Chicago, where needed evidence had been admitted after the arguments had been commenced. It was true this trial had been protracted, but it was not the first time that a great cause had taken a long time for trial. He referred to a case in Brooklyn some years ago—a case in which no man's life was at stake—in which the distinguished gentlemen from New York had taken part, and which had required nearly six months in trial. He referred to the lack of means on the part of the defence to examine the cause. Mr. Scoville, he said, had borne the whole burden of the defence without compensation. He was a hero. He begged the Court, in the name of justice and fairness, to give the defence one more day in which the testimony could be put before the jury. He said the verdict of the jury, which ever way it went, would be more satisfactory if the Court allowed this evidence to be submitted.

Mr. Davidge remarked that the defence desired to re-open the case for the production of no less than nine witnesses. Referring to Dr. MacFarland, he urged that the evidence he proposed to give appeared to be based upon newspaper reports. The defence, he said, had summoned twenty experts, not one of whom had been called to give their opinions based on a personal examination of the prisoner. It was possible that men could be found who had based their opinions on what they read. If the testimony of such witnesses was to be received, when would the trial come to an end? He thought the action of the defence was a concession on the part of the defence that the expert evidence on their side had utterly failed. Three of the remaining witnesses, it was said, had seen the prisoner and formed the opinion that he was insane. With regard to the two officers who took Guiteau to jail, he said the defence had ample opportunity before to make the inquiries. It was so in the case of Messrs. Brooks and Rathbone. The affidavit was wonderful in respect to the statement that the mental condition of the prisoner was such as to render him incapable of assisting his counsel. They all knew what a remarkable memory the prisoner had. The testimony, if it was worth anything at all, was simply cumulative. He contended that the waste of time in this case was without precedent; the unnecessarily protracted cross-examinations of witnesses had been the main cause of the waste of time. He did not believe the prosecution had occupied over two weeks—or a few days more than two weeks. The rest of the time should be charged to the defence. There were instances here where there had been technical omissions, in which evidence had been admitted out of the regular order. There was no shadow of foundation laid for the introduction of the testimony of Dr. MacFarland. It would be a scandal to admit it at this time. He was presented here as a man reckless enough to swear upon what he had read. As to the rest of the evidence it was cumulative. As to the evidence of the persons who had seen the prisoner, the affidavit simply presented conclusions and not facts.

A wrangle ensued between Mr. Scoville and Col. Corkhill, and then Guiteau took a hand in the discussion. With an air of importance, he said: "I did intend to say nothing this morning. I propose to prove by Mr. McElfresh what I said to him when he went with me to the jail. I told Mr. McElfresh that it was the political situation that did it. I propose to show by Mr. Brooks that he came to my cell on the 2d of July, thinking that there was a great conspiracy. I told him I did it, and I told him that it was the political situation, and I did it under Divine pressure."

An officer tried to stop the prisoner while speaking, and he turned, angrily saying: "Mind your own business. I'll shut your mouth."

Mr. Reed, rising in reply to insinuations made against Dr. MacFarland, said he was the peer of any man.

Judge Cox was about to speak, when the prisoner again interrupted with a complaint about the destruction of the note book, and he was, with difficulty, quieted by the officers.

THE COURT'S DECISION.

Judge Cox said he had appreciated from the outset the difficulties under which counsel for the defence labored. Mr. Scoville had come here a stranger to the place and people and to the practice of the Court, and had been comparatively a stranger to the prisoner himself for several years. It was seen at the outset that he could receive very little assistance from the prisoner in the development of the defence. The most serious difficulty that counsel had to encounter was the odium attached to the assassination, and which disinclined people from appearing as witnesses for the defence. These were very great difficulties, and he appreciated them so fully that he felt it his duty (in order to secure the prisoner a fair trial) to give a certain latitude to the defence and such facilities as corresponded with the difficulties. If any new facts were developed now that struck his mind as having an important bearing on the defence or as necessary to a fair presentation of the case, he would deem it his duty (notwithstanding that the testimony for the defense was formally closed) to allow that fact to be given in evidence. Part of the testimony now proposed to be introduced was offered in the character of sur-rebutting testimony and part not. The first was the opinion of a medical expert as to the condition of the prisoner's mind. He understood the law and practice to be simply this: "The law presumed sanity, and the first affirmative testimony on that issue had to come from the defence. Expert testimony was a part of the evidence-in-chief for the defence on that issue, and all the expert testimony on which the defence relied must be offered in chief. Part of it could not be reserved to be offered by way of sur-rebuttal testimony. After that testimony was in, it then became the duty and the right of the prosecution to offer evidence on the general question of insanity. The prosecution was not confined to the mere

GUITEAU, THE ASSASSIN. 605

contradiction of witnesses for the defence; but it might go at length into the question and offer independent and affirmative proof on that question. A part of that testimony was that of medical experts. That testimony was not offered strictly in contradiction of the medical testimony for the defence, because one man's opinion was not a contradiction of another man's opinion; but it was offered as independent testimony. When this testimony was closed on the part of the Government, then the defence was restricted to a contradiction of facts that may have been testified to on the part of the prosecution. It was not allowed to contradict an expert on the part of the prosecution by the testimony of another expert who had a different opinion. If that was allowed there would be no end to the trial. It would run on to rejoinder and sur-rejoinder, and to all the innumerable issues which the ingenuity of counsel might devise. So that the privilege of producing expert testimony was limited to the evidence-in-chief for the defence, and to the evidence-in-chief for the prosecution. He therefore thought that the testimony of Dr. MacFarland could not be received on the question of the prisoner's sanity.

The offer was also made to prove that, immediately after the assassination, the prisoner claimed to have acted under inspiration. When the prisoner was on the stand as a witness he testified that he had committed this act under what he called, indifferently, inspiration or pressure. To rebut that testimony, the prosecution had put on the stand Mr. Reynolds, who testified that he hadhad an interview with the prisoner two weeks after the assassination, and that in that interview the prisoner did not claim to have acted under inspiration but assigned exclusively political motives. It was not the object of the Government to prove that he did not claim inspiration, but simply to ask the jury to infer that the prisoner never did claim this inspiration until several weeks after the assassination, and after he had discovered that these men whom he supposed he was benefiting by his deed had repudiated it and were denouncing him. The hypothetical case put by the prosecution to the experts assumed that no claim of having acted under inspiration was made by the prisoner until two weeks afterwards and up to the time of this interview of Mr. Reynolds with him. It would be an answer to that to show that on the very day of the assassination the prisoner did claim inspiration. As sur-rebutting testimony that evidence ought to be received. It struck him as strictly sur-rebutting testimony. As to the other testimony offered, which was not in reply to anything on the part of the Government, the common law practice was that the Government should summon all the witnesses whose names were endorsed on the indictment, and it was really incumbent on the Goverment as a matter of fairness to summon all the witnesses who had been present at the transaction and had seen it. The Government was not bound, however, to examine all the witnesses summoned; but, as soon as the case for the Government was closed, those witnesses were at the disposal of the defence. The proper time for the defence to call upon them was when the rebutting testimony was in course of presentation. In this case the defence had occupied two weeks in the presentation of its rebutting testimony, and it was at that time that, strictly speaking, this evidence should have been offered if offered at all.

The next question was what consideration should influence the Court in allowing additional evidence which might have been produced if known at the proper time. Such evidence ought not to be admitted if it is purely cumulative. For example, the mental condition of Luther W. Guiteau had been so thoroughly canvassed on both sides that anything more in addition to that seemed purely and exclusively cumulative. Besides it was not a direct fact in issue, but a somewhat collatteral issue. The proof of Luther W. Guiteau's insanity did not prove that of the prisoner. It did nothing more than merely tend to corroborate the direct testimony on that point. He did not think that it ought to be admitted. As to the proposition to offer witnesses who had seen the prisoner in a public park a few days before the assassination, and had gathered from his conduct the impression that he was out of his mind, such testimony was of very vague and uncertain character, and he did not think it sufficiently definite to warrant him in opening the case again. The only thing that he felt any uncertainty about was in reference to the testimony of Detective McElfresh, who conducted the prisoner to the jail immediately after the occurrence. He would like more definite information as to what McElfresh could prove. If he had an affidavit as to what McElfresh would testify to he might be able to decide more satisfactorily, but that at present it seemed to him too vague. He thought, however, that the testimony as to the claim of inspiration made on the day of the assassination or on the day after was admissible as rebutting testimony.

The prisoner.—"That is a sound decision and worthy of your Honor. I would not give a snap for the testimony of these experts one way or another. It is simply a question of dollars and cents with them. You could get twenty of them to swear that I was square as a rule on the 2d of July, when I did the act; while the fact is that I would not do it now for a million of dollars."

Dr. George M. Beard, of New York, was then called by the defence, but his evidence was objected to by the prosecution and the Court sustained the objection.

Mr. Scoville then stated that he desired to make a proposition to the prosecution. There had been numerous experts examined on both sides. They had testified to some extent in contradiction to each other. Drs. Godding, Nichols and Walker had been present throughout the trial, though not summoned by either side. He proposed to the prosecution, who said that they only wanted fair play, that the Court should call these three gentlemen to the stand and question them. Neither the defence or the prosecution would ask a question. Let their testimony go to the jury without note or comment, and let the jury decide upon it. These gentlemen were not paid to come here. He said that he would not have made the proposition but for the intimation thrown out by the District Attorney that he had sent Dr. Gray to jail with instructions to examine the mental condition of the prisoner, and had stated that if he found him insane the case would never have been brought to trial. If that were good law then it was good law now. If it was the proper thing then to rest the case on Dr. Gray's opinion it was the proper thing now to rest it on the opinion of three such men as he had named, in order that this trial should not result—that it should be a shame and disgrace not only to jurisprudence but to the American people.

Mr. Davidge stated that neither the opinion of Dr. Nichols or Dr. Godding could be of any assistance to the defence. The prosecution declined the offer or proposition made by Mr. Scoville, however, on the ground that such a course would delay the trial.

"You are in great haste to close this case," said the prisoner.

Judge Cox remarked: "There is nothing for the Court to decide."

Guiteau interjected: "If you men for the prosecution, want to submit this case without argument after this testimony is in, I am with you. I don't want to argue this case, and I don't want my counsel to argue it."

James J. Brooks, chief of the secret service division of the Treasury, was then called to the stand and examined by Mr. Scoville. He said he visited the prisoner, in company with his son and Mr. Rathbone, in his cell at the jail at midnight on the 2d of July. Mr. Brooks recounted the interview, which was in substance similar to other interviews held with Guiteau at the time. He said he was a Stalwart; that his act was a political necessity. Mr. Brooke told him that he was about to arrest two or three people, and Guiteau responded: "Don't do it, you will arrest innocent people." The next day Mr. Brooks had another interview with the prisoner. He said he had thought and prayed over this for six weeks. He did not remember anything he said in reference to inspiration. When the witness told him that the President was suffering terribly, the prisoner said: "I am very sorry. I wish I had given him a third bullet and put him out of his misery."

The prisoner frequently interrupted Mr. Brooks to make his usual declarations about the political situation and Divine pressure. When Mr. Brooks had related the accounts of the interviews, with the prisoner said: "It is proper for me to say that Mr. Brooks has stated the conversation that occurred between us very correctly."

"Mr. Brooks said," the prisoner remarked a few minutes later, "that the people were against me and I said the Deity was with me."

Mr. Scoville joined with the officers in an ineffectual attempt to silence the prisoner. Turning upon one of the officers, the prisoner said: "I don't want this officer hanging around me, either. He is a nuisance in this case. I talk to 50,000,000 people. What are you? You are nothing."

When Mr. Books left the stand, Mr. Scoville offered to identify now the photograph taken of the prisoner just after the shooting. After a long discussion an objection made to the evidence was sustained by the Court.

Mr. Scoville then read the lette written at Freeport, October 31st, 1875, by L. W. Guiteau to Mrs. Scoville, which related that Charles (the prisoner) had been at Freeport, endeavoring to borrow $25,000 to aid in his *Inter-Ocean* project. The letter said: "To my mind he is a fit subject for a lunatic asylum, and if I had the means to keep him, I would send him to one for a while at least."

Guiteau inquired, with a sneer: "Is your object in reading that letter, Scoville, to show that my father was a crank or that I was? You are a crank. That is my opinion of you. You have no more wit than a ten-year-old schoolboy.

Mr. Scoville.—"I believe the defence is done under the ruling of the Court."

Mr. Davidge.—"I would be glad now to have the proposition of law relied on by the other side. I have our own prepared."

The Court (to Mr. Scoville).—"Have you prepared anything?"

Mr. Scoville.—"Nothing in order. We have varied the detached propositions."

Mr. Davidge then read the following:

GUITEAU, THE ASSASSIN.

PRAYERS OF THE PROSECUTION.

FIRST.—The legal test of responsibility where insanity is set up as a defence for the alleged crime is whether the accused at the time of committing the act alleged knew the difference between right and wrong in respect of such act. Hence, in the present case, if the accused at the time of committing the act charged, knew the difference between right and wrong in respect of such act—that is, if he knew what he was doing and that what he was doing was contrary to the law of the land—he is responsible.

SECOND.—If the accused knew what he was doing and that what he was doing was contrary to the law of the land it constitutes no defence, even if it were true that when he committed the act he really believed that he was thereby producing a public benefit or carrying out an inspiration of Divine origin or approval. Such belief would not afford any excuse nor would such excuse be afforded by the fact that in the commission of the act he was impelled by a depraved moral sense, whether innate or acquired or by evil passion or indifference to moral obligation.

THIRD.—Insanity would, however, constitute a defence if by reason of disease the accused at the time of committing the act charged did not know what he was doing, or, if he did know it, that what he was doing was contrary to law.

FOURTH.—The only evidence in the present case tending to show an irresistible impulse to commit the homicide is the claim of the accused that his free agency was destroyed by his alleged conviction that the death of the President was required for the good of the American people and was Divinely inspired, but such conviction, even if it really existed, could not afford any excuse when the party knew what he was doing and that it was contrary to law. No mere delusion or error of judgment, not even a fixed belief that what is prohibited by the law is commended or approved by Divine authority, can exempt the accused from responsibility for breaking the law. To have such effect, the commission of the act charged must have been the result of an insane delusion which was the product of disease, and of such force as to deprive the accused of the degree of reason necessary to distinguish between right and wrong in respect of the act, so that at the time of committing the act he either did not know what he was doing, or, if he did, that the act was wrong or contrary to the law of the land

Guiteau then addressing the Court, said: "I suppose your Honor thinks that I shall be allowed to go on the stand and review certain parts of this trial in sur-rebuttal of what Reynolds said, of what Shaw said, of what Phelps said, and those kind of men. I hardly think it necessary. I have stated it to the Court and to the jury and the American people and I have stated it in that way on my honor for truth and veracity. The jury will see that."

No notice was taken of his remarks and then in response to a question by Mr. Reed the Court stated that it was the practice here to settle questions of law before the argument.

The counsel for the prosecution declared their willingness to afford the defence ample time to prepare their legal points, and Mr. Porter commended the rule as to the settlement of law propositions before the argument as tending to abridge the arguments and possibly dispense with them altogether.

The Court then, at Mr. Scoville's suggestion, at a quarter to one adjourned until Saturday.

CHAPTER XLI.

The Prayers for the Defence Fourteen in Number Formally Presented to the Court. The Defence Commences the Closing Arguments.

ON Saturday, January 7th, the press for admission to the Court-room was greater than ever, when the Court was formally opened by the comical but well recognized "Oyez" of the quaint Court crier. Guiteau was pounding the dock rail, during an excited colloquy with Mr. Reed.

Judge Cox at once suggested that there was no necessity for keeping the jury in Court to-day, and, this suggestion being acquiesced in by the counsel on both sides, the jury was given leave to retire. Through their foreman, however, the jury expressed their desire to remain.

The Court then stated that he was ready to hear arguments as to the prayers on the part of the prosecution and defence.

MR. DAVIDGE'S ARGUMENT.

Mr. Davidge proceeded to open the argument on the part of the prosecution. He recalled the fact that on Wednesday last he had submitted to the Court four simple, brief prayers for instructions to the jury. The first of those prayers asked His Honor to declare that the test of responsibility, in respect of human intelligence is the power to distinguish between right and wrong. The next prayer declared that if any human being possessed of that degree of intelligence commits a crime he is responsible for it—in other words that the degree of intelligence makes him responsible for the control of his own moral nature, his passions, his emotions, his intellectual nature, his beliefs, whatever they may be. In the third prayer he asked His Honor to define just what legal insanity is—to wit, that it is the product of a diseased mind. And in the last of these instructions he asked His Honor to lay down for the guidance of the jury what is the law in respect of what is called delusion. In the present case the only irresistible impulse was the so-called inspiration. In this last prayer he asked His Honor to say that if the inspiration was a product of the man's depraved and wicked nature it afforded no excuse; and that, to be an excuse, it must be the product of an insane delusion. In order to shut the door upon controversy in respect of those prayers he proposed to read them again.

Mr. Davidge then proceeded to read again the prayers of the prosecution and amplified his previous explanation of them. He did not anticipate any serious controversy in respect of those prayers. He had, however, read in the papers of yesterday a large number of counter prayers intended to be offered for the defence. So far as he had been able to examine those prayers their tendency—as far as they infringed on the rules of law laid down for the prosecution—was simply to produce confusion and obscurity. If what they meant was clearly exhibited by what they appeared to say, there was hardly one of them that in his humble judgment ought to be entertained for an instant by the court. The great central point in the first prayer of the prosecution was, human intelligence, when ought a human being be held responsible for crime? Capacity to make a contract was one thing; capacity to make a will was another thing. A man might make an ordinary contract and not an extraordinary contract. A man might make a very simple will disposing of a cow or a cabbage garden and yet be wholly unfit to exercise testamentary power in respect of any complicated system of bounty. In this case, however, they were dealing with crime. What degree of intelligence ought to make a human being responsible for crime—and such a crime? Surely the law fixed that degree of responsibility. The law in respect of contracts, the power to alienate property, the power to devise it said that a man must be twenty-one years of age. That same law fixed the age when any human being should be responsible for crime—twelve years of age, he thought. It was hardly possible, therefore, that in respect of responsibility for crime the law did not draw the line somewhere. What was the definition of the law in respect of this responsibility? It had been involved in very great doubt until the decision of the judges of England in what is known as the McNaughton case. There the House of Lords, alarmed at the acquittal of a prisoner who under an alleged insane delusion had shot Mr. Drummond in the streets of London, summoned all the judges of the realm (at that time fourteen) and propounded to them certain interrogatories which were answered by the judges. One of them, Mr. Justice Moll, delivered a separate opinion, but the opinions of the others were embodied by the Lord Chief Justice Tyndall. They laid down a rule of responsibility, and that rule from that time to the present had been adhered to by the English Courts. That rule was laid down as far back as 1843—well nigh forty years ago—and from that time to the present the English Courts have seen no reason whatever to depart from the rule. That rule has been adopted almost universally in America. It was a rule of common sense, a rule of human nature. If a child or an ignorant man were asked when responsibility began he would say that it began when the party had sense enough to know the difference between right and wrong. If he had that quantum of human intelligence he was and ought to be responsible. Think of the illustrious victim of this prisoner on the one hand and this assassin on the other. The law drew no line between a low degree of intelligence on the one hand and the highest on the other in respect of responsibility for crime. This prisoner had been portrayed as an imbecile until he went upon the stand and tore himself into shreds and atoms. A man might be peculiar and might even be partially insane, but if he rose to the point of intelligence which enabled him to know the difference between right and wrong and that what he was doing was wrong, then he was responsible before the Court for the wrong.

The Prisoner.—"I didn't know the difference, sir, between right and wrong. I had no choice. If I had had I would not have done it."

Mr. Davidge.—" We will see hereafter whether he had a choice."

Mr. Davidge then stated that in the "McNaughton" case five questions on the subject of insanity had been submitted to the Judges of England. Three of those questions have a direct bearing on this case. The first question was as to the responsibility of a person for an act when at the time of committing the act he knew that he was acting contrary to law, but did the act complained of with a view, under the influence of an insane delusion, to redressing a supposed injury, or of producing some supposed public benefit. The answer of all the judges (excepting Chief Justice Moll) was that they were of opinion that, notwithstanding the party accused did the act with a view, under the influence of an insane delusion, to redressing some supposed injury or of producing some supposed public benefit, he was, nevertheless, punishable according to the nature of the crime committed if he knew at the time of committing such crime that he was acting contrary to law. In answer to the other two questions the Judges stated that the jurors ought to be told that every man is to be presumed to be sane until the contrary be proved, and that to establish a defence on the ground of insanity it must be clearly proved that at the time of committing the act the party was laboring under such a defect of reason, produced from disease of the mind, as not to know the nature and quality of the act.

From that time to the present, Mr. Davidge continued, there had been no departure from the simple rule founded on nature and common sense. There had been a case recently decided in New York (referring to the Coleman case) and he desired to read somewhat at length the able decision of Judge Noah Davis.

Mr. Porter here remarking that it was evident that Mr. Davidge was suffering from his throat, offered to read the case for him and his offer was accepted.

Mr. Porter then read solemnly and dramatically, extracts from Judge Davis' charge to the jury. Among them were the following:—

"The doctrine that a criminal act may be excused on the notion of an irresistible impulse to commit it, when the offender has the ability to discover his legal and moral duty in respect to it, has no place in the law; and there is no form of insanity known to the law as a shield to an act otherwise criminal in which the faculties are so deranged that a man, though he perceive the moral qualities of his act, is unable to control his feelings, and is urged by some mysterious pressure. Under such a notion of legal insanity, the rights of property and life, both public and private, would be altogether insecure, and every man who, brooding over his wrongs, real or imaginary, should work himself up to an irresistible impulse to redress himself, could with impunity become a self-elected judge, jury and executioner. But happily that is not the law of the land. Crime escapes punishment, not through the insanity of the accused, but through the emotional insanity of the Court and jury.

At this point Mr. Scoville made a spirited protest against Judge Porter's "working in speeches to the jury" and asserted that the pretended relief to Mr. Davidge was a mere theatrical trick. Judge Porter indignantly replied that "the farce must end." He said: "we have come to a period in this trial when we stand on our rights and the counsel must not make these broadcast reflections. If he does not receive rebuke from the Court he will receive it from others." After further remarks in which he claimed that the charge was authority and did apply to the case, he waited for the decision of the Court.

Judge Cox said Judge Davis is an eminent judge and his opinion is officially reported. Of course if not applicable to this case it is open to become the subject of comment by counsel.

Mr. Davidge remarked that the charge just read was applicable to the case in which it was delivered—the case of a woman named Coleman, who was indicted for shooting a man whose mistress she had been, and who claimed to have shot him under pressure of an uncontrollable impulse.

The Prisoner.—"That Coleman case was published in all the papers a month ago, and the jury went directly against that charge in the verdict which they found."

Mr. Davidge.—"Here is a man (indicating the prisoner), who, it is contended for the defence, is imbecile."

"Is what!" exclaimed the prisoner (Mr. Davidge having laid the emphasis on the second syllable of "imbecile").

"Now listen to him," continued Mr. Davidge, "and see what a farce has been acted here for these many weeks. He not only knows the difference between right and wrong but he knows the law of the case."

"I do not pretend to be any more insane than yourself, Mr. Davidge," said the prisoner, "and I have not been insane since the 2d of July. It was transitory mania that I had, and that is all the insanity that I claim."

Mr. Davidge.—"He knows the principles of law applicable to the case as accurately as any lawyer."

The Prisoner·—"I do not pretend that I do not. My head is as good as yours or as Porter's. I am no fool. The Lord does not employ fools to do His work."

Mr. Davidge.—"Mr. Scoville has said that this man was a fool for three weeks."

The Prisoner.—"Scoville is a fool himself. (To the deputy marshal) —Keep quiet; let me alone. I repudiate entirely Scoville's theory of the defence. I do not even want him to address that jury. I will do that business myself. Two hours' speech to the jury will settle the question."

Judge Cox (to the prisoner).—"Keep silence, now, and let the argument go on."

The Prisoner.—"That is all right, Your Honor, but I repudiate the idea that I am insane. I never claimed that I was insane."

Mr. Davidge.—"I now desire to read the opinion of Judge Curtis in

the case of the United States against McGlew, 1st Curtis, page 1.
do so in order to stamp out any possible status in respect to the responsibility of the prisoner.

The Prisoner.—"I say that it was God's act, and that He has taken care of it and will take care of it."

Mr. Davidge.—"We will come hereafter to the Deity part of this matter. I am not saying a word about that now."

The Prisoner.—"If you get the Deity down on you He will stick to you all your days, in this world and in the next. I notify you now. You ought to be ashamed of yourself, Davidge, for selling yourself for a little filthy lucre. God Almighty will curse you prosecuting men. That is the opinion of the American press, too. (After a pause)—I want to get a chance at that jury for two hours' talk."

Mr. Davidge.—"If this defence of uncontrollable impulse is to be found only in the absurd pretence of inspiration, I want, by this first prayer, to put the conviction of this defendant beyond the possibility of doubt. I need not have gone so far as I have gone, because we are not trying here a man whose grade of intelligence is merely sufficient to distinguish between right and wrong—to know that he ought not to do the wrong and that he ought to do the right. We are trying a lawyer, a theologian, a lecturer—a man who, although imbecile for three weeks (as claimed by the defence) was transfigured in the estimation of the jury and of the world by his own testimony. Still I want the law to be laid down as it is. I want its simple rules to be given by this Court, because then there is an end of irresponsibility in respect of incapacity."

Mr. Davidge then proceeded to quote from Judge Curtis' opinion in the case of the United States against McGlew, from Judge Clifford's opinion in the case of the United States against Holmes and from other authorities on the subject of irresponsibility by reason of insanity. He then said, I have now presented to you the unbroken current of the English decisions from 1843 to the present time. I have presented to you the unbroken current of the decisions of the judiciary of the State of New York down to the present time. I have presented to you every outgoing from the Federal judiciary, of which you are an officer. I think that I have abundantly established the proposition that insanity, when urged as a defence in a criminal trial, is to be governed by the application of certain rules of law, and those rules are bound in nature and common sense. They are so plain that he who runs may read. They consist simply of two plain propositions, involving—first, the consideration whether the party on trial knew what he was doing; whether even if eccentric, even if queer, even if partially insane, he have sufficient reason and understanding to know that what he was doing was wrong. I shall trouble you no further in respect of the first prayer. The second prayer asserted this simple proposition and nothing more—that where God had given a man that degree of intelligence which enabled him to discriminate between right and wrong he had in his keeping the operations of his own mind and his own moral nature. The third prayer asked the Court to decide what degree of insanity emancipated a human being from responsibility. The fourth prayer asserted that no conviction of an irresistible impulse could afford an excuse if the accused knew that he was doing wrong.

In the further course of his argument Mr. Davidge alluded to the case of Reynolds, the Mormon, decided by the United States Supreme Court, when the prisoner broke in:—"I am glad you refer to the Mormons. They break the law all the time, and the Government does not do anything."

Mr. Davidge.—"They break the law, just as the law was broken here"

After summing up the law asserted by the prayers of the prosecution Mr. Davidge said:—"Such I understand to be the law in the District of Columbia. It would perhaps be improper for me to discuss at this stage the different propositions offered by the other side until I have heard from them. It might, and perhaps would be, under the feeling I was sorry to see existed here this morning, attributed to a desire on my part to forestall Your Honor's judgment, and certainly nothing is further from my mind. So, with these remarks, I submit the prayers of the prosecution, merely adding that these propositions of law ought to be read together, and when so collated I think Your Honor will come to the conclusion that they completely cover the legal requirements of the case."

The Prisoner.—"Mormonism is an institution for the benefit of private lust. My act was a patriotic act for the benefit of the American people; they are well satisfied with my act."

At half-past twelve a recess for half an hour was taken.

After the recess the jury did not return to the Court-room and the proceedings were opened by the formal presentation of the prayers of the defence for instruction to be given to the jury by the Court.

THE PRAYERS OF THE DEFENCE.

First—The legal test of responsibility, when insanity is set up as a defence for alleged crime, is not merely whether the accused knew at the time what he was doing, and that the act was contrary to law, for an irresponsibly insane person may know those things, but was the act done as the result of an insane delusion, or was it committed under an influence or power which the accused could not resist by reason of his unsoundness of mind?

Second.—Although the accused may have known what he was doing, and that what he was doing was contrary to the law of the land, yet if, when he performed the act he really believed that he was thereby producing a public benefit, and was actuated by an insane delusion that he was carrying out an inspiration of Divine origin or approval, and would not have done the act but for such insane delusion, then the accused is not guilty of the crime charged against him, and the jury should find him "not guilty by reason of insanity."

Third—Insanity constitutes a defence if, by reason of it, the accused, at the time of committing the act charged, did not know what he was doing; or, if he did not know that what he was doing was contrary to law; or, if the act would not have been done by him but for reason of his insanity.

Fourth.—The only evidence in the present case tending to show an irresistible impulse to commit the homicide or that the accused acted under the pressure of an insane delusion in doing the act, is found in the conduct and words of the accused as detailed in evidence. The question whether the free agency of the accused was destroyed by a conviction on his part that the death of the President was required for the good of the American people, and that he was divinely inspired to remove him by death, is one of fact to be determined by the jury from all the evidence in the case, and such evidence includes the acts as well as the words of the accused. But such conviction, if it really existed, could not afford any excuse when the party knew what he was doing, and that it was contrary to law, unless it was the product of an insane delusion and he was impelled to do the act by such delusion. Such delusion may exist as to a Divine requirement, or as to an inspiration from God. No mere delusion, unless it be the product of an unsound mind, nor error of judgment, nor even the fixed belief that what is prohibited by the law is commanded or approved by Divine authority, can exempt the accused from responsibility for breaking the law, if at the time he knew what he was doing and that it was contrary to law, and he was not acting under an insane delusion. To have such effect the committing of the act charged must have been the result of an insane delusion of such force as to deprive the accused of the degree of reason necessary to distinguish between right and wrong in respect of the act, as sane people generally judge of such conduct. The delusion must have been such that at the time of committing the act he did not know what he was doing, or, if he did, he must have acted under a controlling conviction that the act was right. Although he may have known that the act was contrary to the law of the land, yet if he did it under the insane delusion that it was commanded to be done by God, such knowledge on his part would not make him liable to punishment.

Fifth —Whether insanity exists or has existed at any time with the prisoner, and the degree of insanity, if any existed or has existed, are questions of fact to be determined entirely by the jury from the evidence.

Sixth.—If the jury find from the evidence that the prisoner was of unsound mind at the time of the doing of the act charged against him as criminal in this case, then it is also the duty of the jury to find whether said act was the result of such unsoundness of mind of the prisoner.

Seventh.—The punishments of the law are intended for rational persons, and no one but a rational person can commit the crime of murder.

Eighth.—Insanity may be interposed as a legal defence in any prosecution for an otherwise criminal act, and if such defence be established by the evidence it takes away the criminality and the act ceases to be a crime in contemplation of law.

Ninth.—If the jury have a reasonable doubt as to the sanity of the accused at the time of committing the act charged against him as a crime, they should give him the benefit of that doubt and should find him "not guilty, by reason of insanity."

Tenth.—The jury are the sole judges of the credibility of witnesses, and have a right to take into account, in weighing the evidence, any apparent feeling or interest manifested by witnesses on the stand, their manner of testifying, their compensation or want of compensation, and any other circumstances connected with their testimony which the jury may think would influence them.

Eleventh.—If the jury believe from the evidence that the prosecution have wilfully suppressed evidence of the mental condition of the accused during two weeks next following the shooting of President Garfield, which it was in their power to have produced on the trial, the jury have a right to take that fact into consideration as raising a presumption that such evidence, if produced, would have been unfavorable for the prosecution.

Twelfth.—If the jury shall believe from the evidence that the prisoner was of sound mind, or not so insane as to be irresponsible for the act at the time of shooting at the President, on the 2d day of July, 1881, and that he then unlawfully and wilfully, but without malice in fact in the District of Columbia, shot at and thereby injured the President, of which shooting and injury the person so injured subsequently died in the State of New Jersey, and within the United States, then the prisoner is guilty of the crime of manslaughter and the jury should so find.

Thirteenth.—The jury are instructed to find a separate verdict upon each count in the indictment, and, inasmuch as it is charged in the first, second, fourth, fifth, seventh and eighth counts of the indictment in this case that the death of the President took place in the county of Washington, in the said District of Columbia, and there is no evidence of such fact, therefore the jury are directed to find the accused not guilty upon each of said counts, separately.

Fourteenth.—Inasmuch as the evidence is uncontradicted in this case that the wound was inflicted upon the President by the accused on the 2d day of July, A. D., 1881, in the county of Washington, in the District of Columbia, and that the President subsequently and in the month of September, A. D., 1881, died of such wound in the State of New Jersey, the jury are instructed that by reason of these facts the accused is not guilty of the crime of murder charged in the indictment, and the verdict must be not guilty—unless the jury shall find him guilty of manslaughter, as charged in the twelfth prayer of the defence.

Mr. Reed then proceeded to open his argument in support of them.

MR. REED'S ARGUMENT.

He prefaced his remarks by the concession that in the use of a deadly weapon in such a manner as to result in death the law presumed malice. That need not be discussed. The question whether or not the killing of the President was done with malice was a question entirely and exclusively for the jury. The defence claimed that the act was done without malice on the part of the defendant. If the jury had a reasonable doubt of the guilt of the accused it was their duty to acquit him. They had no discretion. As to insanity, the modern doctrine, the better doctrine, was that if the jury had a reasonable doubt of the sanity of the accused at the time of committing the act it was their duty to find him not guilty. Formerly the insanity had to to be proved by the defendant beyond any reasonable doubt.

The Court.—"In one State."

Mr. Reed.—"Yes. Then the doctrine began to be modified. In the Roger's case in Massachusetts it was decided that if the insanity was made out by the weight of the evidence the accused should be acquitted. But the courts have advanced from that ground, and the doctrine now held is that if there is a reasonable doubt of the sanity of the accused he is entitled to an acquittal."

Mr. Reed then cited in this connection the case of Happs vs. The People (31st Illinois), in which the Judge in his charge said:—"In every criminal proceeding if a reasonable doubt is entertained of the guilt of the accused the jury is bound to acquit. * * * Sanity is guilt; insanity is innocence. Therefore reasonable doubt of the sanity of the accused must acquit. The presumption of innocence is as strong as the presumption of sanity."

In further support of his position that if there was a reasonable doubt of the sanity of the accused the jury must acquit, Mr. Reed cited from the cases of Richard Done vs. The State, reported in the Tennessee State Reports; The People vs. McCann, 16th New York; Alexander vs. The People, 96th Illinois; The State vs. Bartlett, 43d New Hampshire, and Polk vs. The State, 19th Indiana.

He also quoted from the decision of Chief Justice Cartter, of the Supreme Court of the District of Columbia, in the case of the United States vs. Albert Nicholas, in 1870. It was there held that if the jury had a reasonable doubt on the question of sanity they were bound to acquit the accused.

Mr. Davidge called attention to the fact that the prayers in behalf of the defence spoke of the burden of proof in respect of insanity, treating it generally. In any event His Honor would define it by speaking of doubt in respect of the legal standard of responsibility, and would indicate what was meant by "reasonable doubt."

Mr. Reed.—"I admit that it will be Your Honor's duty to tell the jury what "reasonable doubt" is. The question of what constitutes insanity, we submit, is a question solely for the jury.

The Court.—"The question of responsibility is for the Court, the question of fact for the jury.

Mr. Reed.—"Your Honor will give your views as to what constitutes insanity, but whether this defendant was of sound mind or not is a question for the jury. Is there any argument made against the reasoning of Judge Reese in Illinois, Judge Bellows in New Hampshire and Judge Chalmers, of Mississippi? Ought not that to be the law? It would be monstrous and shocking to the sense of justice of any man that an accused should be condemned to the gallows about whose sanity any reasonable, fair man could have any question. Send a lunatic to the gallows in America? Whether he is a lunatic or not is a question to be decided by the jury. When they consider the evidence in the seclusion of the jury room they may say, "Well, this man committed an awful crime—atrocious, indescribable, unparalleled in history—yet we are not quite certain that he knew that he was doing wrong." Is it not the doctrine of humanity to give the man the benefit of that doubt and hesitation, and for the Court to say to the jury, if you have a reasonable doubt it is your duty to give the benefit of it to the accused? Some men will say that that will turn the man out on the country and he will kill somebody else. That is a question unworthy to be suggested in a court of justice. If the man's mind had been weary and memory had departed from him, should any man say that he ought to walk as a culprit to the gallows? Would any man say that in any enlightened country to-day? Bellingham, tried in England many years ago, after he shot his victim was hurried to the gallows in seven days, and an undoubted lunatic was convicted and condemned—a shame and disgrace to British jurisprudence. In this case, all we ask is that Your Honor shall say to the jury—describing to them, explaining to them what is meant by a reasonable doubt:—"if you, on your oaths, have a reasonable doubt of the sanity of the accused at the time he shot the President, it is your duty to give him the benefit of that doubt and say he is not guilty."

Mr. Scoville rose to close the argument in support of the prayers advanced by the defence, but first commented on the absence of the jury, which had availed itself of the privilege given by Judge Cox this morning, and had not returned to the court room after the recess. He said that he did not complain of it, but it was one of the incidents of the trial which he could not help noticing.

Mr. Davidge promptly objected to these ill-natured remarks, and an acrimonious colloquy ensued between all four of the counsel, Guiteau for once keeping out of the wrangle, and Judge Cox attempting to pour oil on the troubled waters.

Finally Judge Cox said—"I told the jury this morning that they might leave the court room if they chose, but they did not choose to do so during the morning session."

The District Attorney.—"We all agreed that the jury might go this morning."

Mr. Scoville.—"It is only an accident, as I stated, but we have accidents always. I shall not trouble Your Honor with long citations of authorities. I am satisfied that the Court has pretty thoroughly looked into those cases—more carefully and thoroughly than I have had time to do."

Mr. Scoville then went on to argue that the Court should not take from the jury the right to pass upon the question whether the prisoner would have committed the act if he had been of sound mind, and he saw that the decisions, according to the McNaughton case, were just as antiquated as Mr. Porter's style of oratory. They had both started at the same time.

Mr. Scoville went on to say that the only way in which courts had progressed at the present day was by the force of enlightened public opinion crowding them out of the old ruts and obliging them to abandon those precedents which common sense, common reason and enlightened public opinion say shall no longer be asserted in courts ot justice. He then referred to the opinion of Judge Wylie in the Mary Harris case, admitting that the tendency of modern decisions seemed to have set in in the direction of holding that one of the elements of crime was that the person committing it shall be of sound memory and discretion; also to a modern English case (The Queen vs. Davis, reported in 14 Cox's Criminal Cases, page 657), in which the Judge charged the jury that while drunkenness was no excuse for crime, delirium tremens, caused by drunkenness, might be an excuse, if it produced such a state of mind as relieved the man from responsibility.

The language of the Judge in this case is:—"Any disease that disturbs the mind so that a man cannot think calmly and rationally of all the different reasons to which we refer in considering the rightness or wrongness of an act—any disease that so disturbs the mind that it cannot perform that duty with some moderate degree of calmness and reason—may be fairly said to prevent a man knowing that what he did was wrong." "If Your Honor," continued Mr. Scoville, "will charge the jury like that in this case we shall be very well satisfied."

Leaving Mr. Scoville's argument uncompleted, the Court, at three o'clock, adjourned to Monday.

CHAPTER XLII.

The Arguments Continued—Mr. Scoville and Mr. Davidge on the Question of Malice—Colonel Corkhill on Jurisdiction—The Prisoner on Everything in General.

ON Monday morning, January 9th, the beginning of the eighth week of this remarkable trial found an anxious and excited public still clamoring for admission to the Court room. Guiteau on being brought in at once claimed the attention of the audience in as trivial a manner as if the entire business was a mere pastime. He said: "I have about seven or eight hundred letters that I expect to examine as soon as I have time. A good many are from ladies, expressing sympathy and praying that I be acquitted. I desire to thank the ladies of America for their sympathy. On Saturday I received a check for one thousand dollars from the Stalwarts of Brooklyn; also one for five hundred dollars from the Stalwarts of New York. I desire to call on other Stalwarts to show their hands with checks. (Angrily to the bailiffs) Keep quiet and mind your business. Don't interfere with me when I am speaking."

Mr. Scoville resumed his argument, and laid stress upon the proposition that insane men often know the difference between right and wrong, and for that reason conceal their plans; that the benefit of the doubt should attach to the plea of insanity when raised with the same force as when urged in connection with the commission of the crime. Alluding to the decision of Judge Davis, he said the Judge had gone out of his way to pass upon something not involved in the case he was then considering. He further said that the opinion of a man who sat on the same bench with a Barnard and a Cardoza should not be received with much consideration. Judge Porter indignantly interfered, and condemned this false accusation against Judge Davis. After an angry retort from Mr. Scoville and a complaint by Mr. Davidge that not five minutes had been devoted to the proper scope of the argument, the Court warned counsel that they must abstain from personalities. Mr. Scoville concluded his argument at twelve o'clock, and then in the course of a personal explanation, criticised the conduct of counsel on the other side, especially in reference to their custom of bowing to the jury upon entering Court. Judge Porter resented the implications, and then a recess was taken for half an hour.

After the recess the jury did not return, taking advantage of the permission given them to do so. District Attorney Corkhill stated that he had not expected to speak on the legal points, relying upon the assurance of the defence that the question of jurisdiction would not be raised, but as the last two prayers of the defence distinctly made that issue, he felt it his duty to address the Court upon that question. He then occupied the Court for an hour in an exhaustive argument upon the subject of jurisdiction, supporting his position by references, and reading from printed slips.

PRECIS OF COLONEL CORKHILL'S ARGUMENT.

The argument of the District Attorney was almost exhaustive on the subject, but it will be further handled in the address of Judge Porter. The main points were as follows: "As Guiteau fired the pistol in the District of Columbia, and his victim died in New Jersey, the legal point raised is, where was the crime of murder committed? As the common law was at doubt in regard to this subject, the statute of two and three, Edward VI., chapter twenty-four, was passed, providing that the trial should lie in the county where death occurred, though the fatal blow was given in another. This statute was repealed in the reign of George IV., by a statute which provides for the punishment of a crime in either county, when it shall be begun in one and completed in another. This is the present law of England. But it has been settled that these statutes do not apply to the District of Columbia. The question where a wound is given on land in one district and death ensues in another, is not touched either by the Congressional Act of 1790 or 1857. But it will be urged that the case of Guiteau is covered by the thirtieth section of the Act of March 2, 1867, which provides that "When any offence shall be begun in one judicial district and completed in another, every such offence shall be deemed to have been committed in either, and may be dealt with, tried, determined and punished in either in the same manner as if it had been actually and wholly committed therein." Consequently, the direct question as to jurisdiction, which has not as yet been argued by the prosecution. is : Do the District of Columbia and New Jersey constitute judicial districts, ascertained by law, as provided in the Constitution? In the Revised Statutes this law has not been codified as it originally passed, for the words, "Judicial Circuit" are substituted for "Judicial District," so that it reads, "When any offence against the United States is begun in one Judicial Circuit and completed in another, it shall be deemed to have been committed in either, and be tried, determined and punished in either District."

MR. DAVIDGE'S ADDRESS.

The District Attorney having finished his reading, Mr. Davidge rose and after referring to the understanding with Mr. Scoville, that the question of jurisdiction should be waived, and to his own readiness to argue it at the very beginning of the trial, he said: "Ever since I examined this question of jurisdiction, I have entertained a very fixed opinion in respect to a broader ground on which the jurisdiction may be sustained than either of the grounds mentioned in the paper read to the Court. That larger ground has always appeared to me to be this : That the crime mentioned in this indictment is a crime against the Federal Government, and that the Federal Government is not embarrassed in its legislation by the rules and principles of the common law. In the construction of the laws of the Federal Government, we refer to the common law simply to ascertain the meaning of words, and, having ascertained that meaning, we have nothing at all to do with the peculiar policy or processes that govern in States, the jurisprudence of which represents the common law. My view, therefore, has always been, that as to a statute passed by the Federal Government before the cession of this portion of the District of Columbia by the State of Maryland, its language ought to be construed according to its plain, natural and popular signification. We are trying this case under that Federal statute—a statute antedating the cession of this District. The language of that law is that whoever shall commit the crime of murder in any place within the exclusive jurisdiction of the Federal Government shall suffer death. With this intimation of those views of mine, in addition to those presented by the District Attorney, I shall say nothing further now on the subject, but shall defer argument on it until this case shall go to review in the Supreme Court of this district, sitting in banc.

After referring to what he thought to be a misunderstanding by the counsel for the defence of the word "malice" and showing that "malice" in law means simply the intentional doing of an act denounced by the law as a crime, Mr. Davidge continued as follows: I have laid down four simple propositions. In the first place I stated that in this civilized land there was a test of responsibility in respect of human intelligence. I said that we were not here to define what the rule was in respect of civil transactions, but only in respect of crimes, and that the law furnished a rule whereby was established a test of human responsibility for the violation of a criminal statute. I said in the next place that if the party had that degree of intelligence which made him responsible, no mere belief, no intellectual operation of his mind would make him irresponsible. No opinion, however fixed, not even the belief that he was inspired to do wrong by Holy Writ, would make him irresponsible, provided that it was an act of his own mind and the conclusion reached by the exercise of his own reason. In the third place, I said that, as no intellectual error would excuse, a fortiori, no depravity, no moral disease would excuse. I said that the intelligence of a man was king, and that if he had a certain amount of intelligence he was held bound to keep in check, not only the intellectual, but the moral operations of his nature, and that such a monstrous thing as moral insanity was unknown to the law of this District and ought to be unknown to the law of any civilized community. Lastly, I said that the only postulate of irresponsibility was disease ot the mind—insanity—the product of a diseased mind and existing to such an extent as to dethrone reason and to deprive the man of the power to exert his intelligence in respect of the act which is the subject matter of the indictment.

I do not understand that the first proposition is seriously combated on the other side. I do not understand that there is any policy on the other side except to produce obscurity and confusion in the instructions to be given to the jury. All this medical jargon which might be right and proper when applying to an insane person, is manifestly wrong and improper when urged as an excuse for crime on behalf of a man who knew what he was doing and who knew what he was doing was wrong. You have before you here a question of administration and not a question of disease. What we learn from the medical gentlemen in their writings is all very well when the question is whether a party ought to be secluded in a mad house or ought to be treated in any degree; but it is wholly irrelevant and wholly improper when a Court of Justice is called upon to define what the law is—a law enacted for the protection of society. The learned gentleman (Mr. Scoville) treated us to a homily here in respect to public sentiment. Where would his client be if public sentiment could be heard here? How long would he continue in this Court room?

Mr. Davidge then proceeded to criticise in detail the several instructions prayed for on the part of the defence and to contrast with them the four simple propositions prayed for by the prosecution. Continuing, he said: The law lays its hand upon the prisoner and deals with him for the purpose of making an example of him. According to the testimony of one of the medical witnesses, there is in this country one crank out of every five persons. I think that an exaggeration, but undoubtedly the number of cranks is very great, and indubitably there are very many men who are only restrained from crime by example. So that the law doesn't even mean to hurt this man. That is not the object of the law. He will be judged elsewhere, and finally judged. The purpose of the law is to pre_ vent on his part a repetition of the offence, and to prevent an imitation of it by others as depraved and wicked as himself. The law does not want to make him suffer (his very suffering is an accident), but the law punishes him so that society may live.

Mr. Davidge went on to say; We want light. We don't intend to allow this prisoner to escape in a cloud. If we are in error in our prayers, let the error be rectified, but let the outgoings of this Court be plain and perspicacious beyond even the reach of criticism." On the question of "reasonable doubt" Mr. Davidge argued that it must not be a speculation, a theory, a vague suspicion of what might be, but that it must be a solid, well founded doubt. resting on evidence. Referring to one of the prayers of the defence as to the medical testimony offered by the prosecution, he said that that was a mean aspersion upon men as pure and honorable as any men in America. Referring to another of the prayers on the part of the defence, which intimated that there had been a suppression of evidence on the part of the prosecution, he declared that that was another mean and cruel aspersion without the slightest foundation of fact. What motive could counsel for the prosecution have in suppressing anything that would enure to the advantage of the prisoner? Which one of them would do it? ("Corkhill is the man," promptly interposed the prisoner.) Not one scrap, or jot, or tittle that could help him in his dire extremity has been suppressed or kept from the jury.

The prisoner who had constantly interrupted counsel but had been as contemptuously brushed aside as if he were an annoying bluebottle fly, here shouted: "Bailey's notebook was suppressed, but I had Mr. Brooks there as a special Providence on the 2d of July, and I told him all about the inspiration. Corkhill intended to cheat me on that point by suggesting that it was three or four weeks after the act that I first said anything about the inspiration. That shows the iniquity of the prosecution."

Mr. Davidge having closed, Mr. Porter was about to commence his argument when, at the suggestion of the District Attorney, the Court at ten minutes to three, adjourned.

CHAPTER XLIII.

Judge Porter Closes the Arguments on the Prayers—Guiteau Interrupts and "Catches a Tartar"—Judge Cox Gives His Decision on the Prayers.

ON Tuesday, January 10th, a crowded audience with several senatorial and political personages sprinkled through it, gave evidence that something special was expected. Guiteau came in looking pale and nervous, feeling conscious, probably, that Judge Porter had a mental Delaware whipping post and pillion prepared for him. The Court opened promptly at ten o'clock, and shortly after Judge Porter proceeded to close the prosecution arguments upon the prayers. He began his argument shortly after ten o'clock, and scathingly reviewed the conduct of the prisoner and his counsel during the progress of the trial. He dissected the crime in its every phase, and in a masterly manner presented it in all its hideousness. Guiteau attempted several interruptions, but failed to obtain the applause which he coveted, while the rebukes of Judge Porter were received with evident marks of approval. Judge Porter concluded at 11.40 A. M. by reading the letter of President Garfield to Judge Payne, complimenting and thanking him for brushing away the network of sophistries with which it has been customary to envelop the plea of insanity as an excuse for crime. Judge Cox then began the reading of his descision on the prayers of the counsel.

DECISION OF JUDGE COX.

Judge Cox then proceeded to state his views on the prayers submitted on both sides—first giving his attention to the question of jurisdiction. He said that at an early stage in the case he had expressed a preference to hear that question discussed in a preliminary form by way of demurrer, or motion, or plea, because a determination of it adversely to the jurisdiction would have spared all the labor and trouble of the trial. Counsel, however, had the privilege of making the question at any stage of the case. The jurisdiction of the court had been publicly discussed and seriously challenged, and he had felt it incumbent on him not to ignore a question so vital to the rights of the accused. He had deemed it his duty, therefore, to investigate the question thoroughly. After a very exhaustive review of the English and American authorities he expressed his conviction that the English authority was decidedly in favor of jurisdiction where the blow had taken place, and that in this country there was a strong array of authority in the same direction. He felt at liberty to adopt and announce the doctrine (which conformed to common sense) that the jurisdiction was complete where the fatal wound had been inflicted, and that, therefore, the place of death was immaterial. Consequently it would be improper to grant the thirteenth instruction prayed for by the defense, because the offence charged might be tried and conviction might follow under those counts of the indictment which averred the death to have occurred in the District of Columbia. For the same reason the fourteenth instruction relating to jurisdiction had to be denied. When it became his duty to charge the jury in the case it would be his effort to expand and illustrate so much of those instructions as he considered correct, but for the present he merely desired to express his opinion sufficiently to guide the counsel in their arguments to the jury.

Judge Cox then proceeded to consider the first and second prayers of the prosecution in connection with the third, fifth, sixth and eighth prayers of the defence.

The first instruction asked for by the prosecution—namely, that

GUITEAU, THE ASSASSIN.   635

"the legal tests of responsibility where insanity is set up as defence for alleged crime is whether the accused at the time of committing the act charged knew the difference between right and wrong in respect of such acts," he regarded as correct. He reviewed at great length the questions involved in the McNaughton case, and quoted from testimony given by Lord Justice Fitz James Stephen before a parliamentary committee which had before it, in 1874, a bill to define the law of insanity. He referred to this, he said, simply to show that the answers of the judges in the McNaughton case had not since been regarded as clearly establishing the proposition that a mere capacity to know the law of the land subjected persons to criminal responsibility. Since the McNaughton case a number of homicide cases had been tried at *nisi prius* in England, and he had not been able to find one in which a knowledge of the law of the land had been laid down as a test. In the United States there were numerous cases that applied to a knowledge of right and wrong in regard to the particular case, but the instructions had been in the most vague and general terms. He would therefore state his own views, which he did as follows:—To a sane man an act, whether morally wrong or not, is wrong if it is in violation of the law of the land. It cannot be right for him although he may think that independently of the law it would be. It cannot be right for him although he may think it is right notwithstanding the law, and that he may rightfully commit it in violation of the law. But while a sane man is responsible for opinions contrary to law if carried out in practice an insane man is not held to the same responsibility. He may know the law of the land, but in his delusions he may insanely believe that it is not the law for him, but that he is acting under a higher authority which supersedes it. If, therefore, I am to rule upon this proposition as presented I grant it only with a qualification and I give as a substitute therefor my own (marked No. 1) as follows:—

No. 1. The legal test of responsibility where insanity is set up as a defence for alleged crime is whether the accused at the time of committing the act charged knew the difference between right and wrong in respect of such act. Hence, in the present case, if the jury find that the accused committed the act charged in the indictment and at the time of the commission of his crime knew what he was doing and that what he was doing was contrary to the law of the land, he is responsible; unless in consequence of insane mental delusions or other form of mental disorder he was laboring under such defect of reason as to be incapable of understanding the obligation of the law of the land and the duty and necessity of obedience to it, and if understanding that his act was wrong because it was in violation of the law.

I have prepared instruction No. 2, which embodies all that I think is correct in the remaining instructions asked for by the government, and in the first four instructions asked for by the defence. It as follows:—

No. 2. If the jury find that the defendant committed the act charged, and that the time thereof knew what he was doing and that what he was doing was contrary to the law of the land, it constitutes no excuse, even if it is true that when he committed the act he really believed that he was producing a great public benefit and that the death of the President was required for the good of the American people; nor would such excuse be afforded by the fact that in the commission of the act he was controlled by a depraved moral sense, whether innate or acquired, or by evil passions or indifference to moral obligations. And even if the jury find that the defendant, as a result of his own reasoning and reflection, arrived at the determination to kill the President, and as a further result of his own reasoning and reflection believed that his said purpose was approved, or suggested, or inspired by the Deity, such belief would afford no excuse. But it would be different, and he would not be responsible criminally if the act was done under the influence and as the product of an insane mental delusion that the Deity had commanded him to do the act, which had taken possession of his mind not as a result of his own reflections, but independently of his own will and reason and with such force as to deprive him of the degree of reason necessary to distinguish between right and wrong as to the particular act. In such case even if he knew that the act was a violation of the law of the land, he would not be responsible if his reason was so perverted by the insanity that he was incapable of understanding the obligation of the law of the land, and that the act was wrong under the obligation of that law and wrong in itself."

Judge Cox continued as follows:—

In this connection I add the words "wrong in itself," because I can conceive a case in which one might believe, insanely, that the law of the land provided no punishment for murder, and yet the person might be perfectly aware of the moral enormity of the crime. I would be unwilling to pronounce such a person irresponsible.

I have omitted from this instruction one important feature of that asked for on the part of the defence. It is expressed in the first sentence of the first prayer in these words:—"Or was it committed under an influence or power which the accused could not resist by reason of his unsoundness of mind." It cannot be denied that some of the most respectable courts in this country have recognized it as possible that a

man may be driven against his own will to the commission of an act
which he knows to be wrong by an insane irrepressible impulse within
him, overriding his own will and conscience, and those courts maintain
that, as under such circumstances the will to do wrong (which is the
very essence of criminality) is wanting, he ought not to be held criminally
responsible. They, therefore, hold that the test of the knowledge of
right or wrong ought to be qualified by the further condition whether
the person had the power to choose between doing or not doing the
act. The question is a dangerous one alike for courts and juries to
handle, and I do not intend to express an opinion upon it further that
the facts of the case require. Those facts seems to relieve me from
the necessity and the responsibility of discussing it generally. If we
struck out of this case all the declarations and testimony of the defendant himself we have no light whatever upon this subject. There are
circumstances, such as his actions and conduct, which, his counsel
may argue, of themselves indicate some aberration and are corroborative of and explained by his testimony. But of themselves they
would have afforded no indication of the particular motive or special
form of delusion that actuated him. Of this we have no indications
except in the declarations, oral or written, of the defendant himself.
But he has never claimed that he was irresistibly impelled to do an
act which he knew to be wrong. On the contrary, he always claimed
that it was right. He justified it at the time, and afterward, in his
papers as a political necessity and an act of patriotism, and whether
he claimed inspiration, early or late, he has claimed that the act was
inspired, and, therefore, right. He has used the words "pressure" and
' inspiration'' interchangeably, as it were, to express the idea. This
has no meaning unless it be that he was under an insane delusion that
the Deity had inspired and commanded the act. He has certainly not
separated the idea of pressure and impulse from the conviction of inspiration and right and duty. The defendant has asserted no form of
insanity which does not involve the conviction that the act was right,
and I feel sure that I am not transcending the privilege of the court
when I say that there is no evidence in the case outside of his own
declaration tending to prove irresistible impulse as a thing by itself
and separate from this alleged delusion. Therefore, the case does
not seem to me to present or call for any ruling on the hypothesis of
an irresistible impulse to do what the accused knew to be wrong and
what was against his will. Whether there is such a thing as irresistible insane impulse to commit crime and whether it has existed in any particular
case are questions of fact and not of law. In this case, I think, there
is no testimony showing that it can exit by itself as an independent

form of insanity, but rather the contrary. There is, however, testimony tending to show that such impulses result from and are associated with insane delusions, and especially with an insane delusion as that the party has received a command from the Deity to do an act. But if such an insane delusion exists, so as to destroy the perceptions or right and wrong as to the act (which is substantially the defendant's claim), this of itself is irresponsible insanity, and there is no need to consider the subject of impulses resulting from the delusion. On the other hand, if there were no insanity but a mere fanatical opinion or belief, the only impulse that could have actuated the defendant must have been a sane one—such a one as, in the most favorable view of it, a mistaken sense of duty—which impulse the law requires him to resist and control.

In connection with the medical testimony tending to show that these impulses are always or generally associated with some insane delusion, if there are facts tending directly to show the existence or absence of an irresistible impulse they may perhaps furnish some evidence of the existence or absence of insane delusion. But I think, in view of the undisputed features of this case, it would only confuse and perhaps mislead the jury to give them any instruction directly upon the subject of irresistible impulse, and that this particular case does not call for any qualification for the general rule adopted, as I have mentioned, as the text of responsibility.

The twelfth instruction is drawn with reference to section 5,342 of the Revised Statutes. I do not understand that statute to create any new species of manslaughter. It uses the common law definitions or both murder and manslaughter and (perhaps in view of the doubts I have already spoken of) applies them to two cases where the mortal wound was inflicted in one jurisdiction and the death occurred in another. The terms "malice" and "maliciously," used in the statute, would have no meaning except by reference to the common law. We know that the term "malice," in the definition of murder, does not require that proof shall be given of any special hatred or ill-will to the deceased but that the deliberate intent to kill, from whatever motive, constitutes all the malice that the law requires to be shown, and that the term "without malice" in the definition of manslaughter means simply without premeditated intent, as where the killing occurs in the heat of passion or sudden quarrel. All this I will explain to the jury when it becomes necessary to charge them. But the instruction—in its use of the phrase "without malice in fact"—might convey the idea to the jury that if the killing was done from the motives declared by the prisoner, and if he had, as he says, no personal ill-will toward the

President, it was not murder. It is objectionable on this ground, and every object that could be properly sought under this head will be attained by the explanations which I have indicated to be made to the jury. It becomes important, in the first place, to settle the rules of evidence by which the jury is be guided in weighing the proofs.

In reference to the question on whom rests the burden of proof where insanity is relied on as a defence, three different and conflicting views have been held by three different courts. According to one view it is incumbent on the accused to establish the fact of his insanity at the time of commission of the alleged crime by evidence so conclusive as to exclude all reasonable doubt of it. But this view derives so little support from authority that it may be passed over without comment as inadmissible. Another view is that the defence of insanity is an affirmative one, which the party asserting it must establish to the satisfaction of the jury by at least a preponderance of evidence. That is to say, the evidence in favor of it need not be so conclusive as to leave no room for reasonable doubt, but it must have more weight with the jury than the evidence against, so that they would feel justified in finding the fact as they would find any fact in a civil suit, in which all questions of fact are decided according to the weight of the evidence. Still another view is that the sanity of the accused is just as much a part of the case of the prosecution as the homicide itself, and just as much an element in the crime of murder, the only difference being that as the law presumes every one to be sane, it is not necessary for the Government to produce affirmative evidence of the sanity, but if the jury have a reasonable doubt of the sanity they are just as much bound to acquit as if they entertained a reasonable doubt of the commission of the homicide by the accused. After a careful examination of the authorities, some of which are mere dicta and others not well considered or even consistent statements of opinions, I am satisfied that the best reasons and most weighty of them sustain the views which I now proceed to state. I have examined all the authorities with great care over and over again. The cases that are referred to in support of the second rule are somewhat more numerous than the others. Some of them, however, turn on the statutory definitions of the charge of murder. A great many of the cases are mere dicta, and some of them involve utter contradictions. Not one of them contains the least show of argument. With us there is no statutory definition of murder. We have the common law definition of murder as occurring when a homicide is committed by a person of sound memory, discretion, &c. The opinions which support the last view are decidedly entitled to most confidence. They are reasoned out from first principles and their reasonings have been unanswered and are, in my judgment, unanswerable. In the case of Stone, tried in this court a few years ago, the instructions were as follows:—"In a capital case the defence of insanity is required to be made out by most clear and convincing proof. In this case the jury must judge of the evidence offered to sustain the defence; and if, on consideration of all the evidence in connection with the assumption that what a man does is sanely done, the jury entertains a reasonable doubt as to whether the prisoner committed the homicide charged or as to whether at the time of the commission he was in a sane state of mind they must acquit him." I shall, however, adopt the suggestion which is found in some of the latter authorities—that is, not to instruct the jury to acquit if they feel a reasonable doubt about any one fact in the issue; but I shall instruct them as to the nature of the crime and as to all the elements composing it, including that of responsibility. I shall instruct them as to the presumption of innocence and sanity, and shall tell them finally that, on the whole evidence and on the consideration of both these presumptions, if they have a reasonable doubt of the guilt of the prisoner the prisoner is entitled to an acquittal.

The tenth and eleventh instructions asked for on the part of the defence do not involve any serious question. The eleventh instruction asks me to say that, "If the jury believe from the evidence that the prosecution has wilfully suppressed evidence of the mental condition of the prisoner during two weeks following the shooting of President Garfield which it was in their power to have produced in the trial, the jury have a right to take that fact into consideration as a presumption that such evidence, if it had been produced would have been unfavorable to the prosecution."

Any instruction ought to be based on some evidence in the case, and if I were to grant the instruction in that form I would be assuming that there was some evidence in the case tending to show a wilful suppression of evidence by the prosecution. I cannot so assume. It is always, however, open to either side to argue that evidence which might have been produced and which has not been produced should be regarded as injurious to the party refusing to produce it. But I do not think the Court ought to give a formal instruction in the shape of either the tenth or eleventh prayer.

At the conclusion of Judge Cox's decision the prisoner remarked:— "I am satisfied with the law as laid down by Your Honor."

Judge Cox then inquired as to the probable time that would be consumed in the argument to the jury.

Mr. Davidge said he would request three or four hours, possibly a day. Mr. Reed intimated that he would require about the same time. Mr. Scoville said that as he would have to sum up the evidence he would require at least two days, and the prisoner said, in a tone of perfect confidence, that two hours would be enough for him to settle the whole case with the jury.

As Mr. Davidge expressed a desire to have one day for preparation the Court, at half-past one, adjourned the case till Thursday morning, with the understanding that the daily sessions should be from ten to four, with an intermission of half an hour for recess.

CHAPTER XLIV.

Mr. Davidge makes Argument on the Prayers for Instructions—The Question Raised as to Whether Guiteau should Speak—Much Feeling Exhibited by Counsel on Both Sides.

ON Thursday, January 12th, there was again a large audience, and the Marshal gave notice that no one would be permitted to leave the Court till the hour of recess, and ordered the doors locked. A few moments after ten o'clock the Court was called to order, and Mr. Davidge commenced his argument with the statement that he did not intend to make a set speech, but merely desired to aid the jury, whom he highly complimented for their conduct and attention throughout the trial, in arriving at their verdict. He then proceeded to make a masterly resume of the points claimed by the defence, stating that there was but one single point for discussion and consideration —the subject of insanity. He showed that the attempt to shift the responsibility of the President's death upon the medical attendants had been abandoned. He called the attention of the jury to the definition of malice as laid down by the Court, and claimed that the degree of reason necessary to make a man responsible is very limited. "Thus you will see that a man may be here who has been styled a crank, or off his balance, and even partially insane, and yet may be abundantly responsible for crime. What is the act committed here? Murder, murder, murder by lying in wait—what is commonly called assassination. How great a degree of intelligence does it take to inform a man that that is wrong? What degree of intelligence was necessary to make a lawyer know that it was in violation of the law of the land to kill? What degree of intelligence was necessary to make a religious man know that the everlasting edict had gone from Almighty God, 'Thou shalt commit no murder?'" The prisoner repeatedly interrupted, but merely afforded counsel opportunity to call attention to the difference between the state of the man and the condition as set up by the defence. After referring to the question of inspiration, Mr. Davidge asked for a recess of half an hour, which was granted.

After recess Mr. Davidge resumed by taking up what he termed the first branch of the defence —that through disease of the brain, the prisoner when he committed the crime, was unable to appreciate the difference between right and wrong in respect of his act. He considered it almost a mockery to argue upon such a claim, but he felt it his duty to leave no claim unanswered, and expected to make it apparent that this defence was not only a false but a fabricated one. After reviewing the history of the Guiteau family, he proceeded to a review of the life and habits of the prisoner, as exhibited by the evidence adduced. He set aside as unworthy of consideration, the alleged odd conduct of Guiteau at various times and places, and asked: "Is it so very strange, gentlemen, that this prisoner should have appeared queer, when at that very time he was carrying in his breast this monstrous crime?"

After three o'clock Judge Porter suggested an adjournment, which was assented to by counsel for the defence. Some discussion then ensued as to whether the prisoner should be allowed to make the speech which he professed to have prepared, and a good deal of feeling was manifested on both sides. Guiteau became very violent, and repeatedly claimed that he appeared as his own counsel, a position which the District Attorney resented, in view of the abuse and interruptions with which the prisoner had disgraced the Court room. Judge Cox, after intimating that he could not trust the prisoner to keep within bounds, finally desired counsel for the defence to examine the proposed speech and ascertain whether there was anything in it which should be brought before the Court, and report to him in the morning. Without stating, however, whether he would permit the prisoner to speak, Judge Cox ordered an adjournment.

On Thursday, January 13th, on the opening of Court, Guiteau apologized for his remarks against Mr. Davidge the day before, but added that while he was wrong about Davidge, he was right on Corkhill. Mr. Davidge resumed his argument, and dissected the evidence of witnesses for the defence to demolish Mr. Scoville's theory that the prisoner was an imbecile. He said the prisoner upon the stand had shown wonderful memory, logical reason and intellectual ability. In reference to the question of morality, he claimed that the prisoner had been shown to be such a monster of corruption, deceit, depravity and wickedness that the country looked on with a shudder. He cited the *Inter-Ocean* scheme as a proof of the prisoner's audacity and egotism. Commenting upon the testimony of Dr. Spitzka, he said the witness never denied the prisoner's legal responsibility, and even his evidence brought the prisoner within the reach of law and punishment. After recess Mr. Davidge took up the expert testimony, and claimed that of the cloud of witnesses of this class, with two exceptions, they could not take the stand and swear to the prisoner's sanity. The two moral insanity men, neither of whom could or would admit that he believed in a God, were permitted by the defence to retire. In answer to the prisoner's claim of Divine inspiration, Mr. Davidge read the first chapter of the Epistle of James, 13th to 15th verses, inclusive. The prisoner throughout the day offensively interrupted counsel, who took but little notice, except on one occasion, when, turning to the Judge, he said: "Let him go on. I will hang him upon his own testimony." Again to the prisoner's testimony, Mr. Davidge pointedly singled out its various phases and claimed that the true explanation of the crime was to be found in the traits which had been developed of inordinate vanity, desire of notoriety and reckless egotism. Mr. Davidge read in detail the evidence of General Reynolds, during which he was continually interrupted by the prisoner.

In concluding his comments upon the testimony Mr. Davidge said: "Now, one word, and a very short word. I told you in the beginning that I did not come here to make a set speech. I told you that I came here to help as far as I could (and to help honestly) a jury of my country in the discharge of an important and solemn duty. I began my remarks without an exordium, and I close them without peroration, except to say to you that your countrymen and Christendom are waiting for your verdict. I thank you, gentlemen, for the attention you have given me."

The prisoner.—"And I thank you, Mr. Davidge. That is a very light speech. I hope Porter will go light, too. You had better see General Arthur, Mr. Porter, before you begin to talk. I wrote him a note on this matter the other day."

The Court then, at five minutes past three o'clock, adjourned.

CHAPTER XLV.

The Court Refuses to Allow Guiteau to Speak—Mr. Reed makes his Argument—He Also Makes the Startling Discovery that Charlotte Corday was Insane.

ON Saturday, January 14th, the proceedings were as usual opened by the prisoner, who as soon as he had entered the dock, stated that he had received several checks representing fifteen thousand dollars, and supposed that some of them were good.

Mr. Scoville rose and stated that the defence would like to know to what conclusion the Court had arrived in respect to the prisoner addressing the jury. He called the Court's attention to the fact that a precedent for that could be found in the case of Harrington, a former United States Attorney for the District of Columbia.

The Court stated that he had been informed that the prisoner was preparing an address to the jury. He would be loth in a capital case to deny any prisoner an opportunity to present a proper argument in his own behalf. But he was persuaded that any address from this prisoner would partake of the character of his former testimony and interruptions; that it would be a rehash of his testimony. No person had a right to do that.

It would be grossly improper to permit such testimony to go before the jury. The Court would not make the experiment. The counsel for the defence might examine the prisoner's manuscript and, if they thought proper, read it to the jury.

The prisoner in an excited manner claimed to represent himself, and in such capacity as counsel, to take exception to the ruling. He further threatened that the Court would go down to future ages with a black stain upon his name if the ruling was maintained.

Judge Cox without heeding the prisoner's remarks, gave counsel a sign to commence the argument.

MR. REED'S ARGUMENT.

Mr. Reed began by complimenting the jury on the care and attention they had bestowed upon the details of this remarkable trial, and explained that he should simply talk with them on the evidence as between neighbors. Commenting upon the fact that Mr. Davidge had occupied two days with his address, Mr. Reed claimed that this showed the grave apprehension on the part of the prosecution lest something might have appeared in the case which would make the jury say that this man was a lunatic and irresponsible. He said that at the time this awful offence was committed, every one who read the details, instinctively believed that the man must be insane. He believed that if the spirit of the dead President could appear before the jury, he would say to them, "Let him free, he cannot have been sane." If the jury after returning to their room solemnly and seriously came to the conclusion that the man was sane at the time of his offence, they could not hesitate nor falter in saying that he was guilty, but if they had a reasonable doubt of his sanity, it would be best for the cause of free government throughout the world that the jury should say so by their verdict. He then read from the fourth chapter of Matthew as to the healing of lunatics by the

GUITEAU, THE ASSASSIN. 649

Saviour, and adjured the jury to heal this man, not hang him and put him to death. He then went over the history of the prisoner's life, and claimed that the incident of his striking his father was the first proof of insanity, and the raising of an axe against his sister was further evidence of it. He cited the letters of the prisoner at the time he left the Oneida Community as proofs of an unsound mind.

He reminded the jury of the act of Charlotte Corday in poniarding in his bath, Marat, then the chief man of the French nation, and how she was guillotined in four or seven days afterwards. The picture of that fair French girl could be seen in the Corcoran Art Gallery, looking through the bars of her prison, appealing to posterity, insane. Her execution had disgraced the name of the French nation. He also referred to the cases of Lawrence who had fired at President Jackson; Hadfield, who had fired at George III. of England, and Oxford, who had fired at Queen Victoria; in all of which cases, the prisoners had been found not guilty by reason of insanity and had been sent to insane asylums. He drew a parallel between the case of Oxford and the present case. Oxford, like Guiteau, had bought a pistol and practised with it. He had been deliberate, his intention had been fixed, yet he had been acquitted. He also pointed out the similarity existing between this case and the case of William Lawrence, who attempted to shoot President Jackson. He read a number of the interruptions by the prisoner in the latter case and compared them to the frequent interruptions and (to some extent) boisterous manner of Guiteau. Lawrence had been acquitted. He read the Lawrence case to show that the present case was not the only one in which the prisoner had disturbed the peace and quiet of the Court room.

Branching off on to the discussion of the instructions of the Court, Mr. Reed called the attention of the jury to the wording of the instruction defining the test of responsibility for an act to be "whether he knew the difference between right and wrong in respect of that act." Mr. Davidge, he asserted, had repeated and repeated that the test was "whether he knew the difference between right and wrong," and had failed to quote the remainder of the instruction.

Mr. Davidge denied that he had done so, but Mr. Reed declared that he could not be mistaken on that point.

You twelve men, continued Mr. Reed, sitting there to-day on the facts and the evidence are superior to all powers on the earth. No emperor, no potentate, no combination of potentates, no court, no president has any right whatever to invade you upon that question. You are superior to all the powers of the earth on the evidence in this case. Every man of you is a king. No insinuation that you are to be governed by anybody else is to be considered by you. You and you alone are supreme on the question of fact. You and you alone are to say what the evidence is, what witnesses shall be believed, what disbelieved and what weight shall be given to the testimony of one witness or another. Your consciences under your oaths to your God are to be your only guide. If any one man among you, when he shall have seriously and solemnly considered this case in the jury room, shall feel within himself, "I have a fair, honest oubt whether this man was sane at the time," it is the duty of that juror before his Maker to say, "I cannot find him guilty." If one man so feels the other eleven have no right to dictate to him.

He reviewed the expert testimony, and claimed that if the evidence of Detective McElfresh and the stenographer Bailey had not been suppressed by the prosecution, it would have spoken in thunder tones in behalf of the prisoner. He severely condemned Mr. Davidge's statement that the prisoner's family ought to have cast him aside as a wretch, and branded the proposition as simply monstrous and inhuman. He referred to the testimony of Mr. Reynolds as that of a sneak and a spy, yet claimed that that very evidence sustained the theory of mental derangement. In conclusion after drawing a picture of the final scenes in the event of conviction, he asserted that such a verdict and the execution of the consequent sentence would be an infamy beyond description. He thanked the jury for their attention, and said: "I only ask of you pray do that which shall not in after years bring the blush of shame to your cheeks."

The prisoner who had maintained a running fire of interruptions and contradictions throughout the address, now exclaimed: "Reed is a good fellow, but I would not give a cent a bushel for his rubbish. If I could only have a talk with that jury, I could give them the right theory." The Court then at 3.10 P. M., adjourned until Monday.

CHAPTER XLVI.

Mr. Scoville Commences his Argument and Speaks for Five Days—
A General Summary of a Long Argument made Against Time
to Effect Delay.

ON Monday, January 16th, Guiteau, contrary to his usual custom did not make his morning speech, but sat quietly in the dock and at first listened patiently, yet intently to Mr. Scoville's speech.

MR. SCOVILLE'S ARGUMENT.

Mr. Scoville began by thanking the jury for the patience with which they had listened to the evidence, and expressed his obligations to members of the Bar all over the country for the generous, unasked for assistance which they had rendered him, and which had enabled him to present the case not wholly at a disadvantage. He appealed to the jurors to divest their minds wholly of any pre conceived opinions on the case. They should not come to any conclusion until the last word has dropped from the Judge in his final charge. They ought to wait until they went to the jury room and sat down and weighed the facts of the case, and with calm, sincere minds, seek to arrive at what was the truth and nothing but the truth. That was all that the defence asked. He would not attempt to appeal to the sentiments of the jury, the gentleman who would follow him (Mr. Porter) would attempt to influence their emotion; he would address himself to their hearts rather than their intellects ; and if the question was to be decided by emotion, by passion, by prejudice, by fear, then the defendant was lost—the defendant would be hanged. But the jury under their oaths could not be influenced by any such consideration. What was the issue? It was whether or not the prisoner was insane on the 2d of July last when he shot the President. He characterized Mr. Davidge as a fair, honest man, but stated that insensibly he had not in all cases given the jury a fair, full, strict, honest statement of the evidence. Neither had he given them a full, fair, honest statement of the law. He (Mr. Scoville) would before he concluded, take the liberty of criticising the conduct of the other counsel for the prosecution more at length, simply because they deserved it. The speaker claimed that Mr. Davidge had unintentionally misrepresented him in quoting from his opening address, which he proceeded to read somewhat at length in order to place himself in a proper light before the jury. He had not (as Mr. Davidge told the jury he had) characterized the prisoner as a fool. He charged that in this case there had been a conspiracy on the part of the District Attorney, Mr. Porter, Mr. Davidge and the expert witnesses (Drs. Hamilton, MacDonald, Kempster, Gray and Worcester), and the object of the conspiracy was to hang the defendant. He also complained of the conduct of the press in prejudging the case. One of his specifications in the charge against the conspirators in the present case was that they had attempted to pervert the law. Referring to Mr. Porter's repudiation of the idea that Judge Noah Davis, of New York, sat on the same bench as Barnard and Cardozo, Mr. Scoville declared that the two latter judges had never done a more reprehensible thing than Judge Davis did when he attempted to promulgate a judicial decision not bearing on the case before him, but intended to influence this case with which he had nothing to do.

A passing remark from Mr. Davidge brought out the prisoner in one of his usual exhortations. He told Mr. Davidge to shut up and keep quiet. He had talked for two days and had not said anything.

An invitation by Mr. Scoville that he should be corrected by the prosecution if he made any misstatement of the evidence, was declined by Mr. Porter, with the remark that they didn't propose to turn the argument into a town meeting.

"Then," said Mr. Scoville, "I tell you that I propose—if Mr. Porter shall in his closing argument falsify the law or the evidence—to correct him then and there every time."

"So shall I," shouted the prisoner.

"I do not propose," continued Mr. Scoville, "to let Mr. Porter put his own coloring on the facts and to distort them. If he makes a single allegation of facts or of law that is false I shall try to prevent it."

"I will attend to him," the prisoner again shouted.

GUITEAU, THE ASSASSIN.

Mr. Porter (ironically to Scoville).—"Mr. Guiteau will attend to me."

Mr. Scoville proceeded to criticise some of Mr. Davidge's propositions in his argument to the jury, complaining of misrepresentations of the law. One of these propositions was, that the case must turn on "the iron rule whether the man knew the difference between right and wrong." That was not the rule here (Mr. Scoville said), it had been the rule in England 250 years ago, where, if a man had sense enough left to know more than a wild beast, he must be executed. It had been well termed "the wild beast rule." It was not the law of this country, except as laid down by Judge Davis, of New York.

The Prisoner.—"And Judge Davis' jury rebuked him. They had more sense than he had."

Mr. Porter (sarcastically)—"The rebuke consisted in the jury convicting the prisoner."

Mr. Scoville proceeded with his argument. As to the power to discriminate between right and wrong, he argued that from the prisoner's standpoint, from his diseased view of it, the act was not wrong. It was right, and so Mr. Davidge's proposition was not a correct proposition of law. The inmate of an insane asylum when he attacked another inmate or an officer of the institution, knew that he was committing a crime, knew the difference between the right and the wrong of the act; but nobody ever heard of one of these insane people being held to account in a Court of Justice under this "iron rule of law." If he (Scoville) had never studied law, he would still have known enough to be confident that that was not a correct proposition of law.

Mr. Scoville cited several similar quotations from Mr. Davidge's argument, in order to show that the counsel representing the prosecution were wilfully falsifying the law. It occurred some thirty times he said, in Mr. Davidge's argument. The prisoner might have had on the 2d of July last, enough sense and judgment to know that it would be wrong to pick up a pocketbook which he found on a bench in the railroad station and transfer it to his pocket. That was not the question. If the prisoner was on that morning overpowered by the consciousness (coming through his diseased mind) that the Lord was requiring him to do an act for the good of the country and to save the nation from war, then it was the result of a diseased mind, and the act was in the prisoner's view of it, right.

Commenting upon the fact that the prosecution had raked up

every little act in the prisoner's life on which the jury were asked to convict and hang this man, he said there was only one thing in his history for which he should hide his head, and that was the crime of adultery. And even that crime was not one which would justify the hanging of this man; and he recounted the incident of the woman taken in adultery, and how when Christ looked up after writing in the sand, her accusers were all gone.

In commenting upon the expert testimony, Mr. Scoville spoke of Dr. Gray as the big gun of the prosecution—the man who had stood up in the witness box and fired off his testimony with his fingers.

At this stage of the argument, the Court took a recess for half an hour.

After the recess Mr. Scoville proceeded with his argument, pointing out several places in Mr. Davidge's address, in which he alleged there was a deviation from or misrepresentation of the testimony. After speaking some half an hour he was interrupted by the prisoner, who said: "Davidge had better read my speech. It is published in the "New York Herald" this morning, over a page of it. I must have an understanding with his Honor as to whether shall have a chance to deliver it or not."

Mr. Scoville proceeded with his criticism of Mr. Davidge's argument. While he was talking Attorney-General Brewster entered the Court-room and took a seat beside Judge Cox. A good deal of time was spent over the testimony of Stephen English, the prisoner continuing to interject his own remarks.

Referring to Shaw's testimony as to the incident of the oroide watch Scoville said (ironically), "And this is another step in the vast career of crime which leads on to the gallows."

Referring to the testimony of Shaw and his clerk as to the conversation in which the prisoner said he would imitate Wilkes Booth, Mr. Scoville declared his belief that in that matter both those witnesses had perjured themselves. Shaw wanted to bring this man to the gallows. He (Scoville) could honor Mason, McGill and Jones as compared with Shaw. They were willing to take their lives in their hands, if necesssary. They were willing, at least, to stake their personal liberty on the issue. But Shaw sought to hang this man without assuming even the risk of a prosecution for perjury.

"This whole Shaw business," the prisoner interposed, "is a lie from beginning to end, and any decent man will say so."

Then as the Court was declared adjourned at three o'clock, Guiteau said, "I ask your Honor to read my speech this evening, because I want to talk to you about it to-morrow morning."

ON TUESDAY, JANUARY 17th, the prisoner came in very quiet and subdued, but with an expression on his face that must have reminded any close observer of the alleged frog in the fable, just prior to the pretentious and disastrous attempt to inflate himself to the bigness of a bullock. Mr. Scoville rose to resume his address, and then Guiteau leaned forward, enquiring insinuatingly, "Shall I do it now?" All eyes were directed towards him at once, since nobody could divine whether this mental acrobat was about to shoot the judge, turn a somersault, or make a speech. Mr. Scoville replied, Oh yes! I forgot: and then turning to the Court, stated that the prisoner wished to say a few words. Judge Cox wearily nodded assent, and Guiteau posed himself and then proceeded to read in a very pretentious oratorical style, the following statement:

"I intend no disrespect to this honorable Court, I desire no controversy with this honorable Court. In general I am satisfied with the law as proposed by Your Honor. But I have a still broader view of the law which I ask Your Honor to follow—to wit, that if the jury believe that I believed that it was right for me to remove the President because I had special divine authority so to do, and was forced to it by the Deity they will acquit me on the ground of transitory mania. Sickles, McFarland and Hiscock (meaning Cole) were acquitted on the ground of transitory mania. In my speech, published yesterday in all the leading newspapers of the country, and which I presume Your Honor has read, I gave my reasons for asking Your Honor so to charge. Mr. Reed made a brilliant and lawyer-like plea for the defence, and Mr. Scoville is making a strong argument on his theory. But neither Mr. Reed nor Mr. Scoville represents me in this defence. I am here as my own counsel, and have been from the beginning. No one represents me to this jury. I know my feelings and inspirations in removing the President, and I have set it forth in my speech yesterday. And I ask Your Honor, in the name of justice, in the name of the American judiciary, in the name of the American people, to allow me to address that jury of my countrymen in a case where my life may be at stake. If a man upon that jury has a doubt as to his duty to acquit me my speech will probably settle it in my favor. Therefore, in the interest of justice, it is of the greatest importance that the jury should hear me in my defence."

Judge Cox—"I will take the matter into consideration."

The Prisoner—"Thank you, sir."

Mr. Scoville then resumed his argument. He occupied the whole of the morning in complaints of the unfairness of the prosecution, and had some lively colloquies with the opposing counsel. After recess he took up a review of the prisoner's life from about the year 1859, and insisted upon a parallel between Guiteau and his father, who he contended was always on the border-line of insanity, though able to attend to business. He claimed that the failure in business and consequent lack of a steady employment on the part of the prisoner had caused the rapid development of insanity in his case. Mr. Scoville continued in this strain till the hour of adjournment. Guiteau made sarcastic comments throughout the day, but without seriously disturbing the argument.

ON WEDNESDAY JANUARY 18th, as soon as the prisoner entered the Court, he turned to Judge Cox and said: "I presume your Honor will allow me to address the jury when Mr. Scoville gets through?" Judge Cox intimated that he would consider the question at such time.

Mr. Scoville, resuming, discussed the statistics of the insane criminals introduced in evidence by the prosecution. He claimed that it was of benefit to the defence, but an exactly similar case to the prisoner's he did not think had ever existed. He did not think the world had ever seen, or would ever see, a second Guiteau. He proceeded to denounce Dr. Gray as one of the conspirators to hang the prisoner. After depicting the horrors of crime as often shown in the acts of insane criminals, Mr. Scoville went out of his way to denounce certain prominent politicians who were seeking to hide their own shame behind the disgrace of this poor prisoner, and make him the scape-goat of their crimes. He then at some length denounced by name President Arthur, General Grant and Mr. Conkling as being morally and intellectually responsible for this crime. This denunciation created a profound sensation in the court-room, and provoked several heated discussions during the recess. After recess Mr. Scoville continued with a review of the evidence, and called attention to various incidents in Guiteau's life, arguing his insanity as evidenced by the undoubted lack of something in his mental composition possessed by other men. Guiteau called out, sarcastically, "Give them that dog story; it cost Corkhill $200 to get it here." Mr. Scoville continued to speak until three o'clock, when the court adjourned.

ON THURSDAY, JANUARY 19th, the prisoner resumed his practice of opening the proceedings, and exclaimed in a loud tone: "The decision of the New York Court of Appeals comes with so much force at the present moment that I desire to call attention to it. It comes with great grace from the Empire State, from that grand old State of the Republic, the state that sends forth the brains, the money and the commerce of the nation. It is a great step forward in the law of insanity. Hitherto the law has been that the burden of proof was on the defendant, but the Court of Appeals with great magnanimity, says that the burden of proof is on this prosecution to prove that the man not only committed the act, but also that he was sane at the time he committed it. In the name of justice, and in the name of the American people, and in the name of the American Judiciary, I desire to thank those gentlemen of the Court of Appeals of the State of New York."

Mr. Scoville then resumed his argument. He complained that the prosecution had suppressed the evidence of Detective McElfresh, and had mutilated a letter written by the prisoner before producing it in evidence. They had also destroyed their notes of their interviews with the prisoner during the first two weeks after the shooting. He went again over the record of the prisoner's life, interrupted occasionally by the prisoner, and by retorts from Mr. Davidge and Col. Corkhill. Alluding to the evidence of Dr. North, Mr. Scoville complained that the District Attorney had without reason insulted the witness by asking if he had ever been indicted; but the laugh was turned against Mr. Scoville when District Attorney Corkhill said he remembered having tried the man in this court on an appeal from the Police Court. After recess Mr. Scoville continued to complain of the prosecution and criticise its witnesses. He classed Dr. Worcester as one of the government conspirators and continued in this strain until the hour of adjournment, when he stated that he should probably conclude next day.

On Friday, January 20th, as soon as the Court was called to order, Mr. Scoville resumed his address promising that he should endeavor to confine his remarks to the facts as detailed in the evidence of the experts.

He began his review of the medical testimony by commenting upon the evidence given by Dr. Hamilton. If the jury discovered that that gentleman had a disposition to testify in favor of one side or the other that fact must detract from the value of the testimony. The jury could not give it as much credit as if it had been given plainly and frankly. Mr. Scoville then proceeded to dissect the evidence given by Dr. Hamilton in order to show that the witness was strongly prejudiced against the defence, and instanced a single answer given by him whereon he had seventeen times used strong adjectives which could tell against the prisoner where they were not necessary to express his meaning. The use of these adjectives was possibly inadvertent; but still they left the foot tracks by means of which the feeling of the witness could be followed and discovered. He read from the testimony of Dr. Hamilton that the prisoner's head was perfectly symmetrical, and declared that it was not often that a compass and rule could demonstrate that in giving his opinion a man was telling a lie. But he would show the jury a diagram of the prisoner's head as drawn according to rule.

This elicited a sneer from the District Attorney which provoked an angry colloquy until the Court stopped it by sustaining Mr. Scoville's right to illustrate by measurement.

Mr. Scoville then referred somewhat at length to the shape of the prisoner's head illustrating his remarks by an examination of the cast which has been placed in evidence. He ridiculed the testimony of Dr. Kempster upon the subject of asymmetry in heads, declaring that his representation of the shape of the District Attorney's head was no more the shape of it than it was the shape of a square cube. Dr. Kempster's diagram of the prisoner's head was false, and,he (Scoville) would, if necessary, bring the prisoner before the jury, and by actual measurement of his head show that Kempster lied when he said that his diagram was a correct representation of Guiteau's head.

Mr. Scoville in the further course of his review of the medical testimony was charged by the District Attorney with misrepresenting a witness by not reading the whole of one of his answers. In making his charge the District Attorney made the statement of a fact which had not appeared in evidence and Mr. Scoville warned him that he would do the same if the act were repeated. The District Attorney had done the same thing yesterday in reference to the witness Moss, whom he asserted had been tried in this very court upon an information. He (Scoville) had since discovered that Colonel Corkhill's prejudice against the man arose from the fact that he had once been sued by a servant for $3 and had been tried by Moss, who was a Justice of the Peace. That was on record.

The Prisoner—If Corkhill was sued for all he owes it would take all the courts in this city to do the business.

Mr. Scoville continued and dwelt at great length upon the asymmetry of the prisoner's head as compared with other heads, and having mentioned the District Attorney's among others, the prisoner stated that, in his opinion, "Corkhill's is a swell head."

The District Attorney once or twice interrupted Mr. Scoville, and on one of these occasions Mr. Davidge sarcastically exclaimed:— "Don't interfere with Mr. Scoville. I am afraid he will stop if you do. Don't stop, Mr. Scoville." The irony of this remark was appreciated, even Mr. Scoville joining good humoredly in the laughter which ensued.

Mr. Scoville resumed his argument, criticising the testimony given by Dr. Gray, of the Utica asylum, whom he characterized as the big gun which the prosecution had reserved until the close of the case, supposing that he would carry the jury by his grand, round, well proportioned, overwhelming declarations. Quoting the case of an insane man who was thriftless in his family affairs, Mr. Scoville said he supposed that Colonel Corkhill would call it a case of devilish depravity. "Yes," cried the prisoner, "Corkhill is authority on the devil. Gray is a big gun with a big mouth. I will mark him."

The Court then at fifteen minutes past twelve took a recess for forty-five minutes.

After the recess Mr. Scoville, addressing the jury, said that if he attempted to follow out all the evidence and take up the witnesses in detail and point out the inconsistencies in the testimony on behalf of the prosecution, he could easily detain the jury a week longer. But he would detain them but a short time this afternoon and then submit the case to them for their consideration. He would dwell no longer on the facts of the case, but would simply mention some considerations which should be called to their attention. Human laws were made for sane people. Laws were enacted to reward or punish people who were clearly of sound mind.

He then drifted into an argument tending to advocate the abolition of capital punishment. Reverting to the state of the prisoner's mind he contended that the very fact of the prisoner restraining his hand went to prove that he was acting under delusion; for had his act been one of depravity, as the prosecution claimed, he would not have needed another night to allow that depravity to be developed in his heart.

He then passed to an exordium upon the duty of jurors and the great privileges of trial by jury, remarking that he never expected to see the day when jury trial shall be abolished, unless, unfortunately he should live to see the day when civil liberty shall groan in the dust.

In conclusion he said:—You, gentlemen, are liable to err. No twelve men could be collected in the United States who would not be liable to make erroneous decisions; but when we collect twelve men

GUITEAU, THE ASSASSIN. 661

after careful questioning, fellow citizens who understand all our relations of life and society, who know the value of property, the value of liberty, the value of life; men who have had varied experience, who have come here from the East, from the West, from over the seas, in one common citizenship building up, maintaining, resolved to perpetuate these institutions, I feel more secure in the proper administration than I would under any other mode of adjudication. We are safe and shall be safe in the juries of our country so long as they are honest and well intentioned. It is not requisite that you have a high degree of intelligence; it is requisite that you have honest hearts, cool heads and a disposition to do what is right. But above all you should have moral courage, stability of character, moral stamina to determine that what may come, what may be said, you will do what is right and just toward your fellow men and in the sight of your God. That is what I expect of you. I don't ask you now to find for or against this defendant. I simply ask you to take the evidence into consideration; I ask you never to question yourselves as to what will be the result of your verdict in regard to your position in society; as to whether your fellow men will approve it or not; as to the result in any way except that you should believe it to be just. You should not be influenced by any personal motives, by any motive outside of a sincere desire to decide this case according to law and evidence; and when you have reached a conclusion in your own mind I ask that you will render a verdict without fear or without hope or favor of reward, and I believe, gentlemen, that you will do it. I leave the case with you, thanking you for your careful attention.

The District Attorney then rose and called the Court's attention to the desire of the prisoner to address the jury. At the time that the application was made he had opposed it very earnestly. The case had now occupied seventy days, and he did not desire a repetition of it. He did not intend that any error should get into the record upon which there was any possibility that a new trial should be allowed, and he therefore, on behalf of the Government, withdrew all objection to the prisoner being heard.

Judge Cox stated that some of his brethren had very serious doubts whether, in a capital case the prisoner could be denied the right to address the jury. He would permit the prisoner to speak

The prisoner.—"Will your Honor allow me to go on in the morning? My mind is not perfectly clear now."

Mr. Davidge inquired how long the prisoner would require, and Guiteau replied, "About two hours. I talk very fast. I will commence at ten and probably close at twelve."

Mr. Davidge stated that Mr. Porter was in very delicate health and was unable to attend Court to-day. He did not think that the gentleman would care to go on with his argument to-morrow, and suggested that the case go over until Monday.

The prisoner.—"I have no objection to the case going over until Monday morning."

Mr. Davidge.—"Oh, no. We want the prisoner to-morrow."

The prisoner.—"All right, Judge. You be here and hear me."

After another little spat between the District Attorney and Mr. Reed which the prisoner closed by saying, "Don't do that Reed, you will get the Court down on us." An adjournment was taken with the understanding that Guiteau would read his address in the morning.

CHAPTER XLVII.

Guiteau Makes the Closing Argument for the Defence, and Showers His Thanks upon the New York Court of Appeals His Previously Maligned Counsel and the American Press.

ON Saturday, January 21st, the last farcical act of this great drama was played, and the curtain forever rung down on the most sanguinary mime, or most comical criminal that the world has ever seen.

Upon entering the room, Guiteau took a seat in the witness box, remarking as he laid out his papers: "I sit down because I can speak better, not that I am afraid of being shot. This shooting business is getting played out."

At an intimation from Judge Cox, the prisoner carefully arranged his glasses, and with a flourish began to read from manuscript as follows:

> The prosecution pretend that I am a wicked man. Mr. Scoville and Mr. Reed think I am a lunatic, and I presume you think I am. I certainly was a lunatic on July 2d, when I fired on the President and the American people generally, and I presume you think I was. Can you imagine anything more insane than my going to that depot and shooting the President of the United States? You are here to say whether I was sane or insane at the moment I fired that shot. You have nothing to do with my condition before or since that shot was fired. You must say by your verdict sane or insane at the moment the shot was fired. If you have any doubt of my sanity at the moment you must give me the benefit of that doubt and acquit me. That is, if you have any doubt whether I fired that shot, or as the agent of the Deity. If I

fired it on my own account I was sane. If I fired it supposing myself the agent of the Deity I was insane and you must acquit. This is the law as given in the recent decision of the New York Court of Appeals. It revolutionizes the old rules and is a grand step forward in the law of insanity. It is worthy of this age of railroads, electricity and telephones, and it well comes from the progressive State of New York. I have no hesitation in saying that it is a special providence in my favor and I ask this Court and jury so to consider it. Some of the best people of America think me the greatest man of this age, and this feeling is growing. They believe in my inspiration and that Providence and I have really saved the nation another war. My speech setting forth in detail my defence was telegraphed Sunday to all the leading papers and published Monday morning, and now I am permitted by His Honor to deliver it to you. Only I here desire to express my indebtedness to the American press for the able and careful way they have reported this case. The American press is a vast engine. They generally bring down their man when they open upon him. They opened upon me with all their batteries last July because they did not know my motive and inspiration. Now that this trial has developed my motive and inspiration their bitterness has gone. Some editors are double-headed. They curse you to day and bless you tomorrow, as they suppose that public opinion is for or against you, which shows the low grade of their humanity. I desire to thank my brother and sister and my counsel, Scoville and Reed, for their valuable services. I intend to give my counsel ample fees, especially Scoville. He is a stanch man and a hero, and I commend him to the great Northwest as a fine lawyer and a Christian gentleman. We have differed as to this defence. He has his theory and I have mine. I told him to work his theory as he thought best and he has done it in a splendid way, and I commend him for it. Considering his slight experience as an advocate he showed himself as a man of marked resources. In other words, you cannot tell what is in a man until he has a chance. Some men never have a chance and go down in obscurity. There are plenty of brains in this world. Not every man has a chance to develop his brain. It is brain and opportunity under Providence that makes a great man. I return thanks to the Marshal and his aids, to the Superintendent of Police and his force, to the warden of the jail and his keepers and to General Ayres and his forces for services rendered me. I return thanks to this honorable Court and bright jury for their long and patient attention to this case. I am not here as a wicked man or a lunatic. I am here as a patriot, and my speech is as follows—I read from the New York Herald. He then proceeded to read the rambling effusion he had previously given to the Press. In a declamatory manner he rolled forth his sentences, holding the paper in one hand and with the other gestulating and emphasizing his utterances. The words, "Rally round the flag, boys," he repeated in a sing-song tone, waving his arm in the air above his head. "And for this I suffer in bonds as a patriot," he quoted in an oratorical manner, and then repeating the sentence he allowed his voice to tremble so that the words were nearly inaudible. The trembling in his voice continued till he spoke about his mother and declared that he had always been "a lover the Lord," when he broke down completely, and, applying his handkerchief to his eyes, wiped away the tears which, naturally or forced for the purpose of exciting sympathy, coursed down his cheeks. However, he immediately recovered himself, and in his usual tone of voice proceeded with his address. When he came to his description of the attempts made upon his life by Mason and Jones he stood up for the purpose of the more vividly pointing out to the jury the narrow escapes which he had had. With something of pride he held up his arm and showed the rent made in his coat by the bullet fired by Jones and made his old declaration that it was a proof that the Lord was watching over him. A laugh ran through the audience as the prisoner read and reread his declaration that it would be perfectly safe for him to walk the streets of Washington or New York. Coming down to the extracts from his mail he read them with extreme unction, particularly the rhyming one dated, Philadelphia, New Year's Day, 1882, which he read in a sing-song way, which caused a laugh among the audience. Reaching that portion of the speech where an abstract from his address to the American people is inserted, he folded up the paper, took off his glasses and squaring himself in his chair proceeded to repeat the extract from memory. In doing this he assumed his most oratorical style, modulating the tones of his voice, using both arms to aid him in emphasizing his dramatic utterances and as far as possible acting the extract. Coming down to to his quotation from "John Brown's Body," he threw back his head and sang a verse from that old song, much to the amusement of the spectators. He read from his speech:—"Put my body in the ground if you will: that is all you can do. But thereafter comes a day of reckoning. The mills of the gods grind slow, but they grind sure, and they will grind to atoms every man that injures me;" and supplemented it with the remark, "as sure as a hair of my head is injured this nation will go down in the dust, and don't you forget it."

He then proceeded to read his speech to a close, without any noteworthy incident, and then the Court adjourned until Monday

CHAPTER XLVIII.

Judge Porter's Masterly Closing Argument for the Prosecution—The Calm, Consciencious, Comprehensive Charge of Judge Cox to the Jury—Retirement and Deliberation of the Jury for only Thirty Minutes—The Verdict—"GUILTY! AND SO SAY ALL OF US."

MONDAY, January 23d, 1882, will long be remembered as the initiative of the closing scenes of one of the most astounding trials, in connection with one of the most atrocious crimes ever yet brought home to and fixed upon a depraved and desperate human being, the abnormal product of unbounded liberty prostituted to the uttermost limit of devilish license. To say that the Court Room was crowded to its fullest capacity, while thousands vainly strove for admittance, is but to give a faint idea of the anxiety manifested by the public. At ten o'clock, when the prisoner was brought in, he, as usual, gave vent to his egotism by recounting his doings of the previous day, the extent and contents of his mail correspondence, and his feelings of positive repugnance to a suggestion that President Arthur should tender him a Cabinet position. It was the last act of the ghastly farce, and the egotistical, murderous mime played out his part before finally washing off his paint. The Court was formally opened, and at five minutes past ten o'clock Judge Porter began his address. In order to present this masterly effort in its most perfect form, we shall eliminate the continuous, impertinent and blasphemous interruptions of the prisoner, save where they formed the text for Judge Porter's remarks. The terms "liar" and "whelp" were among the mildest epithets which the wretch, in the terror of his desperation, heaped upon the Counsel, as boldly and clearly the revolting outlines of a vicious life were rapidly sketched, and the terrible details filled in, until a perfect picture of the miscreant and his miserable crime had been presented to the jury.

JUDGE PORTER' ARGUMENT.

Judge Porter, whose voice was weak from the effects of his recent illness, commenced by alluding to the weariness, which he shared with the jury, in consequence of the long and tedious trial, and spoke of his own midnight labors in connection with the case, but the nature of the duty imposed upon him was such, that he should have felt as an accessory after the fact of this crime, if he omitted to say such words as his strength permitted to aid the jury in reaching a conclusion. Thus far in this case the trial had been practically conducted by the prisoner and his counsel, Mr. Scoville. Everybody had been arraigned, everybody denounced, everybody interrupted and silenced at their will. He had received notice from both of them that he was to be interrupted and silenced now, and that he was not to be permitted to utter anything which any of them might disapprove. His strength was very much gone, but he believed that what he desired to say to the jury would be said, and that what would be said would be said in no rhetorical form. He would deal only with the evidence. Two days had been spent by Mr. Scoville in the opening for the defence. The purpose of that was obvious.

Mr. Scoville knew, what the prosecution did not, that the trial was to be a long one, and that it was important that he should begin the case with iterations and reiterations, in favor of the prisoner and against the Government. The jury had heard the evidence—much of it over two months ago. They had heard it amid clamor, objections, interruptions, vituperations and blasphemy. The jury were compelled to rely upon their memory for the points of that voluminous testimony. Of course the prisoner's counsel knew that, under such circumstances, the jury could not recall every point made at the time. He knew that at the close of the trial much of that would be obscured, that it was easy to confound statements and impressions made in and derived from the opening speech. He would say, in justice to the prisoner, that of the three arguments which had been made by him and his associate counsel, the one most free from objection was the one delivered by himself. Aside from the impiousness of his statements, it was free from the deliberate misstatements and perversion of testimony that ran through the arguments of his associate counsel. In the addresses of the other two counsel, and especially of Mr. Scoville, there had been an attempt to carry out the plan first proposed, of misrepresentation and perversion of testimony. It was deliberate, designed, cunning, done by subterfuge and indirection. After alluding to the threatened interruptions by the prisoner and his counsel, Judge Porter said : "My relations to this case are simply those imposed on me by the Government, and most cordially accepted by me, because I believe that the interests of public justice demands that the cold-blooded and deliberate assassin of President Garfield shall not leave this dock until he is under sentence of death, that he shall leave off the shackles he wears, only to pass to the shackles of the murderer's cell. He, in the meantime, invokes the mercy of that God who spares even him who spares not. He did not spare Garfield, though he said he was a good man whom he was transferring to Paradise; he did not spare that wife who, by her leaning on Garfield's arm, saved his life on one occasion. He swears that if she had leaned on the President's arm on the 2d of July it would have saved him. He did not spare that aged mother whom the son so loved. Overcome by this overwhelming feeling, even on his inauguration day, after President Garfield had kissed the Book of God and taken his constitutional oath, he with those same lips pressed the lips of that mother in the presence of the American people. He did not spare her. He spared no one. A murderer at heart then, he is a murderer at heart now, and he has shown it. You, gentlemen, have witnessed the daring

GUITEAU, THE ASSASSIN. 669

of this man on this trial. I wish to know if, unshackled and assured of the mock defense of insanity to protect him, he had held the "bull-dog" pistol in his hand, he would not have put an end to this trial the other day when His Honor, in his own personal views of propriety, prohibited him from making a last speech. And His Honor, who had been the object of his fulsome praise, would have become the object of his fiendlike hate. In the violence of his temper he warned His Honor that he would erase from the record he had made for the American people, and for all time, the commendation he had bestowed upon him, and would send his name blackened down the course of history. Do you believe that the man who shot the President, who dogged him at night and went to church to murder him, would not, if he felt safe, instead of sending His Honor's name, coupled with infamy, thundering down the ages, have sent à cartridge into His Honor's breast? This man, who appeals to you in tears and with such pathos, through his counsel, for dew-fallen mercy—this man showed his idea of mercy to others when, on one occasion, he turned to you and said that that God whose name he has so often blasphemed, would interfere to strike down one of your number before you should be able to convict him. This is the man who invokes the tender and merciful consideration of his case. A man, brutal in his instincts, inordinate in his love of notoriety, eaten up by a thirst for money which has gnawed at his soul like a cancer, a beggar, a hypocrite, a canter, a swindler, a lawyer who, with many years' practice, never won a case. Would you know why? No court, no jury, failed to see that he was a dishonest rogue, and such men cannot win cases. A man who has left his trail in various States; a man who has lived on other people's funds and appropriated them to his own use, in breach of every trust; a man who is capable of aping the manners of a gentleman; a man who, as a lawyer, had this notion of morality, that when he had taken debts to collect and collected them by dunning the debtor, held them against his client, and chuckled over the success of his scheme; a man who sold oroide watches, or pawned them to get money through falsehood and misrepresentation; a man who was capable of endeavoring to blast the name of the woman with whom he had slept for years and acknowledged as a virtuous wife; who was capable of fawning himself off on Christian committees and Christian churches as a pure and moral man, who spent six years in fornication at the Oneida Community; a man who afterward, when he wished to get rid of that wife, consulted the commandments of God, and read "Thou shalt not commit adultery," and went out and committed it with a street prostitute. He wanted to remove his wife, but, fortunately for her, it did not come to the necessity of the removal he applied to Garfield. He was content with a removal he could provide for himself. A man so mean and vile, that in a case which showed how rotten hearted he was, he appeared before the judicial referee as a witness to establish the marriage, and produced the prostitute with whom he committed adultery as a witness to prove the prostitution. A man so void of all honor, so possessed of the spirit of diabolism that he was capable, at the age of eighteen, of stealing up behind his father and giving him a blow, and, relying on the fact that he was then a stronger and larger man than his father, exchanged blow for blow with him, and when the old man, by a fortunate blow, drew blood from his nose, whimpered as he whimpered the day before yesterday, and surrendered, coward, murderer at heart. He had no "bull-dog" then, but the spirit in which he fired at Garfield was the spirit in which he struck his father. Mr. Porter then alluded to the incident of the prisoner raising an axe at his sister, whom he (Mr. Porter) esteemed for her loving devotion to her brother, who, a fiend at eighteen when he struck his father, was a fiend at twenty-five, and was a fiend now.

Proceeding with his speech, he eulogized Mr. Garfield as a soldier, a lawyer and a statesman, and said that so high was his reputation he had been elected to the Presidency by a vote so clear and so strong that all the people said "Amen." And that was the man, he said, against whose life this prisoner had been plotting for six weeks, plotting without malice, as he said, plotting, with no counsel except the fiend of darkness, who had prompted the crime. Plotting and plotting for six weeks the murder of this President. Is there any dispute about that? He swears to it. He complains that I call him an assassin. I called him an assassin from the moment that he swore he was one. You call him an assassin. The law calls him one. I tell him that he is a murderer from the moment he says he did commit "so-called" murder. His oath is contradicted by almost every witness he has called to the stand, in one particular or another, which, of itself, condemns him as unworthy of belief. But his testimony is, that for two weeks after he (not God) formed the conception, he knelt every night at the feet of God (with whom he says he is now very well satisfied) and prayed to have him work a miracle in order to find out whether, after all, this was not an inspiration of the devil, and as He worked no miracle he concluded that it was an inspiration from God. This man professes to believe that the God who spoke to Moses and the Christ who spoke to Paul in order to

GUITEAU, THE ASSASSIN.

replace Judas, who had been false to his trust, inspired this murder. He tells you on his own oath that he meditated the means, that he contrived the vindication, that he prepared the papers which were to vindicate him before God and man, that he revised his book (his inspired book) and altered it. What? Altered the inspiration of God, blotting out "hell" in his book, as a preliminary to the murder of President Garfield, and substituting the milder term, "perdition." Does inspiration need alteration by the very man who receives it? Mr. Porter reviewed the history of the case, the purchase of the pistol, the prisoner practising by the river side, the various occasions when he was deterred from the murder, etc. In regard to the incident of the practising at the river side, he said, Who was it that was practising—the Deity or the prisoner at the bar? Who fired at those osiers? Who sent them swerving down as Garfield swerved? Who hit them? Who fired twenty times in order to accustom himself to the noise of the report of the pistol, to the end that it should not stun him when he murdered the President?

As to his being restrained from the murder by the presence of Mrs. Garfield on one occasion, and that of the two boys on another occasion, Mr. Porter remarked that there was no diabolism so complete on this side of the infernal regions that it has not some remaining twinges of conscience, and yet he believed that this statement of the prisoner was as false as anything else he had said. He had been restrained by nothing but cowardice on all such occasions. He knew that if he had murdered the President in his wife's presence, no military force could have prevented the people who were around tearing him limb from limb. And on the occasion when the children were present, they had come surrounded by their friends and domestics. Those boys, though not strong, would on such an occasion, have felt that their arms carried the power of the Almighty in the defence of their murdered father. Mr. Porter also referred to the spirit of vanity which made the prisoner choose a white handled pistol rather than a black one; that it might bear his name and fame "thundering down the ages" and be more conspicuous in the Patent Office. He rehearsed the scene at the railroad depot, and said that after Guiteau fired the bullet he turned to run. Run where? Run to jail? He was careful in the very last moment, of his own safety. He held aloft his letter to General Sherman, asking him to summon instantly to his (Guiteau's) protection, that military force which had not been present to protect the murdered President. This man had appealed to the Court to give him every right, every constitutional right, freedom of speech, perfect impartiality (which would consist in making all decisions in his favor). He had been dictating to the Judge the charge which he proposed the Judge should make to the jury. He had shown himself averse to sitting in the dock, which was a disparagement to a lawyer, a theologian, a politician, a man of God, a man of prayer, a patriot, a man whose name is to go on through all ages.

The prisoner interrupted with the exclamation ; "I am the only man who has not been benefited by the new administration. There is Porter, with his $10,000 fee. He has been benefited, not me. This is a good time to make that point. Everybody else has been benefited by this move but me."

Mr. Porter.—"His benefit will come when the law has been fully executed in his case ; but has he not told you again and again that he was to be benefited, first in the advertisement and sale of his book, and second in the reward which he was to receive after elevating Mr. Arthur to the Presidency ?

The Prisoner.—"I have not got any reward from him, and do not expect any. I would not take a Cabinet commission to-day."

Judge Porter then explained away the insinuations of the defense as to the compensation of the prosecution's counsel and witnesses, and stated that with regard to the experts, those on both sides had been treated exactly alike. Commenting on the intimations of the press that there would be a disagreement of the jury, he remarked that counsel for the defence would not claim that there could be an acquittal ? Why not ? Because it would shock all Christendom. So all the struggle of counsel for the defence had been to lead one of the twelve jurors to differ with his fellows. Mr. Reed had made it very evident that he thought there would be one, or perhaps two, of the jurors who would disagree with the others, and Mr. Scoville had indicated pretty plainly that he thought so too. "I do not," he said, "and have not thought so from the beginning. I know nothing of the antecedents of any of the jurors and have heard nothing that would lead me to suppose that any of them would not find a verdict according to the evidence. But when these attempts are made so persistently and so constantly, when they are circulated by telegraph, when they appear in the newspapers and are the subject of indignant comment throughout the country, I cannot ignore them, especially when I see the last seven days of argument addressed to the same point, of procuring a division of the jury. If there should be such a division it would be very unfortunate. I think it would be unfortunate for any interest that I can conceive of as an honest man. How would the case stand if there were such a

GUITEAU, THE ASSASSIN.   673

division of the jury? It would stand about thus :—Here is a man who swears he is guilty, and here is a juror who says : "I will swear that he is not." The prisoner calls it an assassination over his own signature, and the juror says it is no assassination. Oath to oath opposed. Prisoner, "guilty." Juror, "not guilty." Prisoner, "sane." Juror, "insane." I am dealing with the testimony and I shall demonstrate it clause by clause. The only consequence of that disagreement, gentlemen, would be (under the charge which the Judge will deliver to you) to call the attention not only of this country, but of mankind, to the only human being who is ready to stand by and shield the cowardly assassin of the President of the United States. But what would be accomplished by it? Is it supposed that this Government is not strong enough to press the case to a conclusion? It would defeat the purpose of this particular trial, and it would compel other twelve jurors to be prisoners in their turn as you have been in yours ; to be held away from their families and business, as you have been held away from yours, and to have so much cut out of their lives as so much has been cut out of yours, and all this when the prisoner swears he is guilty. I shall demonstrate that, unless this prisoner is a liar unworthy of belief, he is guilty. The theory of this defence, as presented by Mr. Scoville, was plausible and false. He chose to embark this entire defence on a craft which the prisoner with his own hands has scuttled. This case stands on the single question whether on the 2d of July, 1881, the assassin believed that he was commanded by God to murder the President——"

"The prisoner.—"That is all there is to it, and that is what the jury has to pass on."

Mr. Porter (to the jury).—" You perceive it. He foresaw from the beginning of this trial the weakness of his counsel's theory, and if his counsel had had the brains of the prisoner they would have foreseen it. And they would have concentrated their whole power upon it. Let me suggest to you, gentlemen, that the office of a juror is not a light office. Some one has said (I think it originated with Bacon) that when you come to the Anglo-Saxon race and its form of government, the ultimate decision of all rights and all liberties is to be found in the jury box. In yonder Capitol districts are represented, and States are represented, but not the American people. There are in our Government only two representatives of the American people. The one is the head of the government, the President of the United States; the other is the jury of twelve men to whom, in the last resort, all rights, whether they be of life, liberty or property,

29

come for protection. For that purpose, and under the operation of our law, you twelve men stand to-day as the representatives of the American people. I do not mean that you are to represent them in any other sense than as of them, as bound by the laws which they have ordained, and to uphold the government which they have established. It is true that you are not to be governed by outside opinions, except so far as that outside opinion is exactly in harmony with your own judgment and conscience. But, gentlemen, there are certain questions which rise so immeasurably above minor issues, that upon them great masses are universally agreed. This is one of those cases. It has arrested attention, because it was a crime committed not in the secrecy of night, but under the broad canopy of heaven and in the broad light of day; because it was a crime committed not merely against the murdered victim, but against household relations, family relations, State relations, public relations, the existence and duration of the Government itself—so far, at least, as a change of political administration can be wrought out by assassination. In such a case I deny that any man can ignore the fact, that just as all other men loathe and abhor such crimes, so should you. This prisoner has been blatant in claiming from day to day that the people of this country were on his side: that he was receiving letters and telegrams and contributions expressing sympathy with him; that the newspapers, which he professed to be reading (while he was looking over the top of them and watching the progress of the case), were containing expressions in his favor. While all this has been going on, you might very well have wondered how it was that neither of the counsel for the defence dared to refer to the general judgment of the City of Washington, of the District of Columbia, of the United States, or of manhood. For they had yet to see the first newspaper published in America that ventured to defend this criminal. I have seen occasional articles before the trial, and one or two since, doubting whether he might not have been insane, but all of them denouncing the Court, the administration of justice—everything and everybody— because this man was not tried and hung.

A SCENE BETWEEN COUNSEL.

At this point the prisoner and Mr. Scoville, at one and the same time, addressed the Court, demanding that counsel be restrained from making these statements. Judge Porter declared that he would not allow the misrepresentations of the past few weeks to remain unchallenged and uncontradicted. Judge Cox, after the clamor had continued for some time, ruled that counsel could contradict the prisoner's assertions, that he was receiving commendations from the public and the newspapers, but could not go further and quote the press on the subject. Again the confusion broke out, but Judge Porter managed to say: "I shall not be prevented by clamor from doing my duty. If it were true, as the prisoner has alleged, that the American people and the leading papers of the country are on his side, why was it that his counsel, when they came to sum up to you, did not follow his lead, and why did they insist that you should not be controlled by public opinion?"

Mr. Scoville once more protested, and the District Attorney interpolated a remark, that the prisoner had been allowed to make statements as to public opinion. Judge Cox interposed: "He was not allowed to do so; he did it without being allowed." He then repeated his previous ruling, and Judge Porter, in defence of his own position, proceeded to quote from the report of the trial various statements by the prisoner as to what the newspapers and his own letters and telegrams contained, but he showed such sense of exhaustion and physical weakness that he was forced to desist, and the Court at ten minutes past one adjourned.

JUDGE PORTER'S SECOND DAY.

TUESDAY, JANUARY 24.—At the opening of Court, Guiteau commenced the proceedings by denouncing the alleged actions of some " cranks," and announced that anybody who attempted violence against him would be shot dead.

Judge Porter then said: "As usual the Court has been opened by the prisoner; but, by his permission, I am now at liberty to add a few words. I am grateful to you for the indulgence which has enabled me to proceed this morning. You have been kept here on this trial longer than the fast of the Saviour in the Wilderness, in an air black and putrid with vile calumny and blasphemy, and you will therefore, extend some indulgence to those who speak in behalf of the Government and the law. I endeavored to show you yesterday that this defence was one founded on shams and imposture; on brazen falsehood, which was supposed to acquire force and strength by perpetual reiterations. The disciples of the school of Guiteau have great confidence in a maxim of Aaron Burr, that falsehoods are to be verified by persistency and reiteration. I showed you how the prisoner had belied, by his acts, his profession; how he had belied by his acts, the character given to him by his counsel; how this gentleman, this prayerful man, this moral and Christian man, was a liar, a swindler, and a murderer in heart from the beginning. That this man has grown worse every year that he has lived, we all see and know. That he was a disobedient child; that he was lawless and ungrateful to his father; that he was an unkind brother; that he stung every man who was a benefactor to his youth; that he had inordinate desire for unholy notoriety; that his vanity was boundless, and that his malice was still more unbounded, we all know. All this he was in early life. And I shall now call your attention to some of the evidences that he was growing worse and worse, until his career culminated in cold-blooded assassination. His life was consistent and harmonious from the beginning. There is a self-propagating property in sin and vice and crime, until the man becomes (not by disease, but by culture) what Dr. Spitzka calls a moral monstrosity."

Guiteau here interrupted counsel, and among other insolence called him a wine bibber. Judge Porter smiled calmly, and said: "This Christian gentleman, this moral gentleman, this praying gentleman, who prays every morning before he eats (but nobody hears) makes the suggestion that I am a wine bibber. Perhaps I am. That reminds me of a distich which I heard in a temperance meeting many years ago on a church deacon, who used one of the vaults of the church for storing his wine:

> There's a spirit above, 'tis the spirit divine:
> There's a spirit below, 'tis the spirit of wine;
> There's a spirit above, 'tis the spirit of love:
> There's a spirit below, 'tis the spirit of woe.

It is for you, gentlemen, to judge whether it was the spirit of love or the spirit of wine that led to the murder of your President and mine.

Mr. Porter went on to justify the prosecution from the allegation that they had suppressed evidence which might have been favorable to the prisoner, and claimed that they had only used their undoubted right to judge of what testimony they should present.

As to the suppression particularly of the statement of the District Attorney's stenographer, in which it was asserted that the prisoner had put in his claim of inspiration, he said that he had read that statement, and he denied that it contained any such claim. Mr. Scoville here rose and objected to Mr. Porter making any statement as to the contents of that paper.

Considerable controversy ensued, but Judge Cox finally ruled that he could not allow counsel to quote from that paper, stating in reply to remonstrance on the point that the prisoner had been under oath as a witness, when he made assertions as to its contents.

Judge Porter replied: "He was in the dock, and not on oath." After some further discussion, Mr. Porter proceeded with his argument, in the course of which he referred to a recent case in New Jersey—The State *vs.* Martin—in connec- with the *onus probandi*, where the defence was insanity. Counsel for the defence objected to a discussion of points of law at this stage of the case. After some colloquy on this point, Mr. Porter resumed his argument. He asked who it was that killed President Garfield.

Guiteau shouted: "The Doctors;" and after a short colloquy with the counsel, added: "The Lord allowed them to confirm my act. They were the immediate cause of his death." Judge Porter continued:

"I am afraid the prisoner has not the latest intelligence from Heaven, for he said that the inspiration left him an hour after he killed the President. Who killed Garfield? The prisoner says: "Secretary Blaine." He says, in his testimony: "Secretary Blaine is responsible for the murder of President Garfield." Who else is responsible for the death of Garfield? Mrs. Garfield: because the prisoner swears, that when he saw that honored lady leaning on her husband's arm, her presence on that occasion saved his life, and so if she had been with him on the 2d of July, the prisoner would not have shot President Garfield." [Referring to Mr. Reed's suggestion about Mrs. Garfield praying in behalf of the prisoner, Mr. Porter said]: "Imagine what sort of scenes these are that counsel thus brings up. Imagine the aged mother of the President coming before you draped in black. Imagine, according to the old custom of the English laws, this trial taking place in the presence of the corpse of Garfield, mutilated by the murderer, wrapped in white linen, through which it was supposed the mere approach of the murderer would start the blood to flow. Imagine Garfield lying there, not one of the clavicles of his backbone, but the whole man, cold in death, with the death sweat not even yet dry on his brow, with the expression of agony which this prisoner put there, and with the cowering assassin yonder shrinking from approach to the body which was required by the old process of bier rite. Imagine the aged mother, who had looked to that son to close her eyes in death, bowing with grief at the coffin head with Mrs. Garfield, whose lips were the last that touched the cold lips of the President, sitting at his feet in dust and ashes. If in such a scene Mr. Charles H. Reed stood up and said: "The woman who seems to you to be kneeling only to God in her sorrow, is kneeling to God in prayer that this murderer shall be dealt with leniently;" what would you think of it? It is well for us all, gentlemen, that the law does not call upon jurors to leave the only immortal part of their nature—their moral nature—outside of the court-house when they come to administer justice. Who else killed Garfield? John H. Noyes, says the prisoner. He killed Garfield. He from whom the prisoner stole his lecture on "The Second Advent" and on "The Apostle Paul." Who else killed Garfield? The prisoner's father? That father whom he struck from behind when he was eighteen years of age— ["I never struck him," said the prisoner]—and whom he said he would never forgive—["I never said so;" said the prisoner]—that father with whom he says he was not on speaking terms for the last fifteen years of his honored tife. Who else killed Garfield? The mother of this prisoner, who was guilty of the inordinate atrocity of having a temporary attack of erysipelas just before he was born, and leaving him an inheritance of congenital monstrosity. Who else killed Garfield? This prisoner's drunken and dissolute uncle Abraham who, although he was never insane himself, transmitted insanity to the prisoner, though he was not his father, nor his mother, nor his grandfather, nor his grandmother. Who else killed

Garfield? The prisoner's cousin, Abby Maynard. Who else killed Garfield? The Chicago Convention which nominated him for the Presidency. The Convention was inspired, according to the prisoner's statement. He says: "His nomination was an act of God, and if he had not been nominated and elected I could not have killed him." The prisoner claims that he was appointed by God to kill him—he, with his swindling record—he, a liar from the beginning —he, who struck his father; who lifted an axe against his sister, who struck his brother—he was commissioned to correct the act of the Convention and of the people by murdering the President. These are the defences put forward by this praying prisoner, and by his praying counsel, in order to divert your attention from the fact that the man who killed Garfield sits there (pointing at the dock), and although Garfield is dead, the prisoner speaks and has spoken on the witness stand those words which prove him to be not only the assassin, but the meditating, deliberate, sane and responsible assassin of the President. But that is not enough. The press killed Garfield. The press is solemnly indicted by the murderer and his associate counsel; indicted without the formality of the grand jury; accused by the oath of a murderer; found guilty by the murderer; charged with responsibility by the murderer. But fortunately he no longer holds the "bulldog" pistol in his hands, and the press is only to be convicted of the murder of Garfield by the bad tongue of a murderous liar. This man slaughtered Garfield as he would have slaughtered a calf that he wanted to eat. ["The doctors did that," said the prisoner.] And having disposed of him in that way, in comes his counsel and charges with the crime, those who occupy too lofty a position to notice the vipers that said it, and who would have degraded the dignity of their office by noticing it. One of them is a distinguished American Senator, who at this moment (except that he was too proud and too lofty to accept the office, would be sitting as the Chief Justice of the Supreme Court of the United States; the son of a great and honored American Jurist; a man who still young in years, has commanded more of the attention, at home and abroad, of the admirers of intellectual greatness, of the loftiest eloquence, and of the greatest statesmanship than any man perhaps even of his time; a bitter partisan; a man honest in all that he undertakes; a man faithful to his friends, faithful to his convictions, even though they involve sacrifice; a man who was capable of doing what but few men are—resigning the leadership of the American Senate, and to do it at the peril of his own political destruction; a man of unstained integrity, of a courage and fearlessness and manliness which made this withdrawal a matter of regret even to his political adversaries. Such a man is to-day arraigned before an American jury, and arraigned not by the criminal, but by the criminal's defender ["Without my knowledge," interposed the prisoner] as responsible for the murder of Garfield.

Another of those whom he arraigned is a man more honored in the Confederate States than any American, save their own cherished leader, General Lee; a man who is honored in the Northern States for services rendered—first in war and afterward in reconciling the difficulties which grew out of the war; a man whose life has been without dishonor and reproach; a man elevated to conspicuous positions, the successor of Washington and Jefferson, Jackson and Lincoln; one who, after he left that place was welcomed in every European and Oriental land as one of the noblest men and purest personal characters to be named in the history of the nineteenth century. That man is arraigned by the lawyer of Guiteau as responsible for the murder of General Garfield. More than that, we have the President of the United States, the successor of Garfield and Hayes and Lincoln and Jackson and Jefferson and Adams and Washington, elevated to that position not by an assassin, but by the voice of his countrymen. And when this creature says: "I made Arthur President;" he forgets that General Arthur was made President by the voice of his countrymen; by that very voice which made Garfield President. He was made president under the constitution and the laws. Millard Fillmore was as truly elected by the people as the President whom he succeeded. This man told you in his speech last Saturday, that Garfield might have died from any other cause; that he might have trod on an orange peel, and received an injury which might have caused his death, or that he might have trod upon a rattlesnake, whose fangs might have pierced his heel. Was it the orange peel or the rattlesnake that made Arthur President? Both—because the prisoner has shown himself all his life as slippery as the orange peel and as venomous as the rattlesnake. But in one respect meaner than the rattlesnake, for Providence has provided in respect of that reptile that there shall be a warning at one end, but the venom at the other. This was a rattlesnake without the rattle, but not without the fangs, and when he tells you that he made General Arthur President of the United States, he made him President in just the same sense in which the rattlesnake might have done it by introducing into President Garfield's veins that venom which in eighty days would bring him down to the grave. Mr. Reed, as counsel for the prisoner, has chosen to pose here as a friend of Garfield. I take it for granted that he has read those memorable sayings of President Garfield, simple as childhood, guileless, frank, sincere—his dying utterances between Guiteau's bullet and Garfield's death. In one of his waking hours on the 11th of July, the President asked Mrs. Susan Edson where Guiteau was. This was while he expected to recover. He then remarked that he supposed people would come to him some day with a petition to pardon that man; and he wondered what he should do in a personal matter of life and death. Mrs. Edson told him that she should think he would do nothing at all, and that he surely could not pardon such a man, and the President said: "No, I do not suppose I can." And yet Mr. Charles Reed, to whom the American Bar is indebted for the introduction to its ranks of the prisoner Guiteau, undertook to say that the President regarded him as an irresponsible man.

Passing on to criticize Mr. Reed's argument and his illustration as to Christ casting out devils and healing lunatics, Mr. Porter said: "The Saviour made a distinction between the sick, the lunatic and those that were possessed of devils. The claim here is, that this man was so enormously wicked as to be, in the language of Dr. Spitzka; a moral monstrosity. He represents the class of which the Saviour spoke, not lunatics, but possessed of the devil. A man who was possessed by the devil came to the Saviour and prayed to be delivered. The Saviour granted his prayer and commanded the devil to say who he was. "My name," said the devil, "is Legion." And he prayed to be allowed to go into a herd of swine, because even devils go through a form of prayer. The Saviour consented. What became of the swine after Legion had entered the herd? "They rushed down a steep place into the sea and were choked." Whether the devil that possesses this man is or is not to be choked by the law you are to determine. But the destination of diabolism such as his was thought by the Saviour to be fitting for the swine, and the ultimate destination even of the swine was to be choked in the water.

I have said all that I deem necessary in going over those grounds of the impeachment of this defence. I am here for the purpose of ascertaining whether this man is guilty, and I shall not further discuss these collateral issues. I desire you to recollect, though, that it is a mistake to suppose that you are (as in one of those weak and feeble arguments you have been told you were in a spirit of obsequious flattery) twelve kings and emperors. Does such fulsome adulation commend itself to your taste? If I used such language I trust that you would scorn me. You are no more kings, gentlemen, than Messrs. Scoville and Reed are kings. If that had come from Scoville I would say it had a cheating purpose; but as it came from Reed, I will only say that they did not teach him his lesson well. What was the purpose? The purpose was to lead you to suppose that you can override the judge and the law; that you are at liberty to override the instructions of the Court, and to find your verdict, or refuse to find it, on the ground of speculative doubts not warranted by the evidence, but based on your own view of the prisoner, or on evidence which has not been submitted.

Here the Court took a recess for half an hour.

After the recess Mr. Porter resumed his argument. Referring to the prisoner's desire for notoriety, he said that he had made himself illustrious by having his hand stained by illustrious blood. That man undertook to award immortality to the jury, or immortality to the Judge, and he had through his counsel told them that their names would go down blackened, unless they violated their oaths, and that his (Mr. Porter's) name was to go down blackened unless he came to the rescue of the prisoner. He tells you that even the President and the great men of the country must take heed; that even God Almighty must take heed how he acts towards him. He tells you that, at all events, he is satisfied so far with what the Almighty has done, and that he expects before the trial is done, that if it is necessary the Almighty will take one of you, gentlemen, or will take me, or will take each one of us, rather than that he shall be struck down. The drama is well played, gentlemen. This man is an actor. While in jail he has borne his natural part, but here he has been constantly on the stage posing for you and carrying out the suggestions of his counsel. This man is neither a crowned nor an uncrowned king. Although he has sworn to you repeatedly that he was prepared to meet his God, there is not a soul in this vast assemblage who shrinks with such abject cowardice from confronting the Deity. I believe that there is not a single dishonest juror in that box. There is not one of them a king, not one of them an emperor. They are God made men, and the result will show whether my prediction is correct.

And now I ask not who killed Garfield, but did this man murder Garfield, and did he know what he was doing? If he did, then he is as I understand the law, responsible. Mr. Porter then went on to discuss the points of law as laid down by Judge Cox in this case. After he had disposed of that question, he took up again the question of the responsibility of the prisoner. What household, he said, would be safe, what church would protect its worshippers, if this man were to escape on the plea of irresponsibility? Is it true that any man who has had an insane cousin, an insane uncle, an insane aunt, or an insane ancestor, and who is not himself insane, but knows perfectly that murder is legally and morally wrong, is to escape punishment? May he stab, or shoot, or waylay, or murder in any form by day or by night, and then claim in his vindication, not that he is insane himself, but that somebody else was? If so what is human life worth? Nay, more, if it were true that every insane man, no matter in what degree, no matter whether from melancholia, or from any of those casual or occasional aberrations of mind, is at liberty to commit burglary, to fire your dwelling house, to set the City of Washington on fire, when the frost shall stiffen the water, and when fire is destruction, to ravish your daughters, what security is there? That is the license for which this brother-in-law of Guiteau contends—namely, that the law is intended only for rational men—and that all of these crimes which I have mentioned may be committed by a license, not from the law, but from one of twelve emperors or kings in defiance of the law and of the instructions from the Court. Nay, more. The insane of this country (I mean the undoubted insane, who are inmates of lunatic asylums) are to learn from the verdict in this case, if the theory of the defence shall be sustained, that each of them is at liberty to murder the keeper who restrains him; that they are all at liberty to confederate to open the gates of the asylums and to go out, knife and torch in hand, and spread ruin and conflagration in every direction, and although the law forbids it, an American jury can be found that will sanction the act.

More than that, any man who has insanity in any degree shall be at liberty to murder any other insane man. In the mercy of a good and kind Providence none of us has, as yet, been put in a lunatic asylum, yet there is not a human being in this vast assemblage who is not exposed to this calamity. And then every one of the five hundred or thousand lunatics in the asylum will be at liberty to take our lives. If such were the law, gentlemen, the most benign institution in the country—the institution of asylums for the insane —must be abandoned. Let the lunatics understand that the law has no hold upon them, and that they can commit murder with impunity, and no order of General Sherman, no troops that may be sent to guard an asylum can save the lives of inmates or keepers. And hence it is (as I am glad to learn), that while this case may well produce horror outside of lunatic asylums, it produces more horror inside of them. I believe that if a jury could be empanelled in any lunatic asylum in this country, they would say of this man not only that they would be endangered by his presence, but that he is perfectly sane. The law on the subject is founded on reason. It is announced by the high federal jurist who presides over this tribunal and the law as he has uttered it, is your law and my law.

Was this man insane on the 2d of July? If he was not, you have but one duty, and that is to convict him. He was not insane. Grant, for the purpose of the argument—what not one soul of you believes—that his father was insane. His father did not assassinate Garfield. Grant, if you please, that his uncle Abraham was insane. His Uncle Abraham is not on trial. He did not murder President Garfield. Grant the same of each and all of these relatives, none of them murdered the President. Was he insane, and insane on that day? I aver (what this proof indisputably established) that he never was insane, and certainly not on the 2d of July. On that point the principal claim by the prisoner and his counsel is the atrocity of this particular act. I do not deny his claim of being the most cold-blooded and savage murderer of the last 6,000 years. But he is not alone, as he will find when he comes to those realms where murderers are consigned. The first born of the human race murdered the second born, and the blood of the second born called from the ground. Though the corpse was mute the blood spoke, and the murderer was condemned to live (then a more terrible punishment than death) with a mark upon his brow. Murder has existed in all ages. Four thousand years ago there were inscribed on tables of stone the command to all people: "Thou shalt not kill." But Guiteau says that life is of small consideration. He says in one of his letters of consolation to the widow: "Life is but a fleeting dream. His death might have happened at any time." As he told you the other day Mr. Garfield might have trod on an orange peel or trod on a rattlesnake." But the Lawgiver of the universe entertained different views on the value of human life when he said: "Whoso sheddeth man's blood by man shall his blood be shed." And that man in the dock tells you that the same God that placed that value on human life, placed no value on the life of James A. Garfield, and that as to that life it was but of small value—it was "a fleeting dream." We have had the gospel of Guiteau, and he thinks that this jury will endorse his gospel. Mr. Porter then went on to discuss the question of the insanity of Guiteau's father, and declared that the defence was a falsehood and a fabrication, an imposture and a sham. I do not deny that there are hereditary tendencies to insanity. There is one order of insanity called by this prisoner

Abrahamic, called by him at other times temporary mania, and called by Dr. Spitzka moral insanity. That moral insanity, according to Dr. Barker, consists in wickedness, and is inherited, not from a natural parent, but from another source. Christ, speaking to the Scribes and Pharisees, said: "Ye who claim to be of the seed of Abraham prove it by doing acts of Abraham; but ye are the children of your father the devil, who was a murderer from the beginning." That is the insanity which this man has inherited. The man is a liar as well as an assassin, and he was instigated not by the Almighty, but by the devil.

Judge Porter proceeded then to review the prisoner's life of crime, in which he included adultery; he referred to his life in Washington, living at first-class boarding-houses at the expense of the keepers of the house; punctual at breakfast, at dinner and at tea; careful to take baths, punctual at night, sleeping well, eating heartily, rising early, and spending the day at Lafayette Square, or in making preparations to murder the President, when he should have a favorable opportunity. Was this, he asked, temporary mania, Abrahamic mania, or disease of the brain, which resulted in murder for the benefit of the stalwarts of the Republican party? Gentlemen, if I went no further, do you believe that this man's brain was diseased? I deal with nothing else now. Was his brain diseased? And did the disease come and go according to whether President Garfield went out alone, or went out with his wife, or went out with his children, or went to the Soldier's Home, or went to the railroad depot? Do you believe that the right remedy for a disease of the brain is to make six weeks' preparation for an assassination, and that shooting another man through the spine is a cure for the disease? That is the case as the prisoner makes it out.

A reference by Judge Porter to the prisoner's divorced wife, and his treatment of her, brought out angry rejoinders from Guiteau, whose contemptible conduct was fully demonstrated by counsel. Mr. Porter, referring to the testimony of Mrs. Scoville, paid her a compliment as a sincere woman, and said that she had never noticed insanity in the prisoner until the time when he raised the axe upon her, when he was thirty-five years of age. ["That never occurred;" interposed the prisoner.]

Mr. Porter.—"Your sister swore it did occur, and she is a woman of truth, while you have committed perjury. She came into Court with unbloodied hands, and she went out of it as she entered it—an honest woman, believing what she asserted. I lifted no axe against this sister. He did. There is his own sister, the only one who has stuck by him faithfully and honestly. She tells you honestly that the first time she thought him insane was when he was thirty-five years of age. She says: "I had no thought before that he was not in his right mind."

Mr. Porter went on to criticize the testimony of Reed, ot Amerling, and of North. He said that it would take a thousand Norths to make him believe that Luther W. Guiteau, that calm, quiet, religious man, ever said to an old father and an old mother who had an only son that did not want them to go to the Oneida Community. "Take a knife and slay him, as Abraham did Isaac."

At this stage of Mr. Porter's argument, and at ten minutes past three, the Court adjourned.

THE CLOSING DAY OF THE TRIAL.

WEDNESDAY, JANUARY 25.—As a matter of course, when the Court convened this morning, Guiteau had his opening speech to make, but although he looked defiant and insolent, there was a shadow of doom over him, which somewhat checked his reckless buoyancy. He merely stated, that his sister had been making silly statements in Chicago, but then, he added contemptuously, "though she means well, she is no lawyer." For the moderation of his opening, however, he made ample amends, during the day, his interruptions of counsel being more venomously vindictive than ever before; his bellowings at times resembling those of a caged wild beast.

Mr. Porter then proceeded with his speech. He had reached a portion of the argument which was wearisome to him, and would be still more wearisome to the jury. It was the dry portion of the evidence having no interest but that which resulted from the revulsion of human nature at the facts which had been exposed. He intended, because he had confidence in the jury, to make it brief. If it were possible to condense the few salient points into a few hours, he hoped not to detain the Court even this afternoon. His plan had been otherwise, but he had been admonished by the snow of the change of the season, and he felt that it was important that this trial should come to an end. If he passed hastily over some topics which ought to be considered, he would rely on the jury to supply his deficiency.

Referring to the testimony of Dr. North, he stated that that witness came here to swear this case through by fixing upon his benefactor, Luther W. Guiteau, the guilt of this murder in transmitting his own blood to his son. That witness had left the stand after having planted a quivering barb in the heart of the prisoner. If this man were innocent now, he was guilty then, for he was animated by the spirit of murder when he struck his father, taking him at a disadvantage and fighting him in the spirit of a devil. In his turbulent passion and egotism and wrath and hate of all mankind he turned, in his spirit of selfishness, his hand upon his honored father, and provoked that father to a fight, from which he (the prisoner) retreated with the ignominy of the coward, as—like a coward—he shot the President in the back.

He then referred to the testimony of the prisoner's brother in order to show, as he said, that when the prisoner was forty years of age, when he had murdered Garfield, and when Garfield was dead, this brother, from the circumstances, and from his antecedent knowledge of the prisoner, said that the prisoner was sane and responsible. All that had changed that opinion was the acting of the prisoner himself, and the production of a letter from the father which he regarded as evidence of insanity, but which I regard as evidence of depravity. The jury would recollect that this was a witness who had stood by the prisoner with the fidelity of a brother —who, though wronged, had come here and was ready to contribute from his means, from his energy, from his exertion, from all that he could to save this man's life, and yet he had been compelled to utter this truth before the jury. He believed John W. Guiteau to be an honest man; feeling naturally the bias which inclines one to save a brother's life and to save his father's name from infamy. But this brother was an honest man. Although under the circumstances the opinions of John W. Guiteau were no safe guide to the jury, the facts stated by him were facts that were rooted as the oak tree is rooted and cannot be removed. They might as well attempt to uproot that oak as to uproot that conviction which this testi-

GUITEAU, THE ASSASSIN.

mony must carry to their minds. However it might have been on the 2d of July, prior to that he was no more insane than the jury, the Judge or the counsel. This little circumstance was one of these things that spoke to the consciousness. Was it depravity, weakness or selfishness, or was it disease of the brain, curable in an hour by an act of murder?

In quoting from and commenting upon the testimony of John W. Guiteau, he said that this prisoner, through his counsel, had assailed the men to whom he looked with confidence for acquittal, or failing acquittal, disagreeing : or, failing disagreement, pardon. He had two tones to his voice—two masks to his face, one of the masks shows the sanctity of the Pharisee and the other the hideous grin of the fiend of hell.

Commenting further on John W. Guiteau's testimony, Mr. Porter came to the point where the prisoner had exclaimed; "Jesus Christ struck back, and so do I!" and he said : This prayful Christian struck back at Blaine. He asked Garfield to remove him, under a menace which was unfortunately fulfilled. He struck back at Garfield, and, unfortunately for the nation, for the household and for the victim of malice, he struck home. Commenting upon the expressions of the prisoner excusing his own conduct because he had been imitating the course of Jesus Christ and St. Paul, in going about from town to town and from city to city, Mr. Porter spoke of the prisoner travelling from State to State, swindling women as well as innkeepers, and then quietly saying that he had paid the debt because he had acknowledged it and that it should be charged over to the Lord. Instead of Paul swindling and defrauding while engaged in the mission of his divine Master, he worked at his trade as a tent maker and paid his way. He swindled no Jew, he passed no mock gold watches off as real gold ones. He lived as we are told in his own hired house, and while there were so many opposed to Paul no living being except the assassin of Garfield has charged that he could not pay his rent. Do you doubt that when under your verdict the sentence of the law shall come to be pronounced we shall hear again and again the same language of menace and of hate, and that if he had the pistol with which he aimed at Garfield, in his hand, he would if he dared, send the cartridge home? If he had loved his neighbor, Garfield, as he loved himself—what think you? Would it have been his opinion that this inspiration was of the devil or of God? If he had loved his neighbor as himself how many of his swindled victims would there be in this broad land? Do you believe that He who knows all things really selected the prisoner as the successor of Paul and the junior member of the firm of Jesus Christ & Co., to write a sequel to the Bible and to illustrate the Golden Rule by lying in wait to murder?

Judge Porter then referred to the prisoner's habit of swindling boarding-house keepers, and branching off, quoted ironically from the various statements of the prisoner that the Stalwarts were responsible for President Garfield's murder; that the half-breeds were responsible; that the Democratic and Stalwart press were responsible; that it was the rebels who were not in rebellion. He then went into an exhaustive review of that portion of J. W. Guiteau's testimony in which he refers to a quarrel between his brother and himself. He next alluded to the criticisms on the trial by the English press, remarking with emphasis: "I say that when England claims, as her leading journal claims, that we cannot administer justice in America—that we cannot convict assassins—they belie the Court and the jury.

This remark brought Mr. Reed to his feet with a protest, and another intemperate colloquy, enlivened by the prisoner's choicest epithets, followed.

Mr. Porter, alluding to an insulting reflection on one of the witnesses as a Jew, said: It is no dishonor to any man to be the countryman of the Redeemer of mankind, or to be of the seed of those prophets whose names have come down to us in honor and whom we all agree in holding as the messengers of God. To be one of that Hebrew lineage is no disgrace. The one who sings from week to week in the church the songs of David of Israel, the one who consults the wisdom of Solomon, the man who honors the name of Saul, the one who professes to reverence—as this man does—Abraham, the progenitor of Christianity. But it is convenient for the purposes of the defense in this case to cast discredit on this witness Edwards, and so Mr. Scoville, with the decency of his client, circumcises Edwards in the presence of this Court. He has stripped himself naked, in a moral sense.

The speaker again took up the letter from Luther W. Guiteau to Mrs. Scoville, and repeated those sentences, "Disobedience of authority and rule, disobedience to God and the spirit of truth. * * * * I do know that he has in all this matter (the Oneida Community), as well as in his other acts of disobedience, been instigated by Satan and satanic influence, and I warn whomsoever it may concern to beware how they yield themselves to the wicked one. There, said he, "is the record of this man's insanity. I bring to you also the judgment of his living brother, and also the evidence of his living sister. She swears that she never suspected him of being out of his right mind until 1876. I bring to you also the evidence that there is a step-mother and a half sister of this prisoner whom he calumnates and traduces, and who are kept back from you, and we produced the wife who lay side by side with him, and who, though he professed having been kneeling at his bedside night after night never saw him do so, or else they would have been glad enough to prove it by her.

Another stormy interruption this time from Mr. Scoville and the prisoner was stopped by Judge Cox referring to note and exception.

Judge Porter then took up the evidence of Dr. Kiernan. This expert said he, declared that one person out of every five is more or less insane. Whether I am one of these unfortunate of five I do not know. I do not think however, that Dr. Kiernan would have any difficulty in sending me to a lunatic asylum for believing that this man and not Mr. Corkhill killed the President. I presume that Dr. Kiernan shares the feeling of the counsel for the defence that the man who killed the President is the man who is now personating the prisoner, and that I and Mr. Davidge stood by him with our hands upon our hip pockets ready to shield him after he had shot the President in the back. Passing on to a criticism of Dr. Spitzka's testimony, Mr. Porter continued : I wonder whether if Lucifer happened to be on trial Dr. Spitzka would say of him that he was a moral imbecile, a moral monstrosity. When Satan fell, if we may believe the book of inspiration, he fell from where? From the Empyrean heights, and he sank into the depths from which come those temptations that lead men to crime, and doom them to punishment here and hereafter. But there was a change in Satan. Dr. Spitzka thinks there never was a change in this man. He was a moral imbecile—that is, wicked from the beginning. He commented on Dr. Spitzka's description of the prisoner as a third-rate shyster of a criminal court, and quoted the significant statement of the same witness. "He has always known the legal consequences of criminal actions." Continuing, he alluded satirically to Dr. Spitzka's definition of a rhombocephalic head, and said : I wonder what this doctor would think of a vicious and kicking horse for he has pre-eminently a rhombocephalic head. The owner proposed to thrash the horse and to pass a rope over his back and to punish him, or set him to kicking at an elastic object at his back until he is tired of kicking. Dr. Spitzka would say, "Do not do that, this horse has a rhombocephalic head." It is a case of moral monstrosity, otherwise called moral insanity. Treat the horse gently ; nurse him kindly. No, no! don't shoot him. You would not surely (in the language of my friend, Mr. Reed), shoot a poor common lunatic."

Commenting on Mr. Reed's allusion to Charlotte Corday, Mr. Porter said: The world had lived since the year of the French Revolution in ignorance of the fact that the beautiful Charlotte Corday was insane. It was left to Mr. Reed to announce that fact. She cannot turn in her grave to belie it, but there are some of us who know something of the history of that wonderful woman's true patriotism which led to an assassination that was justified if ever an assassination was justified. She was no sneaking coward. She left the house in which she was reared to deliver France, to stay the hand of revolutionary slaughter; to lay her own head beneath the guillotine in order to save the effusion of blood. She believed it to be her duty to the France she loved, and she made her way with deliberate preparation, sane in mind and devoted in purpose, ready to die that others might live, and she succeeded in finding her way to the man who had in his right hand the lives of millions of Frenchmen, and who by jotting a mark of blood opposite the name could hurry men into a dismal, dark dungeon, from which there was no escape except through the guillotine. She devoted herself to the work not after providing for her own safety; not with the idea of securing rewards from others. This prisoner and his counsel made the discovery at the Corcoran Art Gallery that Charlotte Corday who will live immortal in history as one ready to give her own life for her country was insane. Forsooth, Mr. Reed would place this murderer by the side of that girl who gave her life that others might live. When she was called to execution she rose from her knees with a crucifix clasped to her breast. Another case is that of Wilkes Booth. I confess that while I have a strong conviction that Wilkes Booth was a perfectly sane man, still there were in his case circumstances that tended to mitigate in some degree the horror we feel at his crime. He was a man wholly devoted to the cause which had failed; who looked and rightly looked on Abraham Lincoln—his constancy, his wisdom, his devotion, his patriotism—as the bar which had prevented the Southern States from achieving their independence. Booth had been a play actor. He had been among many temptations. The hate of that bloody war had not passed away. He was eaten up by the love of notoriety which has led to so many crimes. He had an idea of patriotism and he became infatuated—not insanely, but wildly—with the idea that he would render a service to that portion of the country with which he had cast his ortune if he did the act. Of course neither you nor I justify the act It was justified neither by the Confederate army nor by the people of the Confederate States. It was justified by no man North or South ; but I cannot say that I have not now some degree of commiseration for the brilliant life so unfortunately ended and bound to eternal infamy by an act which I readily believe was in some degree at least, influenced by a feeling of misguided patriotism.

But what is this case? Are there in it any of the mitigating circumstances that attach even to the memory of the murderer of Lincoln? No. True, Booth shot from behind, but he felt that he was putting his life in peril for he was in a crowded audience, and yet with the instincts of manhood and believing or feeling that he might be justified by his countrymen, he leaped upon the stage, mounted his horse and rode for life or for death—he rode to death—and within the blazing flames of the building in which he was penned, as God pens murderers, he still presented the lion front of a brave man and although crippled in body he died like a stag at bay. But this man, this coward, this disappointed office seeker, this malignant diabolical, crafty, calculating, cold-blooded murderer, providing for death to his victim and for safety to himself—would you compare him with Wilkes Booth? This man has told you of the preparations he made for murder. He had been making them for years. It was a contingency which he had in view years before, while he was in New York in desperate circumstances. He read the popular literature of the day, and nursed in himself that very love of notoriety which he commended in Wilkes Booth. He had contemplated such a murder as one of his many brilliant conceptions. But, in order to illustrate the peculiarity of this man's mind, his wickedness, his recklessness, his depravity, it is enough that he should even have thought of such a thing. My attention has been called to a dialogue in one of Ouida's novels, which illustrates the topic that I am discussing. The famous John Wilkes had been mentioned as the ugliest man in Europe, and one of the parties to the dialogue said : "Let me be the ugliest man in Europe rather than to remain in mediocrity." There is not a hair breadth's difference between notoriety and fame. Let me be celebrated for something. If you cannot leap into a pit like Curtius, pop yourself into a volcano. Folly is immortal just as much as heroism. The world talks of you and that is all you want. If I could not be Alexander, I would be Diogenes. If I were not a great hero I would be a most ingenious murderer. This love of notoriety, said Mr. Porter, has pursued this man from the beginning. He never earned an honest penny.

This man has been all his life craving money. You cannot find two letters of his in this book in which mention is not made of money. His clamors from the dock have been all money! money! money! According to him the witnesses are swearing for money, the Government is prosecuting for money. He says: "I would not have killed President Garfield as I feel now, for a million of dollars." You have heard that over, over and over again until nauseation. He is "The Honorable Charles J. Guiteau, the Little Giant of the West." He was always glorifying himself. He has been endeavoring to persuade you that Providence wrought miracles in his favor, and the only reason why, when the Stonington and Narragansett came in collision, Providence saved the lives of those on board was because this travelling book peddler and lecturer was on board. That he thinks was one of the cases of special Providence. The leading spirit of the man has been—first, greed of money and the greed of reputation. When Horace Greeley was a candidate for the Presidency, this man was at his heels, an applicant for the mission to Chili. If Mr. Greeley had been elected and the Chilian mission had been refused to this man he would have got a Bulldog pistol and sent a cartridge into the back of Horace Greeley.

Passing on to the expert testimony, Mr. Porter said that every one of the thirteen experts had sworn on personal examination, that the prisoner never was insane, and three of them were witnesses who had come under subpœna from the defence, believing from public rumor that he was insane. They examined him, came to the conclusion that he was sane, and notified the counsel for the defence that they should so swear. Three of them remained and were asked the hypothetical question whether, if the prisoner were insane, he was insane. The others left the city. Those men subpœnaed on both sides, themselves the foremost men in their specialty, and selected because they were so. Men of European reputation all swore that there was no disease of the brain in this man, no insanity, but that he was as sane as any of us.

The Court here took a recess, and after reassembling, Mr. Porter resumed his argument to the jury. He proceeded to analyze the testimony, the various interruptions and the speech to the jury of the prisoner, commenting on various sentences as he went along and was met by constant interruptions and virulent remarks by the prisoner in the dock. At times it was a regular duet between counsel and prisoner, both of them speaking at the same time. Mr. Porter quoted from some scenes in "Othello," between Iago and Roderigo, in order to show that the prisoner had found in Shakespeare the idea of softening down the name of murder into "removal," but the prisoner repeatedly denied that he had ever consulted Shakespeare on the subject.

Passing on to the theory of transitory mania, Mr. Porter read from one of the prisoner's exclamations: "I repudiate the theory of Mr. Scoville. I am not insane now, and I never pretended that I was." Here the prisoner shouted, "I was insane on the 2d of July." Almost every other sentence that was uttered by Mr. Porter was retorted to by the prisoner, until finally Mr. Porter proceeded to close his argument, which he did as follows: Gentlemen, the time has come when I must close. The Government has presented the case before you, and we have endeavored to discharge our duty to the best of our abilities. His Honor has endeavored to discharge his. I know that you will be faithful to your oaths and discharge yours. So discharge it that, by your actions at least, political assassination shall find no sanction to make it a precedent hereafter. He who has ordained that human life shall be shielded by human law, from human crime, presides over your deliberations, and the verdict which shall be given or withheld to-day will be recorded where we all have to appear. I trust that that verdict will be prompt, that it will represent the majesty of the law, your integrity and the honor of the country; and that this trial which has so deeply interested all the nations of the earth may result in a warning—to reach all lands—that political murder shall not be used as a means of promoting party ends or political revolutions. I trust also that the time shall come in consequence of the attention that shall be called to the considerations growing out of this trial, when by an international arrangement between the various governments the law shall be so strengthened that political assassins shall find no refuge on the face of the earth.

The conclusion of the address was marked by a burst of applause which the officers with difficulty oppressed. When order was restored, an almost painful silence fell hushingly upon the eager yet breathless audience, for the next step in the proceedings, Judge Cox's charge to the jury, was felt by all to be an event of deep import in regard to the fate of the prisoner.

THE CHARGE TO THE JURY.

Judge Cox, at fifteen minutes past 3 P, M., proceeded to deliver his charge to the jury. He commenced by saying that the Constitution provides that in all criminal prosecutions the accused shall enjoy the right of a speedy and public trial by an impartial jury in the State or district where the crime shall have been committed. That he shall be informed of the cause and the nature of the accusation against him ; that he shall be confronted with the witnesses against him that he shall have compulsory processes to obtain witnesses in his favor and that he shall have assistance of counsel in his defence. Those provisions were intended for the protection of the innocent from injustice and oppression, and it was only by their faithful observance that guilt or innocence could be fairly ascertained. Every accused person was presumed to be innocent until the accusation was proved. With what difficulty and trouble the law had been administered in the present case the jurors had been daily witnesses. It was however, a consolation to think that not one of those sacred guarantees of the Constitution had been violated in the person of the accused. At last the long chapter of proof was ended, the task of the advocate was done, and it now rested with the jury to determine the issue between public justice and the prisoner at the bar. No one could feel more keenly than himself the great responsibility of his duties, and he felt that he could only discharge them by close adherence to the law as laid down by its highest authorities. Before proceeding further he wished to notice an incident which had taken place pending the recent argument. The prisoner had frequently taken occasion to proclaim that public opinion as evidenced by the press and correspondence was in his favor. Those declarations could not have been prevented except by the process of gagging the prisoner. Any suggestion that the jury could be influenced by such lawless clattering of the prisoner would have seemed to him absurd, and he should have felt that he was insulting the intelligence of the jury if he had warned them not to regard it. Counsel for the prosecution had felt it necessary, however, in the final argument, to interpose a contradiction to such statements and an exception had been taken on the part of the accused to the form in which that effort was made. For the sole purpose of purging the record of any objectionable matter, he should simply say that anything which had been said on either side in reference to public excitement or to newspaper opinion was not to be regarded by the jury.

The indictment charged the defendant with having murdered

James A. Garfield, and it was the duty of the Court to explain the nature of the crime charged. Murder was committed where a person of sound memory and discretion unlawfully killed a reasonable being in the peace of the United States with malice aforethought. It had to be proved, first, that the death was caused by the act of the accused, and further that it was caused with malice aforethought. That did not mean, however, that the Government had to prove any ill will or hatred on the part of the accused towards the deceased. Wherever a homicide was shown to have been committed without lawful authority and with deliberate intent ; it was sufficiently proved to have been done with malice aforethought, and malice was not disproved by showing that the accused had no personal ill will to the deceased, and that he killed him from other motives—as for instance, robbery or through mistaking him for another, or (as claimed in this case) to produce a public benefit If it could be shown that the killing occurred in a heat of passion or under provocation, then it would appear that there was no premeditated attempt and therefore no malice aforethought, and that would reduce the crime to manslaughter. It was hardly necessary, however, to say that there was nothing of that kind in the present case. The jury would have to say either that the defendant was guilty of murder or that he was innocent. In order to constitute the crime of murder the assassin must have a reasonably sane mind—in technical terms he must be "of sound mind, memory and discretion." An irresponsibly insane man could not commit murder. If he was laboring under a disease of the mental faculties to such an extent that he did not know what he was doing or did not know it was wrong, then he was wanting in that sound mind, memory and discretion that was a part of the definition of murder. In the next place every defendant was presumed innocent until the accusation against him was established by proof. In the next place, notwithstanding this presumption of innocence, it was equally true that a defendant was presumed to be sane and to have been so at the time the crime was committed—that is to say, that the Government was not bound to show affirmatively as a part of its proofs, that the defendant was sane. As insanity was the exception, and as the majority of men are sane, the law presumed the latter condition of every man until some reason was shown to believe to the contrary. The burden was therefore, on the defendant who set up insanity as an excuse for crime, to produce proofs in the first instance to show that that presumption was mistaken so far as it related to the prisoner.

Crime, therefore, involved three elements—the killing, malice and a responsible mind in the murderer. After all the evidence was before the jury, if the jury while bearing in mind both those presumptions—that is, that the defendant is innocent till he is proved guilty and that he is sane till the contrary appears—still entertained what is called a reasonable doubt on any ground or as to any of the essential elements of the crime, then the defendant was entitled to the benefit of that doubt and to an acquittal.

It was important to explain to the jury here in the best way that the Court could, what is a reasonable doubt. He could hardly venture to give an exact definition of the term for he did not know of any successful attempt to do so. As to questions relating to human affairs, a knowledge of which is derived from testimony, it was impossible to have the same kind of certainty that is created by scientific demonstration. The only certainty that the jury could have was a moral certainty, depending on the confidence which the jury had in the integrity of witnesses and in their capacity and opportunity to know the truth. If, for example, facts not improbable in themselves were attested by numerous witnesses, credible and uncontradicted, and who had every opportunity to know the truth, a reasonable or moral certainty would be inspired by that testimony. In such a case doubt would be unreasonable or imaginary or speculative. It ought not to be a doubt as to whether the party might not be innocent in the face of strong proofs of his guilt, but it must be a sincere doubt whether he had been proved guilty. Even where the testimony was contradictory and where so much more credit should be given to one side than the other, the same result might be produced. On the other hand, the opposing proofs might be so balanced that the jury might justly doubt on which side under all the circumstances the truth lay, and in such case the accused party was entitled to the benefit of the doubt. All that a jury could be expected to do was to be reasonably and morally certain of the facts which they declared to be their verdict. In illustration of this point, Judge Cox quoted the charge of Chief Justice Shaw, of Massachusetts, in the case of the COMMONWEALTH vs. WEBSTER.

With reference to the evidence in this case, very little comment was required by the Court, except upon one question—the others being hardly matters of dispute. That the defendant fired at and shot the deceased President was abundantly proved; that the wound was fatal had been testified to by the surgeons who were competent to speak, and they were uncontradicted; that the homicide was committed with malice aforethought—if the defendant was capable of criminal intent or malice—could hardly be gainsaid. It was not

GUITEAU, THE ASSASSIN. 699

necessary to prove that any special or express hatred or malice was entertained by the accused toward the deceased. It was sufficient to prove that the act was done by deliberate intent, as distinct from an act done under a certain impulse, in the heat of blood and without previous malice. Evidence had been exhibited to the jury tending to show that the defendant admitted in his own handwriting that he had conceived the idea of "removing the President" as he called it, six weeks before the shooting; that he had deliberated upon it and came to a determination to do it, and that about two weeks before he accomplished it, he stationed himself at certain points to do the act but for some reason was prevented. His preparation for it by the purchase of the pistol had been shown.

All these facts come up to the full measure of the proof required to establish what the law denominated malice aforethought. The jury would find little difficulty in reaching a conclusion as to all the elements that made up the crime charged in the indictment, except, it might be, as to the one of sound mind, memory and discretion, but that was only a technical expression for a responsible, sane man. He now approached that difficult question. He had already said that a man who is insane in the sense that makes him irresponsible cannot commit a crime. The defence of insanity had been so abused as to be brought into great discredit. It was the last resort in cases of unquestioned guilt. It had been an excuse for juries to bring in a verdict of acquittal when there was a public sympathy for the accused, and especially where there was provocation for the homicide according to public sentiment, but not according to law. For that reason the defence of insanity was viewed with disfavor, and public sentiment was hostile to it. Nevertheless, if insanity were established to a degree necessary, it was a perfect defence for an indictment for murder, and must be allowed full weight. It would be observed that in this case there was no trouble with any question about what might be called total insanity, such as raving mania, or absolute imbecility, in which all exercise of reason is wanting and where there is no recognition of persons or things or their relations. But there was a debatable border line between sanity and insanity, and there was often great difficulty in determining on which side of the line a party was to be put. There were cases in which a man's mental faculties generally seemed to be in full vigor, but where on one single subject he seemed to be deranged. A man was possessed, perhaps, by a belief of something absurd which he could not be reasoned out of (what was called an insane delusion), or he might have some morbid propensity, seemingly in harsh discord with the rest of his intellectual and moral nature. Those were cases which for want of a better term were called partial insanity. Sometimes its existence and sometimes its limits were doubtful and undefinable, and in those cases it was difficult to determine whether the patient had passed the line of moral or legal accountability for his actions. The jury would bear in mind that a man did not become irresponsible by the mere fact of his being partially insane. Such a man did not take leave of his passions by becoming insane. He might retain as much control over them as in health; he might commit offences, too, with which his infirmity had nothing to do; he might be sane as to the crime he committed, might understand its nature, and might be governed by the same motives in relation to it as other people, while on other subjects having no relations whatever to the crime, he might be the victim of delusion. Whenever this partial insanity was relied on as defence, it must appear that the crime charged was a product of the delusion or other morbid condition and connected with it as effect with cause, and that it was not the result of sane reasoning which the party might be capable of, notwithstanding his limited and circumscribed disorder. Assuming that that infirmity of mind had a direct influence on crime, the difficulty was to fix the character of the disorder which fixed responsibility or irresponsibility in law. The outgoings of the judicial mind on that subject had not been always entirely satisfactory, nor in harmony with the conclusions of medical science. Courts had in former times passed upon the law in regard to insanity, without regard to the medical aspect of the subject, but it would be only properly dealt with by a concurrence of harmonious treatment between the two sciences of law and medicine. The Courts had therefore adopted and again discarded one theory after another in the effort to find some common ground on which to stand, and his effort would be to give to the jury the results most commonly accepted by the Courts.

It would be well to say a word to the jury as to the kind of evidence by which courts and juries were guided in this difficult and delicate inquiry. That subtle essence called mind, defied, of course, ocular inspection. It could only be known by its manifestations. The test was as to whether the conduct of the man and his thoughts and emotions conformed with those of persons of sound mind, or whether they contrasted harshly with it. By that a judgment was formed as to a man's soundness of mind. And for that reason evidence was admissible to show conduct and language that would indicate to the general mind some morbid condition of the intellectual powers. Everything relating to his mental and physical history was therefore relevant, because any conclusion on the subject must often rest on a large number of facts, and letters spontaneously written afforded one of the best indications of mental condition. Evidence of insanity in the parents was always pertinent, but juries were never allowed to infer insanity in the accused from the mere fact of its existence in the ancestors. When, however, there was evidence tending to show insane conduct on the part of the accused evidence of insanity in the ancestors was admissible as corroborative of the others. Therefore, it was that, in this case, the defence had been allowed to introduce evidence covering the whole life of the accused, and reaching also his family antecedents. In a case so full of detail he should deem it to be his duty to call the attention of the jury to particular parts of it, but he wished the jury to distinctly understand that it was their province, and not his, to decide upon the facts; and if he, at any time, seemed to express or intimate an opinion on the facts, which he did not design to do, it would not be binding on them; but they must draw their own conclusions from the evidence.

The instructions which he had already given to the jury imported that the true test of criminal responsibility, where the defence of insanity was interposed, was whether the accused had sufficient use of his reason to understand the nature of the act with which he was charged, and to understand that it was wrong for him to commit it. If those were the facts he was criminally responsible for the act, whatever peculiarities might be shown of him in other respects. On the other hand, if his reason was so defective in consequence of brain diseases, that he could not understand what he was doing, or could not understand that what he was doing was wrong, he ought to be treated as an irresponsible lunatic.

As the law assumed every one at the outset to be sane and responsible, the question was, what was there in this case to show the contrary as to this defendant? A jury was not warranted in inferring that a man was insane from the mere fact of his committing a crime, or from the enormity of the crime, because the law presumes that there is a bad motive and that the crime is prompted by malice, if nothing else appears. Perhaps the easiest way for the jury to examine into the subject was first to satisfy themselves about the condition of the prisoner's mind for a reasonable period of time before any conception of the assassination had entered it, and also at the present time, and then consider what evidence exists as to a different condition of mind at the time of the commission of the act. He should not spend any time on the first question, because to examine it all, would require a review of the evidence relating to over twenty years of the prisoner's life; and this had been so exhaustively discussed by counsel, that anything he could say would be a wearisome repetition. It was enough to say that, on the one side, this evidence was supposed to show a chronic condition of insanity before the crime, and on the other side, to show an exceptionally quick intelligence and decided powers of discrimination. The jury would have to draw its own conclusions. Was the prisoner's ordinary, permanent, chronic condition of mind such that he was unable to understand the nature of his actions, and to distinguish between right and wrong in his conduct? Was he subject all the time to insane delusions which destroyed his power so to distinguish, and did those continue down to and embrace the act for which he is on trial? If so, he was simply an irresponsible lunatic. On the other hand, had he the ordinary intelligence of sane people, so that he could distinguish between right and wrong as to his actions? If another person had committed the assassination would the prisoner have appreciated the wickedness of it? Would he have understood the character of the act and its wrongfulness, if another person had suggested it to him? The jury must consider these questions in their own mind. If the jury were satisfied that his ordinary and chronic condition was that of sanity—at least so far that he knew the character of his own actions and how far they were right or wrong, and that he was not under any permanent insane delusion, which destroyed his power of discriminating between right and wrong—then the remaining inquiry was, whether there was any special insanity connected with this crime. It would be seen that the reliance of the defence was the existence of an insane delusion in the prisoner's mind, which so perverted his reason as to incapacitate him from perceiving the difference between right and wrong as to this particular act. As a part of the history of judicial sentiment on this subject, and by way of illustrating the difference between insane delusion and responsibility, he would refer the jury to a celebrated case in English history which had already been commented on in the arguments.

Judge Cox here quoted from the opinions of the judges in the McNaughton case, and from some American authorities on the same subject. He went on to say that the subject of insane delusion played an important part in this case, and demanded careful consideration. The subject was treated, to a limited extent, in judicial decisions; but more was learned about it from works of medical jurisprudence, and from expert testimony. Sane people were sometimes said to have delusions, proceeding from temporary disorders and mistakes in the senses. Sometimes they speculated on matters beyond the scope of human knowledge, but delusions in sane people were always susceptible of being corrected and removed by evidence and argument. On the contrary, insane delusions, according to all testimony, were unreasoning and incorrigible. Those who had them believed in the existence of facts which were either impossible absolutely, or impossible at least under the circumstances of the individual. A man might, with no reason for it, believe that another was plotting against his life, or that he himself was the owner of untold wealth, or that he had invented something which would revolutionize the world, or that he was the President of the United States, or Christ, or God, or that he was inspired by God to do a certain act, or that he had a glass limb—and those were cases of insane delusions. Generally the delusion centered around the patient himself, his rights or his wrongs. It came and went independently of the exercise of will and reason, like the phantasm of a dream. It was, in fact, the waking dream of the insane in which ideas presented themselves to the mind as real facts. The most certain thing was that an insane delusion was never the result of reasoning and reflection; was not generated by the mind, could not be dispelled by them. A man might reason himself, or be reasoned by others, into absurd opinions, and be persuaded into impracticable schemes, but he could not be reasoned or persuaded into insanity or insane delusions. Whenever evidence was found of an insane delusion, it was found that the insane delusion did not relate to mere sentiment, or theory, or abstract questions in laws, politics or religion. All these were subjects of opinions, and were founded on reasoning and reflection. Such opinions were often absurd in the extreme. Some persons believed in animal magnetism, in spiritualism and other like matters, in a degree which seemed absurd to other people. There was no absurdity in regard to religious, political and social questions that had not its sincere supporters. Those opinions might arise from natural weakness, bad reasoning powers, ignorance of men and things, fraudulent imposture, and often from perverted moral sentiment, but still they were opinions founded on some kind of evidence, and liable to be abandoned on better information or on sounder reasoning; but they were not insane delusions. An insane delusion was the coinage of a diseased brain, which defies reason and ridicule and throws into disorder all the springs of human action.

Before asking the jury to apply these considerations to the facts in this case, he wished to premise one or two things. The question for the jury to determine was, what was the condition of the prisoner's mind at the time when this project was executed? If he were sufficiently sane then to be responsible, it mattered not what might have been his condition before or after. Still evidence had been properly admitted as to his previous and subsequent condition, because it threw light, prospectively and retrospectively, on his condition at the time. Inasmuch as these disorders were of gradual growth and of indefinite continuance, if he were insane shortly before or shortly after the commission of the crime, it was natural to infer that he was so at the time. But still all the evidence must centre around the time when the deed was done. The jury had heard a good deal of evidence respecting the peculiarities of the prisoner through a long period of time before this occurrence, and it was claimed, on the part of the defense, that he was, during all that time, subject to delusions that were calculated to disturb his reason, and to throw it off its balance. The only materiality of that evidence was the probability which it might afford of the defendant's liability to such disorders of mind, and the corroboration which it might yield to other evidence tending to show such disorder at the time of the commission of the crime. The jury must determine whether, at the time the homicide was committed, the defendant was laboring under any insane delusion prompting and impelling him to do the deed. Naturally they would look first to any explanation of the act that might have been made by the defendant himself at the time, or immediately before or after. Several papers had been laid before them that had been in the prisoner's possession, and that purported to assign the motive for the deed. In the address to the American people, of the 16th of June, he said: "I conceived the idea of removing the President four weeks ago. Not a soul knew of my purpose. I conceived the idea myself, and I kept it to myself. I read the newspapers carefully, for and against the administration, and gradually the conviction dawned upon me that the President's removal was a political necessity, because he proved a traitor to the men who made him, and thereby imperilled the life of the nation." Again, he said in this address: "Ingratitude is the basest of crimes. The President, under the manipulation of the Secretary of State, has been guilty of the basest ingratitude to the Stalwarts. His express purpose has been to crush General Grant and Senator Conkling, and thereby open the way for his renomination in 1884. In the President's madness he has wrecked the once grand Republican Party, and for that he dies." And again: "This is not murder; it is a political necessity. It will make my friend Arthur President, and save the Republic." The other papers were of similar tenor. There was evidence that, when arrested, the prisoner refused to talk, but said that the papers would explain all. On the night of the assassination the prisoner had said to the witness Brooks, that he had thought over it, and prayed over it for weeks; that he was satisfied that he had to do the thing, and had made up his mind and had done it as a matter of duty. He had made up his mind that the President and Secretary Blaine were conspiring against the liberties of the people, and that the President must die. In addition to this, the jury had the important testimony of Mr. Reynolds as to the prisoner's statements, oral and written, about a fortnight after the shooting. There he was found reiterating the statements contained in his other papers, and saying that the situation at Albany suggested the removal of the President, and that as the faction fight became more bitter, he became more decided; that he knew Arthur would become President, and so on.

Judge Cox proceeded to quote from the address to the American people, which was written and given to Mr. Reynolds. "I now wish to state distinctly why I attempted to remove the President. I had read the papers for and against the adminisration very carefully for two months before I conceived the idea of removing him. Gradually, as the result of reading the newspaper, the idea settled on me that if the President were removed, it would unite the two factions of the Republican Party, and thereby save the Government from going into the hands of ex-rebels and their northern allies. It was my own conception, and, whether right or wrong, I take the entire responsibility."

A second paper, dated July 19th, addressed to the public, reiterated these statements, and added: "I have got the inspiration worked out of me."

The jury had now before it, His Honor said, everything emenating from the prisoner about the time of the shooting. There was nothing further from him until three months afterwards. And now he would pass to consider the import of all this. The jury would consider, first, whether this evidence fairly represented the feelings and ideas that governed the prisoner at the time of the shooting. If it did, it represented a thing which he (Judge Cox) had not seen characterized in any judicial utterance, as an insane illusion. They would consider whether it was evidence of insanity or whether, on the contrary, it showed an ample power of reasoning and reflection on the arguments and evidences for and against, resulting in the opinion that the President had betrayed his party, and that if he were out of the way, it would be a benefit to his party, and would save the country from the predominance of their political opponents. So far there was nothing insane in the conclusion. It had doubtless been shared by a good many heated partisans who were sane people, but the difference was that the prisoner reached the conclusion that to put the President out of the way by assassination, was a political necessity. When men reasoned, the law required them to reason correctly, so far as their practical duties were concerned. When they had the capacity to distinguish between right and wrong they were bound to do so. Opinions, properly so-called—that is, beliefs resulting from reasoning, reflection and the examination of evidence—afforded no protection against the penal consequences of crime. A man might believe a course of action to be right, and the law might forbid it as wrong. Nevertheless he must obey the law, and nothing could save him from the consequences of the violation of the law except the fact that he was so crazed by disease as to be unable to comprehend the necessity of obedience. (In this connection Judge Cox quoted the decision of the Supreme Court in the Mormon case.) In like manner, he said, a man might reason himself into a conviction of the expediency and necessity of protecting the character of a political association, but to allow him to find shelter from punishment behind that belief would be simply monstrous. Between one and two centuries ago, there had arisen a school of moralists who were accused of maintaining the doctrine that whenever the end to be attained was right, any means necessary to its attainment were justifiable. Consequently they incurred the odium of nearly all Christendom. By that method of reasoning the prisoner seemed to have gotten the idea that in order to unite the Republican Party and to save the Republic, whatever means were necessary would be justifiable; that the death of the President by violence was only a proper and necessary means of accomplishing it, and was therefore justifiable; and that, being justifiable as a political necessity, it was not murder. This appeared to be the substance of the idea which the prisoner had put forth to the world, and if this was the whole of his position, it presented one of those vagaries of opinion, even if it were sincere, for which the law had no accommodation and which furnished no excuse whatever for crime.

There was undoubtedly a form of insane delusion, consisting of a belief by a person that he was inspired by the Almighty to do something—to kill another, for example—and this delusion might be so strong as to impel him to the commission of crime. The defendant in this case claimed that he labored under such a delusion at the time of the assassination. His unsworn declarations in his own favor were not, of course, evidence, and were not to be considered by the jury. A man's language, when sincere, might be evidence of his condition of mind, but not evidence in his favor of the facts declared by him. He could never manufacture evidence in that way in his own exoneration. The law allowed a prisoner to testify in his own behalf, and therefore made his sworn testimony on the witness stand legal evidence, to be received and considered, and given such weight as it deserved. No verdict, however, could be safely rendered on the sole evidence of an accused party under such circumstances. Otherwise, a man on trial for his life, could secure his acquittal by simply testifying that he had committed the crime under a delusion or inspiration or irresistible impulse. That would be to proclaim a universal amnesty to criminals in the past, and unbounded license in the future, and courts of justice might as well be closed.

He would say a word about the characteristics of that form of delusion. The idea of being inspired to do an act might be either a a sane belief or an insane delusion. A great many Christian people believed not only that events were providentially ordered, but that they themselves received special Providential guidance and illumination in respect both to their inward thoughts and their outward actions. But this was a mere sane belief. On the other hand, if a man sincerely, though insanely, believed that, like St. Paul on his way to Damascus, he had been smitten to the earth and had seen a great light, and had heard a voice from heaven warning and commanding him to do a certain act, that would be a case of imaginary inspiration amounting to insane delusion. The question was, whether the case of this defendant presented anything analogous to that. The theory of the Government was, that the defendant committed this homicide in full possession of his faculties and from perfectly sane motives; that he did the act from revenge, or perhaps from a morbid desire for notoriety; that he calculated deliberately on being protected by those who were to be benefited politically by the death of the President; that he made no pretense of inspiration at the time of the assassination, nor until he had discovered that his expectations from the so-called Stalwart wing of the Republican Party were delusive, and that then, for the first time, he broached this theory of inspiration and irresistible pressure to the commission of the act. Whether this was true or not, the jury must determine from the evidence. It was true that the term "inspiration" did not appear in the paper first written by the defendant, nor in those delivered to Mr. Reynolds, except at the close of one dated July 19th, in which he said that the inspiration was worked out of him (although what that meant was not clear), and it was true also that that was after he was informed that he was being denounced by the Stalwarts.

In this connection Judge Cox referred to the testimony of Dr. Noble Young, Dr. MacDonald and Dr. Gray, and this, he said, was about the substance of what appeared in the case on the subject of inspiration.

Judge Cox went on to say that the question for the jury was whether, on the one hand, the idea of killing the President first presented itself to the defendant in the shape of a command or inspiration of the Deity, in the manner in which insane delusions of that sort arose ; or whether, on the other hand, it was a conception of his own, and whether the thought of inspiration was not simply a speculation, a theory, or theoretical conclusion, of his own mind. If it were the latter, it was nothing more than one of the vagaries of reasoning, which he had already characterized as furnishing no excuse for crime. He had dwelt upon the question of insane delusion simply because the evidence relating to that was evidence touching the defendant's power, or want of power (from mental disease), to distinguish between right and wrong as to the act done by him. This was the broad question for the jury to determine, and was what was relied upon by the defence.

It had been argued with force on the part of the defence, that there were a great many things in the defendant's conduct which could not be expected of a sane man, and which were only explainable on the theory of insanity. There were strange things in his career, and whether they were really indications of insanity or could be accounted for by his ignorance of men, by his exaggerated egotism or by his bluntness of moral sense, it might be difficult to determine. The only safe rule, however, was for the jury to direct its attention to the one test of criminal responsibility, namely—whether the prisoner possessed the mental capacity, at the time the act was committed, to know that it was wrong : or whether he was deprived of that capacity by mental disease. There was one important distinction which the jury must not lose sight of, and they must decide how far it was applicable to this case. That was the distinction between mental and moral obliquity, between the mental incapacity to distinguish between right and wrong, and the moral insensibility to that distinction.

In conclusion he said:—From the materials presented to you, two pictures have been drawn to you by counsel. The one represents a youth of more than average mental endowments, surrounded by certain immoral influences at the time his character was being developed, commencing life without resources, but developing a vicious sharpness and cunning, conceiving "enterprise of great moment" that indicated unusual forecast, although beyond his resources, consumed all the time by unsated egotism and a craving for notoriety ; violent in temper, selfish, immoral and dishonest; leading a life of hypocrisy, swindling and fraud, and finally, as a culmination of his depraved career, working himself into the resolution of startling the world with a crime which would secure him a bad eminence.

The other represented a youth, born, as it were, under malign influences—the child of a diseased mother and of a father subject to insane delusions, reared in retirement and imbued with fanatical religious views ; subsequently his mind filled with fanatical theories, launched on the world with no guidance save his own impulses, evincing an incapacity for any continuous employment, changing from one pursuit to another—now a lawyer, now a religionist, and now a politician, unsuccessful in all, full of wild, impracticable schemes for which he had neither resources nor ability, subject to delusions, his mind incoherent and incompetent of reasoning coherently on any subject, with a mind so weak and a temper so impressionable that he became deranged, and was therefore impelled to the commission of a crime the seriousness of which he could not understand.

It is for you, gentlemen, to determine which of the portraits is the true one. And now, gentlemen, to sum up all I have said to you, if you find from the whole evidence that, at the the time of the commission of the homicide, the prisoner was laboring under such a defect of his reason that he was incapable of understanding what he was doing, or of seeing that it was a wrong thing to do—as, for example, if he were under the insane delusion that the Almighty had commanded him to do the act—then he was not in a responsible condition of mind, but was an object of compassion and should be now acquitted. If, on the other hand, you find that he was under no insane delusion, but had the possession of his faculties and had power to know that his act was wrong, and if of his own free will he deliberately conceived the idea and executed the homicide, then whether his motive were personal vindictiveness, political animosity, a desire to avenge supposed political wrongs, or of a morbid desire for notoriety ; or if you are unable to discover any motive at all, the act is simply murder, and it is your duty to find a verdict of guilty as indicted. Or (after a suggestion from Mr. Scoville to that effect) if you find that the prisoner is not guilty by reason of insanity, it is your duty to say so. You will now retire to your room and consider your verdict.

THE JURY OUT.

During the delivery of the charge, which occupied until twenty minutes to 5 o'clock, P. M., an unbroken stillness obtained, save on two occasions when the prisoner, with more mildness of manner than he had ever before exhibited, respectfully suggested points which he conceived he had a right to claim. Slowly the jury filed out of the Court room and many of the audience also gladly availed themselves of the opportunity to terminate their self-imposed incarceration. The Court was occupied with some routine matters for a brief period, and then some twenty minutes after the jury had retired, took a recess until 5.30 P. M.

Within ten minutes afterward the jury summoned the bailiff in charge and stated that they were ready with their verdict, having thus been but thirty minutes in consultation. They were informed of the recess taken by the Court and of the fact that Judge Cox had left the building; consequently they waited in their room for the official summons. But the fact that they had agreed, speedily leaked out, and like a returning wave the impatient mass of humanity surged back upon the Court room, apparently conscious that the promptness of the jury could only mean a verdict of guilty.

It was a scene never to be forgotten. Strangely enough the gas man has never yet invaded this antiquated, musty court-room, and the gathering darkness of a winter afternoon was but partially combatted by the fitful glimmer of primitive candles, planted here and there on the desks of the Judge, the clerk, the counsels and the well-nigh wearied out journalistic corps. "Ever been at an inquest in a village?" was the whispered query of one loquacious scribe. "Yes!" was the softly muttered response. "I was down at Vineland after Landis murdered Carruth." "Ah!" yes!" remarked another scribe, as he thoughtfully sharpened his Faber; "but this alleged lunatic won't have Landis' luck." Further comment was cut short by the stern. "Order! order!" of the Court officers, as Judge Cox, with impressive solemnity, took his seat. At twenty-five minutes to six o'clock the jury returned to their seats, and again a great hush fell upon the densely packed audience. Slowly and firmly the clerk in the usual formula inquired of the foreman whether the jury had agreed upon their verdict. With equal distinctness and firmness came the reply: "We have." Then again the clerk asked: "What is your verdict—guilty, or not guilty?" The intense silence at this moment was as deep as that darkness in Egypt—it could be felt? With a clear, metallic ring came the answer:

"**GUILTY AS INDICTED!**"

There was an immediate demonstration of applause on the part of the audience, which was promptly and properly checked by the officers. In the meantime, Mr. Scoville and the District Attorney were each claiming the ear of the Court. The latter asserted his routine rights, however, and said: "Wait till we have the verdict complete and in due form of law." The clerk then put the formal question to the jury collectively, in the following words: "Your foreman says: 'Guilty as indicated,' so say we all of us?" The collective response came without hesitation: "We do."

Mr. Scoville still insisted on his privilege and demanded a poll of the jury. Each juror was then called by name, and each firmly and unhesitatingly responded: "Guilty."

Guiteau, who had keenly watched each of the twelve as the names were called, shrieked out, as the last response was given: "*My blood will be upon the heads of that jury. And don't you forget it.*"

Mr. Scoville again addressed the Court, saying: "Your Honor, I do not desire to forfeit any rights I may have under the law and practice in this District. If there is anything that I ought to do now to save these rights, I would be indebted to your Honor to indicate it to me."

Judge Cox assured him that he should have every opportunity; that the charge would be furnished to him in print to-morrow, and he would be accorded all the time allowed by law within which to file his exceptions, and that he would also be entitled to four days within which to move an arrest of judgment.

Once more Guiteau interrupted, with a parting broadside as from a sinking pirate ship: "God will avenge this outrage."

Judge Cox then turned to the jury and said: "Gentlemen of the jury, I cannot express too many thanks for the manner in which you have discharged your duty. You have richly merited the thanks of your countrymen, and I feel assured you will take with you to your homes the approval of your consciences. With thanks, gentlemen of the jury, I dismiss you."

It was over, the dismal, weary farce of many anxious days, the unparalleled judicial forbearance of ten long weeks, and the over-strained audience passed quietly out with the solemn conviction that the law had been vindicated, and the outrage upon the American people was in a fair way to be atoned for. Not less anxious were the jurymen, and courteously, but firmly, declining the Marshal's invitation to an elegant dinner, they hastily betook themselves to their long neglected homes, each feeling, or being entitled to feel, that he had by his patience, his attention and his sterling integrity earned the gratitude, respect and admiration of every honest fellow-citizen of this great Republic.

The prisoner was manacled and led away, looking like a man upon whom some unjustifiable indignity had been perpetrated, and as he passed the reporter's table he bent over and with an air of seeming contentment, remarked: "The Court in banc will reverse all this business."

As Guiteau was put into the van and driven away, the hooting, jeering and yelling of the men and boys must have convinced him that his boast: "The American people are with me," was but an empty mockery.

CHAPTER XLIX.

Argument for a New Trial—Some Lively Scenes between Counsel—
Judge Cox Takes the Papers.

ON Friday, February 3d, when the prisoner was brought in, he was, as usual, placed in the dock, but in a deferential manner applied to the Court, for permission to sit at the counsel table. Judge Cox said he had no objection if counsel were not opposed to it. Turning blandly to the District Attorney, Guiteau asked: "You have no objection, Colonel?" "No, sir!" replied Colonel Corkhill, and the prisoner was led to his old seat. He began at once, however, to attempt an address to the Court.

Mr. Scoville (interrupting).—"I think that that is improper. I think we ought to go on with this motion. I desire, if the Court please, to make a further motion this morning for leave to file additional grounds for a new trial (and I have an affidavit in support of this case), which have come to my knowledge since the motion was filed."

Mr. Scoville then read the affidavit filed by himself as counsel for the defendant. It states that other facts have come to his knowledge since the filing of the motion for a new trial, which he deems it material should be properly shown to the Court, as follows, to wit: That during the trial of this case and while the jury were guarded at the National Hotel, out of Court hours, they were visited by one William McFeeley, a clerk in the Treasury Department, and one John J. Downs, an employee in the Signal Service of the United States, for the purpose of "seeing the boys" and taking cigars to them; that on their second visit they were accompanied by Benjamin Miller; that at such visit they were permitted by the bailiffs to have, or without the knowledge of the bailiff had, conversation with one or more of the jurors relating to this case and to the action of the jury. The affiant further says, that on the afternoon of the 2d of February, 1882, he received information by mail, that four different persons would testify to declarations by one of the expert witnesses of the prosecution made since the trial that he thought the defendant insane, but he thought it would be damaging to him in business and public estimation to appear as a witness in behalf of the defendant, which expert witness testified that the prisoner was sane. The affiant further says, that he does not know the names of these four persons, but believes that he can obtain them within three or four days. They had expressed their willingness to give their testimony.

Mr. Scoville (continuing).—" On that affidavit I ask leave of the Court to file the additional grounds thereon indicated in support of the motion for a new trial, to wit: Unauthorized conversation with jurors by outside parties, and the subsequent admissions by one of the experts who testified unequivocally on the trial that he was convinced that the prisoner was sane, who now says that he considers him insane. The Court will see that ir this affidavit I have contemplated that additional time will be given for argument. There are three reasons for that. First, it is uncertain whether, if this matter now before the Court is properly investigated, it will not take two or three days to determine. My opinion is that it will. Another ground is that I have assurance from a prominent member of the bar, that if his engagements permit—and he thinks they will—by the middle of next week, he will come in here and help me."

The District Attorney.—"Who is that?"

Mr. Scoville refused to give the name of the lawyer, but stated that he would give it to the Court in confidence.

The third reason presented by Mr. Scoville in his motion to file additional grounds for a new trial was that the decision of this motion could not in any way facilitate the final judgment of the Court one day or one hour. It seemed to him that that was a consideration which should appeal to the Court.

The Court stated that Mr. Scoville might proceed with his argument, and in the meantime he (the Court) would take this new matter into consideration.

Mr. Scoville then read the affidavits filed in support of his motion which were in effect that on a certain day in December, one Frederick Snyder, passing room 92 in the National Hotel, where the jury were lodged, found the door open, saw a copy of the *Evening Critic* lying on the table and entering the room, took it and brought it away. That there were marks in writing on the margin of the paper, being the signatures in whole or in part of some of the jurors, etc.

When the reading was concluded he said that he thought they presented a question which he did not think could be properly determined on *ex-parte* affidavits, and suggested that an examination be instituted by the Court. He proposed to place before each witness the signatures on the newspaper and the signatures of the jurors in autograph albums, and ask them whether, from a comparison, they were of opinion that the signatures on the paper were genuine. He asked the Court to take such steps as would probe the question to the bottom. He was perfectly willing that His Honor should call in experts and let them compare the signatures on the newspapers with those in the autograph albums.

I am accused by the District Attorney, he continued, of procuring a forgery to be made in this case, and the charge of forgery is made against a reputable citizen of New Jersey, a man against whom I defy any proof of misconduct to be produced. He is accused of forgery, and it has gone out to the world that he has committed a forgery without any motive, because counsel will not dare to intimate that there has been any money used on behalf of the defendant in this case. It appears that his sole and only purpose in picking up a paper from the jury room and handing it to me was to subserve the purpose of justice, and that the motive and conduct of this gentleman should be recognized publicly by the Court as being in accordance with principles of justice and in aid of the Court arriving at a proper judgment in this case. The District Attorney grautitously stated that this gentleman had been arrainged for forgery. I am informed that this is not the fact. I am informed by a gentleman on the Grand Jury who had the matter in charge that when a charge was made against this man for purloining letters the Grand Jury became satisfied that it was a matter of personal pique between two individuals and refused to receive it. That is all the foundation for the allegation against that gentleman.

The District Attorney declared that in his belief the signatures upon the margin of the newspaper were base forgeries, but that he did not believe that they had been perpetrated by Mr. Scoville. He thought, however, that he could convince Mr. Scoville of the fact; that he could convince the Court of it, and that he could convince the country of it. The District Attorney then proceeded to read a number of affidavits made by the jurors and bailiffs.

The first affidavit sworn to by Foreman Hamlin, states his belief that the signatures on the *Evening Critic* are forgeries; that he noticed Snyder at the hotel, thought his conduct suspicious and warned the other members of the jury against him. The other affidavits of the jurors were similar in effect. Those jurors whose names are on the margin of the paper swear that those names are forgeries, while the other jurors declare their belief that they are forged. Juror Browner's affidavit differs from those of his associates in this only, that on one occasion he noticed Mr. Scoville passing through the passage in the National Hotel engaged in earnest conversation with some one to affiant unknown, and that his conduct was such as to raise a suspicion in affiant's mind as to the purpose for which he was there.

The next affidavit read was signed by Norman Wiard. He states that he has known Frederick H. Snyder for fifteen years: that he does not think him worthy of belief; that he is a well-known detective, whose business it is to suborn perjury; that he is a thief, a forger and a blackmailer: that he once stole some letters from affiant's room and affiant had him arrested for larceny

Affidavits filed by detectives McElfresh and Sargeant, of Washington, simply stated the fact that in 1875 they arrested Frederick H. Snyder on the charge of larceny.

Mr. Scoville inquired whether His Honor would take under consideration the question as to whether he would allow evidence to be taken as to the genuineness of the jurors' signatures on the margin of the newspapers taken from room No. 92.

The Court replied that he could not admit affidavit or oral evidence tending to show that the disputed writing was the writing of the jurors by simply comparing it with other papers produced for that purpose.

Mr. Scoville cited some authorities to the Court on the question as to whether it was not competent for the Court to inquire into the conduct of the jurors.

Mr. Davidge then proceeded to argue against the motion for a new trial. The subject of newly-discovered evidence was touched upon briefly, Mr. Davidge holding that the evidence which the defence desired to bring in, was simply cumulative and of the weakest kind. As to the matter of the finding of the newspaper in a room to which the jurors had access during the trial Mr. Davidge criticized severely the conduct of Snyder in going into a room which he had no authority to enter and taking therefrom an article he had no right to.

Any fair minded man would concede that the status of Snyder was one of suspicion. Even granting that the paper had been found in the room it did not follow at all that any of the jurors had ever read the newspaper. It was remarkable how glibly that fact was assumed. It seemed a most natural thing to Mr. Scoville, that a man who inscribed his name on a newspaper must *necessitate rei* have read the contents of that newspaper. He (Davidge) contended that the presumption of law is the other way. In the course of further criticism of Snyder's conduct, Mr. Davidge sneeringly referred to his entering a strange room, when the prisoner suggested that the door of the room was open.

Mr. Davidge.—"Yes, and many private doors are open; but what would you think of me if I went mousing around private rooms?"

The prisoner.—"If you had been in Snyder's place you would have done what he did."

Mr. Davidge.—"Suppose that it was something of more value than a newspaper he had taken away?"

Mr. Davidge then commented upon the circumstance of the finding of the newspaper in the jurors' quarters having been known by Mr. Scoville in December, and upon that gentleman's failure to bring it to the attention of the Court at that time.

The Court.—"It is due to Mr. Scoville to say

that he did bring it to my attention at the time. I made inquiries of the Marshal and discovered that it was an error."

Mr. Davidge — "These papers do not show that Mr. Scoville brought it to the attention of the Court and jury, but took the chance of the trial, and after that was decided against him revamped it as a ground for a new trial."

Mr. Davidge, continuing his argument, contended that it was no evidence that the jurors read the *Evening Critic* because their names were upon it.

Mr. Davidge characterized the proposition for the appointment of a commission to inquire into the matter as simple, unqualified nonsense, and protested against the final action of the jury being impeached by a miserable and despicable trick. He referred to Snyder as being spotted as a leopard in this business, because a man cannot touch filth without being defiled. He touched briefly upon the motion submitted by Mr. Scoville to be permitted to file additional grounds for his motion for a new trial, but after a short review of the points submitted, dismissed them with the remark, that they amounted to nothing. In conclusion he said: "If ever a case was fairly tried it was the case of the United States against Charles J. Guiteau. Certainly he can lodge no complaint against the liberality, patience and justice of this Court, and I humbly submit that public policy and the administration of justice alike demand that the trial shall come to an end and the motion for a new trial be overruled."

Mr. Scoville then indignantly replied to the criticisms which had been made against Snyder both by counsel for the prosecution and by affiants. He had been maligned and traduced. The Court must assume that he was an honest man, and every step he had taken was consistent with that assumption. What he had done had been imperative upon him as an honest man. In the course of his remarks Mr. Scoville intimated that the affidavits of the jurors had been drawn up under the direction of Mr. Davidge. This the latter denied, but stated that whatever the jury swore he would endorse.

After a few sarcastic interchanges between the counsels generally, Mr. Scoville continued to argue that it was improbable that Mr. Snyder had "put up a job" in this matter, and stated that when the case came before the Court in banc he should make a point whether the Counsel for the prosecution have any right, at every stage of the case, to denounce and villify not only the defendant but the witnesses for the defence.

The District Attorney also placed in evidence the certified record of the Police Court in the case of the *United States* vs. *Frederick H. Snyder*, where the defendant was held in bail for the action of the Grand Jury.

The affidavit of George C. Curtis, was then read. He stated that he was one of the bailiffs in charge of the jury; that he occupied Room 92, in which Snyder swears he found the newspaper; that he did not purchase a copy of the *Evening Critic* during the trial; that there never was a copy of the *Critic* in his room, unless placed there by some person with a sinister motive; that Mr. Scoville had been seen in the corridors of the hotel upon two occasions, and that he (the witness) had examined the copy of the paper and did not believe the signatures thereon to be the signatures of the jurors.

Allan R. Searle, another of the bailiffs in charge of the jury, swore that he noticed three persons at the National Hotel on one occasion, whose actions attracted his attention; that they were Frederick H. Snyder, George Scoville and J. E. Hayden; that this matter was the subject of criticism and remarks, and that at the hour when Snyder says that he took the newspaper from room 92, the jury were in their rooms, and that it was therefore impossible that he could have done so.

The last affidavit read was that of Henry Bragden, one of the witnesses whose evidence Mr. Scoville desired to bring in as newly discovered evidence, who denied that he ever saw the prisoner, except one day while he was being taken from the Court room to the van. He stated that last June he did see a man in Lafayette Park who may have been this prisoner, and that he remarked that he must be either a disappointed office seeker or a lunatic. He denied, however, the statement made by Mr. Scoville in his affidavit, that he was frightened out of the Park by the crazy conduct of the prisoner.

The District Attorney then stated that he had nothing to add to those affidavits. He thought they completely disposed of the motion for a new trial.

Mr. Scoville.—"I desire to move to expunge from those affidavits, certain portions of them which the District Attorney, it seems to me, must have known were not proper to be included therein. It is not right to place on the record here such vague allegations affecting the character and integrity of a citizen as has been included in these affidavits, without being called for, without being permissible therein for any purpose."

Judge Cox.—"There is a good deal in the affidavits, particularly in regard to Snyder, which is not competent evidence, and will not be considered by the Court at all."

After a long argument and an admission by the District Attorney that there was a good deal of testimony in the affidavits which was not legitimate, the Court ordered the affidavit of Mr. Wiard to be expunged, except so far as it impeached the credit of Snyder for truth and veracity. The Court further stated that with the exception of the affidavits filed by the defence, he had not read the affidavits read here this morning. They were new to him, and he did not feel that he ought to act upon the motion without taking it under advisement until the next day. If counsel had any question of law or fact which they wished to discuss meanwhile, it might be well to do so.

The prisoner, who, when not engaged in impudent or blasphemous interruptions had been busy in comparing the names of the jurors on the margin of the newspaper with their names as they appeared in an autograph album, exclaimed, "Any one can see that they are in the same handwriting. A hundred experts would testify to that. I know something about handwriting myself."

The District Attorney.—"Yes, they are very clever forgeries."

Judge Cox then asked Mr. Scoville to hand him certain authorities from which he had quoted (20 Iowa and 43 Connecticut), and this being done the Court adjourned.

CHAPTER L.

The Application for a New Trial Refused—The Prisoner Sentenced to be Hanged on June 30—End of the Trial.

ON Saturday morning, February 4th, for the first time in the whole course of the trial, there were some vacant seats in the auditorium of the Court room. Shortly after ten o'clock, the prisoner was brought in and allowed to take his seat at the counsels' table. Mr. Scoville attempted to interject some alleged new evidence as to the conduct of one of the bailiffs in charge of the jury, but the District Attorney protested strongly, urging that it was unfair to attempt to put the bailiffs and the jury on trial.

Judge Cox sustained this view, and then proceeded to deliver his decision on the motion for a new trial.

THE COURT'S DECISION.

Judge Cox said that the motion to set aside the verdict and grant a new trial had been based on various grounds, only two of which were made the subjects of discussion and used to be considered by the Court.

The first ground in substance was that certain newspaper matter calculated to prejudice the minds of the jury against the prisoner was found in one of the rooms assigned to the jury, and passed under their examination and inspection. Undoubtedly if any undue influence had been used to bring about the verdict, it would be good ground for setting it aside, and the fact that matter in writing or print calculated to prejudice the jury came into their possession and was examined by them, was ordinarily considered as a sufficient ground to vacate the verdict. But the legal intendment was in favor of the verdict, and no verdict ought to be disturbed (and certainly none which had been effected after so much time and labor as this one), without a clear and satisfactory reason for it. Some pertinent observations on this subject were found in THE PEOPLE vs. GAFFNEY, 1st Sheldon's Rep., in which it was decided that justice should not be defeated on the mere suspicion of improper influence on the jury.

The first testimony relied upon in support of this alleged ground was the affidavit of Snyder, to the effect that a certain paper was found by him in one of the rooms occupied by the jury. To the mere fact that, in the absence of the jury, a paper, of whatever character, was found in the vacant room, the Court could attach no significance or weight, for the reason that it was within the power of anybody to place the paper there. It was in the power of any friend of the prisoner to do so. It was in the power of the affiant himself to do so. He might have placed it there and afterwards found it, and that fact would not be inconsistent with the truth of the affidavit. He (the Court) did not mean to express any opinion as to Snyder's complicity in this transaction, but he simply stated this to show the facility with which this state of facts could be brought out designedly. A prisoner would have nothing to do but to get a friend to commit the very trick that is suspected and charged by the Government in this very case, and that fact alone would not influence the Court in the slightest degree, and affidavits of the bailiffs and the jury showed that this was not the room of any of the jurors, but was the room of the bailiffs, to which the jurors resorted occasionally for the purpose of signing their autographs, but always under the observation of the bailiffs.

It was further testified, however, by Mr. John W. Guiteau that certain signatures appearing on this paper were in the handwriting of the jurors. If that were true, it would follow that the paper was under their observation and in their hands. It was somewhat surprising at first to find the averment that the affiant was acquainted with the handwriting of the jurors, for obviously that knowledge could not have been acquired in the ordinary way—in the regular course of business or social intercourse. It did not appear, except by statements at the bar, how that knowledge had been acquired. The inference was that it had been acquired by procuring the autographs of those jurors for this special purpose. When it was acquired did not appear, and that might be an important question. It might have been acquired before the making of the affidavit, for the express purpose of allowing the affidavit to be made, and there was great doubt whether knowledge acquired in that way would qualify a person to testify as to handwriting. Such a case appeared in Doc vs. Scyamore, 12 Adolphus and Ellis. It was a subject of doubt whether if this knowledge had been acquired for the express purpose of qualifying affiant to testify in this case, it made him a competent witness, and it was obvious that this knowledge was acquired under a certain bias and under circumstances which took away from the influence which would attach to it if acquired in the regular way. Therefore it was that he thought this affidavit was one of doubtful competency and doubtful weight. He had not given close criticism to the writing on the paper, but his eye had been attracted by one or two circumstances which were somewhat suspicious.

The letter "H," in the initial of Mr. Bright's name, was written in two or three different ways, and Mr. Heinline's name was spelled in two ways, and each wrong, which made it extremely improbable that those gentlemen could have written their names themselves. On the other hand, as opposed to the affidavit of Mr. Guiteau, were the affidavits of the four gentlemen whose names were purported to be on the paper, and who testified that the names were not in their handwriting. The other jurors did not pretend to know the handwriting of their co-jurors, but united in swearing that no such paper was in the room at all.

And still he could conceive that these jurors were honestly mistaken; he could conceive the state of facts as was supposed by the counsel for the defence, that this newspaper, nearly a month old at the time it was said to have been found, was lying in the room of the bailiff, and that those gentlemen before writing their autographs tried their pen or ink by scribbling on the paper, and yet were so unscrupulous as to ignore its presence and to be conscientiously convinced that no such paper was there at all. He could conceive that state of facts to exist, but could hardly believe it existed after the unanimous affidavits of the bailiffs or jurors that no paper came under their observation at all.

Supposing such a state of things to exist, what could be the consequence? The only effect of that fact would be to raise a suspicion or a probable inference that the contents of the paper were brought to the notice of the jury; but that was a suspicion and an inference that might be repelled. In this case there was no conflict of testimony as to the contents of the paper having been seen by the jurors. It was the unanimous testimony of all of them that neither that nor any other paper was read by them. There were several cases reported on the books, in which it appeared that newspapers or other forbidden matters had found their way into the jury's room, and yet the verdict had not been held to be affected by that circumstance. The Court here quoted the case of HICKS vs. DUERING, 5 Pickering where, though a forbidden paper had been found in the jury room, upon the jurors representing that they had not read it, the Court sustained the verdict. In regard to the question whether this paper was read by the jury, it was the unanimous testimony of all of them that they saw no newspaper at all while they were engaged in that case, and about that he did not think there was any room for mistake. He had not the slightest ground for suspecting the integrity or veracity of these gentlemen, who made this statement under oath. Nothing was presented which threw a suspicion on the good conduct of the jury in regard to the matter now charged.

It had been suggested that a commission should issue to take testimony; that was a practice entirely foreign to common law courts. Even if he felt that he had the discretion to do so, was the matter before him such as would call for the exercise of such discretion? There was no suggestion that there would be any witness who would swear that the names on the margin of the newspaper were in the handwriting of the jurors. Even if this were true it would not influence the decision of the Court, unless it could also be shown that the paper had been read by the jury. It had been suggested that there might be witnesses who were deterred from voluntarily coming forward by public clamor, but who, if a commission were issued, would be compelled to appear and testify. But there was no averment that in point of fact any such witnesses existed; it amounted to an application to the Court to send out a roving and fishing commission to seek evidence to invalidate the verdict, and even if he had the power he would not be justified in granting that application.

One of the additional grounds for the motion made yesterday was that information had reached counsel of conversations between the jury and other parties. That was stated simply on information— on the say so of a third person not named. Information of that sort would be coming to counsel all the time, but no Court could act except upon sworn statements.

Then, again, it had beeen suggested that the Court subject the jury to a cross-examination. It had always been a question whether a voluntary affidavit on the part of a juror as to the conduct of another juror could be received. The general rule was that it could not. He had never yet heard of a practice of compelling a juror to testify as to misconduct in the jury box. He did not see anything in the paper that required inquisition into the conduct of the jury. There was nothing suspicious about their affidavits; but they bore every evidence of sincerity and truth.

Another ground alleged was discovery of new evidence; and the evidence in question was simply that of two individuals who, it was said, would testify that between the 15th and 28th of June the prisoner was seen by them in Lafayette Square, and that his conduct and actions were such as to excite their suspicions of his sanity. In this connection it was well to consider what evidence had already been introduced on the part of the defence in the same direction. They had introduced evidence touching the prisoner's conduct and actions covering the period from the first of March down to the day of the assassination. The evidence now proposed to be offered was exactly of the same character as that already introduced and therefore was essentially cumulative evidence. There was another consideration, and that was whether such evidence if introduced would be likely to change the result. It seemed to him that this evidence was so light and inconclusive that there was no probability that it could have affected this case. It might be very well understood that the manner, restlessness and excitement of the prisoner on that occasion would engender a suspicion as to his sanity in the minds of persons who knew nothing about his circumstances; but when it was known that at that time he had resolved upon the commission of homicide and was awaiting his opportunity, all this restlessness would be quite compatible with sanity. He (the Court) could not conceive that evidence of this kind could operate to bring about a different result. In addition to this it might be remarked that the affidavit now filed by Mr. Bragden on the part of the prosecution showed that the defence would be disappointed with his testimony and would lessen the weight of what might be said by other witnesses.

It was further alleged that the defence might be able to prove that one of the expert witnesses had admitted since the trial that his opinion was different from that which he had given at the trial. It was a general rule that newly discovered evidence, going to impeach a witnesss, was not a ground for a new trial under any circumstances, but least of all when it went to admission of a witness, after the conclusion of the trial. That would place it in the power of any witness to set aside a verdict founded upon his own testimony after the trial was over. No evidence of that kind could be considered by the Court in regard to a new trial. He had considered all the matters which had been presented and was compelled to overrule the motion for a new trial.

Mr. Scoville noted an exception to the ruling of the Court and also requested the Court to rule upon the motion to expunge certain matters in the affidavits reflecting upon the witness Snyder.

The Court stated that he had already ruled that whatever related to Snyder in the affidavits, except such matters as went to his credibility as a witness, should be suppressed, but he did not think that the portions of the affidavits of the jury in relation to Snyder were improper. The affidavit of Snyder attacked the jurors, and they had the right to say that they regarded his conduct as suspicious. There was nothing slanderous in their averments.

Mr. Scoville thought that a mere statement of a conclusion without a ground to support it was improper.

The Court did not think it was so slanderous that it ought to be expunged. The jury had a right to express an opinion. The Court did not pretend to express any opinion himself on that subject, he did not think it necessary.

Mr. Scoville then filed a motion in arrest of judgment, which was overruled by the Court, and exception taken.

After some discussion during which Guiteau violently abused his counsel and then appealed to the Court to preserve all his rights in banc, it was finally arranged between the Court, the District Attorney and Mr. Scoville, that the latter should have till the 1st of March to file his bill of exceptions.

The District Attorney then said: "The duty is now imposed upon me to ask the Court to pass sentence in accordance with the verdict.

The prisoner.—"I ask your Honor to defer that as long as you can."

The Court (to the prisoner).—"Stand up." (The prisoner rose). "Have you anything to say why sentence should not be pronounced?"

Quietly at first, but gradually getting excited the prisoner said: "I am not guilty of the charge set forth in the indictment. It was God's act, not mine, and God will take care of it. He will take care of it, and don't let the American people forget it. He will take care of it and every officer of this Government from the Executive down to that Marshal, taking in every man on the jury and every member of this Bench will pay for it; and the American nation will roll in blood if my body goes into the ground and I am hung. The Jews put the despised Gallilean in the grave. For the time they triumphed, but at the destruction of Jerusalem forty years afterward the Almighty got even with them. I am not afraid of death. I am here as God's man. Kill me to-morrow, if you want. I am God's man and I have been from the start."

THE DEATH SENTENCE.

Judge Cox then proceeded to pass sentence, addressing the prisoner as follows:

You have been convicted of a crime so terrible in its circumstances and so far-reaching in its results that it has drawn upon you the horror of the whole world and the execrations of your countrymen.

The excitement produced by such an offence made it no easy task to secure for you a fair and impartial trial, but you have had the power of the United States Treasury and of the Government in your service to protect your person from violence and to procure evidence from all parts of the country. You have had as fair and impartial a jury as ever assembled in a court of justice. You have been defended by counsel with a zeal and devotion that merits the highest encomium, and I certainly have done my best to secure a fair presentation of your defence. Notwithstanding all this you have been found guilty. It would have been a comfort to many people if the verdict of the jury had established the fact that your act was that of an irresponsible man. It would have left the people the satisfying belief that the crime of political assassination was something entirely foreign to the institutions and civilization of our country, but the result has denied them that comfort. The country will accept it as a fact that that crime can be committed, and the Court will have to deal with it with the highest penalty known to the criminal code to serve as an example to others. Your career has been so extraordinary that people might well at times have doubted your sanity. But one cannot but believe that when the crime was committed you thoroughly understood the nature of the crime and its consequences, and that you had moral sense and conscience enough to recognize the moral iniquity of such an act. Your own testimony shows that you recoiled with horror from the idea. You say that you prayed against it. You say that you thought it might be prevented. This shows that your conscience warned you against it, but by the wretched sophistry of your own mind you worked yourself up against the protest of your own conscience. What motive could have induced you to this act must be a matter of conjecture. Probably men will think that some fanaticism or a morbid desire for self-exaltation was the real inspiration for the act. Your own testimony seems to controvert the theories of your counsel. They have maintained and thought honestly, I believe, that you were driven against your will by an insane impulse to commit the act, but your testimony showed that you deliberately resolved to do it, and that a guilty and misguided will was the sole impulse. This may seem insanity to some persons, but the law looks upon it as a willful crime. You will have due opportunity of having any errors I may have committed during the course of the trial passed upon by the Court in banc, but meanwhile it is necessary for me to pronounce the sentence of the law—that you be taken hence to the common jail of the District, from whence you came, and there be kept in confinement, and on Friday, the 30th day of June, 1882, you be taken to the place prepared for the execution, within the walls of said jail, and there between the hours of 12 and 2 P. M., you be hanged by the neck until you are dead, and may the Lord have mercy on your soul.

The prisoner who had twice addressed the Judge, but without disturbing him, during the passing of the sentence, now broke out in a tone of intense hatred. "And may God have mercy on your soul. I had rather stand where I am than where that jury does, or than where your Honor does. I am not afraid to die. Confound you— (he cried, violently struggling with the Deputy Marshals, who were endeavoring to repress him)—leave me alone. I know where I stand on this business. I am here as God's man and don't you forget it. God Almighty will curse every man who has had anything to do with this act. Nothing but good has come of General Garfield's removal, and that will be posterity's view of it. Everybody is happy here except a few cranks. Nothing but good has come to this nation from his removal. That is the reason the Lord wanted him removed."

Mr. Scoville then took an exception to the judgment and sentence of the Court.

The now convicted and sentenced felon then again broke out savagely; "I'd rather a thousand times be in my position than be with those devils who have hounded me to death. I will have a flight to glory, and I am not afraid to go. But Corkhill and the others are. There is no let up on Corkhill, the scoundrel. He has a permanent job down below. I will go to glory whenever the Lord wants me to go, but I will probably stay down here a good many years and get into the White House. I know how I stand on this business and so does the Lord and He will pull me through with the help of two or three good lawyers, and all the devils in hell can't hurt me."

The Court then, at a quarter to twelve, adjourned.

The long sustained suspense of an outraged public was over and the audience quietly dispersed as Guiteau struggling violently with his guards, heaping curses on the Court and counsel vainly endeavoring to strike one of the officers until securely handcuffed.

He was driven safely to the jail, the death watch was placed over him, and thus ends the trial of GUITEAU THE ASSASSIN.